THE BROTHERS MANKIEWICZ

HOLLYWOOD LEGENDS SERIES
CARL ROLLYSON, GENERAL EDITOR

THE BROTHERS MANKIEWICZ

Hope, Heartbreak, and Hollywood Classics

SYDNEY LADENSOHN STERN

UNIVERSITY PRESS OF MISSISSIPPI / JACKSON

The University Press of Mississippi is the scholarly publishing agency of the Mississippi Institutions of Higher Learning: Alcorn State University, Delta State University, Jackson State University, Mississippi State University, Mississippi University for Women, Mississippi Valley State University, University of Mississippi, and University of Southern Mississippi.

www.upress.state.ms.us

The University Press of Mississippi is a member of the Association of University Presses.

Manufactured in the United States of America

First printing 2019

∞

Library of Congress Cataloging-in-Publication Data

Names: Stern, Sydney Ladensohn, author.
Title: The brothers Mankiewicz : hope, heartbreak, and Hollywood classics / Sydney Ladensohn Stern.
Description: Jackson : University Press of Mississippi, [2019] | Series: Hollywood legends series | "First printing 2019." | Includes bibliographical references and index. |
Identifiers: LCCN 2019009744 (print) | LCCN 2019019569 (ebook) | ISBN 9781617032684 (epub single) | ISBN 9781496824691 (epub institutional) | ISBN 9781496824707 (pdf single) | ISBN 9781496824714 (pdf institutional) | ISBN 9781617032677 (hardcover : alk. paper)
Subjects: LCSH: Mankiewicz, Herman J. (Herman Jacob), 1897–1953. | Mankiewicz, Joseph L. | Motion picture producers and directors—United States—Biography.
Classification: LCC PN1998.2 (ebook) | LCC PN1998.2 .S732 2019 (print) | DDC 070.4/49320922 [B] —dc23
LC record available at https://lccn.loc.gov/2019009744

British Library Cataloging-in-Publication Data available

To Jon

CONTENTS

PROLOGUE

HERMAN

THE MANKIEWICZ BROTHERS OF HOLLYWOOD

JOE

EPILOGUE

PROLOGUE

CHAPTER 1

The End: Joe, 1993

ON FEBRUARY 9, 1993, THE FAMILY OF THE LATE JOSEPH LEO MANKIEWICZ assembled in the Bedford, New York, churchyard of St. Matthew's Episcopal Church to bid Joe farewell. It was an unlikely resting place for the avowed-atheist son of Jewish immigrants, but like so much about Joe, it was complicated. Joe wanted to be buried next to his wife, Rosemary, and Rosemary was the daughter of a Church of England archdeacon. The fact that formally becoming Episcopalian made Joe officially not-Jewish was just a side benefit. Besides, as their daughter, Alex, joked, her atheist father probably didn't mind a bit of insurance.

Wherever he was going, Joe would not be lonely. He had always wanted to be buried with his cherished pipes and his favorite Barking Dog tobacco ("matches will not be necessary"), but now there was his beloved black Lab, Cassius, whose ashes he had saved in a tin. Originally it seemed that Cassius would not be allowed to accompany him: animal remains were prohibited in the cemetery.

Yet there lay Joe, surrounded like an Egyptian potentate with his favorite books, plays, pipes, and tobacco pouch, secretly enjoying the last laugh. Because instead of Barking Dog tobacco, the pouch now held dead Labrador retriever ashes. As his son Tom said, "Dad always hated to lose."

Joe's death also concluded the story of the Mankiewicz brothers of Old Hollywood, brothers whose lives and careers spanned the history of Hollywood's studio system. Joe and his older brother, Herman, started in the 1920s, writing titles (captions) for silent pictures. When movies exploded into sound, they wrote screenplays and became renowned for their witty dialogue. They wrote, directed, and produced some of the most memorable pictures of the industry's Golden Age of the 1930s and 1940s, and were still there in the early 1950s, when the studio system began its decline. Each left behind one of Hollywood's most iconic films.

Despite opposing career trajectories, Herman and Joe had much in common, and not just because they were brothers. They were first-generation Americans who hungered for their father's approval, but not enough to conform to the career path he intended for them. They were brilliant students who expected their entire lives to fulfill their early promise. They were German Jews who resolutely defined their background as a religion, not a race. They were both erudite intellectuals and avid sports fans; irrepressible wits, quite capable of wounding; family men who caused their families great pain. Both embraced life with gusto yet spent their years in Hollywood yearning to return to New York. Both hoped to write a Great American Play, or at least a successful one, yet both achieved immortality through the medium they scorned for much of their lives.

After the service Joe's family and friends gathered in his book-lined study, filling the room with talent as they admired the four Oscars on the mantel. All of Herman's children and several of his grandchildren had become writers, for print and television as well as for motion pictures. Two of Joe's three sons and his artist daughter had followed him into the business. As they visited, their common ancestor gazed out from the wall above Joe's writing chair. Herman had commissioned their father's portrait by designer Jo Mielziner, and Joe had worked beneath it for nearly forty years. Now Rosemary and Alex were ready to pass it on. But for all their pride in their heritage, none of Pop's descendants seemed eager to take their progenitor home. Finally Rosemary decided Herman's son Don, now the senior member of the Mankiewicz family, was its most appropriate custodian. Besides, Don wasn't there to refuse it.

Pop had been an eminent and beloved personage in his field, but it was Herman and Joe who made the Mankiewicz name into a valuable Hollywood heritage. Ironically, it all began by accident. Herman went to Hollywood on a short writing assignment, planning to stay just long enough to earn the $2,200 he needed to pay off a debt.

But as Joe liked to say, life has a way of lousing up the script.

CHAPTER 2

The Beginning: Herman, 1926

HERMAN MANKIEWICZ LIKED TO SAY THAT EVERYONE ORIGINALLY came to Hollywood "in pursuit of a lump sum."

Of course, Herman's "everyone" was not really everyone who poured in during the 1920s motion picture gold rush. It did not include the pitiful characters flocking in to follow their dreams, whom Nathanael West portrayed in *The Day of the Locust*. Nor did it include many members of the movie colony's elite, some of whom were having the time of their lives. Herman's "everyone" meant people like himself, fellow writers like his boss and role model, George S. Kaufman, and friends like Dorothy Parker and F. Scott Fitzgerald, who considered themselves slumming but could not resist Hollywood's lucrative payouts.

Like his friends, Herman aspired to higher things and considered money merely an unpleasant necessity of life. However, the longer Herman enjoyed his hefty Hollywood paychecks, the longer his list of life's necessities became, and the harder it became to leave. Herman was hardly the only screenwriter who came to loathe himself for prostituting his talents, but Hollywood did not send Herman on his path of self-destruction. Herman's drinking and gambling led him there in the first place.

Herman was only twenty-eight when he arrived, and he anticipated a quick return to his Algonquin Round Table friends; his job at the *New York Times* as Kaufman's assistant theater editor; his position as the *New Yorker*'s first drama critic; his ongoing theatrical collaborations with Kaufman and Marc Connelly; his identity as Central Park West Voltaire. In short, a return to the life he loved and the profession he deemed worthy of his gifts.

One observer in particular watched Herman and hoped, possibly more anxiously than Herman, that he would grab that lump sum and return as quickly as possible. Professor Frank Mankiewicz, aka "Pop," understood that, for all of Herman's irreverence, his son was an original and erudite thinker, and he fervently wanted Herman to apply that penetrating intellect to worthwhile endeavors.

For Pop, there was no higher calling than teaching and no worthier existence than a life of the mind. He had given up imagining that Herman would follow him into academia and transferred that particular aspiration onto seventeen-year-old Joe. But Pop dared to hope that upon his return, Herman might shift his professional attention to subjects weightier than the Marx Brothers. Perhaps Herman would fulfill his own dream of writing theatrical work of merit. Or use his considerable knowledge of political history to shine in the world of journalism.

Pop's love for his children was beyond doubt, but there was also a dark side to the admirable Frank Mankiewicz. He was a hot-tempered parent with impossibly high, Old World standards, and his harshness had already generated in Herman a sense of inadequacy and self-hatred that never left him. Herman always regretted the damage he wreaked on himself and his loved ones, but he never managed to overcome his cycles of self-destruction. Even knowing they practically guaranteed fulfilling the terrible image of himself Herman imagined he saw in his father's eyes.

CHAPTER 3

The Real Beginning: Pop, 1891

IF POP IS THE KEY TO HERMAN—AND A KEY TO JOE—HOW FAR BACK to go? Perhaps a good place to start is 1913, when Herman, not quite sixteen, and Pop, almost forty-one, enroll at Columbia University. Herman is a freshman and Pop a candidate for a master's degree. Both will leave that august institution with an education, an abundance of friends and contacts, and the valuable Ivy League imprimatur they will treasure for the rest of their lives.

They were unlikely students, so short of funds that Herman's shabby suits changed color when it rained, and Pop lined his shoes with cardboard to make them last longer. Herman was accustomed to relative impecuniousness after years as a scholarship student at Harry Hillman Academy, in the Pennsylvania mining town of Wilkes-Barre. But at Hillman, Herman had been one of the smartest. At Columbia, Herman, like college freshmen then and ever after, found himself surrounded by classmates who were just as smart or smarter, often more affluent or more sophisticated, and in many cases, more talented.

Pop paid little attention to classmates. He was too busy supporting his family of five. While amassing a nearly perfect academic record, he substitute-taught all over the city during the day, instructed immigrants in English as a second language at night, and translated German travel brochures on the fly. By February 1914, Pop was a German teacher on the faculty of Manhattan's prestigious Stuyvesant High School, coaching the slow students (gratis) and visiting the promising ones at home to convince their parents to send them to college even if they thought they couldn't afford it. As for his family, Pop treated his own bright college student like an intellectual rival and as his vocation grew from a calling to an obsession, he practically ignored the rest of them.

Pop finished his master's degree in February 1915 and earned his doctorate from New York University in 1924. Starting in 1927, he headed

Franz and Johanna, New York 1903.

James Monroe High School's modern languages department while teaching at City College of New York and other universities, including University of Southern California and UCLA (after Herman and Joe moved west). When City College made him an associate professor of education at the age of fifty-nine, and again in 1936, when he was promoted to full professor, hundreds of students, former students, and colleagues gathered to honor him at testimonial dinners. The 1936 group included Mayor Fiorello LaGuardia and Pop's old friend Professor Albert Einstein.

The widely beloved and respected Professor Mankiewicz was the apotheosis of Pop's particular American Dream, and that Pop—that admirable, idealized father—lived on in both sons' psyches throughout their lives. And not just in their heads. Pop never stopped urging them to transcend their Hollywood careers and aim for higher things.

Actually, the story should begin further back, when Franz Mankiewicz arrived in New York in November 1891, a few weeks shy of his nineteenth birthday, hoping to find work as a journalist. He had studied French and German at University of Berlin, and with both parents dead, he left behind only two sisters teaching school in Berlin.

A typical German Jew (more German than Jewish), Franz later told Herman, Joe, and their sister, Erna, that his German family's Polish surname originated when his father's family lived in Posen, which later became part of Poland. Posen's Jews were not required to take surnames until the nineteenth century, so when he needed one, Franz's father, Jacob, adopted the name of "a nice man who lived on a hill nearby." When Joe and Erna later claimed their family was originally Catholic, perhaps they were thinking of that nice man on the hill. Pop also told his children one of their ancestors had furnished Napoleon with a carriage during his 1812 retreat from Russia; given Napoleon's route back to Paris, that is at least possible.

On New Year's Eve 1896, Franz married Johanna Blumenau, a dressmaker who had emigrated from Kurland, a German-speaking area of Russia (later Latvia). Herman arrived on November 7, 1897, followed on February 27, 1901, by Erna Caroline. Joe would be a later surprise.

Hanna was considerably less educated than Franz. She signed her 1898 passport application with an "X," and the family's 1900 census record describes her as unable to read or write. But the lively blue-eyed blonde was clearly intelligent, and responses to census takers could be unreliable. She actually may have been able to read and write German—Kurlanders tended to be educated—and at some point, Hanna mastered English. Hanna's accent was stronger than her husband's, and when she became upset, she would mix German and English, with more expletives in German. Then she would laugh.

Her children's recollections are characteristic. Erna recalled her mother reading and arguing out loud with *New York Times* editorials. Hanna especially adored New York's colorful mayor, James (Jimmy) Walker, telling her teasing family, "You can't tell me in politics they're not all crooked, but I would rather have a crook who helps poor people as well as himself." Herman described Hanna to a *Life* reporter in 1951 as "a round little woman who was uneducated in four languages. She spoke mangled German, mangled Russian, mangled Yiddish and mangled English." Herman's biographer, Richard Meryman, quoted that description in his 1978 biography, and Joe, ever vigilant to any hint of Jewishness, annotated his copy: he marked an "X" over "Russian," drew a line through "Yiddish," and wrote in the margin next to the offending passage, "not one word did either of them know."

Besides her considerable gifts as a seamstress, Hanna was a born storyteller. If their father dominated his sons' psychological landscapes, they acquired their sense of humor—and their distinctive sense of comic hyperbole—from their mother. They also absorbed Hanna's ability to use humor to mask anger, though sometimes the mask slipped. Among her grievances was her husband's inattentiveness, and one Sunday afternoon, as little Joe looked on in terror, she pulled her husband's books from the shelves and hurled them all over the floor. Joe developed a protective shell to tune out his parents' frequent arguments and later recollected the few good times as examples of his mother's angry humor.

> The intermittent times of relaxed tensions at family gatherings, as I recall them, were—if ever happy ones—those given over to one of Mom's descriptive fantasies woven from some ordinary happening or perhaps a fanciful characterization of some family acquaintance—and, more often than not, a funny and biting savaging of one of Pop's female teacher-pupils. An example I can remember of the latter was a shockingly ugly pedagogical slavvy of Pop's . . . Mom used to work over mercilessly the ill-favored and overripe [Ms X], particularly in Pop's presence (I think Mom suspected, with some justification, that she lusted after a type of enlightenment from Pop that was more akin to the slap-and-tickle to the foreskin rather the sheepskin), to the entertainment of us all. I can recall . . . Herman chuckling and egging Mom on—Erna giggling—Pop smiling and smoking away, even while being ribbed.

Once Joe was in school, Hanna created more of a life for herself outside the home. She became deeply involved helping disabled children, leading her family to joke that Mom took care of children's crippled bodies, and Pop their crippled minds. Despite her strong accent, she also became a skilled and fearless fund-raiser. "When you go to a rich man and ask for a donation to buy braces for crippled children, or to serve milk in public schools in the Bronx, you're not asking for you," she told Erna. "This is for the children that you're asking, and if that man says no to you, then he is the one who should be embarrassed, not you."

Despite his frequent obliviousness, Pop was acutely aware of those whose good opinions he valued, especially members of New York's German intellectual elite, whose *Stammtisch* (regulars' table) he joined when he could. During his early years in New York, they gathered at Luchow's, a German restaurant near Union Square, and if funds were particularly scarce, he would stay away or time his appearances to avoid the actual lunch meal. In his more successful years, he founded his own *Stammtisch*, in the Roerich Museum near Columbia, which included Einstein, among others.

In early years, Franz was frustrated by his inability to advance professionally and sometimes retreated into alcohol. Herman later recalled his father saying that drinking made him feel like a new man—and that new man wanted a drink. But Franz's drinking was no joke. Alcohol shortened his already-short fuse, and his family bore the brunt of his temper. Hanna did not shrink from fighting back, but the abuse took its toll, especially on their firstborn, from whom Franz always expected much.

In 1905 Franz became editor of *Demokratischer Wachter*, a German language weekly newspaper serving Wilkes-Barre, Pennsylvania's sizable German-speaking community. There, Americanized as Frank, he served as secretary of the Gesangverein Concordia (a men's singing and social organization) and chaired the local Democratic club, which enabled his family to meet national figures like William Jennings Bryan. To supplement his income, he began tutoring Hillman Academy boys in German and French, and found he liked it so much that when Hillman's modern languages teacher left, Frank left the newspaper to become a teacher.

Within a few years teaching became his calling. He founded a boys' German club and staged German-language productions so popular they attracted Wilkes-Barre's greater German American community. He also took students to Europe during the summer vacations, which enriched the boys' education, supplemented his family's income, and financed his own trips to visit relatives.

Even with more satisfying work, Pop remained a harsh parent. If Herman excelled in school, Pop shrugged it off as a function of his ability; if his performance was less than perfect, Pop excoriated him in front of the other boys in class. A ninety-two on a test would evoke, "Where are the other eight points?" In later years Pop asked the same question of Erna and Joe, as well as of his regular students and even his student teachers, but he asked the others with a smile. With Herman he didn't smile. If Herman protested that his grade was the highest in class, Pop would shout, "Don't tell me you were the best in the class. There were plenty of boys who deserved that grade much more than you, because you didn't do any work. You're just telling me you're in a class with a lot of inferior minds." Herman couldn't win.

In addition to stinting on praise and doling out public shaming, Pop did not spare the rod. Whether or not he had done anything wrong, Herman was spanked several times a week, sometimes merely on general

Herman and his bicycle, which was not named Rosebud.

principles. Pop's unrelenting demands and cruel punishments were terrifying, and Herman's anger at the injustice mingled with his eagerness to please his charismatic father. Outside the family, Herman learned to use wit and humor to attract friends. He helped classmates with their work, and though he was a mediocre athlete at best, he always loved sports.

Pop was an avowed atheist, but to expose them to their heritage, he sent Herman and Erna to Reform Jewish Sunday school. That experiment was short lived. The rabbi sent them home one day, and when Herman told his mother, "Dr. Salzman says I can't come to Sunday school anymore," Hanna feared the worst. However, when Herman explained, "We're not good Jews because we have a Christmas tree," that was the end of the Mankiewicz children's religious education. They continued to celebrate Christmas and Easter, and one of Herman's Christmases became part of film history.

When he was about ten, Herman begged for a bicycle, and his parents promised him one for Christmas. On Christmas morning, however, there was no bicycle, and though he got one a few weeks later, Herman never forgot the intensity of his disappointment. Once he had it, he reveled in the freedom a bike provided, and his parents enjoyed their new source of leverage. One day when Hanna had grounded him, Herman simply waited until she left, then rode to the public library, where he loved to

Wilkes-Barre, 1909.

lose himself in books for hours at a time, but on that occasion his bicycle was gone when he emerged.

His parents refused to replace it, and despite the logic of their reaction, Herman experienced that loss so profoundly—and remembered those feelings so vividly—that he utilized them more than three decades later in *Citizen Kane*: "Rosebud," moans Charles Foster Kane with his dying breath, and his beloved sled, Rosebud, becomes a powerful symbol of the lost familial love for which he yearns. Like Hanna, Charlie Kane's mother does what she thinks best for her son. Like his creator, Kane becomes a self-destructive adult who never quite fills the void.

Generally, Wilkes-Barre provided pleasures of small-town life, like baseball and a comfortable house with a porch and a yard; and aside from his eruptions, Pop approached parenthood conscientiously and thoughtfully. He taught his children to respect authority but also to question even authorities if their facts or conclusions seemed dubious. Pop loved arguing and Joe said he never saw his father lose an argument, even if he was wrong. Herman frequently adopted outrageous positions, just for the fun of arguing, and according to Joe's children, Joe also was never wrong. (Herman's oldest son was offered a debate scholarship to Stanford, so, nature or nurture, that affinity survived at least unto the third generation.)

In 1908 Hanna, thirty-seven, learned that what she had assumed was menopause was actually pregnancy, and on February 11, 1909, she gave birth to Joseph Leo. Eleven and a half years younger than Herman, and eight years younger than Erna, Joe became their petted toy. He retained few memories of Wilkes-Barre, but he did recall Herman taking him to watch the luxurious Black Diamond Express train pass through on its way between New York and Buffalo. Both teenager and toddler loved watching the dining car, full of finely dressed people eating dinner off white tablecloths, and though it was not the world to which Pop aspired, its distant glamour called out to both his sons.

Herman started high school a couple of months shy of his twelfth birthday, and as he whizzed through in three years, Pop decided he should take the entrance examination for Columbia University in New York. Pop was taking correspondence courses from the University of Chicago and Lycée Français and wanted to attend Columbia himself, so he resolved that if he and Herman were both admitted, they were going. He would find the money somehow.

Herman passed the examination at thirteen and graduated at fourteen, the youngest prep school graduate in the history of Luzerne County. He also won prizes and spoke at graduation ("The Value of a Great American Navy"). He could not attend Columbia until he was fifteen, and Frank and Hanna sent him to work for a year. In an experience he always valued, Herman exchanged companions from the city's elite for the camaraderie of coal miners. Working as a surveyor's assistant, he wore a head lamp and accompanied them into the mine at dawn. In return, the miners taught Herman to drink beer and smoke cigarettes, skills he absorbed better than many of Hillman's academic offerings.

The family left Wilkes-Barre in 1913, one step ahead of the bill collectors. As usual, Frank left Hanna the job of convincing their landlord their check was in the mail (it wasn't). Joe was only four, but Wilkes-Barre left its mark, even on him. Over the years both Herman and Joe inserted the city's name into their films whenever they could. The humorous quality of the name amused them, and they used it as shorthand for small-town provincialism: Wilkes-Barre became the Mankiewiczes' Peoria.

HERMAN

CHAPTER 4

Herman's Life Begins

NOT ALL OF HERMAN'S COLUMBIA UNIVERSITY SCHOOLMATES WERE privileged. Many also needed scholarships or patched together a variety of jobs. But Herman must have recognized his lack of social graces and decided the best defense was a good offense—literally. One college friend recalled that "people were pretty rude to him because he really was a boor. He'd push his food on his fork with his fingers, would belch, use words forbidden then, like 'half-assed.' He wanted to be known as an eccentric, and he enjoyed shocking people."

When he wasn't offering up a caricature of himself, Herman enthusiastically immersed himself in academic life. Students could study comparative literature with Henry Wadsworth Longfellow Dana, a grandson of the poet; listen to Charles Beard's economic interpretation of the Constitution; absorb Elizabethan literature at the feet of John Erskine, whose esteem for the great works of Western civilization led to Columbia's famous core curriculum and beyond, to the Great Books movement. Erskine established the Boar's Head Society, a literary club for students interested in writing, then led protégés through Homer and Virgil to newer poets like Robert Frost and Amy Lowell. He taught discipline and craftsmanship to the twenty or so students he admitted to his writing classes and became an important mentor to Herman and, later, to Joe.

To save tuition, Herman raced through college in three years, but those three years were packed. He joined Columbia's honors program and, despite a keen interest in politics and history, majored in German and English. He took every possible English course and would devour literature his entire life. He demonstrated no interest in activism. One of Herman's classmates was Howard Dietz, future lyricist and longtime publicity chief at Metro-Goldwyn-Mayer (Dietz created MGM's Leo the Lion and coined its slogan, "Ars Gratia Artis"), and as he recalled, "Mank was not a joiner; his ambition was to be a freeswinging heckler. . . . Having views was a form of intellectual therapy. It was clear, he said, that he was against the Right, the Left, and the Center, and the best party was one that was pro-Mank." In short, even as a teenager, Herman masked passion with humor. Sincerity risked exposing vulnerability; satire allowed him to puncture targets with his intellect.

Herman's extracurricular activities anticipated his future interests. After spending most of his first year at the Boar's Head Society, he added the Deutscher Verein (German Club) and Honors Forum, all agreeably commensurate with Pop's plan that Herman follow him into teaching. But he was also drawn to the fast-paced, irreverent world of journalism and humor. After writing for the campus humor magazine, the *Jester*, he progressed to editing "The Off-Hour," the humor column of *Columbia Spectator*, the school's daily newspaper. That position allowed him to combine his powers of observation with his analytic abilities and biting wit while providing an enjoyable rise in stature in a community he respected.

Not that he disdained shortcuts. Dietz, who also had literary aspirations, was impressed by Herman's poetry until he came across some of Herman's cleverest lines in *Life Sings a Song*, a 1916 book of poetry by theatrical agent Samuel Hoffenstein. When confronted, Herman explained that Hoffenstein was a Wilkes-Barre family friend, and though Herman believed in plagiarism on principle, in this case he had traded some ideas for the verses, an exchange Hoffenstein later confirmed.

Herman also created a magazine—for one issue. Throughout his life, Herman rarely met a target he could resist ridiculing, no matter how laudable its goal—in fact, the more laudable the goal, the more irresistible the target. In 1916 it was *Challenge*, a new, intercollegiate, supposedly radical left magazine created by two of his friends, Max Schuster (eventual co-founder of Simon and Schuster), and Morris (Morrie) Ryskind (who later wrote Marx Brothers material and won a Pulitzer Prize with George S. Kaufman and the Gershwins for *Of Thee I Sing*). When *Challenge* attracted *New York Times* and *New York Tribune* coverage, Herman countered with *Dynamite*, which drew at least the *Tribune*. Besides predictable college-magazine pieces like "Graft among Professors," which accused professors of failing to provide what students actually came for (a good time), *Dynamite* offered ten tips on how to have a radical mind: "Blame everything on conditions. Never mind what a condition is. No one else knows, either. . . . Remember that the essence of radicalism is to state the trite in terms of the sensational. . . . Be personal. Everybody assaults institutions."

Dietz, Ryskind, and Herman were also focused on the world beyond Columbia, regularly submitting items to "The Conning Tower," Franklin P. Adams's (F.P.A.) column in the *New York World*. F.P.A. specialized in light verse and quips from pseudonymous contributors, both published writers and unpublished hopefuls, and to receive a nickname from F.P.A. was a badge of honor. Dorothy Parker was Dottie. Howard Dietz was Freckles. Morris Ryskind was Morrie. Herman was Mank.

Herman also fell in love with theater and gravitated to a group of likeminded friends, including Oscar Hammerstein II and Lorenz (Larry) Hart. Although Hammerstein's grandfather was a well-known theatrical impresario, young Oscar had promised his parents he would go to law school. Hart, who had been writing songs and stories since childhood, had a Tammany Hall–connected father who revered his son's talent and welcomed his friends to their house on nearby West 119th Street. The group often stayed up all night talking, and according to Henry Myers, another member who went on to a successful screenwriting career, "A great deal of theatrical practice and theory that later developed in the New York theater was developed right there in that back room in that brownstone house."

Although Herman graduated in 1916, he was considered a member of the class of 1917, so having his musical chosen for Columbia's prestigious Varsity Show was a particular honor. They were usually not written by undergraduates, much less juniors, and Herman's was the first politically oriented selection. *The Peace Pirates* spoofed Henry Ford's "Peace Ship," a much-ridiculed 1915 initiative launched by the industrialist in hopes of ending the war. Herman wrote the book and lyrics, and Ray Perkins, who had spent the previous year playing piano on the vaudeville circuit to finance the rest of his Columbia education, wrote the music.

In the play, a group of men and women crossing the Atlantic Ocean on a mission to avert war are captured by pirates and taken to a South Sea island. The eloquence of "perpetual candidate" William J. Tryan saves them, and the second act finds them on the Connecticut country estate of Andrew Rockyford ("a jitney pacifist") and Mrs. Rockyford ("his better 99/100"). Other characters include Pirate Chief Captain Kidd (he "put the pie in pirate"); Mrs. Kidd; some little Kidds; and R. L. Perkins, an entertainer. Hammerstein wrote and performed a blackface scene as a character called Washington Snow. Hart played Mrs. Rockyford (all women's parts were played by men). The story also featured twenty chorus "girls" and a pony ballet. It was a heady beginning to Herman's theatrical career.

The cast for Herman's first produced show included (standing, left): Oscar Hammerstein II ("Washington Snow") and Larry Hart ("Mrs. Rockyford").

Herman also demonstrated an aptitude for publicity, linking the musical to a popular fund that had been inspired by a thirteen-year-old Brooklyn girl named Marjorie Sterrett. In a letter to the *Tribune*, Marjorie had offered her hard-earned dime toward building a battleship to help the United States prepare for war, and she wanted the battleship named *America*. After former president Theodore Roosevelt sent a dollar, and dimes poured in from everywhere, Congress passed a law allowing the navy to accept the fund's $20,000 donation.

Pledging part of their opening-night revenues to the fund, the students invited Marjorie and called it "Battleship Night." The show ran for a week at the Hotel Astor's Grand Ballroom, and according to the *Tribune*, "Mr. Hart did a stunning imitation of five Broadway favorites, so good that many people in the audience recognized the favorites, although they had never seen them" (including Mary Pickford and Ethel Barrymore). Herman and Perkins were also lauded: "The authors of the entertainment are by no means unknown. Ray Perkins has achieved considerable fame as a vaudeville pianist on the subway circuit, and H. J. Mankiewicz is rumored to have gotten a contrib into F.P.A.'s column several years ago. Both are members of the staff of 'Jester,' the university comic monthly, which was on sale in the lobby."

Herman also pursued time-honored college activities like drinking and gambling, and more than once Pop and Hart's father joined forces to scour bars in search of their sons. Herman always liked intelligent women, and though he was a bit awkward, women always liked Herman. He didn't date much, because dates cost money, a shortfall Herman often exacerbated by trying to gamble his way out of poverty. He lived at home, idolized by Erna as well as Joe, and contributed what he could to family funds. He typed theses for other students; worked in a city playground; and, with a rabbinical school dropout, co-managed a newsstand so lucrative that when the dropout was drafted in 1917, his brother took his place.

Dietz also recalled Herman running a lending library of dirty books, beckoning potential readers, "Come In and Enjoy Yourself," at "$1 an hour for *Fanny Hill,* 50 cents for *The Memoirs of Josephine Mutzenbacker.*" Dietz may have exaggerated about Herman's career as a pornography purveyor, but what is not in doubt is that Herman was a champion moocher. Once the coal miners introduced him to the pleasures of nicotine and alcohol, Herman smoked and drank for the rest of his life. The caption below his Columbia senior yearbook entry read, "We'll say this much for H. J. Mank: When anybody blew, he drank."

Despite his often slovenly appearance, Herman's yearbook photograph portrays a serious honors graduate, his tie neatly tied, his hair smoothly combed. That summer and into the fall, he combined news work and politics, working as a press agent for President Woodrow Wilson's 1916 reelection campaign, which meant doing everything from arranging speeches to buying extra socks for prominent supporters. In deference to Pop, he returned to school as a fall 1916 graduate student in English, but he dropped out after one term.

Within a few months, he had jobs at two publications, both employers unaware of the other. At the *New York Tribune,* he started writing articles, book reviews, and short essays and by June had theatrical feature stories on the front page of the Sunday entertainment section. He was also assistant editor at the *American Jewish Chronicle,* a small weekly magazine founded by the Zionist intellectual Dr. Samuel Max Melamed to advocate for "the rights of Jews after the close of the European war." There, Herman wrote about politics and theater, and even a short story or two.

Herman was nineteen and frequently facetious, but his natural sympathy sometimes poked through. His aptitude for vivid characterization was already apparent. In a July *Tribune* piece, he described actors seeking work:

> During the busy parts of the day almost all of the booking agencies' offices are crowded with [unknown aspirants], waiting their turn to be heard and to hear, in all probability, that there is "nothing today." There is the girl with the Mary Pickford curls, who is sure she would make good if she were only given a chance. (Probably she would; therein lies the tragedy.) There is the faded old fellow who played with [renowned actor Edwin] Booth (in spite of the mathematical absurdity, the number of those who played with Booth is growing each year). There is the fresh young lad with the white socks who can't realize that George M. Cohan had other equipment besides a gray bowler and a cold in the head. . . . There is the large, red-nosed person who talks familiarly of Lee [Shubert] and Charlie [Frohman] and Martin [Beck—all important producers] and the rest. There is—but what's the use? You've probably seen them all yourself; they were all there yesterday; they will all be there tomorrow.

More typically ironic was "The Tubercular Cow," a *Chronicle* short story about a thirty-four-year-old man who starts drinking to attract the affections of a young woman: "Madelein, it was plain, had a brewery complex. Madelein was interested solely in men who drank." The narrator's title is a metaphor based on the idiosyncrasies of a journalist he knows who is obsessed with tubercular cows because healthy cows bore him:

> There are so many of them, you know. And so it was with Madelein. As a healthy cow, I was worth little more than passing attention. My merits, sad to relate, as dancer and conversationalist are limited, if not non-*existent*. As a tubercular cow, with the tuberculosis, so to speak, of Münchner Beer and Apricot Brandy, I was decidedly worth while. Madelein, in other words, was determined to reform me.

Herman's formerly abstemious narrator eventually becomes so enamored of drinking that he loses Madelein rather than foreswear alcohol.

Herman retained his passion for theater, and Samuel Hoffenstein, the poetry-writing theatrical press agent from Wilkes-Barre, introduced him to some of the most important figures in his life, including Alexander

Woollcott and George S. Kaufman. Woollcott was then the *New York Times* theater critic, and Kaufman, who moved to the *Times* at the end of 1917, was working hard to become a playwright himself.

In February 1918 Herman, twenty, went to Washington, D.C., to cover a speech by Dr. Melamed at George Washington University, and at the social hour afterward, he met an interesting pair of sisters. Naomi Aaronson was studying to become a teacher. Her younger sister, Shulamith Sara, was Herman's age, but her father had kept her out of college to help him at his box factory. Herman managed to wangle an invitation for dinner, and as they walked, he entertained them with stories of New York theater, describing the lead in a recent production of Ibsen's *Doll's House* as "a fat, elocuting Nora, who in a self-respecting household, would have been munching poisoned macaroons ten minutes after the curtain went up." His insider gossip had the desired effect, at least on the younger sister, who will henceforth be known as Sara.

"By the time we got home," she told Herman's posthumous biographer, "I was absolutely in a dreamworld. I'd never heard anything like such talk." (Joe had known Sara almost sixty years by the time the biography appeared, and his marginalia provide entertaining color commentary. Next to the account of his pseudo-sophisticated brother's ability to impress the Aaronsons, Joe wrote, "a good minor league pitcher throwing against a pick-up team of Girl Scouts . . .")

After dinner Sara, her four sisters, and one brother gathered around the piano to sing popular songs, and Herman further impressed them by knowing the verses as well as the choruses. Herman was captivated by the warmth of Sara's family and by tiny, attractive, intellectually curious Sara. Pressing his advantage, he invited her to a local musical comedy the following night.

When he arrived for their date impressively attired in a tuxedo, Sara had no idea Herman wore it only because he had ripped his suit slacks. Without shoes to match, Herman had painted his brown shoes black and the polish reeked so strongly that people edged away from them in the theater. Sara could hardly miss the odor, but she simply giggled adoringly. She was already so in awe of Herman's wit and sophistication that she could hardly wait to get to work the following morning to write Herman's name at the top of her list of suitors on the bathroom wall and cross off the rest.

Although they agreed to write, Herman enlisted in the Army Air Service a few weeks after they met and started flight training. He was too young to be drafted, but he wanted to fly airplanes. Unfortunately, the

Private Mankiewicz, Altwied, Germany, 1919.

flight simulator made him throw up, so he switched to the Marines. The next time he saw Sara was six months later, when he stopped between trains on his way to basic training. Sara's mother accompanied her to the station to chaperone their visit.

By the time Herman's division landed in Brittany on November 3, the war was practically over, and when the Armistice was signed on November 11, they were en route to Germany. Because he spoke German, Herman and a friend named McCoy were sent ahead to assess conditions. He wrote his family that he and McCoy were not only the first Allied soldiers to enter Cologne (population 700,000), they were so far ahead of their division that they "saw the German army in retreat and "reviewed them in front of the Cathedral with Cardinal Hartman [archbishop of Cologne]." He had much more to tell them, he added, but, as he had already written in a separate letter addressed to "Howard A. Mankiewicz" (with instructions not to open until he returned): "It would be both tedious and unpolitic to repeat the story here—-I'll have to save it for that glorious night when, the fire having been lighted, the last Creploch devoured and the bottle of Scotch dragged from its hiding place, I shall proceed to recount my travels. This sentimental feeling of mine for the dramatic accounts for my leaving out so much in my letters to you—-the censorship must account for the rest."

His unit settled in the southwestern area of Rhineland Pfalz, near France and Luxembourg, and on Christmas Eve, Herman and McCoy were sent to the local castle to ask the Prince of Wied for firewood. The prince was unavailable, but they did meet the princess, whose father was King William II of Württemberg. "Some painter, I believe, ought to immortalize the scene: Herman J. Mankiewicz, leather neck, accompanied by the trusty McCoy, each with their full retinue of cooties [lice], trying in his patois German, to bum the daughter of a reigning monarch for a couple of sticks of wood. I am, by the way, getting to be an expert at Platt [idiomatic German]. . . ."

His German also enabled him to follow the local news, and he relayed what he thought would pass the censor. On January 1 he reported that the German mark was already falling, and the "German debacle is more than complete . . . everything is falling to pieces. . . . the first act of Hoffmann, the new Kultur minister, was to abolish Religionsunterricht [religious instruction] in the schools. . . . Berlin is very unquiet, and I am afraid it is going to be in for a regular reign of terror very shortly. Verbum sapienti [enough said]—I have written to Aunt Anna out in Michigan." (He may have meant he was trying to contact Pop's sister, Tante Anna, who lived in Berlin.)

He was rescued from the tedium by John Erskine, who hired him to teach English and journalism in Beaune, France, at the American Expeditionary Forces' AEF University, a postwar educational program Erskine had developed with the YMCA. Anticipating the prospect of a million or so soldiers idly awaiting demobilization, the military had decided to offer them educational opportunities, and the courses ranged from art, agriculture, and law to English, journalism, and medicine (for premeds only—cadavers were deemed inadvisable after what the soldiers had been through). At its peak 380 teachers instructed soldiers whose education ranged from illiterate to postgraduate, and Herman sent Sara a photograph of the faculty, inscribing on the back, "My other faculties will follow in due course." Some of the professors found the experience exhilarating. Herman was so unimpressed that he disparaged the entire program in "The University in Khaki," in the January 1920 issue of the *World Tomorrow*, a pacifist monthly edited by socialist Norman Thomas, with contributors like theologian Reinhold Niebuhr and artist Rockwell Kent.

Noting that by the end of the term, the university was left with only half the students who had started, he added, "It is only fair to those students who remained to say that they had absolutely no opportunity to leave." Private Mankiewicz had many criticisms, but he objected most vigorously to the university's combination of "universal military training and education." When the university's president learned that some of the teachers had discussed issues like Prohibition and universal military service in class, he proclaimed, "Discussions are not encouraged at military posts. The wise teacher will conduct his classes without discussion," an edict that so appalled the indefatigable debater and educator's son that he condemned the university as "a fraud and a farce."

Mostly, Herman focused on getting home and escaping war's destruction.

> I am now teaching a course in the short story to replace Corporal Herbert Davidson, who left here the other day for the States. HIS FOLKS GOT HIM THE DISCHARGE. . . . I cannot get myself to believe, when everyone else with even the slightest pretense to pull is going home, that you are doing all you can. Don't take "no" for an answer. Go to Washington personally with [Judge Leopold] Prince. By this time you'll know whether the Germans are going to sign peace—and if they don't, little Herman is scheduled for another winter in the Rhineland. See Sam Koenig [Republican operative], see [Columbia Dean] Keppel, see everyone you know. If you learn that the Germans have not signed and that we are moving in, go to the New York Tribune, tell them that I resigned from their paper to enlist in the aviation corps, and that I want them to get me out. I have already written them to that effect. See F.P.A.—he will remember me.

He was homesick. "Somehow, Mama, much as I miss you all, I think I miss you most. At all events, there is no doubt that I worry more about you than the rest of the family put together. Try to get a letter through to me. And let me know that you're still playing bridge and winning cut glass and darning socks and wiping Joe's nose and practicing at Perrogen and Kreploch for the day of my return."

Herman had not seen combat, but he had seen enough:

Erna's line about the death of Freddy Gudebrod . . . has awakened in me a line of thought that sometimes clouds my mind whole weeks at a time. The futility, the sheer waste, of war is brought home best when one thinks of Freddy Gudebrod—I have known no one who loved life more than he did. And with Freddy barely decently buried, the Vultures and The Messiah are doing their damnedest so to arrange things at Paris [Versailles negotiations] that more Freddies should leave the life they love—and, as I see it, very likely even in our time. Not being either an officer or a war correspondent, I have had to satisfy my conversational desires with the common people of France and Germany, and it is wonderful to see how much of one mind they are. The fourteen points, disarmament, self-respect to each nation—-they want nothing more. And all the time the conference awards Fiume to the Italians, Dantzig to the Poles, the Saare Basin to the French, disregards the fourteen points, and the peace treaty, as a French soldier told me last night, will be signed with the blood of the generations to come and not, as it should be, of the generation that is past.

But none of this, I know, is particularly new to you. As I gather from occasional articles of the New Republic and the Nation that I see, there is still a little—though a precious little—independent thought left in America. Perhaps it's just as well that I am safely over here under iron-clad military discipline—I'd probably be in jail now if I were home, or at all events in deep disgrace with all the "nice" people. All the same, when I look at the outline of the Peace Treaty and then think of Freddy Gudebrod and Joyce Kilmer and Jeff Healy and Herb Buermeyer and the hundred others that I knew and of the millions of other Freddy Gudebrods and Kilmers and Healys and Buermeyers that I didn't know, my blood boils.

Once the Germans signed at Versailles, Herman sailed home, ready to give his war souvenirs to little Joseph and get on with his life. When Hitler began his rise to power a decade later, Herman found little pleasure in his prescience. Instead, he struggled to raise the alarm about the Nazis. But when he failed, Herman remained adamantly opposed to US intervention, casting about for alternatives, anything that might avert another war, with its inevitable and terrible cost, especially to the young.

CHAPTER 5

Glorious Adventures

FOR A SOLDIER SO EAGER TO GET HOME, HERMAN TOOK HIS TIME, and six months later, he was back in Europe.

But first he had a girlfriend to see. He detoured to Washington on his way north from Quantico, and found Sara Aaronson still smitten. Years later, screenwriter Herman dramatized their third meeting, a walk in Washington's Rock Creek Park:

> H.J.M.: (just returned from the wars) "Have you ever thought seriously of getting married?"
> S.A.: "Oh, Mr. Mankiewicz, how you carry on."
>
> Silence. Mr. Mankiewicz realizes that something is wrong and inwardly curses Moses, whom he suspects to be responsible for his not being allowed to smoke on Shabbos.
>
> H.J.M.: (swallowing several times and remembering rather humorously that he is a Marine.) "Could you learn to love me?"
> S.A.: "Probably. I learned Hebrew once."
>
> Silence. Mr. Mankiewicz suspects that all is not going well. The suspicion dawns on him that the quarter he paid for "Advice To Young Gentlemen and Young Gentlewomen on how to propose and how to receive proposals including three specimen letters and a cure for boils" is a dead loss. He swallows again and looks fervently at the calm, majestic brow of his beloved idol.
>
> H.J.M.: (suddenly and with the voice of a sick calf) "Shulamith!"
> S.A.: "Mank!"
>
> Clinch

Engaged, 1919.

Actually, Sara told Herman's biographer, Herman tried to kiss her as soon as they were alone and she refused, insisting she would not kiss a man unless she were going to marry him. So Herman proposed. Then he got his kiss. He also acquired a fiancée, and whether or not that had been his intention, he was exhilarated.

Sara's family was considerably less enchanted. "Marry him!" her father snorted, "You don't even know him. You don't know anything about his father, his family."

Displaying the will for which she would become renowned, Sara said, "Poppa, you can investigate the family. I'm going to marry Herman."

Determined to charm them, Herman joined the Aaronsons for a summer weekend at the New Jersey shore, then wrote to his parents in Connecticut. His prospective father-in-law now believed "that I'm a decent enough sort of person "mit a kluger Kopf" [with a good head] and is willing enough to entrust his Shulamith to my tender care," but he wanted to meet them. "Shulamith left for Washington yesterday with Ruth and Mattie, which leaves an even twenty immediate relatives still around. Among other things, there is an uncle, Will Milwitzki, of about your own age, Columbia '93, a teacher of French in Barrington High School,

Newark, who thinks he's met you at Modern Language meetings. . . . Please think this over and let me know your decision. It is of importance to me."

He added, "I dispelled an illusion that a Jacob Mankiewicz, a shoemaker, gentleman and Talmudist known to Grosspa Milwitzki in Russia, whence he moved to Germany and America, where he died about ten years ago, was your father."

Without that meeting, Sara's father remained apprehensive, and Sara's sisters shared his concern, worrying that her suitor possessed a less than sufficient supply of "solidity, sobriety, maturity, and Jewishness." Herman tried to reassure them, explaining that "the problem arises from my unwillingness to take unimportant things seriously and my desire to avoid appearing sentimental by making bad jokes. The fact is that I am the most serious man in the world, even when I'm joking." Although religion meant nothing to him, he promised he would always respect Sara's desire to practice in the ways that were important to her and her family. It was one of the few promises Herman actually kept.

He returned to the *Tribune*, but always in need of more money, he took his first job in the motion picture industry, freelance writing German publicity for the films Famous Players-Lasky (Paramount's predecessor) was sending to Germany. He and Sara continued their epistolary courtship, and that fall Sara, escorted by her uncle, ventured to New York to meet her future in-laws. After climbing three flights of stairs at 44 St. Mark's Place, she met a "stout, big bosomed woman" and a "big powerful man with a booming voice," who rendered her "scared out of my wits. I almost fainted." Years later Sara speculated they probably had feared Herman would bring home a chorus girl, or worse. When they became formally engaged, Herman gave Sara a ring made from one of Hanna's earrings.

Herman started working on a newsletter for the Red Cross and transferred to Washington within a few months. He moved into Sara's neighborhood and began joining the Aaronsons for nightly dinners as if he were their second son—which, to Herman, meant that he engage Sara's father in the same ritual he shared with his own father, nightly arguing. He recalled their exchanges as "painstaking debating whether the grass is black or yellow, he saying black and I yellow."

When the Red Cross offered him a promotion and the opportunity to work in its Paris press office, Herman leapt at it and spent the next six months enjoying France. After stopping in Berlin to visit relatives, he arrived in Washington on June 30, 1920, the day before his wedding. He brought Sara a beautiful pair of silver candlesticks as a wedding present, though he spoiled the effect a bit by handing them to her in two brown paper bags. Sara treasured them forever.

They were married in an Orthodox ceremony at the Aaronsons' home and spent their wedding night at an unprepossessing local hotel. Both families saw them off at the station the following day, with Sara's mother and sisters all in tears. Because it was Friday, they scheduled their arrival before sundown and stayed in a hotel within walking distance of Pennsylvania Station. The first dinner of their marriage was a perfect preview of their subsequent life together—or became so, in Sara's account half a century later.

Herman spent their train ride reading newspapers and ignoring Sara. When they arrived, he bought an evening newspaper, folded it vertically and read it as they ate side by side at the counter of a Penn Station restaurant. As Herman consumed a full-course dinner, Sara, who ate only kosher meat and did not like fish, made do with Grape-Nuts cereal while asking herself, "My heavens above! Is this what being married means? No Sabbath dinner? No candles? No nothing?" She recalled, "I felt so sorry for myself, so bereft—until I took a look at him. He was so intent on this newspaper. And all my pride in him came back in a minute. I thought, 'You've just married the greatest guy in the world. He's not just a ninny who's going to make love to you in the railroad station.' And I felt so full of love."

In short, a simulacrum of the marriage of Herman and Sara: Herman sins. Sara suffers. Sara punishes Herman (passive-aggressively or, in this case, posthumously). Punishment duly administered, the loyal and adoring Sara restores her brilliant Herman to the pedestal they both believe he deserves. And all conveyed with self-deprecating good humor.

They honeymooned in Far Rockaway with Herman's parents and Joe. To Sara, eleven-year-old Joe was an adorable, new younger brother, and she concocted games for them like Race to the Mailbox. Six weeks later, she and Herman began their first glorious adventure. The year was 1920, and the worlds of science, architecture, art, music, literature, and theater were exploding. Young and in love, Herman and Sara traveled first class to Europe: they were going to live in Berlin, where Herman would work for the *Chicago Tribune*. Berlin was both a red-hot center of modernity and a bastion of Old World culture, and Herman and Sara spent the next two years absorbing avant-garde art and Old Masters, traditional and innovative theater, sexual decadence rooted as much in desperation as liberation.

Underlying the spectacular flowering of the arts was the precarious postwar economy, especially in Germany, where Weimar Republic officials attempted to forge a recovery beneath the Versailles Treaty's crushing reparations requirements. Among their many visitors were Edna Ferber and Alexander Woollcott, and Ferber later recalled the way American tourists, whose dollars bought practically anything for practically nothing, seemed oblivious to the effect on the locals trying to live on such worthless European currencies. "Berlin was prophetic enough for anyone who cared to read the writing on the wall," she recalled in 1938, after the Nazis had risen to power on the tide of economic and political chaos.

Herman understood the economic and political fragility, but Sara arrived agog and starry-eyed, about Herman as well as Europe. Her education regarding the former began aboard the SS *Kroonland*. That Herman used part of her $2,500 dowry to finance their luxurious cabin concerned Sara not a whit—his prospects were excellent. But when he finished off both of Sara's small bottles of sacramental port in one night, Sara, who had never seen Herman drink more than a token amount, was shocked. She hadn't known nice Jewish men did such things, much less her own husband.

There were many more things Sara didn't know. Contrary to what he had told everyone, Herman did not really have a job with the *Chicago Tribune*. He had experience at the *New York Tribune* and other publications; extensive newspaper contacts; a track record of good jobs; offers of help from his Paris Red Cross press office; fluency in German; various contacts through his Berlin relatives; and, not inconsequentially, a gambler's sense of optimism. Herman certainly hoped to get work at the *Tribune*, but as yet the *Tribune* had not hired him. Nor had anyone else. Herman had no job at all waiting for him in Berlin.

He had planned to tell Sara on the way over, but somehow he kept losing his nerve. Sara was still unenlightened when they arrived at the kosher pension Herman's aunt had chosen and found it so infested with bedbugs, prostitutes, and customers that Sara could only laugh. At that point, confessing seemed out of the question. So when it was time for Herman to go to work, he put on a suit and tie and pretended to leave for the *Tribune*. Then he took the first job he could find, which was unloading trucks for a department store. Berlin's cost of living was low in 1920, but it was not so low that carton-unloading could support them. Nor was it a viable route to writing the great American novel, the great American play, or even a great American news story.

Chancellor's Garden Party, Berlin, 1921.

So while Sara visited museums and imbibed culture with Tante Anna, Herman pursued one scheme after another. These included, but were but not limited to, equipping a flower cart near the University of Berlin; selling German war planes to "an unsavory Pole"; exchanging tourists' currency on the black market and investing their marks on the German stock market. All the while, Herman kept his eye on the goal. He hung around the large, elegant Hotel Adlon, unofficial headquarters for Berlin's American correspondents and theater people, talking to reporters in the bar and acting as if he were one of them, and soon he was. By fall 1920 Woollcott and Kaufman were running his "News of the Berlin Stage" columns in the *New York Times*.

He started with reports on American producers' search for Berlin material but soon progressed to reviews and disquisitions on any element of theater that intrigued him, from actors' performances to the state of German commercial theater. Because he lived to debunk, he took frequent aim at the renowned director and impresario Max Reinhardt. The prestigious association was welcome, but Herman could not live by *New York Times* columns alone, especially when they paid only eight dollars apiece, "with deductions for dashes, as is the benevolent custom of the office," as Kaufman wrote.

With Jack Dempsey and the Berlin press corps, 1921.

A month into their stay, Herman finally told Sara the truth about the *Tribune* job—or at least part of it. He admitted that he had not arrived with a *Tribune* job (true). But (again transforming wishful thinking into fact) the bureau chief had since offered him a job as his assistant (false). That meant Herman actually was a foreign correspondent (also false). On the other hand, Herman had befriended *Tribune* chief George Seldes, and *Tribune* reporter Sigrid Schultz, two of the most skilled journalists in Europe. Seldes had been moved by Herman's tale of "a New York *World* job in Paris that had fallen through [false], his arrival in Germany with a new bride and no money [almost true], and a Berlin bank president uncle, whom Herman was too proud to approach [possibly true—he was related to a prominent Berlin bank director]." Herman spent so much time at *Tribune* headquarters that Sara, who often met him there in the evenings, believed that version for the rest of her life. Seldes and Schultz insisted to Herman's biographer that he had not written for the *Tribune* as a staff member until the winter of 1922, but Meryman suspected Herman actually did contribute to Seldes's pieces as a legman.

Visiting relatives in Frankfurt. Erna stands beside Herman. Joe is seated. Behind Sara is Rene Harald Mankiewicz, who fled the Nazis with his family, first to France and later, to China. Joe helped them when they emigrated to the US. They settled in Canada, and their son, Francis, became an esteemed director.

In January 1921 Schultz found Herman a fifteen-dollar-a-week job as the Berlin stringer for *Women's Wear Daily*. As she later explained, "I did it partly for his wife. I liked her, and I thought she had a problem with that husband." Sara had no idea she was an object of pity, or that her situation was instrumental in securing a job for her husband. Nor had she any inkling that this would happen again and again over the years. Sara's pitiable plight became an unpleasant but fundamental aspect of her identity, and on the occasions when she could see no other alternative, she learned to play the sympathy card, effectively and with grim determination.

It wasn't the *Times* or the *Tribune*, but *Women's Wear Daily* was a business publication covering political and economic news as well as fashion. Its all-important press credentials allowed Herman to meet with Weimar Republic officials and industrial leaders and discuss Germany's attempts to rebuild its economy. Although his stories ran either under the name of the paper's Berlin correspondent, Bertram Perkins, or without a byline, Herman did much of the actual reporting, because Perkins did not speak German. Then he started repaying Schultz's kindness by missing deadlines so regularly that Schultz started shutting him in the *Tribune* office until he produced his weekly file.

Money worries aside, their Berlin years were a glorious adventure, and they reveled in their opportunities. But Herman gambled and spent so profligately that when Sara became pregnant in 1921, he had to generate extra income. Always a skillful publicist, he represented popular world heavyweight champion boxer Jack Dempsey while he toured Berlin, and planted stories for the Moscow Art Theatre.

Herman was still so broke that when their son Don Martin was born in January 1922, he had to borrow the funds to get Sara discharged from the hospital. By the time dance pioneer Isadora Duncan and her young Russian poet husband, Sergei Yesenin, arrived a few months later, Herman was searching for a way to get back to New York, and working for her seemed like his lucky break. Touring Europe with Duncan and her entourage should have earned him enough to send Sara and Don home, but once he joined them, Herman realized Duncan was even worse with money than he was, or maybe equally disastrous but on a larger scale. Herman routinely had to beg her to pay him, and when she did, it was always less than she had promised.

Finally he left the tour and returned to Berlin, where the three remained stranded until Herman's parents came to the rescue. They had visited with Joe that summer, but Pop returned alone and took Sara and Don home, leaving Herman to find his own way. Herman took up a collection from his poker friends, and after he departed one asked the others, "By the way, besides what we just gave him, does Herman owe you money?" Every man raised his hand.

CHAPTER 6

Central Park West Voltaire

UNFAZED BY HIS IGNOMINIOUS RETURN, HERMAN WAS ELATED TO BE back. New York was home, and the Roaring Twenties suited him perfectly. Herman was in his twenties for most of that decade, and it shaped his sensibility for the rest of his life. Much of Herman's humor was 1920s humor, and Prohibition affected him profoundly. The Eighteenth Amendment took effect on January 17, 1920, so living in Paris and then Berlin, Herman missed most of Prohibition's first two years. By the time he returned, speakeasies were in full swing, hip flasks and bathtub gin de rigueur. Like Pop, Herman needed no encouragement to drink. His drinking problem preceded Prohibition, but Prohibition's illegality added the fillip of the forbidden, prolonging adolescent attitudes toward boozing among the adults who swarmed into nightclubs and speakeasies and rubbed elbows with bootleggers and other gangsters.

After parlaying freelance writing assignments into a *Times* column, Herman expected a warm embrace from the newspaper world. Kaufman had assured him he planned to recommend Herman as his replacement when he quit to write full-time, and with his and Marc Connelly's 1921 comedy, *Dulcy*, a huge critical and commercial hit, Kaufman expected to leave in about a year. However, in 1922 Kaufman was not quite ready to leave the security of his job. He was not quite ready for the next eight years, about eighteen plays later.

Instead, Kaufman sent Herman to see the *New York World*'s executive editor, Herbert Bayard Swope, who employed some of the dailies' most talented writers. Winner of the first Pulitzer Prize and considered "the foremost newspaper reporter of his generation," Swope lived so grandly, even as a reporter, that F. Scott Fitzgerald had modeled Gatsby's parties after his. Swope hired Herman for a measly twenty-five dollars a week (top reporters made one hundred), and instead of the German economy and the state of the Berlin theater, Herman covered mostly local news.

Herman's role model, George Kaufman, rarely smiled and never smoked. This was a gag photo.

At one point, he went undercover to write about the Ku Klux Klan in New York—the *World* had won a Pulitzer Prize in 1922 for its 1921 coverage of the group, so Herman continued the investigation.

He and Sara could only afford to rent the second floor of a two-family house in Brooklyn's Flatbush section, but that did not prevent Herman from making the most of his connections. He socialized with some of the most eminent members of the staff, including Swope himself, the revered Franklin P. Adams (F.P.A.), Heywood Broun (sportswriter/drama critic/columnist), and Deems Taylor, a music critic and eventual composer.

In 1923 Kaufman hired him as *New York Times* assistant section editor and drama reporter, which meant Herman wrote brief items for the daily paper and longer pieces for weekend editions and served as third-string critic. The section's chief critic was John Corbin, an erudite and highly educated man about Pop's age. Kaufman wrote reviews and other short pieces, oversaw the department, and edited the Sunday section. The department's day-to-day operations were maintained by Sam Zolotow, a cigar-chomping, Runyonesque copy "boy" (he was two years younger than Herman), who outlasted them all to become the section's indefatigable theater reporter and columnist.

Louise Brooks was one of Herman's favorites.

Kaufman was extremely conscientious about his duties and famously disciplined—he had three plays produced in 1923 alone. Eight years older than Herman, he was lean, nervous, and often unsmiling. Herman was stocky, gregarious, and notoriously undisciplined. Both popped in and out several times a day to check for releases, write pieces, and work the telephones. Herman liked to drop in on rehearsals and visit friends like W. C. Fields and publisher Horace Liveright, who loved theater as much as Herman. Liveright kept an open house in his office at the end of the day and was known for the quality of his parties as well as the quality of his books. In the evenings, the critics ordinarily attended openings, then returned to the office to type their reviews.

Herman also hobnobbed with showgirls and actresses. Former Martha Graham and current Ziegfeld Follies performer Louise Brooks was a particular favorite, probably because she was just Herman's type, intelligent as well as attractive. She and Herman constituted two-thirds of the

Louise Brooks Literary Society, which Herman created for Brooks and another Ziegfeld beauty named Dorothy Knapp. Brooks recalled, "We had a big dressing room on the fifth floor of the New Amsterdam Theatre Building, and people like Walter Wanger and Gilbert Miller would meet there, ostensibly to hear my reviews of books that Herman gave me to read. What they actually came for was to watch Dorothy doing a strip-tease and having a love affair with herself in front of a full-length mirror. I get some consolation from the fact that, as an idiot, I have provided delight in my time to a very select group of intellectuals."

Actually, Brooks's ignorance was as feigned as the pseudo-intellectual interests of her audience. She spent much of her Wichita, Kansas, child-hood in her lawyer-father's library, reading Carlyle, Thackeray, Emerson, and Twain, and in a memoir described herself as "an inhumane executioner of the bogus." She played hooky from the Follies to accompany Herman to the opening of *No, No, Nanette* and took notes for his review because he was too drunk to stay awake.

Herman relished his job's side benefits. Besides enjoying the pleasure of pulchritudinous company, he was intoxicated by having his reviews mined for blurbs in theatrical advertisements and seeing his name displayed alongside such estimable critics as Heywood Broun and Alexander Woollcott. He loved being able to help. When Joe's friend Chester Eckstein was interested in a Broadway career, Herman changed his name to Erskine (after the brothers' beloved Professor Erskine) and found him a job.

He also delighted in the power of his position. Kaufman firmly guarded his integrity and refused to write about shows with which his friends—and especially, himself—were connected. Hired to publicize Kaufman's *To the Ladies,* John Peter Toohey asked Kaufman how to get the name of their star, Helen Hayes, into the paper. "Shoot her," Kaufman said.

Herman was less fastidious. When his college friend Henry Myers needed work, Herman telephoned the press office of powerful theater owner-producers Shubert brothers, and an impressed Myers listened to Herman's side of the conversation: "Claude, this is Herman. I'm reviewing a play of yours that is opening tonight."

Claude had already left tickets for the show.

Herman already knew that. He was calling because his friend needed a job.

Claude had no openings.

Herman: "You didn't hear what I said. I'm reviewing a play of yours tonight."

Herman's extortion worked. Despite Myers's total lack of press experience, the Shuberts hired him.

As usual, Herman's *Times* salary did not begin to cover his expenditures, so during the summer of 1923 he took a leave of absence to work as press agent for Max Reinhardt's American production of *The Miracle*. From Berlin, Herman had declared Reinhardt professionally dead several times over, but either Reinhardt did not hold a grudge or he considered Herman's early dispatches beneath his notice (probably the latter). In *The Miracle*, a nun in the Middle Ages runs away with a knight, and the convent's statue of the Virgin Mary comes to life to take her place. The grandiosity of the production made Herman's job easy and probably quite enjoyable—how else to explain a *Times* item reporting that producer Morris Gest planned to become an "American Ambassador of Artistry" and that the production would be "as effective in the cause of international friendliness as a League of Nations"? (Herman probably considered the jab at the League a fringe benefit.)

He returned to the *Times* a few months later but continued to freelance, and when their second son, Frank Fabian, was born on May 16, 1924, the family moved to an apartment on Central Park West in Manhattan. The neighborhood was more convenient for carousing with his friends, and Herman spent as much time as possible with the Algonquin Round Table regulars. The group revolved around Alexander Woollcott, F. P. Adams, Kaufman, and Dorothy Parker, with John Peter Toohey, Heywood Broun, Robert Benchley, Robert Sherwood, Marc Connelly, and Harold Ross as its inner core. The larger group included Ross's wife, journalist Jane Grant; Kaufman's wife, Beatrice, an editor, among other things; poet and playwright John V. A. Weaver; actresses Margalo Gillmore, Tallulah Bankhead, and Peggy Wood; Harpo Marx; novelists Edna Ferber and Alice Duer Miller; writers Donald Ogden Stewart, Charles MacArthur, Frank Sullivan, and Deems Taylor.

Magazine illustrator Neysa McMein provided an away-from-the-Algonquin salon at her Fifty-Seventh Street studio, where Helen Hayes met her future husband (MacArthur), and outsider regulars like Otto Kahn, George Gershwin, and Jascha Heifetz dropped in. Group members saw one another at "21" and speakeasies like Tony Roma's and Texas Guinan's ("Hello, suckers"), as well as at the offices of publisher Boni & Liveright. A few founded the Thanatopsis Literary and Inside Straight Club, where Ross, Kaufman, and Harpo Marx allowed a few select others, like Ring Lardner and baking company heir Raoul Fleischmann, to join marathon poker games that could drag on for more than a day.

Algonquin Table friends for life: Alexander Woollcott, Charles MacArthur and Helen Hayes, and Dorothy Parker.

Although Herman was among the youngest, they respected and liked him, and he fit in easily, drinking, playing poker, and exchanging quips. Despite their apparent viciousness (they called themselves the Vicious Circle for a reason), the irreverent sophisticates of the Algonquin set and the hard-drinking newspapermen-turning-playwrights like Ben Hecht and Charles MacArthur remained Herman's cherished friends and most important influences for the rest of his life. Well beyond his twenties, Herman struggled to reconcile the frivolity his friends espoused with his desire for serious achievement, both for himself and to impress his father. Amidst the disappointments of his later years, his connection with the Algonquin group was a comforting validation.

Of course their frivolity was a pose. They were actually fiercely ambitious, but like English aristocrats they concealed genuine effort, feigned anti-intellectualism, and affected a lack of interest in success. Many sank into alcoholism and died relatively young. The heavy drinking that had contributed to their cohesion also contributed to their deaths.

In a 1925 letter, Ring Lardner describes a typical escapade to F. Scott Fitzgerald (Lardner was an alcoholic who died in 1933 at the age of forty-eight). Distressed to see Dorothy Parker so depressed over her current love affair, Lardner and his wife invited her to visit them in Great Neck, a Long Island New York suburb, where they lived down the street from the Swopes. Parker stayed for two months, and, Lardner reported, he was "constantly cock-eyed, drinking all night and sleeping all day and never working."

When Herman came to visit them one evening, the three went drinking at Durand's, a nearby speakeasy filled with big, husky Irishmen. Seeing them, Lardner wrote, reminded Herman that "he had been in the Marines and ought to prove it by licking all the inmates of the joint." After Lardner broke it up, Herman spent the night at the Lardners' and, upon awakening the next morning at ten, said he needed to get right back to New York to work on the Sunday editions of the *Times*. Then Lardner's wife gave him "a few highballs to brace him up," and he stayed until five that evening.

Sara had mixed feelings about Herman's celebrated friends. She was proud of their regard for Herman, worried about their influence, and intimidated by their cruelty. Some of Herman's other friends were less impressed. "Among the Woollcottians," wrote Ben Hecht, "the bedazzling of the uninvited was made easy by the fact that nearly all of Alec's captains conducted gossip columns in the press and magazines. F.P.A., Broun, Ross, Frank Sullivan, Miss Parker, Corey Ford and Woollcott himself wrote about each other swooningly. . . . Though most of the talent of the day (in fact nearly all of it) was missing from their salons, this Algonquin school of wags offered itself as the artistic vortex of the town. Among the missing . . . were Thomas Wolfe, Sandburg, O'Neill, Sherwood Anderson, Willa Cather, Mencken, Nathan, Hemingway. . . . Edith Wharton, Edna Millay . . . et cetera. The artist was wise who was absent."

Like Herman, Hecht was a soft-hearted, iconoclastic curmudgeon, and despite Herman's regrettable regard for characters Hecht deemed unworthy, Hecht considered Herman the most clear-eyed of observers and certainly one of the wittiest. Dubbing Herman the Voltaire of Central Park West, he wrote that his dear friend "could puncture egos, draw blood from pretenses—and his victims, with souls abashed, still sat and laughed. The swiftness of his thought was by itself a sort of comedy. Never have I known a man with so quick an eye and ear—and tongue, for the strut of fools."

On a less exalted note, Hecht and Herman also shared a penchant for shortcuts, as in 1925, when they decided to strike it rich by publishing a magazine. Hecht had created the *Chicago Literary Times* with poet Maxwell Bodenheim, and while it had not made their fortune, Hecht hoped Otto Kahn's backing would make a difference. In exchange, Hecht

Visiting Coney Island with Ben and Rose Hecht, 1926.

agreed to help Kahn's teenaged, saxophone-playing son, Roger, write a Broadway show. Hecht and Herman formed the Bozo Publishing Corporation and operated out of the back of Le Perroquet de Paris, a nightclub Roger would open the following year.

In May they published volume 1 of *The Low Down: A Magazine for Hypocrites*. It included both published and rejected work from Hecht's previous magazine; drawings by George Grosz that they captioned; a fake gossip column; and poems they wrote jointly under the name of Alfred Pupick. After a June issue that recycled some of May's, the publication (not surprisingly) died.

The more time Herman spent in the theatrical world, the less content he became merely to critique others' creations, so he and poet John V. A. Weaver, decided to produce *Love 'Em and Leave 'Em*, Weaver's play about a flapper. They were such a bust in Asbury Park, New Jersey, that they never made it to Broadway, and Herman had to figure out not only how to pay the actors but how to return them to New York, and how to pay Weaver his $500 royalty. How he solved the first two is lost to history, but Herman found the royalty fee by borrowing it from actress Peggy Wood, also known as Mrs. John Weaver.

His instincts were correct, however. George Abbott helped Weaver revise the script and, in his directorial debut, directed it; it was produced by

Jed Harris, in his producing debut. The new, improved *Love 'Em and Leave 'Em* ran for 152 performances and spawned two successful Paramount films, a 1926 silent version starring Louise Brooks, and a 1929 sound-and-titled version, *The Saturday Night Kid*, with Clara Bow, Jean Arthur, Jean Harlow in her first credited role, and titles written by twenty-year-old Joseph Mankiewicz, in one of his first movie assignments.

Herman tried again, directing as well this time. The Algonquin group had staged two revues in 1922, so Herman decided to produce one with S. Jay Kaufman, a New York *Telegraph* writer, whose column, *Round the Town*, provided their title. The Algonquin set had little respect for Jay Kaufman (George Kaufman derisively called him "the *nice* Kaufman"), but they were fond of Herman, and they were show-offs. So Kaufman and Marc Connelly, who had just ended their writing partnership, reunited to write a parody of their current *Beggar on Horseback*, entitled "Beggar off Horseback." Kaufman collaborated with Herman on "Moron Films, Educational, Travel and Topical." Robert Benchley performed "The Sex Life of the Polyp" in their Newark previews but dropped out after local critics called his monologue dirty. Dorothy Parker, Robert Sherwood, and Heywood Broun contributed as well.

As a director, Herman was a disaster. Assigned to cast a chorus line of sixteen beautiful girls, he chose sixteen unbeautiful, untalented dancers because he couldn't bear their sob stories. Why that one? Sara asked, of a particularly egregious choice. "Sick mother," Herman admitted.

They set curtain time for eleven o'clock to attract the after-theater crowd but had to close after fifteen performances. Otto Kahn covered Herman's share of the losses, a loan Herman actually repaid, and though the revue is long forgotten, some of the responses to its sheer awfulness have lived on. It was *Round the Town* that prompted a friend to entreat Actor's Equity president John Emerson (Anita Loos's husband), "If you want to be a public benefactor, call a strike before the second act."

It was also *Round the Town* that provoked Chicago critic Ashton Stevens's infamous wire "The play ran late, the audience early."

Herman was disappointed but not devastated. He always believed his real calling was writing, and he turned out material continually. He sold sketches to the Ziegfeld Follies and other variety revues; he began (though didn't finish) a play about newspaper magnate William Randolph Hearst; and he poured his heart into an expressionist political satire called *We, the People*. During the summer of 1925, he took it along during a visit upstate with Ben Hecht and Charles MacArthur. However, he also brought along a suitcase full of Scotch, so instead of working on the script, the three of them collaborated on the Scotch, reminiscing about the war and old newspaper days.

Herman eventually finished his satire of American gullibility and attracted a producer, but when it failed to get to production, Herman decided that perhaps he, like Kaufman, needed a writing partner. And who better than his ideal, role model, and mentor? Kaufman was amenable because, despite his run of hits, he was still so insecure that he preferred to collaborate. The fact that he chose to work with an assistant whose habits he knew better than most showed his clear regard for Herman. Besides their *Round the Town* sketch, they had written a sketch about a shady pawnshop called "Nothing Coming In" (a sign in the shop read, "Particularly High Loans on Anything from the Metropolitan Museum"). Herman had also helped Kaufman with the only play he wrote alone, *The Butter and Egg Man* (1925), a satire whose plot anticipated Mel Brooks's *The Producers*. (The prolific Kaufman wrote yet a third play in 1925, the Marx Brothers' *The Cocoanuts*, with Irving Berlin and Morris Ryskind, which became such a colossal success that Paramount turned it into their first film, in 1929.)

Kaufman and Herman started during the summer of 1925, working from an idea of Herman's about a lodge master ("Grand Napoleon") of a Wilkes-Barre, Pennsylvania, chapter of the Ancient Order of Corsicans. They assumed that the rituals and costumes of lodge culture would offer easy pickings, but developing a protagonist who was simultaneously sympathetic and a bragging boor turned out to be more difficult than they had anticipated. Kaufman wrote some of his best plays with Edna Ferber, whose strengths were characterization and love scenes. They were not Kaufman's and, unfortunately, they were not Herman's, either.

With enough hard work, they might have overcome the play's weaknesses but despite the honor of working with his boss, Herman showed little interest in putting in the time. He disappeared for hours on end and airily read newspapers when they were together. Eventually they completed *The Good Fellow*, and despite its obvious problems, *The Butter and Egg Man*'s producer, Crosby Gaige, agreed to produce it.

Herman also started working with Marc Connelly on *The Wild Man of Borneo*, about Dan Thompson, a semiretired con man who supports his unsuspecting daughter by secretly working in a sideshow. Connelly had stopped collaborating with Kaufman because he did not want to work as hard as Kaufman, so when easygoing Connelly joined lackadaisical Herman, their progress was snaillike. Connelly later blamed Herman, whom he described as "a born kaffeeklatscher," though one he enjoyed: "He

Collaborator Marc Connelly (r.) with Robert Benchley.

was born to sit of an afternoon and talk. . . . He was noisy. He was vigorous. He was witty and full of fun. . . . And it wasn't until we were half way through that I realized he had taken an idea I had for a skit that I had written for Bea Lillie and W. C. Fields. And I think Mank contributed about five minutes to it."

Herman began a third collaboration that year, with Marion Spitzer, an old friend who worked as a publicist for producer Edgar Selwyn (Edgar and his brother, Archibald, provided the "wyn" that Samuel Goldfish adopted to become Goldwyn). Crosby Gaige agreed to produce it, but they never finished.

At the end of 1924, Harold Ross invited Herman to be theater critic for a new magazine he was setting up. In Paris during the war, Private Ross had edited the US military's newspaper, *Stars and Stripes*, and his staff had included Captain Alexander Woollcott and Private Franklin P. Adams, who both considered their boss a Colorado yokel. After the war, the yokel joined his new friends in New York, where he edited a humor magazine called *Judge* and amused them and their friends by carrying around the tattered prototype of the sophisticated, urbane magazine he wanted to create. When Ross finally published thirty thousand copies of the *New Yorker*'s initial February 21, 1925, issue, the eighteen thousand copies available in New York sold out in the first thirty-six hours.

Harold Ross, the "yokel" who founded the *New Yorker*.

Even with that auspicious beginning, failure was the most likely outcome for new magazines, so Herman's position was a dubious honor, unaccompanied by much money. Except for Dorothy Parker, most of the Algonquin crowd waited until the magazine had proved itself to offer submissions but Herman, who had more to gain and less to lose, helped out in a number of ways. He joked to Ross, "The part-time help of wits is no better than the full-time help of half-wits," and reminded of the remark years later, Ross recalled, "God knows I had both kinds."

Because Ross considered "Talk of the Town" the magazine's signature, he closed the section at the last minute, and Herman often came in to assist with rewrites. He enjoyed helping, but his position as critic elated him. Necessarily relegated to leftovers at the *Times*, Herman could review the season's most important plays in the *New Yorker*, and despite the facetious tics typical of the magazine's early days, his observations were often astute. When Ross allowed it, he expounded on other matters theatrical and plugged friends like W. C. Fields, and friends' shows, even Kaufman's *Butter and Egg Man*.

He took on the mighty, with harsh critiques of both George Bernard Shaw, who would receive the Nobel Prize for Literature the following year, and Eugene O'Neill, two-time Pulitzer Prize winner for drama. He was not above racist jokes (he routinely ridiculed all groups, including his own), but Herman also called attention to the casual racism of underpaying black comedians because of their race.

The *New Yorker* was a heady platform, but Herman's day job was at the *Times*, and at the end of 1925, he almost lost it. Covering a vanity production of *The School for Scandal*, he was appalled to see the role of eighteen-year-old Lady Teazle played by a fifty-six-year-old amateur whose husband had financed the production. By the time he returned to the office to write his review, he was so drunk that he managed only a few paragraphs beyond "Miss Gladys Wallace, an aging, hopelessly incompetent amateur . . ." before passing out at his desk. Sara, who frequently met him at the office, failed to revive him, so when Kaufman arrived to write his own review, Herman was still unconscious and slumped over his typewriter with the review unfinished.

The ordinarily controlled Kaufman lost his temper and sent them home, and they assumed Herman would be fired. After sending the assistant managing editor the bizarre gift of a bottle of Scotch, Herman returned to the office to clean out his desk. Then he telephoned Horace Liveright, who, to his astonishment, offered him a job at twice his *Times* salary. Once offers from press agents and even the Shuberts also started pouring in, Herman stopped worrying and enjoyed the attention. Then Kaufman forgave him. Herman could stay at the *Times*, and Kaufman even wanted to continue collaborating.

In sum, Herman's reprehensible behavior was rewarded. Instead of slinking away beneath a cloud of shame, Herman sailed through the ordeal atop a wave of triumph. Furthermore, although the *School for Scandal* review that actually ran in the *Times* was unsigned, it is impossible to imagine anyone but Herman writing it. Following several paragraphs that damned the acting with faint praise, it noted, "The brocaded broadcoats, the rococo waistcoats, the furbelows, laces, silks, wigs, Gainsborough hats, ruffles and flounces quite outdo mere necessity and keep the stage aglitter with extravagant investiture." As for Lady Teazle, "Mrs. Insull is as pretty as she is diminutive, with a clear smile and dainty gestures. There is a charming grace in her bearing that makes for excellent deportment."

Not only that, the emboldened Herman struck again (and again) in the *New Yorker*. In December he included a brief review in his section, describing the production as "decidedly spotty" and Mrs. Insull as "dainty, earnest and high-minded, but scarcely the type." His February piece about Chicago ("A New Yorker in the Provinces") observed, "Chicago has no waggish weekly of its own, but on the bill-boards there are thousands of posters that advertise 'Mrs. Insull in "The School for Scandal," direct from her triumphant three months engagement in New York.'"

Of course Herman understood that he had gotten a free pass, and when he recycled the incident in *Citizen Kane*, he administered consequences and added complexity. In the film, Kane's best friend, Jedidiah Leland (Joseph Cotten), has to review an excruciating operatic performance by Kane's wife, Susan, and, like Herman, Leland both sticks to his principles by writing a scathing critique and passes out before finishing it. Unlike Herman, who felt only simple indignation at the notion of an actress's buying her way into a part, Leland's situation is more complicated. Kane is Leland's friend as well as his employer, and he pities Susan, who performed only because Kane forced her to, to satisfy his own ego. To maintain his integrity, Leland has to injure Susan, who does not deserve it, and sacrifice what is left of his and Kane's friendship, as well as his job. In life, Herman escaped punishment. In art, Herman punished everyone.

All that lay in the future. In 1925 Herman was a promising young writer, albeit a writer who drank too much and gambled away funds his family needed to live. Given those propensities, he naturally was intrigued when a Metro-Goldwyn-Mayer (MGM) press agent said he could make a fortune in Hollywood. And when "a fortune" turned out to mean $500 a week for writing a scenario, the offer certainly seemed too good to refuse. Other writers were selling their plays' screen rights; why shouldn't he also benefit from the industry's fabulous payouts?

Only embarrassment made him hesitate. By 1925 a number of fine films had been made in Hollywood and abroad, but Herman and his friends, who regarded theater as Art, no matter how silly the play, considered motion pictures déclassé. However, little by little, they were overcoming their scruples, and Herman actually had an idea about the Marines he thought would make a good movie. He just made sure friends knew he had thought of it while sitting on the toilet.

Besides, he would be gone only long enough to earn the $2,200 he needed to cover a debt. As he later observed, everyone who went to Hollywood initially set out "in pursuit of a lump sum." Indebted though he was, Herman went in style. He took the luxurious Twentieth Century

Limited to Chicago, where he stopped for a few days to scoop up another lump sum. Dr. Morris Fishbein, editor of the American Medical Association's journal and author of medical articles for popular magazines, had invited Herman to address Chicago's Book and Play Club on the subject of New York theater. They had met in Liveright's office, and once Herman took Fishbein home to dinner, he had become an ardent fan of Sara's as well as Herman's.

Herman enjoyed both the honor of following such illustrious predecessors as Carl Sandburg, Sherwood Anderson, and Edgar Lee Masters in addressing Chicago's Algonquin equivalent, and the pleasure of turning down a job offer from the *Chicago Tribune*. Then he entered a two-dollar-limit poker game and lost his entire $300 honorarium.

He wired home for funds to finish the trip, then stayed on for another couple of days to win back his fee, and lost that, too. Fishbein cheerfully staked him to the rest of the trip. "Herman Mankiewicz was one of the most brilliant conversationalists I have ever known," he later wrote, recalling that "the literati constantly argued whether Ben Hecht or Herman was the greater in this art . . . it was always a dead heat."

Reaching Los Angeles, Herman was captivated by its mild climate and profuse flowers, though he also experienced a preview of the capricious ways of studios. MGM no longer wanted a scenario on the Marines; they wanted a new story for Lon Chaney, the so-called Man of a Thousand Faces. Herman obligingly invented Singapore Joe, a one-eyed villain who sacrifices his daughter to give her the chance at a better life and later saves her from disaster by murdering the man she is about to marry. Chaney used a full-eye white contact lens to cover one of his eyeballs, and *The Road to Mandalay* (1926) became Herman J. Mankiewicz's first contribution to American cinema.

His California idyll ended abruptly in February 1926, when he lost his job at the *New Yorker*. Harold Ross so feared conflict that he had waited until Herman was on the other side of the continent before firing him by mail. Stunned, Herman assumed he could talk Ross out it. That was a "low, dirty piece of behavior," he remonstrated, for which he deserved an explanation.

> Four days before I left for California you assured me flatly and positively that my job would be waiting for me upon my return. (This assurance, as you know, had much to do with my decision to take the trip West.) . . .

> . . . There has been a lot of bushwah around about the lateness and unreliability of my copy. You write that "we had so damn much trouble with your deadlines, the Goings-On blurbs, etc. that we construed it as lack of interest on your part." The actual fact is that three times in a year was my copy in after the arbitrary time limit set by your efficiency experts, and then it was in in plenty of time. I hereby agree to write you ten full-length casuals free if you can show me one instance in which the New Yorker was inconvenienced, except conversationally among the busy yes-men, by a delay in my copy—one instance in which the make-up or printing was held up for a second.

He dismissed his probable successor: "I ask you to toy with the weird notion that to mention me and Gabriel [Gilbert Gabriel, theater critic at the *Evening Sun*] in the same breath as writers on the theatre for civilized audiences is to expose yourself to history's definitive judgement as one of the worst judges of dramatic criticism of all time."

He reminded Ross of his loyalty: "I ask you to remember who it was, in the early, struggling, hopeless days of the New Yorker, who showed up at MacMurtrie's on press night and wrote pieces on the premises so that you could publish at all. You forget very easily, Ross."

As a plea for reinstatement, Herman's response left much to be desired, and Ross did not mince words:

> I will not discuss the merit of your dramatic criticism which, of course, was a factor. Aside from this, I was forced to the conclusion three months ago that it would be impossible indefinitely to continue relations. Your disposition and your attitude seemed to make it impossible. My accumulation of grievances was too preposterously great. . . . I will tell you now, Mank, that I had no confidence that they would stand on more than a temporary basis and doubted if they would last out the present season. When you decided to go west, I told you that your going would not affect your status. You assumed that I "assured you flatly and positively that my job would be waiting" upon your return. I didn't, because I know what was in my mind, and I wanted to be careful not to mislead you. I thought this over and, two or three days later, decided that I had better tell you before your departure that we were making new arrangements. This, so that there would not be any misunderstanding, and

it was not, then, the result of a chance meeting a day or two before you left.

... I am still grateful personally for the help in the early days, but I sincerely feel that your subsequent omissions and actions removed that obligation a hundred times over. I would point out too that I am responsible for other persons' property, other persons' money. . . . Damn it, we are not playing magazine, and we are not children.

A few specific things: You drew $100 a week . . . with the understanding that you would do the criticism and considerable other work. . . . In fact, while you were neglecting this you were actually writing pieces for other magazines. Unpardonable breach of faith.

... You denounced me to contributors we were trying to line up. A dirty game. . . .

You were negligent in your covering of shows, being inexcusably late with important reviews. We have the statistics on this.

Your personality is such that you cannot be fitted into an organization. You are too disturbing—announcing to the assembled staff that you were resigning and coming into my office to paste me one in the mouth, haggling boyishly about things such as the Fields profile, etc. etc. My god, Mank, you resigned publicly at least six times.

Even for a crowd that valued outrageous behavior, Herman's was so egregious that Ross had needed only a few months to decide Herman was not an organization man. But Ross had indeed deceived him, and Herman decided to confront his former boss in person.

Once he returned to New York, Herman charged into the magazine's office brandishing a cane and vowing to administer justice. Ross, who had been warned, hid in a coat closet, so Herman used his cane to administer justice to Ross's desk instead and left. When he returned a second time, Ross faced him in the publication's main office while the magazine's entire four- or five-member staff eavesdropped breathlessly from behind a partition. Ralph Ingersoll, the young managing editor at the time, recalled the scene: "After Mank's 'But you *can't* fire me' reaction, and as they got madder and madder, roaring at each other, first ties, then coats—and could be a shirt—came flying over the partition." The men were "stripping out of sheer excitement, much to our delight." Eventually a "red-with-rage Mank came flying out in tatters." From then on Ross forced Ingersoll to convey bad news. "Firings were too much for Harold after Mank's."

Herman and Ross eventually reconciled. Herman pitched stories, and the *New Yorker* occasionally ran his work. Ross saw Herman when he was in Los Angeles, and when they played cards, Herman usually lost large sums, but Ross had trouble collecting on the debts. Losing his job at the *New Yorker* gave Herman the push he needed to make a change. His plays with Kaufman and Connelly were progressing, but he assumed he could commute between coasts, and Sara loved the idea. The money was welcome, but she also hoped a change of scene might induce Herman to reform, especially by separating him from his alcohol-soaked New York friends.

Before he left, Herman carefully avoided burning his bridges. He checked with his *Times* editor and received his assurance that if the experiment did not work out, he could indeed return to his eighty-dollar-a-week job.

THE MANKIEWICZ BROTHERS OF HOLLYWOOD

CHAPTER 7

In Pursuit of a Lump Sum

MGM BEGAN PRODUCTION OF *THE ROAD TO MANDALAY* IN APRIL 1926, but Walter Wanger, a handsome, cultured, longtime New York friend of Herman's, had become Paramount's general manager of production, and he convinced Herman to work for Paramount. Sara and the boys spent the summer at the New Jersey shore while Herman started work in Los Angeles, at $400 a week, plus $5,000 bonuses for every scenario Paramount used, with a guarantee of no less than four a year. He returned in the fall to fetch his family, and as they made their way west on the train, Herman and Sara enjoyed elegant dinners in their private compartment while Don, six, and Frank, four, rode in a separate car with a nanny. A studio limousine met them in Pasadena—it was considered déclassé to ride all the way downtown to Union Station.

Sara loved Los Angeles from the start and moved them through a series of apartments and houses until she found the right home. Once they lived next door to actor Edmund Lowe, who kept his pet canary supplied with marijuana seeds. Another house resembled a castle, complete with a spiral staircase leading to a turret Herman used as an office. Eventually they rented 1105 Tower Road, a large Mediterranean-style house in Beverly Hills, with a porte-cochère, a free-form swimming pool, and an office for Herman over the three-car garage. A huge screened sleeping porch topped a latticed area where Sara installed a ping pong table. The owner was a Canadian woman whose guardians were unable to agree on a rental price, so they rented at a nominal rate for years until the woman died. Then they bought it from her estate.

Emulating many Hollywood couples, they took separate bedrooms. Sara decorated hers to resemble a glamorous Paramount set—large and white, with a fireplace and a huge walk-in closet. Herman's was smaller, darker, and smoky from his Camels. He cared more about his library, which they housed in the downstairs study, but he too began savoring

With Don and Frank, Los Angeles.

his newfound riches. He bought new clothes, golf clubs (though he didn't play golf), and director Ernst Lubitsch's Cadillac convertible limousine. They hired a series of couples, many of them German, though the first was an Irish chauffeur with a wife who cooked. Sara supplemented the couples with a series of "Frauleins" to take care of the children. With Sara's Chrysler and Herman's Buick two-seater, their fleet of three cars was excessive for that era (even in Beverly Hills), but Herman's Buick didn't last long. Always a terrible driver, when he saw a policeman and could not resist yelling, "Look! No hands!" he ran into a telephone pole.

They became sought-after guests, with dazzling new friends and neighbors. Greta Garbo, who lived with their neighbor, actor John Gilbert, swam in the nude, played fierce tennis with Herman, and laughed uproariously at his jokes even when she didn't understand them. If he was at a party, George Gershwin usually sat down at the piano and played for the rest of the evening. Mary Astor, Oscar Hammerstein, and John Barrymore lived nearby, as did David and Irene Mayer Selznick and agent Leland Hayward and his wife, Margaret Sullavan, who became lifelong friends. They gave costume parties and entertained friends from back east like Dorothy Parker and F. Scott Fitzgerald, who brought his daughter Scottie and, later, Sheilah Graham, who devoted an entire column to a dinner party that featured fried chicken for the Selznicks, Haywards, and Harpo Marxes, plus Irving Berlin, Sidney Howard, and of course, Fitzgerald.

Herman and Sara had no idea they would be there for the rest of their lives. They also were unaware that revolution was just around the corner. Talkies were about to sweep the nation, and as the silent-movie era sputtered to a close, there would be winners like Herman, whose intelligence and wit were invaluable once spoken dialogue was required, and losers, mostly actors who were better seen than heard. Because Herman did not regard movie work as his real life, he delighted in what he imagined was his temporary sojourn in the lap of luxury. All he had to do was what came naturally.

Writing scenarios was easy—he already entertained friends with elaborate fantasies that went far beyond wisecracks. "He could improvise in a way that just held you spellbound," Nunnally Johnson recalled years later. The intertitles or titles, the onscreen captions that conveyed dialogue or explained the action, were actually very important, because they could make or break a movie. That was why top title writers were so highly paid. To Herman, they were as easy as captioning comic strips; coining clever ones was just an extension of what the epigrammatic Herman did for fun every day.

At Paramount, the most sophisticated of the major studios, Herman reported to Benjamin (B. P.) Schulberg, a literate former newspaperman who had started his career as F.P.A.'s copy boy, and Schulberg treated Herman like a star. Instead of a tiny office in the writers' warren, Herman had a secretary and a spacious office suite in the administration building. Working only a few hours a day, Herman spent the rest of his employer's time reading newspapers, both trade and general; collecting and disseminating Hollywood gossip; placing bets with bookies and friends; wandering around the Paramount lot; playing and gambling with other writers; and punctuating long lunches with witticisms that were repeated all over town.

Naturally, there was a trade-off to be made in exchange for the enormous salary and luxurious perquisites. Like theater, moviemaking was a collaborative process, but the difference in status between screenwriter and playwright was profound. Theater evolved from Sophocles and

Shakespeare. Theatrical backers, producers, directors, or actors might ask—or even insist—that a playwright make changes. But a play's script remained the playwright's, and the playwright remained a respected member of the creative team.

Movies grew out of peep shows and vaudeville. They started as commerce and developed into art. Studio chiefs respected literature and theater and had no objection to producing art—as long as the art made money. Most of them had started as theater owners and ran their studios like the factories that they were: studios existed to supply products that would pull audiences into their theaters. Screenwriters were studio employees, cogs in the picture-manufacturing machines. Their scripts were studio property. Studio executives could do whatever they chose with them and routinely did. As Herman put it, "When the producer says to you, 'Now in Reel Three the fellow shouldn't kiss the girl, he should kiss the cow,'" that fellow was going to kiss the cow and there wasn't a thing the writer could do about it.

In the beginning Herman was more amused than indignant, since he viewed himself as a playwright and critic, temporarily slumming for the money. His collaborations with Kaufman and Connelly were his real work, and both plays were moving toward fruition. "If this play fails, I'll never speak to you again," Kaufman warned Herman before he left for the coast, the first of many threats Kaufman made to collaborators. But once *The Good Fellow* went into production, Herman realized his job on the other side of the country was more than an inconvenience—it directly affected the production. Herman had strong opinions about what the play needed, but when they started summer previews in Long Branch, New Jersey, he could only wait anxiously on the sidelines.

The response was not encouraging, so Kaufman worked on revisions and tried again in Atlantic City. Its audiences also were not amused. When Kaufman complained about their lack of merriment to actress Ruth Gordon, who was also trying out a play there, she grumbled that her audiences were laughing, but the play was a tragedy. "Let's switch audiences," Kaufman suggested.

In October 1926 Kaufman took it to Broadway anyway, with John E. Hazzard, a musical comedy performer and playwright, in the lead. Herman considered Hazzard a poor choice to begin with, and because he frequently forgot his lines, he threw off the other actors as well. Their subject also seemed to be a dud. Satire about lodges bored New Yorkers and offended lodge members. Critics generally liked Hazzard, so they blamed the script for the play's shortcomings. They closed after only seven performances, but Kaufman never did stop speaking to Herman. Instead, he offered help with *We, the People*.

Even with capable actors and a first-class producer, Herman and Marc Connelly's *The Wild Man of Borneo* also floundered. After a brief 1926 tryout in Boston, they shelved it and tried again in Washington, D.C., the following year. They planned a September opening on Broadway, but Herman wired Connelly:

> AFTER STUDYING THE PLAY CAREFULLY . . . I DON'T THINK IT IS IN ANY SHAPE TO GO INTO REHEARSAL. . . . I THINK IT IS UNDERWRITTEN THROUGHOUT AND THOMPSON'S ROLE IN PARTICULAR IS DANGEROUSLY LEFT TO THE AUDIENCE'S IMAGINATION RATHER THAN OBJECTIVELY AND STRENUOUSLY PRESENTED STOP I MEAN THAT YOU AND I KNOW HE IS A BOISTEROUS LIAR FULL OF GUSTO BUT THE AUDIENCE HAS LITTLE BEYOND OUR WORD FOR IT STOP I ASSUME YOU HAVE BEEN IN REHEARSAL SINCE MONDAY WHICH MEANS REHEARSALS COULD BE CALLED OFF WITHOUT DAMAGE AND RENEWED IN ANOTHER WEEK OR TEN DAYS STOP IF YOU AGREE I WILL DEVOTE ALL MY TIME FOR NEXT WEEK TO SUPPLYING THE COMEDY AND CHARACTER LINES I THINK ARE MISSING FROM THOMPSON'S ROLE STOP PLEASE UNDERSTAND I AM WILLING TO YIELD TO YOUR GREATER EXPERIENCE IF YOU THINK I AM WRONG BUT I FELT I SHOULD SPEAK OPENLY.

Connelly disagreed, so they opened September 13. Herman wired, "YOU HAVE WORKED LONG AND FAITHFULLY AND IF IT WERE HUMANLY POSSIBLE I'D WANT THE WILD MAN TO BE A HIT TONIGHT MORE FOR YOUR SAKE THAN FOR MINE STOP AS IT IS YOU GET AT LEAST A FIFTY BREAK IN MY HOPES STOP ONCE AGAIN MY SINCERE THANKS." (He also wired Pop, "BEST WISHES FOR MY SUCCESS TONIGHT.")

Afterward, Sam Zolotow from the *Times* wired, "CONFIDENTIAL FIRST TWO ACTS BAD STOP THIRD ACT SWELL STOP AUDIENCE APPLAUDED ONLY THIRD ACT STOP SHOW IS FLOP NO USE KIDDING YOURSELF STOP." They closed after fifteen performances.

So that was that. Herman had worked with two masters of the theater and failed both times. He framed Zolotow's wire alongside one from Kaufman, printed "R.I.P." between the two, entitled it "The Lamentable Condition of the American Theatre," hung it in his office, and moved on.

Despite those disappointments, Pop continued to urge Herman to return to more worthy pursuits, though he seemed inspired to pursue the good life himself, with a small cabin in Mt. Tremper, a Catskill Mountains hamlet in upstate New York. It lacked basic amenities like indoor plumbing, and Hanna and Joe both hated it. But Pop loved it and even embarked on cockeyed moneymaking schemes like raising chickens. Unfortunately, he bought twenty-five roosters and one hen instead of the reverse, so they eventually had to eat them. Worse, Hanna had to do all the slaughtering because Pop couldn't bear to watch.

Joe, who venerated Herman's occupation as much as Pop disdained it, strove to retain his eminent brother's attention. Stuck in the cabin with his parents during Easter vacation 1927, the eighteen-year-old college junior reported: My dear Brother and Gossip,

> As I write this, I am seated at a most quaint old writing table in the right wing of the Willhouse, a most quaint old tavern situated in a most quaint old nook of the upper Catskill mountains . . . the house guests number among them the mater and the pater and the two darling childhood friends Lord and Lady Neustaeder of Boro Park [Brooklyn]. You can imagine my feeling of intense gratitude at their kindness in bringing with them their twelve year old son as my playmate! And after the evening meal—a splendid repast of botrost, gugumber salat, bodadoes and more wegetables—Lady Neustaeder in the fat Jewish glory of her sesqui-centennial marriage anniversary, dispatched Willie to my chamber to help me with my home study!
>
> . . . I wonder will they miss Willie and if they do, will they think to look in the cistern.

By Christmas, Joe was in a better mood, thanking Herman and Sara for sending their mother a Christmas box of fruit and their father a check. "He needed it and it came just at the right time—which, by the way, is all the time."

Even before theatrical failures dimmed his dreams of escape, Herman had decided he could bring New York to Hollywood by importing some of his friends. If Ben Hecht couldn't write him a good script, Herman told Schulberg, then Schulberg could tear up Herman's two-year contract and fire them both. His boss could hardly refuse a bet like that, so Herman wired, "Will you accept three hundred per week to work for Paramount Pictures. All expenses paid. The three hundred is peanuts. Millions are to be grabbed out here and your only competition is idiots. Don't let this get around."

Hecht, who later claimed that Herman's telegram arrived just in time to avert a financial disaster so severe that he had taken to his bed with Gibbon's *Decline and Fall of the Roman Empire*, hurried west to enroll in

Herman and Ben Hecht create a spoof-film for B. P. Schulberg for Christmas. The waiter's recommendation is an enema.

what he called the Herman Mankiewicz School of Screenwriting. As the Master told him:

> I want to point out to you that in a novel a hero can lay ten girls and marry a virgin for a finish. In a movie this is not allowed. The hero, as well as the heroine, has to be a virgin. The villain can lay anybody he wants, have as much fun as he wants cheating and stealing, getting rich and whipping the servants. But you have to shoot him in the end. When he falls with a bullet in his forehead, it is advisable that he clutch at the Gobelin tapestry on the library wall and bring it down over his head like a symbolic shroud. Also, covered by such a tapestry, the actor does not have to hold his breath while he is being photographed as a dead man.

Herman's apt pupil went a step further. Dispensing altogether with a hero, Hecht wrote *Underworld* in a week, creating a new genre, the gangster story, and earning the industry's first Academy Award for screenwriting. Schulberg gave Hecht a $10,000 bonus, but before he could enjoy it, Herman snatched it away to pay some of his own gambling debts. He took so long to repay it that Hecht dragged him into their boss's office, where Herman talked Schulberg into giving him a $500-a-week raise, payable to Hecht. That simultaneously repaid Hecht and made Herman the studio's highest-paid writer, at least for a while.

None of them imagined Ben Hecht would become so prolific that he could make enough money in Hollywood in half a year to live in New York the rest of the time and write what he wanted. But he clearly was so valuable that Schulberg sent Herman back to New York to find more like him. In April 1927 Herman wrote Sara that he had lined up a number of writers, including S. N. Behrman, Oliver H. P. Garrett, and Nunnally Johnson, who became one of Herman's best friends. Although most were newspapermen like Herman, he impressed them. "I was about twenty-three or twenty-four when I first saw him and so was he, but he was four times as sophisticated as I was," Johnson recalled. By May, Herman had eight writers working on a five-week deadline to write an acceptable story for Paramount.

In the fall Warner Brothers released *The Jazz Singer*, whose spoken dialogue and singing by Al Jolson changed the world of movies forever. Because the industry needed time to develop the sound technology, and theaters had to acquire equipment to project it, the changeover took a few years. But with sound, plots became more complicated and dialogue more important. So back went Herman, on another hunting expedition, always happy to visit his New York haunts, especially on a Paramount expense account. "I've got to find five writers to bring back," he told Wells Root, *Time*'s theater and film critic, when they ran into each other at the "21" Club. Root went.

The recruiting trips became known as the Herman Mankiewicz Fresh Air Fund for Writers or, more modestly, the Paramount Fresh Air Fund for New York Newspapermen, and Schulberg made Herman head of Paramount's scenario department. The influx of so many former newspapermen brought a wisecracking, irreverent, flippant sensibility to film that replaced sentimental melodrama in setting the tone of many of Hollywood's most successful films. The boomtown atmosphere also attracted writers like William Faulkner and F. Scott Fitzgerald, who were drawn to the large rewards for what seemed like minimal effort. Some took the money and ran. Some enjoyed their time in Hollywood and stayed. Some, like Herman (and eventually Joe), scorned the movies, took the money, and stayed.

Helping populate Hollywood with former newspapermen became one of Herman's most lasting contributions to Hollywood's Golden Age of films, but his primary job was titling silent pictures. Herman's movies starred old New York friends like Louise Brooks and W. C. Fields, and new film stars like Adolphe Menjou, William Powell, and Clara Bow. He helped adapt *Fashions for Women*, the first solo directing assignment for Dorothy Arzner, an early and rare female director. He collaborated with Anita Loos to adapt her own *Gentlemen Prefer Blondes*, which he had praised in a 1925 *Times* book review. He had shared theater critics' aversion to the long-running Broadway hit *Abie's Irish Rose*, but when Paramount paid a record price for film rights, Herman titled it. He titled films about chorus girls, French nobility, chorus girls plus French nobility, madcap heiresses, and backwoods mountain families. When he titled *The Mating Call*, a 1928 Howard Hughes production that Paramount distributed, he appeared as an unidentified newspaperman. (He also delivered a credible performance as a speakeasy customer in the 1931 adaptation of Hecht and MacArthur's *Front Page*. Told Hildy Johnson is on the wagon, he says, "*I* ain't," and talks his way inside.)

Many silent films are lost, but one of the more prestigious ones Herman titled survives. Directed by Josef von Sternberg, *The Last Command* (1928) starred German actor Emil Jannings as Grand Duke Sergius Alexander, formerly a Russian general in the revolution, now reduced to working as a Hollywood extra. William Powell played Leo Andreyev, a former revolutionary leader and adversary of Alexander, who has become a Hollywood director. While casting a film about the Russian Revolution, Andreyev recognizes Alexander's photograph and hires his former enemy to play a general. As satirical scenes depicting the Hollywood film world alternate with flashbacks to Grand Duke Alexander's traumatic revolutionary experiences, the former general loses his sanity. When he finally dies in the arms of his former adversary, the director declares, "He was more than a great actor—he was a great man."

New York Times critic Mordaunt Hall, Herman's former colleague and a veteran title-writer himself, wrote that Herman's titles reminded him of the "'little girl with the curl in the middle of her forehead,' for when they are good they are very, very good, but when they are bad they are awful." Hall's idea of very, very good was, "And so, with the flames of war crackling along a two-thousand-mile front, troops bitterly needed to defend Russia played parade for the Czar." Awful was, "Is that beard supposed to be Russian? It looks like an ad for cough drops."

Von Sternberg (who had supplied his own "von") was widely detested in the industry, but Herman played poker with him and kidded him that he was circulating stories as part of a "Get von Sternberg Week." Herman also titled von Sternberg's detective story *The Drag Net*, which Paramount

Fredric March won an Oscar nomination for impersonating John Barrymore in *The Royal Family of Broadway* (1930). Barrymore loved it. March also starred with Nancy Carroll (r.), one of Herman's favorites, and Diane Ellis in *Laughter* (1930), which Herman supervised.

hoped would be another *Last Command*. It was not, but Herman again joined the team of von Sternberg, writers Charles and Jules Furthman, and actor George Bancroft, to write dialogue for von Sternberg's first sound film, *Thunderbolt* (1929). (Theaters were offered a silent version, too, with titles by Joe.)

When he had the choice, Herman wrote about what interested him. Because he liked boxing, he wrote the story and dialogue for *The Man I Love* (1929), about a small-town boxer (Richard Arlen) who moves to New York with his genteel bride (Mary Brian). After they shot the fight scenes on location at Madison Square Garden, Arlen told the press most of the dialogue was ad libbed: "Mary and I said just what came into our heads at the moment." Herman, whose reaction can be imagined, had already joked in the *New Yorker* that Groucho Marx wrote his own lines. (Joe also joked about actors believing they wrote their own lines in *All About Eve*.)

Paramount relied on Herman to pep up even the silliest pictures. In *Love Among the Millionaires* (1930), Clara Bow's pesky younger sister (Mitzi Green) so exasperates Bow's hapless suitors (Skeets Gallagher and Stuart Erwin) that one finally tells her, "If I'm ever electrocuted, I'd love to have you sitting in my lap." He adapted some plays he had reviewed favorably, like *The Vagabond King* (1930), and sometimes his Algonquin friends' work. He and Gertrude Purcell turned *The Royal Family*, Edna Ferber and George S. Kaufman's play about the Barrymores, into *The Royal Family of Broadway* (1930), an assignment Herman particularly enjoyed, because Paramount shot it in their Astoria, Queens, studio and wanted Herman on the spot.

He went east again during the summer of 1930 to supervise production on *Laughter* (1930). Director Harry d'Abbadie d'Arrast, a former assistant to Charlie Chaplin, collaborated with screenwriter Douglas Doty on the story, and Donald Ogden Stewart wrote the dialogue. Herman contributed dialogue as well, but the other three were nominated for an Academy Award for best original story. *Laughter* was one of the few films Herman enjoyed discussing in later years and critics loved it. Audiences did not, and Herman later speculated that they had been too far ahead of their time in anticipating madcap comedies like *It Happened One Night* (1934) and *My Man Godfrey* (1936).

As the Depression deepened in the fall of 1930, Paramount sent Schulberg, Wanger, Sam Jaffe (Schulberg's brother-in-law, who headed Paramount's Hollywood production), Herman, four other writers, and director Ernst Lubitsch to New York to try to keep the Astoria studio running.

They failed, but Herman used the opportunity to work with a producer, who wanted to open *We, the People* around Christmastime. Reporting on the plan, a *New York Times* theater columnist noted that Herman, who now "roamed through the cinematic vineyards," had previously collaborated with "the Messrs. Kaufman and Connelly in a couple of half-forgotten plays." Kaufman wrote to protest the characterization of *The Good Fellow* as "half-forgotten': "I have been conducting some inquiries, and am pleased to say that I find no one who remembers it at all. I think you should be a little surer of your facts before rushing into print."

We, the People was not produced, but Herman kept at it and by 1932 had decided he would update it to reflect the state of the nation in the 1930s. He did not, and in 1933 Elmer Rice, who almost certainly influenced Herman, wrote, produced, and directed a play of that very name. (It ran for forty-nine performances.) However, in May 1932, Herman was working on another route back to Broadway. Lawrence Langner, founder of the Theatre Guild and New York Repertory Company, announced that his Westport, Connecticut, summer session would feature *The Devil's Album,* an adaptation by Herman of a play by playwright/screenwriter Leo Birinski. Herman failed to revise it in time, but after Langner dropped him, another producer took it on. He, too, failed to produce it, though Herman eventually adapted a Birinski story into a successful 1934 MGM film, *Stamboul Quest,* starring Myrna Loy. In contrast to his theatrical disappointments, Herman's screenplays were increasingly successful. Two of his original 1931 pictures, *Man of the World* and *Ladies' Man,* were sophisticated, poignant, and comedic like *Laughter,* but much more popular. William Powell's ability to render Herman's gigolos-in-love simultaneously reprehensible and sympathetic probably helped.

Despite his unceasing efforts to write his way back to New York, by 1931 Herman could hardly fail to notice he was putting down roots. Reporters back east linked him to Hollywood and he contributed Hollywood news to the *New York Times*. Although Pop continued to hope he would return to newspaper work, Schulberg promoted him to producer, and Herman also brought Joe (and, for a while, Erna) into the business. Sara preferred the West Coast, though the move was not all she had hoped. Hollywood Herman was just like New York Herman, except with more money. He did not require the presence of his alcohol-soaked Algonquin friends to drink, and when opportunities were not readily available, he created them. He hid bottles around the house (which Sara watered down if she found them) and used his wit to deflect wagging tongues. With admirable economy and unerring aim, Herman lacerated his targets (including himself) with bon mots that made the rounds from coast to coast

One of his most-repeated wisecracks originated at a dinner party hosted by Arthur Hornblow Jr., a cultured and talented producer so sophisticated that he and Myrna Loy celebrated their divorce with a party at the Mocambo nightclub. The elegant Hornblow was known for lavishing care on his food and wine, but on that occasion, Herman drank so much that he had to bolt from the table to vomit. "Don't worry, Arthur," he airily told his host afterward. "The white wine came up with the fish."

Gambling wreaked even more damage. Because Hollywood salaries raised the stakes for everyone, the ability to lose large sums became a way of showing off. Herman was a Clover Club habitué and played cards regularly with Schulberg and Schulberg's friends, who earned far more money than Herman and were better players. He lost frequently and Schulberg, who had a gambling problem himself, had no problem taking his protégé's money. With typical logic, Herman considered his losses a reassuring form of job security. "They can't fire me," he told Sara. "I owe them too much money." (When Kaufman, a serious and expert bridge player, had the bad luck to draw Herman as a partner one day, he asked irritably, "I know you just learned to play, Herman, but what time today?")

Herman's son Don, who became an expert gambler himself (and who also had to dig himself out of trouble more than once), said his father got in trouble not only because he would bet on anything, but because he did not really understand the concept of odds. To Herman, every event (or card) had even odds: either it would happen or it wouldn't. Even poker pots mystified him. After losing almost $4,000 in one night, he sent director Lewis Milestone twelve checks totaling $3,040 with a note asking "Millie" to accept them on an installment plan.

"I have absolutely no money, but I have a regular income from Paramount, out of which I am willing to set aside almost an eighth for some time to come to satisfy my debt to you." Milestone returned the checks, explaining that "there were seven other players in the game. You don't owe me a dime dear fellow—you've bought your chips from the banker and obviously it is to him that your checks should be made payable."

Herman was also unlucky. Proud of his fund of political trivia, he was always on the lookout for a mark and once bet a man in a bar that he couldn't name William Jennings Bryan's 1908 vice-presidential nominee. "John Worth Kern," said the man in the bar, who added that he ought to know, since he had nominated Kern at the convention.

His most painful loss had to be from the 1934 Rose Bowl. The ordinarily dismal Columbia University football team came to town to play Stanford, and Herman headed the local Columbia delegation. He welcomed the visiting alumni at the train station in the pouring rain, accompanied only by his two sons and a timid, mangy mountain lion on a leash. Columbia's actual mascot was a lion, but he could not find a real lion available for rent. To the complete shock of everyone except Herman, Columbia defeated Stanford in the biggest upset in Rose Bowl history, and Herman should have collected thousands. Unfortunately, Sara had talked Herman's bookies into removing his bets.

Sometimes Herman acknowledged his self-destructiveness with perverse pride. Sometimes it was defensive anger. Occasionally, humiliated penitence. Whatever his reaction of the moment, he always milked it. When he ran into an old friend one day, he casually saddled Sara with a moniker that lasted the rest of her life. When the friend asked after Sara, Herman affected ignorance.

"Who?"

"Sara," his confused interlocutor explained. "Your wife."

"Ohhhh," drawled Herman, as if the light had only just dawned. "You mean Poor Sara."

With his usual economy, Herman compressed into two words both his own habits and Sara's martyrdom, and the label stuck forever. "Poor Sara" was funny, but Sara's quandary was not. She loved and respected Herman, and it was mutual. With all their conflicts, their marriage was a reservoir of strength for both. "Remember me to the kids, and I love you, love you, love you," he wrote in one letter, adding at the bottom, "* * * Guess what these are. No, not kisses—better even."

Furthermore, when Herman wasn't picking a fight or jeopardizing their financial wellbeing, life as Mrs. Herman Mankiewicz was stimulating and fun. Herman was her ticket to friends like George S. Kaufman, F. Scott Fitzgerald, and William Randolph Hearst, though the price of the ticket seemed be doubling as Herman's target and Herman's jailer. Sara periodically threatened to leave, and divorce was mentioned more than once. Sometimes she actually did leave, but she always returned. Using the language of addictions treatment one of her grandsons described Sara as a classic enabler, and Sara herself later speculated that perhaps she had been too good, too reliable, too virtuous. But her choices were not easy.

Herman and Sara did not live in the princely style of the Schulbergs, but their lives were luxurious even during the Depression. Schulberg

Mexico-bound in 1929.

became Herman's friend, mentor, and protector as well as his boss, and Schulberg's wife, Adeline, took Herman and Sara under her wing. They were even closer to Ad's younger brother, Sam Jaffe, and Sam's wife, Mildred, and Sara's sister, Mattie, and her husband, Dr. Saul Fox, who had followed them to Los Angeles after Herman promised to send movie folks his way. Saul became a beloved and respected doctor to the stars, and Mattie became famous (or infamous) for her skilled impersonations. The Jaffes collected modern art because they loved it, long before it became fashionable. Sara, Mattie, and Mildred became a formidable trio, a sort of Respected Wives Club.

Of all the friendships Herman and Sara developed in that most fanciful of cities, the most fantastical was with William Randolph Hearst and his mistress, actress Marion Davies. Hearst's San Simeon castle was halfway between Los Angeles and San Francisco, and on a number of occasions, they boarded his private train late in the evening and rode up the mountainside to the ranch, as he liked to call it. They would arrive at four in the morning and sip champagne while servants unpacked their luggage. Herman and Sara were usually assigned the bungalow with Cardinal Richelieu's ornate bed—or what they thought was Richelieu's bed. Hearst's builder actually named many of the beds himself, and only the Gothic Suite's bed had really been slept on by its royal namesake, Henry VIII. The lions, leopards, giraffes, and zebras that roamed the ground were genuine, however.

Herman was as fascinated by Hearst as everyone else, though he was more interested in Hearst's brilliance than his extravagant spending. Even during house parties, the newspaper magnate maintained constant contact with his businesses and monitored world affairs. Herman loved exploring Hearst's extensive library and mingling with senators, editors, world leaders like Winston Churchill and former president Calvin Coolidge, and Hearst himself. Hearst often seated Herman next to himself at dinner with his guest of honor on the other side, though, as Sara later observed, "I don't know how complimentary it was. Because the rest of the party was sometimes quite uninformed, let us say, about all these things, and Herman was a very astute student of politics and literature and . . . really everything that was of interest in the world."

Herman was also fond of Hearst. A decade after he wrote *Citizen Kane*, he said, "I couldn't imagine anyone who didn't have affection for him. There were many who differed from him politically. Personally he was, and is, one of the most charming men I have ever known—manners, courtesy such as I had ever known. It was impossible not to be completely captivated by him, though you differed violently with what at the moment he stood for politically, which on the other hand, might be the exact opposite the next morning."

With Davies's nephew, screenwriter Charles Lederer, Herman wrote parodies of Hearst's newspapers for his amusement. Because Davies treated her nephew like a son, the two felt free to joke even about Davies's famous stutter. "D-D-D-Davies Returns," read a headline in their mock *Herald-Examiner*. Like everyone else, Herman adored her. A former Ziegfeld chorus girl thirty-three years Hearst's junior, Davies was charming and silly and virtually devoid of intellectual curiosity, but she was also unfailingly kind and generous to friends and even acquaintances in need.

Hearst's *Los Angeles Examiner*, September 24, 1931, displays cohosts feting Marion Davies (though Hearst paid). Seated from left: Mona Maris, Gertrude Olmstead (Mrs. Robert Z. Leonard), Virginia Bushman (Mrs. Jack Conway), Eleanor Boardman (Mrs. King Vidor), Frances (Mrs. Samuel) Goldwyn, Marion Davies, Louella Parsons, Diana Kane (Mrs. George Fitzmaurice), Sara, Kathryn Carver (Mrs. Adolphe Menjou), Aileen Pringle, Hedda Hopper. Standing: Clarence Brown, Robert Z. Leonard, Jack Conway, Irving Thalberg, Adolphe Menjou, King Vidor, Samuel Goldwyn, George Fitzmaurice, Herman, Harry Martin (Parsons's husband), John Gilbert, Lloyd Pantages.

Despite her habitual stuttering and blinking, she was a gifted comedienne, though Hearst unintentionally sabotaged her career by forcing her into weighty dramas. As a fellow alcoholic, she joined forces with Herman to sneak alcohol past the tee totaling Hearst. Davies eventually grew to love Hearst, but Herman and Sara suspected she drank because she was bored and feared life was passing her by. Herman was only one of her many drinking companions, but by the end of the 1930s, Hearst no longer wanted him around her.

At the beginning of that decade, Herman had started working on Paramount's Marx Brothers films. He had admired them since their early days on stage, and after shooting their first two pictures in Astoria, Paramount was filming their first original, rather than an adaptation of a live show, in Hollywood. They lacked even a script when Herman was assigned to supervise the picture from screenplay through production, a task so challenging that it probably accounted for his official promotion later that year, from writer to producer. (Employees shepherding pictures through production during the silent era were called supervisors. When sound pictures increased the complexity of the production process, their responsibilities expanded, and they became known as "producers," with a concomitant rise in power and importance.)

Working with the Marx Brothers was not unlike appearing in a Marx Brothers movie: they could be as maniacal in person as they were on stage or screen. One day when Schulberg called them into his office, they grabbed him, removed all his clothes except his underwear, and departed—and Schulberg was their boss. Their first Hollywood writing staff was S. J. Perelman, twenty-seven, and Will Johnstone, fifty-two, two writer/illustrator/humorists Groucho originally had hired to write for their radio series. When they suggested making the Brothers stowaways on an ocean liner, Groucho considered the idea too good for the radio and told them to turn it into a feature film.

Arriving in Hollywood, the neophyte screenwriters reported to Herman, whom Perelman later recalled as "a large, Teutonic individual with an abrasive tongue," whose "fondness for cards and good living kept him in a state of perpetual peonage and had made him a sort of Johnsonian figure in the industry." Herman told them to "proceed as fancy dictated" but cautioned that "in any case, the Marxes would keelhaul us."

The writers assumed Herman was exaggerating when he explained: "They're mercurial, devious, and ungrateful. I hate to depress you, but you'll rue the day you ever took the assignment. This is an ordeal by fire. Make sure you wear asbestos pants." Then they attended his first story conference. In attendance were Herman, Joe, and a few other "cold-eyed vultures obviously dispatched by the studio"; the Marx Brothers' father and their father's pinochle-playing friend; Zeppo, Zeppo's wife, and a brace of Afghan hounds; Harpo and "a couple of blond civilians he had dined with"; "the Chico Marxes" with "a scrappy wirehaired terrier" that began fighting with the Afghans; Groucho and his wife; three gagmen with wives or girlfriends; and finally, "an unidentified rabble I took to be relatives." Johnstone read their first effort to an audience of twenty-seven people and five dogs.

Groucho's reaction—"It stinks"—emptied the room, and the writing staff expanded to include new gag men hired by each Marx Brother. Chico brought in former law student Nat Perrin; Harpo hired cartoonist J. Carver Pusey; Groucho hired former newspaper writer Arthur Sheekman. Eventually five writers; the Brothers; the Brothers' uncle, vaudevillian comedian Al Shean; and Herman gathered in Herman's office to hash out the screenplay. Herman started the action by pulling out a well-worn deck of cards for a game of casino at ten dollars a hand. Eventually a script took shape, and as Marx Brothers historian Joe Adamson reconstructed it, it was "written chiefly by Perelman and Sheekman, with sight gags by Johnstone, contributions by Perrin, and intrusions by Groucho, Harpo, and Herman Mankiewicz." When Sara visited, the brothers treated her no differently from their onscreen victims: they would goose her from behind; Harpo would leer at her and toss her to Chico; Chico would toss her to Groucho.

Herman was genuinely fond of Harpo, who had been part of the Algonquin group, and he socialized with the others on occasion. He and Sara included Harpo and Groucho in the family's Passover seders, and Harpo spiced up the evening by donning a green roulette baize as a yarmulke and leading Don and Frank around the room in Indian war dances.

Herman and Groucho both belonged to the West Side Asthma and Riding Club, along with other eastern transplants like Donald Ogden Stewart, Ben Hecht, Robert Benchley, Samson Raphaelson, Don Marquis, and Perelman. Groucho's real club (which he joined, though it accepted him as a member) was Hillcrest Country Club, Los Angeles's first Jewish country club, where he habitually entertained colleagues at its famous comedians' table. By the time Herman produced Paramount's second Marx Brothers film, he realized Groucho was regaling his friends with jokes from the script, then ordering new material because what he had just used at the club seemed stale. So Herman started withholding new jokes until they were ready to shoot.

Monkey Business emerged with a minimum of plot. Herman considered it an unnecessary hindrance and fought off Sheekman's attempts to have a gangster plot. "If Groucho and Chico stand against a wall for an hour and forty minutes and crack jokes, that's enough for me," he said, and subsequent audiences have agreed. As Adamson wrote, "In *Cocoanuts*, Groucho was even burdened with running a Florida hotel. The glory of *Monkey Business* is that all four of them run nothing but amok."

Instead, *Monkey Business* has situations: the Brothers stow away on a ship in barrels labeled "Kippered Herring." They are discovered. They act as if they own the ship. They work as bodyguards for rival gangsters. Zeppo gets a love interest. Harpo crashes a puppet show and imitates a puppet so convincingly that his pursuer joins in as well. They steal Maurice Chevalier's passport and each takes a turn wearing a straw hat and crooning "You Brought a New Kind of Love to Me" to convince immigration officials that he is Chevalier. Harpo nails it until the singing slows and he turns around to reveal a Victrola strapped to his back.

Four Marx Brothers pretend to be Maurice Chevalier in *Monkey Business* (1931).

Shooting a Marx Brothers film was also hazardous, because the comedians clearly considered production an ad hoc activity. Norman McLeod, a minister's son, had been a college boxer, a war hero, an illustrator of cartoon backgrounds for film titles, an assistant to other directors, and a cowriter with Joe when he agreed to direct the Marx Brothers—after turning it down three times. "Each one of the brothers had three or four 'gag' men in tow," McLeod told the press when the film opened, and when their friend Eddie Cantor dropped by to watch, he contributed some lines as well. When they finished, the Marx Brothers were $200,000 richer, and McLeod was eleven pounds lighter.

Monkey Business was both a critical and popular success, a film both of its time (Groucho: "The stockholder of yesteryear is the stowaway of today") and timeless (when the captain threatens to lock him in irons, Groucho says, "The skipper cannot do it with irons. It's a mashie shot if the wind is against you, and if the wind isn't against you, I am"). Herman and McLeod were duly rewarded—or punished, depending on one's perspective—by assignment to the next Marx Brothers film. (Perelman figured Paramount knew they needed a tough boss to control their "anarchical troupe.") In the interim Herman wrote *Dancers in the*

Herman impersonates three Marx Brothers at once, in Harpo's wig, Chico's hat, and Groucho's mustache and coat.

Dark for Paramount and, on loan out to RKO, *The Lost Squadron* and *Girl Crazy*, which he adapted from the Broadway show featuring songs by the Gershwin brothers. All opened in 1932, and none was particularly successful.

Paramount gave Herman a new contract in March 1932, and along with his Marx Brothers picture, he was assigned to produce (supervise) both *Million Dollar Legs*, written by Henry Myers and Joe Mankiewicz (by then, writing scripts), and *The Phantom President*, a satirical musical that was Broadway star George M. Cohan's first film. Richard Rodgers and Lorenz Hart were writing songs, and Cohan was to play two roles, a boring presidential candidate and his double, a medicine show huckster. With Jimmy Durante as the carnival man's sidekick and Claudette Colbert as the love interest, the picture seemed perfect for Herman. But Cohan was difficult, and Herman was taken off the picture.

Depression earnings continued to spiral down, and Paramount's earnings worsened along with the rest of the industry. In May 1932 Jesse Lasky was pushed out of the studio he had helped found. Schulberg was forced out in June. Herman resigned in mid-July and proceeded almost directly into Cedars of Lebanon Hospital for an appendectomy.

Herman's second Marx Brothers film opened the same month. In *Horsefeathers*, Groucho plays Professor Wagstaff, president of Huxley University, with Zeppo as his son who has been matriculating for twelve years; Chico is a bootlegger masquerading as an iceman; Harpo is a dog catcher. The picture includes some of the Marx Brothers' most famous sight gags. When a man on the street asks for money for a cup of coffee, Harpo pulls a steaming cup, complete with saucer, from inside his coat. When Groucho says he cannot burn the candle at both ends, Harpo pulls a candle burning at both ends from that same coat pocket.

Even before *Horsefeathers* became a hit, *Time* featured the Marx Brothers on its cover. But one picture could not rescue Paramount, and that September, Herman signed with Metro-Goldwyn-Mayer (MGM or, in the industry, Metro). Paramount borrowed him back to supervise its next Marx Brothers picture, *Cracked Ice*, a takeoff on Arctic epics that morphed into the political satire *Duck Soup*. It seemed perfect for Herman, but by then he had grown so cynical that he spent the first few weeks playing darts with their new director, Leo McCarey, and taking tap-dancing lessons from Harry Ruby, one of the writers.

Herman did check in long enough to deflate Harpo's pretensions. After visiting the Soviet Union, Alexander Woollcott had returned convinced that Harpo, given his surname of Marx and his status as the world's greatest pantomimic artist since Charlie Chaplin, really should visit the Communist capital. He had Harpo so persuaded he was a serious artist that Harpo told Herman he couldn't play his part unless he had a better understanding of his character.

"You're a middle aged Jew who picks up spit because he thinks it's a quarter," Herman retorted. Harpo went back to work on his own antics.

As cantankerous as Herman could be, he shared the Marx Brothers' sensibility. Overhearing Chico complain about a potential candidate for their female lead because "she's old and has big tits," Herman admonished him, "I resent that. My mother is old and has big tits." But early in 1933, Paramount took Herman off that picture, too, and he made his way back to MGM. The Marx Brothers followed soon afterward, and their MGM pictures under Irving Thalberg made much more money than the Paramount pictures Herman had supervised. To attract more women, Thalberg added plots, romance, and other straight material, and road-tested their jokes. Herman disapproved, and Marx Brothers fans differ on which pictures are superior.

As for Herman, his mind was elsewhere. Observing the rise of Hitler and Mussolini, he despaired that no one seemed to be paying attention. If no one else was going to sound an alarm, Herman felt he had to do something. But what?

CHAPTER 8

Gold Safe, However

WHEN HERMAN LEFT PARAMOUNT FOR MGM, HE LEFT BEHIND ONE OF his most valuable contributions to motion picture history. The Herman Mankiewicz Fresh Air Fund's youngest recruit had worked as a newspaperman in Germany (like Herman); translated titles into German (courtesy of Herman); and returned to New York broke and in need of a job (like Herman). But Joe Mankiewicz did not arrive in Hollywood aboard a private railway car, courtesy of Paramount. He crossed the country in an upper berth on a train called the Apache, on the Rock Island Line, for the cheapest fare Pop could find. Nor had Joe spent four years in New York making such a name for himself that Paramount guaranteed him $40,000 a year. Paramount gave Joe a sixty-five-dollar-a-week job in exchange for Herman's promise to stay sober long enough to finish a Claudette Colbert script the studio needed. Paramount never made a Colbert film by Herman, but Joseph L. Mankiewicz, not quite nineteen, would have been an excellent investment at twenty times the price.

Siblings often have such different childhood memories that they joke that they must have grown up in different families. Herman and Joe essentially did. Herman was born in the nineteenth century to newlywed immigrants struggling to make their way in hurly-burly New York City. Joe was a 1909 surprise arrival into a family of four, headed by an important personage in Wilkes-Barre, Pennsylvania. When they moved to New York in 1913, Herman, Erna, and Pop were out all day and many evenings.

Joe, who felt very close to his mother and ignored by his father, recalled himself as "a midget in a family of giants—all highly articulate, opinionated, extroverted, argumentative and given to much bellowing." He "withdrew into a defensive stance of apparent dependency upon each and all—manipulating them into spoiling me." He tuned out his parents' discord by developing a protective shell "and finding the release for my own ambition and aggression in a private world of endless fantasies and day dreams." In New York they moved frequently, so Joe never stayed long enough in a neighborhood to make close friends or put down deep roots. As the perennial new boy, he became adept at fitting in by observing and learning to read people, which Joe recognized as valuable skills for writing and directing. But he also believed his isolation left him incapable of forming deep friendships as an adult. Adding to his alienation, he developed double pneumonia and pleurisy, which kept him out of school for a year.

Even losing a year, Joe graduated from junior high school at eleven, so Hanna and Joe spent six months in Europe before he entered high school. Besides sending his son to mark time in Europe instead of coal mines, Joe's Pop also drank less. So rather than struggling to please an angry, inebriated taskmaster, Joe was able to enjoy quiet eavesdropping on his father's friends' reminiscences of Pop's drinking, hearing stories "lurid enough to be held up against many of Herman's later escapades."

When Joe entered Stuyvesant High School, where Pop was teaching, Joe's more benign Pop did not bully his son in class. Herman and Joe both put Pop on a pedestal, but Joe had a second, more accessible idol. Herman was a glamorous older brother and sympathetic father figure all in one. If Joe stayed outside too late or was upset, he waited on the stoop for Herman. Like Herman, Joe gravitated toward writing and even won twenty dollars in a citywide *New York World* essay contest. He graduated at the age of fifteen, like Herman, the youngest member of his class.

Following Pop and Herman to Columbia, Joe was attracted to medicine and envisioned himself as a psychiatrist, until he performed so poorly in college physics that his professor gave him an F-, explaining that he had to give Joe the minus to distinguish Joe's total lack of comprehension from an ordinary F. Aside from physics, Joe's college years were considerably easier than Herman's (and Pop's). Joe's family could afford to buy him better clothes. Handsomer and more athletic than Herman, he played baseball and pledged a fraternity. His father was a respected educator on friendly terms with Columbia's faculty and administrators, and his brother was a *New York Times* critic and reporter, an Algonquin habitué, and then a Hollywood screenwriter. Joe edited the same *Columbia Spectator* humor column as Herman, but when he submitted his first piece of commercial writing to *Life*, a humor magazine for which Herman had written, he signed it "Joe Mason." He wanted to see if he could sell it on his own, and when *Life* accepted it, Joe was thrilled with his seven-dollar fee.

Despite his disappointment with Herman, Pop confidently expected Joe to follow him into academia, but Pop really never had a chance. While Pop was educating young people and convincing their parents to send them to college, Herman was educating Louise Brooks and exchanging witticisms with the likes of George S. Kaufman, H. L. Mencken, and Dorothy Parker. When Herman arranged for Joe to interview W. C. Fields for his high school newspaper, Fields wrote Joe a thank-you note. When Marc Connelly lectured at Columbia, he had tea with Joe. When Joe needed a summer job, Herman got him hired as the drama and baseball counselor at a camp partially owned by the Marx Brothers. (Zeppo insisted Joe play him at first base instead of a camper, and Groucho later liked to claim he had given Joe his start in show business.)

Joe pretended to acquiesce to Pop's plan to support him while he studied at University of Berlin, the Sorbonne, and Oxford, but just before graduation he wrote to Herman and Sara, begging them to help him get work instead. "[C]ontrary to papa's ideas, I have no idea of staying in Germany or any other country for a year and a half, merely absorbing their food, language, and atmosphere to achieve that cosmopolitan touch. I am impatient to get started: I know I have something to offer and the sooner I can start peddling it, the better." He added that the *New York Times'* managing and city editors had promised to write letters of introduction to the paper's Berlin office and that he hoped to get work from *Variety*.

Herman and Sara sent praise, a $100 check, and a request for specifics. Joe's itemized list included letters to Paramount in Berlin and "any other European city," and to Mr. Silverman of *Variety* to help "my campaign to dislodge the persevering Hooper Trask from his job. . . . I can write what *Variety* wants from Berlin, and he can't." Despite his confidence, Joe still needed guidance. "How do I go about writing articles to Sunday drama pages and things? Merely send them on with a prayer or does one arrange for their disposal before-hand? The New Yorker has a weekly Paris letter. Would a Berlin one go?"

By September 1928 Joe was in Berlin and went immediately to the *Chicago Tribune*'s office to meet Herman's previous savior, Sigrid Schultz. Now its chief correspondent for Central Europe, Schultz hired Joe as a cub reporter, which was all Joe needed to call himself an "assistant correspondent." He became *Variety*'s Berlin stringer and used Herman's name to get in to see Erich Pommer, chief of Universum *Film*-Aktiengesellschaft (UFA), Germany's largest motion picture company. Paramount distributed UFA's pictures in the United States, and Pommer was not pleased to find a young man in his office who was not Herman. However, Joe managed to fast-talk himself into a job translating German titles into English, giving him three jobs that combined to bring in about a hundred dollars a week. With those, Joe could live luxuriously, enjoying Berlin's "absolute intoxication of theater, excitement, glamour, and sex." He made friends like composer Franz Waxman and fell in love with Pat Kendall, who was half of an English sister–brother dancing team and the aunt of actress Kay Kendall.

His Berlin revels ended abruptly when Joe overdrew his bank account by about seventy-five dollars and his bank manager uncle refused to cover the shortfall. According to Joe (though the story sounds a bit draconian), his uncle sent the overdraft to the police. Whatever his Teutonic relative actually did, Joe wired Herman for money, and when it arrived hied himself to Paris, leaving behind a few other debts as well. Herman sent him a second check, along with a letter exhorting, "For Christ's sake, come out to Hollywood!"

Joe was ready, though after cautioning Herman and Sara not to tell their parents, he confessed that leaving his true love was the worst part of being in Paris: "This is my third day here and I have written her six letters as compared to one to New York and one to you. She is of the firm belief that in two years time I shall be in a position to marry her—and God help me, I am very often of the same opinion."

Even as he bemoaned his misery, Joe entertained them with an account of *la vie bohème* in Montparnasse.

> I have a little room, which is comfortable enough and cute, on the sixth floor of this hotel, for which I pay 80 cents a day. To my left is a lad who received a violin for his birthday and who has been practising what sounds like Hah Tikvah for the past three nights. (He practises from 2 A.M. to 5 A.M. when he leaves off to practise his homework in carpentry.) To my right is a boychek who is not quite sure whether it is an Assumption or an Annunciation he is creating for posterity, and the result has been a horrible stink of Turpentine all over the place. Just a stone's throw away from here is the celebrated Café du Dome where for the price of a Cognac I can listen to all the arguments about God and the foreshortening of a horse's behind, I want to.

He resented those he regarded as the no-talent rich, playing at artist while he, who had so much to offer, had to languish in impecuniousness.

> Hundreds of perfectly good doctors, lawyers, teachers, business people who, just because their papas have money and they got A plus for drawing a bird house in the sixth grade, live here month after month in berets and corduroy pants,—kidding themselves along day after day in the belief that . . . they are each a Messiah of culture. And then when they see themselves as the perverted Dulcies [the fatuous, breezy character from F.P.A.'s column and the Kaufman/Connelly play] they really are—it's too late and they go home and open French restaurants.

Joe always recalled his sojourn in Paris as one of the worst times of his life, but it was hardly interminable. He arrived late in November 1928. By January 17, 1929, he was on the train to Hollywood.

As Joe's Apache neared the end of its journey, he wired Herman: TWO HOURS LATE HORSES EATEN BY WOLVES GOLD SAFE HOWEVER JOE.

Joe's train turned out to be nineteen hours late, and by the time he arrived, Herman had shown his brother's witty telegram all over town. Herman and Sara had a party to attend that night, and like Herman a lifetime ago, Joe painted his brown shoes black to coordinate with Herman's tuxedo. But this time, the tux was Herman's extra dinner jacket, and the occasion was a party given by Herman's boss's boss, Jesse Lasky.

When Joe stepped into Jesse Lasky's Santa Monica beach house, he felt he was walking into a movie. There were famous faces everywhere he looked. Gary Cooper. Kay Francis. William Powell. Clara Bow. The setting was equally cinematic. B. P. Schulberg earned $11,000 a week and lived like a king. Schulberg's boss owned three Rolls-Royces; his staff included two butlers, two cooks, two chauffeurs, one lady's maid, and athletic trainers for his daily workouts.

Joe handed his hat to the butler—his first real butler and his last time wearing a hat in Hollywood—and plunged into the party. Almost immediately, he ran into someone he knew fairly well. The same John Erskine who had mentored Herman at Columbia and hired him to teach soldiers in France had also extracted Joe's solemn promise he would never go to Hollywood. Oblivious to his vertiginous fall from Joe's pedestal, Erskine greeted his former student warmly and asked him where he was working, matter-of-factly informing Joe that he was at Warner Brothers.

When Joe actually reported for work, he entered considerably less exalted circles. His office was not next to Schulberg's; it was on the fourth floor of Paramount's writers' building with all the other writers. He was assigned to work under William S. (Bill) McNutt, Grover Jones, and

Percy Heath, who schooled him in the art of pitching stories in story conferences. McNutt and Jones were masters of winging it, because they frittered away most of the day playing poker and shooting craps. Neither usually remembered afterward what they had said in the conferences, but as they explained to Joe, their bosses wouldn't either, and it hardly mattered anyway. Whether or not scripts had anything to do with what had been promised, they were routinely worked over.

Joe absorbed the lessons but not the cynicism. In addition to responding enthusiastically to every management memo inviting suggestions, he submitted a steady stream of unsolicited ideas. When the studio put him in its junior writers group—an in-house training program for the Ivy League graduates Walter Wanger had hired—Joe determinedly wrote his way out of the pack. In 1929 many theaters still lacked sound facilities, so the studios also produced silent versions of their talkies. Joe titled nine in his first year alone, setting a company record by finishing six in eight weeks. Three were written by Herman, including *The Dummy*, which was Fredric March's film debut and the talking debut of Broadway actor Jack Oakie, a comedian known for his double-takes. Joe titled *The Virginian*, which was Gary Cooper's breakthrough role, and appeared onscreen himself, as a reporter in *Woman Trap* (1929), prompting the director, William Wellman, to offer him a personal contract to act. Joe was not tempted.

With silent pictures on the way out, Joe knew it was only a matter of time before he had a chance to write words that actors actually spoke, but Herman gave him his first opportunity. He was adapting *Elmer the Great*, a Ring Lardner play about Elmer Kane (Kane!), in which a small-town baseball player recruited by the Yankees lets success go to his head. The director was Edward (Eddie) Sutherland, a close friend of Herman's from their New York days, and when he needed Herman to remove some of the script's long speeches, Herman resisted. As Sutherland recalled, Herman was "one of the nicest men I've ever known but he'd rather argue for eight hours than rewrite one line." Sutherland finally complained to David O. Selznick (Schulberg's assistant at the time), and Selznick ordered Herman to stop being so stubborn. "Let Joe rewrite it for you," Herman countered.

Sutherland didn't care who rewrote it as long as it got done, so Joe threw himself into the assignment with impressive results. As shooting progressed, Sutherland went back to Herman. "Look, you're being very cavalier with your kid brother, but I want to tell you this is going to be a pip. You'd better get your own credit back."

Joe's first spoken dialogue for *Fast Company* (1929) put him on a list of the year's top ten dialogue writers, alongside veterans like Frank Capra.

"Forget it," Herman said. "Let the kid have it."

Fast Company made a star of Jack Oakie, launched the team of Oakie and (Skeets) Gallagher, and won Joe promotion to full-fledged writer. His two-year contract made Joe the youngest writer at Paramount, but Joe recalled the picture for another reason. He was on a date with Paramount star Mary Brian when, halfway through the movie, he felt a tap on his shoulder. Sutherland's assistant beckoned him outside, and telling him, "Sutherland wants you right now," he put Joe in a cab.

They were shooting at night because Paramount's new sound stage had been destroyed in a fire. Until they could rebuild it, they had to shoot outdoors, and the city was quietest at night. Joe arrived to find everyone at a standstill because the comic scene Oakie and Gallagher were supposed to perform had no dialogue. Joe had written, "And now follows a comedy sequence between the two comics, at the pleasure of the comedians." As he later explained, "That was the first time I learned that 'Yeah?'/Oh Yeah'/Is that so?'/'Yeah' type of dialogue was actually written. I didn't know they wrote that kind of crap. I always thought, as

Seeing off Erna and Joe Stenbuck at Glendale Station.

many people think, that comics like the Marx Brothers made up their lines." So while the cast and crew waited, Joe sat down at a typewriter and pounded out the necessary lines.

Joe's dialogue combined with Lardner's witty play to earn him a spot on the *Los Angeles Record*'s list of 1929's top ten dialogue writers, alongside luminaries like Frank Capra and George Abbott, and he celebrated his contract in true Hollywood fashion, by treating himself to a huge, open Buick Roadster at a cost of $2,327.65, payable in installments over the next year and a half.

Joe's success also set Herman thinking. If two Mankiewiczes could make their mark in pictures, why not three? So in 1930 Herman brought Erna to Paramount, too. Unfortunately, Erna lacked her brothers' witty creativity, and Paramount let her go. Herman got her another job at Columbia Pictures by paying her salary himself, but Erna eventually returned to New York, where she helped with their parents and became the only family member to follow Pop's avocation. She became a successful teacher and married Joseph B. Stenbuck, a prominent doctor her

Writing *Skippy* (1931) earned Joe his first Oscar nomination. It also launched Jackie Cooper (left), who was nominated as best actor. Skippy's friend Sooky is Robert Coogan.

entire family liked and admired so much that they were amazed he had married Erna.

Like Herman, Joe became skilled at creating dialogue and bits of business for children. For director Norman Taurog and cartoonist/writer/director Norman McLeod, he wrote *Skippy* and its sequel, *Sooky*, which were based on the adventures of a fifth-grade character from a nationally syndicated comic strip by Percy Crosby (who influenced Charles Schulz). To play Skippy, Paramount borrowed Taurog's nine-year-old nephew, Jackie Cooper, from Warner Brothers, where he had been appearing in *Our Gang* comedies, and the role made Cooper a star.

"Joe Mankiewicz ruins you for anyone else," Taurog recalled decades later. "When he didn't think [something] was working, he'd ask for more time to change and polish it." Basing a feature-length film on child actors and dogs was no small undertaking, and after a month of shooting, they were three weeks behind schedule. To speed things up, Taurog and Joe started offering a daily award of twenty cents to the child who produced the best performance, and as Taurog recalled, the children worked harder for that twenty cents than they did for the hundreds of dollars they actually earned.

Skippy was nominated for four Academy Awards: Jackie Cooper for best actor (competing with Lionel Barrymore, Fredric March, and Adolphe Menjou); best director; best picture; and best story. Oscars were not as important in 1931 as they later became, but even then a nomination was a tremendous honor. Awards were presented at a banquet with nominees eating at tables on a dais encircling the room. As they awaited the awards, US vice president Charles Curtis droned on so long that many slipped out of the room, and Jackie Cooper fell asleep in best actress nominee Marie Dressler's lap.

Studio representatives counted the votes during the banquet, and at one point, *Skippy*'s producer Lewis "Bud" Lighton walked by Joe's table and whispered that Joe was way ahead in the voting. Joe began mentally composing his acceptance speech, reminding himself to be humble, especially because he was so young. When Taurog won for best direction, Joe became even more expectant. Then, Joe recalled,

> an old-time, famous screenwriter, Waldemar Young, got up to make the writing awards. As he opened the slip of paper, he smiled a little in my direction and said that the choice was particularly pleasing to him because it was a friend of his—which I was, a young friend—but also because the subject was so American and so fresh within the memory of some of us, and went on describing *Skippy*. Then he announced, "Ladies and gentlemen, the Best in Screenplay Award goes to . . . ' and I stood up, 'Howard Estabrook for *Cimarron*," and there I was standing with egg dripping off my face. Fortunately, God put Howard Estabrook right in front of me on the next level down, so I did the big ham bit of reaching over and shaking his hand, when I actually hated the son of a bitch. That was my most embarrassing moment—standing up just before my name was not called.

Although Joe didn't win, Herman considered his nomination reason enough to badger Schulberg to give him a raise, and when Schulberg resisted, Herman threatened to resign. Finally Schulberg capitulated, giving Joe a seven-year contract that raised him to "somewhere between $75 and $100," with $50 raises a year. The money was especially welcome, because Joe was falling in love again. He had rented a furnished house in Beverly Hills with his closest friend among the younger writers,

With Bill and Greta Wright, Joe and Frances Dee were a foursome until Dee jilted Joe for Joel McCrea.

William B. (Bill) Wright; and Joe, Wright, Wright's German girlfriend (and eventual wife), Greta, and Joe's girlfriend, actress Frances Dee, became a foursome.

Dee, who exuded a calm beauty, was Joe's age and had studied at University of Chicago before starting in Hollywood as an extra. Once Maurice Chevalier asked Paramount to cast her in *Playboy in Paris* (1930), she was assigned parts like the society girl in Josef von Sternberg's *An American Tragedy* (1931). During the three years she and Joe were both at Paramount, she starred in two of Joe's films, *June Moon* (1931) and *This Reckless Age* (released January 1932).

Joe wrote four films for Paramount in 1932 (his productivity assisted by his delighted discovery of Benzedrine), and one remained a lifelong favorite. With the 1932 Olympic Games scheduled for Los Angeles, Schulberg solicited suggestions for a picture tie-in, and Joe suggested a parody instead of the usual feel-good story of underdogs overcoming odds. Schulberg paid him an extra $2,500 to write the story, "On Your Mark," then assigned Joe and Henry Myers to collaborate on the screenplay and Herman to produce it.

Angela (Susan Fleming, later Mrs. Harpo Marx) and brush salesman Migg Tweeny (Jack Oakie) cheer on Angela's father, Klopstokia's president (W. C. Fields), in *Million Dollar Legs* (1932). Man Ray called it a surrealist masterpiece.

The studio also assigned them Nick Barrows, a gag man who typically punched up the action or dialogue. According to Myers, Barrows methodically examined their script to ensure that it was grounded on a solid storyline, and once he signed off, Herman told Mack Sennett–comedy-veteran director Edward Cline to shoot exactly as it was written. Joe remembered differently. He recalled Paramount considering it "a minor 'B' double-feature" to which Eddie Cline "'made alterations'" and said that "much of the action was quite rightly improvised on the set (together with Nick Barrows, we were assigned as 'gag men' throughout the shooting)." Both writers agreed that an early preview audience was unsure whether or not to laugh, and Joe remembered Herman saying, "Thank Christ my name isn't on this one." To clarify their intentions, they added opening titles: "Klopstokia . . . A Far Away Country. Chief Exports . . . Goats and Nuts. Chief imports . . . Goats and Nuts. Chief inhabitants: Goats and Nuts." From then on, viewers roared.

Klopstokia is bankrupt and needs $8 million to survive. Its president (W. C. Fields) keeps his job only as long as he continues to win at arm wrestling. When traveling Baldwin Brush salesman Migg Tweeny (Jack

Oakie) falls in love with the president's daughter, Angela (Susan Fleming, later Mrs. Harpo Marx), he learns that all Klopstokian women are named Angela, and all Klopstokians are outstanding athletes. He decides to rescue Klopstokia by entering it in the Los Angeles Olympics, because if they win, they can collect a cash prize offered by his boss, Mr. Baldwin. The villains include a mysterious man who skulks around with a notebook (Ben Turpin, cross-eyed and heavily mustached) and the secretaries of the Klopstokian cabinet, who plot to hire spy Mata Machree (Lyda Roberti) to seduce the team members, so they will fight over her and lose at the Olympics.

When the secretaries arrive to hire the seductive spy, they encounter a sign warning: "The Woman No Man Can Resist. Not Responsible For Men Left Over Thirty Days." As they try to enter, they are turned away by her butler, who explains, "Madame is only resisted from two to four in the afternoon." Then he leads them through a set of sumptuous rooms to the foot of a stairway typical of glamorous musicals. Mata appears at the top of the stairs and, evoking Garbo and Dietrich, descends to the tune of Elgar's "Pomp and Circumstance," until, hips swaying sinuously, she breaks into a cheery rendition of, "When I Get Hot." As the popeyed secretaries gape, she sings,

It's terrific when I get mean,
I'm just a woman made of gelatin.
I've got a thunder like a tambourine, Ai yi yi when I get hot . . .

The uncredited lyrics are by Lorenz Hart, who was at Paramount with Richard Rodgers, writing songs for Maurice Chevalier and Jeanette MacDonald in *Love Me Tonight*. Hart's brother, Teddy, also uncredited, plays secretary of the navy.

Time's critic described the picture as "a Marx Brothers comedy without the Marx Brothers." Reviewers generally loved it. From Paris, Man Ray proclaimed it a surrealist masterpiece. Rural America gave it a pass, and it was not commercially successful.

Joe also wrote several episodes for *If I Had a Million* (1932), a collection of stories about the beneficiaries of a millionaire's random checks. In "Rollo and the Roadhogs," W. C. Fields and Alison Skipworth play two portly, retired vaudevillians. Rollo is a former juggler (like Fields), and Emily had a bird act. Now they run a tea shop. When the couple's new car is demolished by a reckless driver, they use the rest of their windfall to send a fleet of drivers to hunt down other reckless drivers and crash into their cars.

After they finished shooting, Fields appeared in Joe's office to buy "that material."

What material? Joe asked, confused.

Fields explained, "That 'My little magpie, my little chickadee, my little tomtit.'" The lines were particularly funny because Rollo's Emily was anything but little.

The dialogue was not his to sell, Joe explained. He was a contract writer. Everything he wrote belonged to Paramount.

Yes, he knew, Fields said. His lawyer had told him. But he pressed a fifty-dollar bill on Joe anyway, explaining it would make him feel better, because "then I'd know it was mine."

Finally, Joe gave in. "I could put up only so much resistance at that age—it was almost my full week's salary at Paramount."

The anecdote was a favorite of Joe's, but when Fields biographer James Curtis compared the script with the film, he found "my little chickadee" nowhere in the final script. He knew Fields had added "Did you chirp for me, my little wren?" to his entrance and concluded that "it was Fields, and not Mankiewicz, who substituted the word "chickadee" for "bird" and created a line associated with him the rest of his life. Because Fields was a gifted (and incorrigible) ad libber, that is most likely "chickadee's" true origin, though Joe certainly believed he had contributed it.

Joe wrote another political satire in 1932. Sam Jaffe had moved from Paramount to RKO, and at Herman's suggestion, he borrowed Joe to write a script for the comedy team Wheeler and Woolsey. Because Joe's "In the Red" spoofed the League of Nations, Paramount executives accused him of plagiarizing the studio's next Marx Brothers picture, *Cracked Ice* (later *Duck Soup*, with which Herman was involved). Joe angrily resigned in December, but once the various lawyers resolved the issue, Jaffe hired Joe and Henry Myers to finish it, and the result was *Diplomaniacs* (1933). Wheeler and Woolsey were not the Marx Brothers, and *Diplomaniacs* is no *Million Dollar Legs*, but it has its moments. The comedians play a pair of unsuccessful barbers who work on an Indian reservation until the Indians send them to a League of Nations conference in Geneva as their diplomatic representatives.

Depression-related losses sent Paramount into receivership in 1933, but Joe returned to the studio while his agent Myron Selznick (David's brother) arranged a ten-week loan out to MGM. Selznick wanted to

David O. Selznick and Herman confer with Walt Disney (center). Perhaps Herman is asking to borrow Mickey Mouse for *Meet the Baron* (1933).

improve Joe's bargaining position to get him a higher salary at Paramount. But when the powerful MGM producer Harry Rapf assigned Joe to *Hollywood Revue of 1933*, Joe considered the concept so ludicrous that he assumed it was a joke and burst out laughing. Furious, Rapf sent Joe back to RKO.

There, Joe wrote *Emergency Call*, a grade B film, before returning to MGM, where David Selznick wanted him to help with *Meet the Baron*, a comedy Herman had written with Norman Krasna and was producing. Intended as a vehicle for radio comedian Jack Pearl, the story revolved around one of Pearl's radio characters, "Baron von Munchausen" (who bore only a passing resemblance to the actual seventeenth-century German storyteller).

Years later, screenwriter George Seaton recalled the scene. A junior, thirty-five-dollar-a-week writer at the time, Seaton arrived in Selznick's office ("a little larger than Mussolini's") to find Herman presiding over a small crowd. Director Walter Lang; Jack Pearl and his gag writers; comic Ted Healy (creator of the Three Stooges); and writers Krasna, Allen Rivkin, P. J. Wolfson, Arthur Kober, and Joe had spent the last two weeks trying to come up with a motivation for the Baron. Seaton stayed up all night and eagerly returned the following day with two ideas, one of which Herman approved immediately. Then he deflated the neophyte, telling him, "It's not that I liked it. I just wanted to get out of Selznick's office."

The cast was even more crowded than the writers' room, including Jimmy Durante, the Three Stooges, Edna May Oliver, and Zasu Pitts. They had songs by Jimmy McHugh and Dorothy Fields, and a mule named Rosebud (probably named by Herman). At one point, they even tried to convince Walt Disney to loan them Mickey Mouse. Critics generally panned the film, though many predicted big things for the Three Stooges.

Joe managed to duck out of that too, but Rapf, magnanimously overlooking Joe's past offense, assigned him to work for comic Ed Wynn, another radio star Joe could not stand. So despite the loan out, the twenty-four-year-old walked out of MGM, treated himself to a trip to Europe, then returned to Paramount long enough to finish out his contract with two more pictures. *Too Much Harmony* was a sequel to *Close Harmony*, starring Bing Crosby (whom Joe loved to impersonate) and Jack Oakie. *Alice in Wonderland* was more prestigious than successful. Along with Marc Connelly and William Cameron Menzies, Joe and many others labored over the script, and its cast included most of Paramount's stars: Gary Cooper (White Knight), Cary Grant (Mock Turtle), W. C. Fields (Humpty Dumpty), and Edward Everett Horton (Mad Hatter). Joe later described it as "a well-intentioned disaster." Critics disapproved and audiences, who were bored with the jumble of characters and scenes from both *Alice in Wonderland* and *Alice Through the Looking Glass*, could not even see their favorite stars, because their cumbersome costumes disguised them.

In 1933 Joe proposed to Frances Dee and meticulously planned their honeymoon, a summer road trip through New England, where they would stay in inns and bed-and-breakfasts. But that spring Paramount loaned Dee to RKO to make *The Silver Cord* with Irene Dunne and Joel McCrea; shortly afterward, Dee and McCrea eloped. When they went on the honeymoon Dee and Joe had planned, Joe was so devastated that he had to be hospitalized for a "partial nervous breakdown."

Dee and McCrea's marriage lasted over fifty years. For years, David Selznick had been telling McCrea he knew the perfect match for him, and McCrea had resisted, saying, "David, you cast the movies. I'll cast my life." Bill Wright told Joe's biographer, Kenneth Geist, that he thought the shock had left Joe determined to end all romantic relationships before he could be jilted. That infuriated Joe when he saw it in Geist's prepublication galleys, though he did not dispute Wright's description of his devastation. He did object to Selznick's story about the three of them that Geist included. Selznick liked to tell people that Dee chose McCrea "when she came to the realization that her attraction to Mankiewicz was purely physical, while McCrea appealed to her intellectually."

Joe insisted Geist change "intellectually" to "spiritually," which eliminated the joke and made little sense. Joe was handsome, but McCrea was movie-star handsome; McCrea may have been intelligent, but he did not match Joe's intellect. However, where Geist wrote, "Some time later Mankiewicz confessed to an intimate that Frances Dee 'was the great love of his life,'" Joe merely circled it and wrote in the margin, "pretty close."

CHAPTER 9

Mad Dogs

JOE WAS STILL FINISHING OUT HIS CONTRACT AT PARAMOUNT WHEN Herman arrived at Metro-Goldwyn-Mayer in March 1933 and departed on a leave of absence only a few months later. Fifteen years after World War I, Herman's anger at war's profligate waste of human life had not abated, and as he watched the Nazis tighten their stranglehold on Germany, he could no longer bear merely to sit on the sidelines. For the first time in years, Herman abandoned humor, irony, sophistication, and his theatrical aspirations to write passionately and from the heart—in the medium he had been deriding for the last six years.

In 1933 the general US public seemed oblivious to the threat, but Herman recognized every milestone in Adolf Hitler's route to power for what it was, and in *The Mad Dog of Europe*, he wove them into a pair of fictional narratives. Set in "Transylvania," one storyline traces the rise of former housepainter "Adolf Mitler." The other follows a pair of families, one Jewish and one Christian, who live in Gronau, Transylvania (Gronau was an actual German town).

It opens with an "earnest and impressive" voice reciting: "This picture is produced in the interests of Democracy, an ideal which has inspired the noblest deeds of Man. It has been the goal towards which nations have aspired—one after the other having asserted a determination to overthrow tyrants and erect a government 'of the people, by the people, for the people.' Today the greater part of the civilized world has reached this stage of enlightenment."

Onscreen is: "THE INCIDENTS AND CHARACTERS IN THIS PICTURE ARE OF COURSE FICTITIOUS. IT IS OBVIOUSLY ABSURD TO ASK ANYONE TO BELIEVE THEY COULD HAPPEN IN THIS ENLIGHTENED DAY AND AGE."

To accompany the sarcastic disclaimer, he wanted the haunting melody of the Kol Nidre, the prayer associated with the holiest day of the Jewish year, "with the military phrases of DEUTSCHLAND UEBER ALLES audible as an undertone." Then, "A large swastika fills the screen, upon which the title is superimposed. The swastika gradually fades to the form of a cross with a figure crucified upon it. . . ."

The first story opens in 1914 in the middle-class Gronau home of Professor Mendelssohn ("Jean Hersholt type"), his wife, their daughter, and three sons. When their oldest son, Karl, announces that despite his exemption, he has enlisted to fight, his father endorses his patriotism.

The other story opens on a pair of housepainters, and the "dark little fellow" (Adolf Mitler) gets his colleague fired. A close-up of Mitler's arm "sawing up and down with a paintbrush" dissolves into an arm "still going up and down without brush," in a beer hall. Mitler's first audible line is, "The French are a nation of niggers. We must exterminate them."

Back in Gronau, little Ilsa Mendelssohn plays with Heinrich and Fritz Schmidt, whose father owns the local newspaper and is a close friend of her father's. Ilsa's two older brothers die in the war, and Heinrich enlists. When the war ends, Heinrich returns, bitter and angry. Newsreel shots depict scenes of unemployment, and before Heinrich leaves Gronau to make a name for himself, he asks Ilsa to marry him when he returns. Ilsa agrees out of pity, though she actually loves his brother, Fritz.

The two narratives merge when Heinrich becomes Mitler's follower and watches him develop his political party. After a recreation of the 1923 Beer Hall Putsch that sent Hitler to jail and inadvertently gave him the opportunity to write *Mein Kampf*, Heinrich accompanies Mitler to a country-club-like prison where Ilsa and Fritz visit him.

> HEINRICH (*proudly*): I have learned what it means to be a Transylvanian.
>
> ILSA: I'm a Transylvanian, too!
>
> HEINRICH (*bitterly*): You're a Jew!
>
> ILSA (*stunned*): What—
>
> HEINRICH (*parroting Mitler*): No Jew can be a Transylvanian. They are enemies of Transylvania—parasites feeding on Transylvania's blood.
>
> ILSA (*furiously*): How dare you say that? My brothers died for Transylvania."

When this momentarily stops Heinrich, Mitler, who has been watching, tells him, "Don't lower yourself by arguing with a Jew."

After they leave, Fritz tells Ilsa that Heinrich is like so many others who came back from the war, "beaten—hurt . . . they want to hurt someone else to get even."

When Ilsa worries that they will get into power, Fritz laughs. "Here in Transylvania? How could they? They don't even make sense. No thinking person would listen to them. They go around making speeches to each other and being put in jail."

The pair confess their feelings for each other, but Ilsa refuses to marry Fritz because being married to a Jew could make life difficult for him. Fritz prevails.

Real and fake newsreels and trick shots convey events from 1924 to 1929, including, "Shots of Nazi disturbances being quelled by police clubs. . . . to show the illegitimacy of the movement." And "Famous Americans arriving in Transylvania . . . i.e., Dempsey, W. R. Hearst, Charlie Chaplin, etc."

To depict the 1929 "world crash," he wanted newsreel footage of panics and bank closings, followed by another trick shot: "Money being sucked back from Transylvania. Under the force of this suction several cracks appear in the surface. Across the bottom of the film the rats are swarming. As the cracks widen, they swarm up through them to the top, overrunning the whole surface. "

Then impressionistic shots of Mitler addressing larger and larger groups of people.

Following milestones like the Reichstag fire and "Mitler's" election, Herman wanted a public book-burning scene like those held all over Germany in May 1933, to showcase Erich Maria Remarque's *All Quiet on the Western Front*—"a traitor to Transylvania—and still alive!" Albert Einstein's *Quantum Theory*—"a Jew . . . and still alive!" Sigmund Freud, Heinrich Heine, Karl Marx, Upton Sinclair . . . and finally, the Bible.

Under Mitler, Heinrich returns to run Gronau and encounters his father. The two embrace, then begin to argue. When a four-year-old boy wanders in, Heinrich teaches him to give the Nazi salute and say "Heil Mitler." Once Ilsa and Fritz appear, Heinrich realizes with horror that the boy is theirs. "You're through with her," he tells Fritz. "With her and her Jewish brat."

Professor Mendelssohn is harassed in the street. In his classroom, a little boy sits in a corner wearing a dunce cap with the word "JEW." "His shirt is torn. He screams as a pen strikes and imbeds itself in his shoulder. He pulls it out, wet with blood." Another student writes, "My teacher is a Jew," on the blackboard. The students eventually drive teacher and student from the classroom.

One of the headlines in Herr Schmidt's newspaper protests the firing of Professor Mendelssohn. Another announces: "MITLER DECREES ALL ARYANS MARRIED TO JEWS MUST SEPARATE OR BE SENT TO PRISON CAMPS."

After Ilsa's brother Hans is killed, Fritz tries to convince her to cross the border. They learn that both their fathers have been killed, and Frau Mendelssohn shoots herself.

They despair of finding a way out when Heinrich arrives at Fritz and Ilsa's, swastika flags waving on his official car. Handing them false passports, he urges them to take his car. He will pretend they stole it. Seeing his father killed was the turning point: "Before my eyes . . . I have been blind—insane. How could I think that was the way to help Transylvania—by killing the finest man that ever lived. And Herr Mendelssohn—and Johann, and those thousands of others. But he made me see . . ."

As troops approach, Heinrich assures Fritz and Ilsa he will try to join them at the frontier and hands them a clutch of money. The Nazis begin to close in, and Heinrich throws himself in their path. He dies shooting at them, and the story ends with Fritz and Ilsa "speeding away to safety."

From the beginning, Herman understood that the powers in Hollywood would consider the very idea of such a portrayal of those events dangerously incendiary and assumed he would have to produce it himself. After telling the press he had already arranged financial backing and distribution, he went to New York to find it. Despite prodigious effort, he failed, and because he could not afford to go without a paycheck for long, Herman was back at MGM by the end of June 1933, working on *Meet the Baron*.

Sam Jaffe was equally anguished. Less than two weeks after Herman's return, he took out full-page advertisements in the trade newspapers announcing that he had acquired the rights to Herman's "anti-Hitler motion picture depicting the sacrifices of the Jews and Catholics in a Central European Nation and the indignities to which they are being subjected." Jaffe also announced that he had resigned from RKO "to devote [his] entire time and attention to this project" and had hired "one of America's foremost dramatists" to help.

Herman remained involved, but opposition was formidable. Although the studios' top executives were almost all Jewish, they were well aware of anti-Semitism's prevalence in American culture and the dangers it posed to them. While leaders in other industries were praised for fulfilling the American Dream, successful motion picture business executives were routinely portrayed as ignorant, jumped-up former garment merchants–"pants pressers, delicatessen dealers, furriers, and penny showmen"—as Karl K. Kitchen wrote in *Columbia*, the official Knights of Columbus magazine. Rather than as captains of industry, they were characterized as "moguls," Oriental, Asiatic despots. They were maligned as greedy capitalists whose sensational products corrupted wholesome Christian Americans, especially during a time when the Depression fueled so many resentments. (Perversely, the same greedy capitalists exploiting the ignorant public would later be condemned as godless communists whose radical internationalism threatened the nation's fabric.) They knew that if they depicted Nazi abuses, they risked being branded as warmongers, trying to pull the United States into a European problem to help their co-religionists.

Studio executives also faced economic pressure. Most of the major studios were owned by publicly held corporations, so even if the studio chiefs wanted to proceed, their corporate bosses would not allow them to jeopardize foreign markets. As one historian put it, the motion picture business was "an industry largely financed by Protestant bankers, operated by Jewish studio executives, and policed by Catholic bureaucrats, all the while claiming to represent grass-roots America."

The Catholic bureaucrats in question staffed the industry's trade organization, Motion Picture Producers and Distributors of America (MPPDA), which was often called the Hays Office, after the organization's president, Will H. Hays. Besides representing industry interests, the MPPDA operated as a self-censoring body, created by the industry to forestall national and local censorship efforts. MPPDA was supposed to be the industry's advocate, but its employees' sympathies ranged from well-meaning to avowedly anti-Semitic, and the latter were not above exploiting studio Jewish executives' apprehensions. When Nazis assaulted American Jewish employees of American film companies and pushed them out of Germany in 1933, the MPPDA spokesman presumably charged with protecting industry interests said only that "these men left the country willingly and have since returned to work there."

Created in 1930, the Code by which the MPPDA regulated its members' pictures reflected the Catholic values of the Code's creators, addressing issues of profanity, alcohol and drug use, respect for clergy, nudity, sex outside of marriage, homosexuality, respect for the flag, miscegenation, and the sensibilities of other nations. MPPDA did not enforce effectually it until July 15, 1934, when Hays's assistant, Joseph I. Breen, took charge of the MPPDA's newly formed Production Code Administration (PCA). That meant Herman's *Mad Dog* script was submitted during the interval between 1930 and mid-1934, a period film historians now fondly recall as Pre-Code Hollywood. During those early Depression years, studios pursued diminishing audiences with increasingly sensational films and stories filled with gangsters, violence, and less censorious treatments of sexual mores.

A week after Jaffe's announcement, Hays summoned Herman and Jaffe to his office and accused them of greed: they were exploiting "a scarehead situation for the picture which, if made, might return them a tremendous profit while creating heavy losses for the industry." Then he threatened, even if they found a studio willing to rent them production facilities, how could they exhibit the film if all the major theaters refused them? Jaffe responded that even if he had to contend with higher costs and lower revenues, he would exhibit in smaller theaters in lesser markets.

Herman, who was as averse to admitting a noble purpose as he was addicted to insulting more than one target at a time, undercut Jaffe's honorable declaration by seeing and raising Hays's accusation of (Jewish) greed. He said he had written *Mad Dog* with "the esthetic tastes of the public" in mind and "for the same reason that Hollywood producers had made *Baby Face, Melody Cruise* and *So This Is Africa.*" With his usual economy, Herman simultaneously repudiated his and Jaffe's obvious idealism; ridiculed the industry for the triviality of its output; mocked the MPPDA for hypocrisy; and exposed its regulatory code as ineffectual. All three of his examples were major studios' recent releases; all three were MPPDA-approved; and all three pushed sexual, rather than political, boundaries. Only Warner Brothers' *Baby Face* was even a drama (Barbara Stanwyck's character slept with men for advancement, and the picture became a prime example of pre-Code Hollywood). The other two were silly sex comedies. Hays was not amused.

As Jaffe set up an office and hired Lynn Root to work on the script, a number of Jewish organizations mobilized. They, too, wanted Americans informed about Hitler and the Nazis, but they wanted the word spread by non-Jewish messengers. The Anti-Defamation League (ADL), which had been organized in 1913 specifically to combat anti-Semitism, joined studio heads and the MPPDA in actively opposing *Mad Dog*. They feared it would provoke accusations of Jewish warmongering, and they worried that if it failed commercially, it would demonstrate American apathy to Hitler or even pave the way for pro-Nazi films. After Jaffe showed the Los Angeles ADL the script, some members thought it might be effective if toned down, but officially the organization opposed it.

In August 1933 Herman and Jaffe conceded defeat. They might use the title at some future time, Herman told a Los Angeles ADL official, but if they did, they would make it more a "newsreel type" picture. ADL officials took the precaution of alerting potential sources of money anyway, in case Jaffe tried again.

By September, Jaffe also needed to get back to work, so he sold *Mad Dog* rights to Al Rosen, a tough agent eager to make his mark as a producer. Rosen went to Paris to meet with Billy Wilder, Paul Kohner, and Sam Spiegel, all Austrian or Austro-Hungarians, but he too was unable to secure funding. After that he embarked on one scheme after another, including hiring a Hitler lookalike to generate publicity. Eventually, he convinced New York philanthropist Samuel Untermeyer to finance it, but ADL members interceded and Untermeyer withdrew. In October 1933 Herman asked to have his name removed.

Once the new Production Code went into effect in mid-1934, Rosen had to deal with Joseph Breen, a known anti-Semite, who pulled no punches. He objected, "Because of the large number of Jews active in the motion picture industry in this country, the charge is certain to be made that the Jews, as a class, are behind an anti-Hitler picture and using the entertainment screen for their own personal propaganda purposes. The entire industry, because of this, is likely to be indicted for the action of a mere handful." That the mere handful were trying to save the lives of multitudes was apparently not an argument the Jewish executives dared venture, especially when Breen added that some believed "that such a picture is an out-and-out propaganda picture" that "might establish a bad precedent. The purpose of the screen, primarily, is to entertain and not to propagandize. To launch such a picture might result in a kind of two-edged sword, with the screen being used for propaganda purposes not so worthy, possibly as that suggested by THE MAD DOG OF EUROPE idea."

As the ADL executives had feared, Breen explicitly suggested anti-Semites deserved equal time. "It is to be remembered that there is strong pro-German and anti-Semitic feeling in this country, and, while those who are likely to approve of an anti-Hitler picture may think well of such an enterprise, they should keep in mind that millions of Americans might think otherwise." By then, he had reinforcements. Nazi censors were already screening everything coming into Germany, but to stamp out offending material at the source, they sent German consul Dr. Georg Gyssling to Hollywood to work with studios on scripts before they were even produced.

Rosen did not give up. In 1935 Italy invaded Ethiopia, and the press began referring to Benito Mussolini as the mad dog of Europe, but Al

Rosen kept at it. Again announcing production plans, he said the picture would be accompanied by a novel of the same name. In July 1935 Joseph Goebbels and the German Film Board of Censors notified MGM's foreign department that "photoplays written by Herman J. Mankiewicz" would not be allowed into Germany unless Herman's name was removed. There was no accompanying explanation.

Herman had spent the last two years turning out MGM fluff, and, if anything, his 1934 *Stamboul Quest*, a caper starring Myrna Loy, was a sympathetic portrayal of an actual World War I German spy. He had written yet a third adaptation of *The Show-Off* for Spencer Tracy, and *After Office Hours*, a Clark Gable/Constance Bennett newspaper murder comedy so silly that more than one critic complained of its excessive whimsy. (It may have been too much Mankiewicz—Joe contributed dialogue as well.) Herman's most recent picture was *Escapade*, an adaptation of Walter Reisch's turn-of-the-century Viennese drawing room romance, *Maskerade*. A number of censors had objected to the line "A woman in that condition should be seen by two men only; her husband and her doctor, and I am both," but that risqué reference to pregnancy hardly seemed sufficient to trigger a Nazi ban from the highest level, and only against Herman.

The *New York Times* coyly speculated that since Herman's films "contained no references to the present German Government or any of its officials," perhaps its ad hominem ban was attributable to "the writer's 'non-Aryanism.'" Or might it be because "the writer contemplated a film production of 'The Mad Dog of Europe' a few years ago." It was "generally understood" that he abandoned the project "on the advice of influential American Jews," who feared "bitter consequences for their coreligionists in Germany." As the only screen writer the Nazis singled out, Herman wore the distinction with honor.

With membership in the Hollywood Anti-Nazi League exceeding four thousand in 1936, Rosen approached the US State Department about the film and came close to convincing Sol Lesser to produce it at RKO. Then the State Department contacted the MPPDA, and Breen sent the State Department and Lesser his 1934 memo, and again killed the project.

In 1937 Rosen announced that after conducting a poll to measure the appeal of an anti-Nazi film with a script "by Herman Mankiewicz, Lynn Root and [Albert] Rosen," he planned to proceed without the blessing of a Production Code seal. Furthermore, he would not reveal casting until shooting began, "because of the incident in which Dr. George Gyssling, local German consul, figured in connection with 'The Road Back.'"

When Universal adapted Erich Maria Remarque's sequel to *All Quiet on the Western Front,* Gyssling had pressured Universal but also had warned individual actors and technicians that if the film offended the Germans, Germany would not only ban that picture but might ban their past, present, and future films. Universal capitulated, transforming Remarque's anti-Nazi, antiwar film into a comedy.

That attempt failed as well, and by then events were overtaking the screenplay. A January 1938 episode of *Time*'s "March of Time" newsreel/documentary series revealed more about Hitler and the Nazis than the public had hitherto seen, and refugees were trickling into the United States. Despite the fact that income from the countries under fascist rule had already dried up, the major studios continued to reject hard-hitting projects, though they released a few that were at least implicitly anti-Nazi, including *The Three Comrades* (1938), which Joe produced. Rosen published *Mad Dog* as a novel, supposedly written by the pseudonymous "Albert Nesor" (Rosen spelled backward).

In 1939, six long years after Herman had first tried to warn the public, Al Rosen continued to publicly credit Herman, Lynn Root, and himself as *Mad Dog*'s creators, and to milk every name or connection he could conjure. He even tried hiring Hitler's sister-in-law as the film's advisor. Finally, Breen grudgingly approved the script as a "fair" representation of "prominent people and citizenry," though he cautioned that such a film was "enormously dangerous from the standpoint of political censorship outside the United States," so Rosen would likely encounter "serious difficulty" in marketing it overseas.

Then Breen engaged in the usual Code negotiations, and his objections, given the subject matter, can only be described as bizarre. Rosen was to remove the "obvious homosexual" character—"I think you know that any suggestion, or even the slightest inference, of sex perversion is not acceptable." Expletives "For God's sake," "Oh God," and "God" were to be eliminated. Breen also warned, "political censor boards" frequently eliminated "blood suckers" and would likely also delete the image of a swastika fading into the figure of a crucified Christ. He noted that the British censors were unlikely to allow the recitation of the Lord's Prayer, and he urged Rosen to shoot the riot scenes so that they were not "too realistically brutal or gruesome"—they should show no dead bodies, either in those sequences or in the morgue.

Then there was Breen's attention to national sensibilities: "It is our thought that even though the expression "the French are a nation of niggers" may be an authentic quotation [of Hitler], its repetition is likely to give offense to the French nation and people, and it might be well for you to consider dropping the expression entirely."

It appeared as if production would begin at last at Denham Film Studios outside London, with distribution by Columbia Pictures. But *Mad Dog*'s moment had passed. *Hitler, Beast of Berlin* opened in October 1939, with a press kit suggesting exhibitors hang photos of Hitler, dress a young man as a storm trooper, and build a concentration camp torture box. In 1940 MGM released *The Mortal Storm*, a Nazi era love triangle among a Jewish woman (Margaret Sullavan), a Christian Communist (James Stewart), and a Christian Nazi (Robert Young) that bore some resemblance to *Mad Dog*. Although it had been adapted from a 1938 Phyllis Bottome novel, Rosen filed suit in 1943, alleging plagiarism by Loew's (Metro-Goldwyn-Mayer's parent company), the film's writers, director, and producer. Second Circuit Court of Appeals judge Learned Hand finally decided against Rosen in 1947—two years after the Nazis were finally vanquished.

When Herman gave up on *Mad Dog* in 1933, he hardly shed his concern. As Nazi devastation spread throughout Europe, he quietly sponsored refugees and found them jobs when he could, pledged financial support when it was needed (whether he had the money or not), and contributed generously to all kinds of relief efforts. But those were mostly private efforts. In public, Herman spent the years leading up to the war vociferously opposing US involvement, and his manner of opposition was often, to put it mildly, offensive. Ordinary hypocrites espouse honorable sentiments in public and behave reprehensibly in private. Not Herman. His private actions were noble, his public pronouncements frequently repugnant.

Herman had written *The Mad Dog of Europe* in an effort to prevent another war, not to encourage US involvement, and his reaction to the previous war remained visceral. Upset at hearing he had been characterized as a Nazi to Irving Berlin, he wrote his old friend in October 1941, explaining his views. "Somewhat over-simplified, I would say in general that I feel this was not America's war and that it still need <u>not</u> be (though our own behaviour constitutes a grave danger that it may <u>still</u> be). If this should happen, I believe that the worst will have happened for America, win, lose or draw. And so it is for this reason that I oppose, with my own puny strength, any and all efforts to associate ourselves with the war."

Herman objected for many reasons, including political beliefs of long standing. Along with Progressives like Senator Robert La Follette, Herman favored a relatively weak central government, and wars tipped the balance toward the federal government by strengthening what President Eisenhower would later call the military-industrial complex. Herman originally had supported Franklin Roosevelt, but when the New Deal began expanding the federal government and FDR tilted toward intervention by calling the United States an "arsenal of democracy," Herman turned against Roosevelt and began snorting about a "horse's arsenal of democracy."

Internationally, as much as Herman feared Hitler, he also distrusted Hitler's most powerful opponents. He objected to aiding the United Kingdom and its colonies, and he abhorred the prospect of American sacrifices on the Soviet Union's behalf.

Third, Herman considered himself an adherent of Realpolitik. In this case, that meant he supported the anti-interventionism of both Charles Lindbergh and the US ambassador to Britain, Joseph Kennedy, who urged the United States to stay out of the conflict because it could not win. As Herman liked to put it, "Would you go into the ring with Joe Louis?" Herman was well aware that Lindbergh and Kennedy, like many isolationists, were also anti-Semites, which made their defeatism a bit too convenient. He cozied up anyway. Calling himself an "ultra-Lindbergh," he condescendingly explained, "The strength of the so-called Rome–Berlin Axis is so overwhelming as to make the thought of conflict the work of a madman. I suggest that the American public return to its worries about the World Series, the chance that the Goldbergs will really be able to pay off their mortgage, and schemes for getting the government, or the state, or the city, or the township, or the ward, to pay them one thousand dollars every Monday, Wednesday, and Friday."

In short, Herman adopted some strange bedfellows. Even granting him the benefit of some sincere, long-standing beliefs, Herman's fundamental orneriness should not be overlooked as yet a fourth contributor. "His views changed a lot, depending on who he was talking to," his son Don recalled. "As he saw it, there were vast quantities of bullshit and he was there to put things right if he thought they were unreasonable. But if he was on the other side, he would argue that side. He didn't care much which side it was." Don speculated that perhaps Herman expressed his contrarian views so vehemently that he eventually began to believe himself.

Perhaps. Don's anti-bullshit theory links up nicely with Herman's aversion to suffering fools gladly. Herman could not tolerate the idea that he had anything in common with the ignorant, the fatuous, or the too ready to adopt the fashionable opinions of the moment, and by the mid-1930s, those categories had come to include large segments of the population who now embraced the positions Herman had tried unsuccessfully to disseminate only a few years before. Being in that company annoyed Herman, especially because he saw them being used without their knowledge by popular front organizations like the Hollywood Anti-Nazi League for the Defense of American Democracy.

On the other hand, he joined a gathering of several hundred at the Hotel Roosevelt in September 1936 to pledge opposition to fascism, Nazism, communism, "and all other dangerous isms," and when Don, still in high school, asked to join the Hollywood Anti-Nazi League, Herman consented, reasoning, "Oscar Hammerstein and Philip Dunne are members so though it may be a Communist front, it's not just that." He even allowed Don to go undercover to infiltrate the local Bund organization's version of the Nazis' Brown Shirts. Don was terrified but thrilled, later describing them as the 1930s equivalent of skinheads. To explain driving such an expensive car to meetings, he told the group his father was a chauffeur working for a Jew who let him use his car.

When he returned in 1939 from his first year of college, Don was worried about being exposed and wanted to quit. Herman chuckled, "If there are ten of you, probably four of them are from the FBI and another four are also infiltrating." Don went downtown anyway and, to his surprise, had to join a long line of members also there to resign. The Nazi–Soviet Non-Aggression Pact had been announced the day before, so the good Communists were following instructions to quit because Nazis were no longer the enemy. (The remaining members renamed the organization and continued their work against fascism.) Two years later the Nazis invaded the Soviet Union, and Herman joked that John Howard Lawson (head of Hollywood's Communist Party) was probably on his way to the Lockheed plant to put the bolts back into airplanes that he had taken *out* the day before.

Those were the oases of calm. In between, Herman often ranted himself into what Joe called his "binges of perversity and extremism," insulting friends with comments like, "Idiocy is all right in its way, but you can't make it the foundation of a career." He was so offensive on one occasion that Ernst Lubitsch ordered him out of his house. On another, he interrupted an old friend describing the situation in occupied France to exclaim that Hitler was right: "All the doctors, lawyers, and professional men in Germany were Jews and they were getting too strong a hold." At a dinner party of Mattie and Saul Fox's, some of their guests walked out, telling Mattie not to invite them again if Herman was to be present.

Then the Japanese bombed Pearl Harbor, and forty-four-year-old Herman tried to enlist. Hoping for a job with the Marine Corps's intelligence department, Herman reviewed his entire work history, starting with his honorable discharge "at Quantico, Virginia, on July 12, 1919." He concluded, "There are, perhaps, other ways in which I could serve my country, but my first—and I believe natural—desire is again to wear the uniform I wore twenty-five years ago."

The military rejected him. Bad kidneys.

CHAPTER 10

The Tiffany of Studios

WHEN HERMAN STARTED AT METRO-GOLDWYN-MAYER IN MARCH 1933, David O. Selznick had just arrived, and Herman replicated the same close relationship he had enjoyed with B. P. Schulberg at Paramount. Selznick made Herman a $1,000-a-week supervising producer and installed him in a large, luxurious office next door with his own secretary. That was $250 lower than his Paramount salary, but it crept back up. Selznick later hired Joe as a $750-a-week writer, and Joe used secretaries from the pool.

At MGM, Louis B. Mayer, and his production chief, Irving G. Thalberg, had utilized Henry Ford's assembly line techniques to create what was generally regarded as the Tiffany of studios. Mayer combined genuine kindness with ruthlessness, charm with histrionics (he could cry, faint, and even foam at the mouth at will), and ruled over an almost self-sufficient society: four thousand employees, 117 acres, twenty-three sound stages, outdoor lots filled with houses, a jungle, and a small lake. They provided employees with a dentist's office, clinic, barbershop, and—for child actors like Elizabeth Taylor, Mickey Rooney, and Judy Garland—a Little Red Schoolhouse. Appealing food and professional camaraderie enticed most employees to eat at the commissary, which boosted productivity.

Although designers and craftsmen were given whatever they needed to create the studio's characteristically lavish productions, directors and writers were regarded as unpleasant necessities who needed to be tightly managed. Thalberg respected creativity, but, in contrast to Paramount, which was considered the directors' studio, and Twentieth Century Fox, which under Darryl F. Zanuck became known as the writers' studio, MGM was called the producers' studio, because MGM producers were so powerful. All the major studios followed the basic system (hence the name "studio system"), but Mayer and Thalberg did it best. At the end

In an early product tie-in, cast members from *Dinner at Eight* (1933) enjoy "the pause that refreshes with ice-cold Coca-Cola." Seated from left: Madge Evans, Louise Closser Hale, Billie Burke, Marie Dressler, Karen Morley, Grant Mitchell. Standing: Edmund Lowe, director George Cukor, Lionel Barrymore, Jean Harlow, Phillips Holmes.

of 1932, with a third of the nation's population out of work and theater attendance plummeting, every major studio except MGM was in the red.

Insulated up to a point, MGM's writers toiled in golden handcuffs. They enjoyed comfortable, spacious offices, first-rate secretaries, reasonable hours, and the prestige of knowing they were at the top studio. The company at the writers' commissary table was stimulating, though that pleasure was tempered by its tradition of throwing dice to determine who paid for the entire table's lunch. In exchange, the writers functioned as cogs in Thalberg's dehumanizing machine: he routinely shifted them from project to project and assigned more than one writer to the same picture at the same time, often without their knowledge. Writers needed credits to get their contracts renewed, so if ten different writers contributed to a picture, they needed to hop on at the right time to get the credit, which was no easy feat in a zero-sum game.

Herman's son Don, who became a successful screenwriter himself, summed up the dilemma: "You have to care about your work, but you can't care too much." Not surprisingly, the studios' demeaning conditions drove Herman and many of his colleagues to take childish pride in working as little as possible on their assignments. Ironically, as much as they disparaged the work, successful screenwriters also looked down on colleagues who couldn't make it, like restaurant patrons complaining that the food was terrible and there wasn't enough of it.

Eager to overcome the stigma of nepotism ("The Son-in-Law Also Rises," quipped the *Hollywood Spectator* when he was hired), Selznick wanted to start with a first-class production. He chose Edna Ferber and George F. Kaufman's 1932 Broadway hit, *Dinner at Eight*, which also enabled him to test Mayer's promise of access to the studio's top stars by using many of them in one picture, as Thalberg had done the previous year with *Grand Hotel*. Selznick borrowed George Cukor to direct Wallace Beery, John and Lionel Barrymore, Jean Harlow, Billy Burke, Edmund Lowe, Phillips Holmes, Madge Evans, and the number one box office star at the time, Marie Dressler, and assigned Herman and Frances Marion to adapt the comic drama about a dinner party on the eve of the Depression. The picture was an enormous hit, and Cukor, Herman, and Sara became lifelong friends. Herman adapted another Broadway hit, *Another Language*, for Helen Hayes, then left to work on *Mad Dog*.

Joe, twenty-five, was more enthusiastic, and fortuitously, his first MGM film became an outsize success. He and Oliver H. P. Garrett (another of Herman's Paramount recruits), were assigned to write a Warner Brothers–style crime drama, and their clever screenplay, combined with Arthur Caesar's Academy Award–winning story, a Rodgers and Hart song that later became "Blue Moon," and skillful performances by Clark Gable, Myrna Loy, and William Powell, made *Manhattan Melodrama* (1934) both a critical and popular hit. Then, two months into its run, federal agents shot and killed John Dillinger, aka "Public Enemy Number One," as he left a Chicago theater after viewing the film. That catapulted *Manhattan Melodrama* onto the front page and into the history books.

On the side, Joe contributed dialogue to King Vidor's eventual classic, *Our Daily Bread*, about a collective farm during the Depression. Vidor financed it himself, and Joe initially agreed to waive half his $5,000 fee until the film broke even. Vidor, who was a friend of Herman's, later dismissed Joe's contribution. "He didn't do anything more than just take the script and go over it. . . . If someone read the script, and they could not think of anything else to say, they would comment that the dialogue might be improved. That's what Mankiewicz did." Vidor added that he didn't remember what Joe had written, "but we weren't enthused about everything he wrote. We might have kept a few lines." When Joe's biographer disparaged the picture's dialogue as "banal and synthetic, lacking Steinbeck's ear and feeling for the poetic commonplaces uttered by laborers of multiple nationalities," Joe wrote next to Geist's comment, "Nor did I win a Nobel Prize."

Joe's next MGM assignment was adapting *Forsaking All Others*, a 1933 Broadway comedy about a love triangle among three childhood friends. The woman in the play (Tallulah Bankhead) is jilted at the altar and later jilts the jilter, but Joe spiced up the script with adventures, slapstick, and so much wit that his producer, Bernie Hyman, talked Mayer into upgrading the cast. "My boy," Hyman told Joe excitedly, "instead of Loretta Young, you've got Joan Crawford. Instead of George Brent, you've got Clark Gable, and instead of Joel McCrea, you've got Robert Montgomery." (Since Joel McCrea got Frances Dee, perhaps Joe was doubly gratified.)

Hyman sent Joe to "Miss Crawford's house" to read her the script, and the terrified young writer followed her butler into a spotless white drawing room filled with Crawford's favorite gardenias. When the star entered in a flowing chiffon costume and bade him begin, Joe started out nervously. Soon Crawford was chuckling and laughing, which encouraged Joe to calm down and throw himself into the reading. When he reached the line "I could build a fire by rubbing two Boy Scouts together," Crawford threw up her hands in such delight that one of her red fingernails went flying through the air and landed on her white carpet. Joe, who had never knowingly encountered false fingernails, was rattled, but Crawford urged him on, and when he finished, she exclaimed, "Quite marvelous, Joe, dear," and kissed him on the cheek.

Crawford later dismissed the picture as little more than a "fashion layout," but audiences loved it, and critics generally agreed, though some thought it exceeded its quota of whimsy. Though he considered it so "smart" that it would be a great hit of the season, Richard Watts Jr. of the *New York Herald Tribune* warned, "The collective efforts of Donald Ogden Stewart, Philip Barry and Alexander Woollcott, mounted on one kiddie-kar, could hardly arrange more whimsies than have been devised by the individual striving of Joseph L. Mankiewicz, author of the screen script," and conjectured that its "fantastic obeisance to the worst side of A. A. Milne" might drive "rational filmgoers" to "homicidal frenzies."

As far as MGM was concerned, if one Joe Mankiewicz romantic comedy worked, two would be better, so Joe was assigned another Joan Crawford society-girl romance. *I Live My Life* also culminated in a wedding scene, though only one this time.

Perhaps all those weddings were catching, for despite being jilted practically at the altar himself in 1933, and despite Pop's advice that he give

Joe's script for *Forsaking All Others* (1934) was so witty that MGM upgraded the stars to Robert Montgomery, Clark Gable, and Joan Crawford.

himself a few years to mature, Joe rebounded enough to marry another actress in mid-1934. Joe had met Elizabeth Schermerhorn Young, a lively, petite former New York debutante with piercing blue eyes, not long after his breakdown. Her father was a children's court judge; her mother, whose best friend was Millicent (Mrs. William Randolph) Hearst, was related to Mrs. Astor and was herself a former Schermerhorn.

Many socialites and heiresses were flocking to Hollywood at the time, but Elizabeth had arrived with a Paramount contract. She had been in three Broadway plays, and the studio touted her as a potential Katharine Hepburn, a "new type of actress coming into vogue in the movies." Shortly after her screen debut as Richard Bennett's daughter in *Big Executive* (1933), director Rouben Mamoulian saw her in the commissary and borrowed her to play Greta Garbo's lady-in-waiting in MGM's *Queen Christina*. Given the oversupply of ingénues, winning the second female role in a Garbo vehicle was a coup, even if her appearance rather than her acting had triggered it, and Elizabeth's future looked as bright as Joe's.

Joe marries Elizabeth Young on May 20, 1934, in Herman and Sara's backyard, attended by Gail Patrick and Phillips Holmes.

They were both busy six days a week, outside the studios as well as within. For a production of *The Stooge* at the Threshold Theater, a small "try-out" house, Joe collaborated with Claude Binyon, a Paramount screenwriter and former *Variety* writer who had written the classic headline "Wall St Lays an Egg" (in 1929). Elizabeth was in loftier company, appearing in the Los Angeles production of Howard Lindsay's Broadway hit *She Loves Me Not*, which Paramount was concurrently shooting with Bing Crosby and Miriam Hopkins.

Elizabeth even worked on her wedding day. She was on loan out to Universal for *There's Always Tomorrow*, and to meet their deadline they had to shoot even on Sunday. So after Elizabeth shot a romantic scene with Robert Taylor in the morning and Taylor, Frank Morgan, and Binnie Barnes sent her off in a hail of old shoes, twenty-year-old Elizabeth married twenty-five-year-old Joe in Herman and Sara's backyard that afternoon. Their attendants were Gail Patrick, a Paramount actress who went on to a long, successful career, and Phillips Holmes, an actor who died early in World War II.

Even Louella Parsons waxed syrupy over their marriage, though newspapers across the country carried an Associated Press report that "Herman Mankiewicz, writer," was marrying "Elizabeth Young, motion picture actress." Joe was not surprised, though after five years in the business he was getting tired of being identified as Herman's younger brother. He sometimes joked his tombstone would read, "Here lies Herm—I mean, Joe—Mankiewicz."

Although Elizabeth was pregnant by the end of 1935, she starred in Universal's *East of Java* (1935). Neither she nor Joe had any idea her career was ending just as Joe's was heating up.

When Joe's second Joan Crawford picture delivered his third hit in a row, he gathered the courage to approach Mayer about directing his own screenplays. He longed for control over his work—or at least as much control as an MGM director could manage. Directors had great leeway to treat scripts as they pleased, and sometimes more than one director worked on the same picture. But Joe labored over his, and he wanted to bring them to the screen as he had imagined. Mayer turned him down flat and made him a producer instead. "You need to learn to crawl before you can walk," Mayer intoned, an admonition Joe quoted for the rest of his life as the best description of a producer he had ever heard. Mayer was grooming Joe as a possible successor to the frail Irving Thalberg, but Joe regarded the promotion as a punishment.

Herman had been promoted to producer more than once, and though neither brother was above enjoying the power or perquisites of the job, both found administrative duties tedious, and the necessity of policing others downright unpleasant. Their individual responses were characteristic. Herman rebelled, often by creative self-sabotage, so that either Herman or his boss demoted him back to writer. Joe resignedly accepted the hand he was dealt, played it skillfully, and looked for ways to improve it.

The brothers' first few years at MGM coincided with a national surge in labor organizing, sparked by Roosevelt's election. The same March 1933 week that Herman started at MGM, Roosevelt declared a bank holiday, and the MPPDA imposed a blanket wage cut on the industry. Although MGM was profitable, Mayer manipulated most of his employees into accepting the cut anyway. Only the International Alliance of Theatrical Stage Employees (IATSE)—the theatrical projectionists, engineers, grips, electricians—refused. Their example was not lost on the screenwriters, who were already meeting to discuss the idea of creating an organization to represent their interests more effectually than the two writers' groups already in existence.

One was the Writers Club, led by Rupert Hughes (uncle of Howard), which functioned as a social group for homesick New York writers. The other was the writers' group within the Academy of Motion Picture Arts and Sciences (AMPAS, or simply the Academy). Studio heads had founded the Academy in 1927 specifically to head off the formation of craft unions like Actors Equity and the Dramatists Guild, so the Academy's writers' group was essentially a company union. Even so, under Academy auspices, a group of screenwriters had gathered in 1931 and 1932 and negotiated with a producers' group to carve out some writers' rights. As chair of the subcommittee on credits, Herman had put Joe on his committee, and they extracted a few concessions from the producers, though nothing meaningful.

When the wage cut ended, only Samuel Goldwyn reimbursed his employees. The other studios simply pocketed the savings. So on April 6, 1933, in the wake of the wage cut and amidst the pro-labor ferment of the New Deal, a newly formed Screen Writers Guild (SWG) elected John Howard Lawson as its first president and Joe as its first secretary. Studio executives and producers fought back angrily, and a number of writers sided with them, including Herman.

As the son of ardent Democrats (Hanna as well as Frank), and the veteran of Wilkes-Barre coal mines, Herman genuinely sympathized with workers. He insisted Sara never dismiss servants unless they had another job and infuriated her during wartime by encouraging their employees to take the opportunity to make much more money elsewhere. He also believed in collective bargaining. But to Herman, creative professionals were not workers like miners and factory laborers, and even if other types of writers formed guilds, he considered the idea of screenwriting as a branch of writing, pretentious. He told Don, "You can't have a literature of screenwriting because it would be like a literature of comic books." Besides considering it ludicrous, he regarded the idea as potentially dangerous to their wellbeing. Of all writers, screenwriters were paid sums beyond their wildest imaginations—and in the middle of the Depression, no less. "Chasen's can dispense the vichyssoise on the picket line," he jeered.

> I want to see the accounting of the first guy who applies to the union good and welfare fund—two hundred dollars a week for school tuition, a hundred twenty dollars for the psychiatrist, three hundred dollars for the cook. . . . You'll all go out on the streets carrying big signs saying, "Help! Help! We're only being paid seven

> and a half a week." And everybody will say, "How about those poor guys? Seven dollars and fifty cents a week." And then somebody else says, "No, seven *hundred* and fifty *dollars* a week." And then duck because you'll all be stoned to death.

Herman also distrusted communists, some of whom were the most active and effective organizers. So, with his usual economy, he annihilated several birds with one *Variety* advertisement urging, "Writers of the world unite—you have nothing to lose but your brains." When Dorothy Parker tried to convince Herman to join for other writers' sakes, pleading, "We're both making over a thousand dollars a week. I'm concerned about the $35 a week writer," Herman simply scoffed, "I'm not concerned about him because he's getting $750 in this business." When they talked about pushing for a five-day week (most studios required writers to work on Saturday), Herman said, "A five-day week? Goddam if I'm coming in on Friday."

Naturally, he also tagged them as village idiots, asking what kind of writers failed to notice that Screen Writers Guild needed an apostrophe, and in 1936 he joined the competing union endorsed by the studios. Screen Playwrights (SP) offered membership by invitation only and required three screen credits within the past three years. Histories of the competition between Screen Playwrights and Screen Writers Guild often pigeonhole Herman with reactionaries and redbaiters like Rupert Hughes, but SP members and their motives were more varied. Morrie Ryskind, like Herman, worried that the Guild would do more harm than good.

The producers recognized SP immediately and began negotiating with them. They even granted them a few concessions they would never have conceded to the Guild, though nowhere near what writers wanted. The competition, which continued for the next few years, evoked angry confrontations among the writers. Studios and producers heavy-handedly backed Screen Playwrights, luring some writers with lucrative contracts and intimidating others with retaliatory firings and an undeclared blacklist. Redbaiting was common and, in some cases, ended careers.

Given the bitterness of the struggle, Herman's affiliation shocked some in the business, though close friends understood the nuances of his thinking (and recognized the possibility of knee-jerk orneriness). Herman's actual enthusiasm for SP was questionable, and the much-repeated story that he hid in an air-conditioning duct to eavesdrop on a Guild meeting is almost certainly apocryphal. As Joe pointed out, "My brother was a large man who was always sitting or lying down. The image of him crawling into a duct is hilarious. If he was in there, he must have gotten drunk and somebody pushed him in." In 1938 writers voted by a huge margin to have the Guild represent them, though the studios and producers managed to avoid signing a contract until 1940.

Throughout the controversy, Herman had it both ways. He mocked his fellow writers' adversarial stance toward management but did so as a privileged insider. Using another leave of absence in 1935, he took Sara and the boys to Italy where he was to write a picture. When the Italians invaded Ethiopia, however, they had to suspend shooting. So they went to London instead, where Herman wrote *Three Maxims*, a film about trapeze artists in Paris. It was released in the US in 1936 as *The Show Goes On*. Still in London when King George V died, they enjoyed a ringside seat to history, watching the funeral from Hugh Walpole's balcony, and relishing insider gossip about the new king, Edward VIII, from Herman's friend Thelma Furness (Gloria Vanderbilt's twin sister). She had been Edward's mistress herself, until she had to leave town for a while and asked her friend Wallis Simpson to look after him.

Back at MGM, Herman floated from assignment to assignment, working without credit on MGM pictures like *San Francisco* and *The Emperor's Candlesticks*, and outside the studio on movies like Sol Lesser's *Rainbow on the River*. For B. P. Schulberg, now an independent producer, he wrote *John Meade's Woman* (1937), a portrait of a cruel lumber baron that anticipated *Citizen Kane*. So did *The Tree Will Grow*, a play he started about John Dillinger, which began with Dillinger's death and attempted a composite portrait through the reactions of others in his life.

Herman never finished *The Tree Will Grow*, but in 1936 he did complete another play, *The Meal Ticket*, about Dorothy Sinclair, a successful young movie actress who supports her family of former vaudevillians. When Dorothy decides to marry an idealistic young doctor and follow him to Africa, her parents try to talk her out of leaving. Her grandmother Rose urges her to follow her heart. Herman was only in his late thirties, but his portrayal of Rose's regret anticipates his more polished depiction of nostalgic yearning in *Kane*:

> ROSE: It's life—and people thinking about life—and people living their lives—that don't make sense. Because there's always something that you should have done and didn't do. Then what you did do, why, if you know what's good for you, that's what you make up your mind you should have done. Because it's what you *have* done—whether you like it or not.

DOROTHY: It's easy enough for *you* to say not to do a thing—and just make up your mind you *couldn't* do it—and take what you *did* do. You're old and it doesn't make so much difference.

ROSE: *That's* where you're wrong. It's when you're *old* that it don't make sense that there's something you should have done—but you did something else. When you're young, there's something you should have done—and you didn't do it—but there's a lot of time ahead of you to do something else that's just as good—maybe even to do the thing you missed, only later. The might-have-been is terrible and bitter when you're old, Dorothy—not when you're young. Why, with you, there isn't any might-have-been. Whatever might have been can still be—with you.

With John Hay (Jock) Whitney's backing, Herman planned a March 1937 Broadway run and went east to supervise rehearsals. The Philadelphia tryouts were so disappointing that they postponed the opening until September, and Herman started revising. The September deadline came and went. George Abbott took it up in 1938, again raising Herman's hopes, but it was never produced.

As the 1930s passed, Herman's credits dwindled, and he feared he would never write the great work he felt he had in him. Ben Hecht feared so, too. To Hecht, Herman's profligacy with his gifts was almost another addiction: "I knew that no one as witty and spontaneous as Herman would ever put himself on paper. A man whose genius is on tap like free beer seldom makes literature out of it." Even Herman's public persona began to fray, sinking from a Johnsonian wit admired for his insightful aphorisms to a Falstaffian character with amusing foibles—or tragic flaws.

He devised an all-purpose, not-particularly-penitent, fill-in-the-blanks bread-and-butter letter to cover embarrassing evenings, and Katharine Hepburn saved this from August 31, 1934 (italicized portions filled in by Herman):

Dear *Miss Hepburn*,

I want to thank you for the lovely evening I spent at your home. Particularly do I appreciate the little thoughtfullnesses [Herman's spelling] that characterized your reception of me. How, for example, did you know that the *baked beans* you served on *that* evening was my favorite *entre-met*? And the *milk*! Yummy!

Thank you again, dear *Miss Hepburn,* and remember me to your charming *house-guest.*

Yours,

Herman J Mankiewicz

A few months later he wrote again:

My dear Kate,

Are you married to Leland? Are you married to Laura? Are you married?

I will give you an idea of the kind of answers I want. For instance, suppose you were asking me the questions. The answers are: No. No. No.

You will understand that this is only a sample and does not apply except where it is in accord with the facts.

Yours,

Mank [signed]

Herman clearly was flirting with Hepburn, though philandering was not high on his list of dissipations. He liked going out with women who were not Sara, and he did wander into extramarital relationships, but they did not seem emotionally engaging or even necessarily sexual. Herman's biographer's term, "platonic retinue," seems a bit forced—one senses the presence of Sara looking over Meryman's shoulder—and perhaps there was a bit of sex here and there. Or maybe not. When asked if they thought Herman had actual sexual affairs, both Don and Frank answered "yes" and "no" on different occasions (I inquired more than once). Joe thought he did not and disparaged his brother for wasting his opportunities. More than one relative mentioned his fear of angering Sara. Anyway, philandering would have been hard to fit into Herman's busy schedule. When he wasn't at work or with his family, his gambling, drinking, and schmoozing took a great deal of time as well as energy.

Platonic or not, Herman did enjoy the attention and affection of beautiful young actresses, and he seemed to favor a particular type. Like Louise Brooks, they were intelligent and strong minded (which to the studios often meant 'difficult'), and red hair didn't hurt. Paramount actresses Nancy Carroll and Miriam Hopkins were two, and Sara methodically befriended any she considered potential threats. Herman was close to Geraldine Fitzgerald as well, but his favorite was Margaret Sullavan, who lived nearby while she was married to Leland Hayward. She was

Margaret Sullavan and Herman adored each other. Together at the annual Beverly Hills tennis tournament with Sullavan's current husband, Leland Hayward.

a complicated woman whose four husbands included Henry Fonda and William Wyler, and whose many lovers included the difficult Jed Harris.

According to MGM's chief, Eddie Mannix, Sullavan made Louis B. Mayer nervous: "She was the only player who outbullied Mayer—she gave him the willies." Herman and Sullavan loved to play backgammon and laugh together, and Herman tried to join her and Hayward in taking flying lessons, until Sara convinced Mayer to talk him out of it. Herman called her "Missy" and "you goddam southern belle," and Sullavan gave him a photograph of herself signed, "From lover number two." At one point Sara asked her outright if she and Herman had slept together. When Sullavan denied it, Sara considered the subject closed. As she told Sullavan's daughter, Maggie was her friend.

In that case it probably was the truth, but, like Herman's ability to convert disaster into humor, Sara's capacity for denial was a valuable coping skill. When Herman's debts became insurmountable, Sara rented out their house and moved the family to an apartment (though, broke or not, she took along servants and continued her daily French lessons). On one of those occasions, Hedda Hopper relayed the "nifty" tale to her readers, barely bothering to mask its underlying gravity.

> Mrs. Herman Mankiewicz, the wife of one of the ace writers at Metro-Goldwyn-Mayer Studios, wanted a trip to New York, but she didn't want to leave hubby in the big house, so she rented the house, got him an apartment, installed a cook, and sailed away. Well, Herman took a gang home to celebrate, but the dinner was not up to par, and the next day on the lot, he ran into his brother, Joe, and poured out his woes. Joe cracked out with, "well, what kind of a cook do you expect from the Pinkerton Detective Agency?"

The more they had to lose, the more reckless Herman became, though they kept the boys oblivious to his drinking problem and lived like a normal family much of the time, albeit a normal family who entertained guests like F. Scott Fitzgerald and Dorothy Parker. Motion picture business was not discussed at the dinner table. Instead, Sara exposed them to music, and Herman imparted his love of history, politics, and sports. He told such engaging newspaper stories that for three years, starting when they were twelve and nine, Don and Frank published their own *Beverly Hills Weekly Journal*. (With Herman selling subscriptions, readers included friends like John Lee Mahin and David Selznick.)

His discussions of politics were so enthralling that from the age of sixteen, Don hoped to run for office. Herman had words of wisdom to cover any number of subjects. He habitually divided people into garage mechanics and Jewish tailors, and his rules of life included, "Never pay bills on time because the first time you are late, they will put you into bankruptcy," and "If you see a man in white socks, he's from out of town."

Despite its outward normality, Sara's edifice rested on a fragile foundation. Out for lunch, Herman would tell Ben Hecht, "Pick a subject for debate, and I'll take the other side," and they could enthrall an audience for hours, talking and drinking the day away. Ordinarily, Herman telephoned Sara at least twice a day, so if he failed to call after lunch, she started worrying. If she couldn't reach him by telephone at haunts like Romanoff's, Brown Derby, and Lucey's, she drove around until she found his car. Then, like Pop in Herman's student days, she marched in like a truant officer and took him away. Occasionally he was in such bad shape that she dropped him at her sister Mattie's to dry out for the night—one morning his nephew found him sleeping it off in the bathtub.

In Berlin, Sara had unwittingly motivated Sigrid Schultz to find Herman a job; by the 1930s her unwitting days were long past. Now she had the starring role in the grim drama of damage control. When Herman blew up at Paramount, Sara went to see Ben Schulberg. When he exploded at MGM, she visited David Selznick or Bernie Hyman or Herman's close friend, story editor Eddie Knopf, or if she had to, even Mayer himself. Making excuses and turning on the charm, she would beg them to give Herman another chance.

Even Sara could not save Herman from his most infamous firing. After Joe called him in an effort to find Herman work, Columbia Pictures story editor Sam Marx urged studio chief Harry Cohn to hire him. Marx, who had worked with Herman at MGM, did not consider it charity—he admired Herman's work. But because Cohn surpassed even Mayer in his capacity for rage and cruelty, Marx and his colleagues warned Herman to stay away from Cohn. Marx knew warning Herman away was really just asking for trouble, but he did comply for a while. Finally he could not resist lunch in the executive dining room, but when he ran into executive producer William Perlberg on the way in, he solemnly promised to keep his mouth shut, no matter what the provocation.

Then Cohn started talking about "the lousiest picture I've seen in years," Ernst Lubitsch's *Bluebeard's Eighth Wife*. One of his producers protested: Cohn might have reacted differently if he had seen it with an audience. No, Cohn insisted. He had a foolproof method for separating good films from bad, even in his projection room. "When I sit still, it's a hit. When I'm antsy like I was last night, it's a sure flop."

"In other words," Herman said, unable to resist, "you have a monitor ass wired to a hundred million other asses."

Joe believed Herman used alcohol and gambling and getting fired, both to lash out "at Sara, his father, the Establishment, Louis B. Mayer," and to protect himself from failure by "rendering himself unable to prove he could achieve—and in the end, destroying himself without guilt." The toll Herman's vicious cycles took on Joe was second only to what Sara endured. Joe had always revered his brother, and he appreciated all Herman had done for him. But once he brought Joe to Hollywood, Herman always expected him to come to the rescue. Actually, Herman expected everyone to rescue him, but especially his family, and the constant threat drained Joe: "When Herman kept demanding money, my rage and fear were so intermingled that I thought it would go on for the rest of my life and there was no way I could stop it. I was terrified of Herman. I never felt I could call on him for help. Everybody else in the world could. But if I did, somehow he'd bawl me out for what was happening to me."

Joe's rise at MGM triggered the family's next Oedipal drama, but this time the protagonists were Herman and Joe instead of Herman and Pop. By the mid-1930s, Herman was in his thirties and Joe in his twenties, and their eleven-year difference was becoming less of a generation gap. But at the same time their relationship began to evolve from quasi-father–son to older brother–younger brother, Joe began to pass Herman professionally. The shift was neither instantaneous nor immediately obvious. Herman was still a senior personage in the industry, and Joe a young man on the rise.

But the ground was shifting. Joe was very publicly being groomed for higher things, and neither Sara nor Herman had any inkling that Joe was desperately unhappy as a producer. Although the disparity rankled Sara, whatever competitiveness Herman felt—and he would have been inhuman not to—his feelings were always leavened with loyalty and pride. Notwithstanding his references to "my idiot brother" (Herman called everyone idiots), Herman continued to applaud Joe's brilliance and achievements. Besides, to an extent, Joe's success reflected glory on him. The two were so clearly brothers. Their family resemblance was not confined to square jaws, stocky builds, and their half-smiling, so-called Mankiewicz leer. Despite contrasting temperaments, their affect was similar, as were their wit, erudition—and arrogance.

But markers of success were hard to miss. Herman's publicly listed 1935 salary was $65,000, and Joe's was $50,000. By 1937 Herman's had drifted down to $61,000, which was still a handsome sum, especially during the Depression, but Joe's rose during the same interval to almost $87,000; the following year Joe made $3,000 a week. Furthermore, in May 1937 Herman was so mired in debt that Pop instructed Joe to make sure Herman repaid Erna and her husband their $3,500 loan, plus interest, by June 1.

If Herman's improvidence punished Joe, at some level that was probably part of the point. Becoming his brother's keeper was not the role he had envisioned for himself, and it was certainly unpleasant for both brothers. But Joe considered himself fortunate to have escaped the damage his father had inflicted on Herman and, to a lesser extent (it seemed to Joe), on his mother and sister. Not that he considered himself completely unscathed. Joe was the abstemious, disciplined Mankiewicz brother, but he too battled internal demons—along with a healthy collection of external demons that included the frustrations of work, pressure from his father to embark on more worthwhile ("literary") writing, and, of course, Herman.

On one hand, Joe rationalized, "I found myself not unhappy that my need for my father's love had gone unnoticed, rather than to have had it brutalized into a malignancy that, in the end, destroyed not only

Herman's need for Pop's love but along with that destruction—Herman himself." On the other, he understood that the shell he had erected around himself, helpful though it had been in tuning out the discord between his parents, bought his protection at a cost: "my quickly-acquired defensive detachment brought with it not only the security of emotional uninvolvement but also the discomfiting presence of an enormous void."

Herman's slide was not unremitting, and despite his disdain for motion pictures, he still had fun. In 1937 he wrote a minor picture, *My Dear Miss Aldrich*, for Edna May Oliver, who was one of his favorite actresses. The long-faced character actress specialized in acidulous old-maid types, and Herman created a madcap newspaper caper in which she played Lou Atherton, the puzzle-crazed aunt of Martha Aldrich (Maureen O'Sullivan), a Nebraska schoolteacher who inherits a New York newspaper. The editor, Ken Morley (Walter Pidgeon, in his first starring film role), disapproves of female reporters, but Martha convinces him to let her try reporting and gets a scoop. On the trail of another story, Martha is captured, and when Aunt Lou and Morley try to rescue her, they are captured as well. Their ruses to escape include faking smallpox, and though Herman had to cut most of it, he inserted some trenchant observations about prejudices against women, and other social anomalies he considered worthy of ridicule.

Also in 1937 Herman and Sara became new parents. At the age of forty with sons seventeen and fifteen, they were stunned at the idea of starting over, but once their blue-eyed, blonde daughter arrived, they were both enchanted. They named her Johanna after Herman's mother and provided her with a fairytale Hollywood childhood, complete with elaborate birthday parties and friends whose parents had world-famous faces.

Herman observed the milestone of turning forty by writing a satirical piece for the *New Yorker*. To his chagrin, Harold Ross rejected it, and he could only place it in the *Hollywood Reporter*, a dispiriting comedown. In theory, Herman was better equipped to deal with the disappointment at that point, because by then, he was seeing a therapist. Psychoanalysis had become wildly popular in Hollywood, and though Herman hated doing what the crowd did, he felt he owed his family the effort.

He had chosen Ernst Simmel, a prominent German psychiatrist who had been associated with Freud and other pioneers of psychoanalysis and seemed to be a good fit. Simmel was interested in problems of gambling and alcoholism and, during World War I, had headed a psychiatric hospital in Posen, Hanna's former home. He treated so many of Herman's friends that Herman suggested they all wear sweatshirts with an

S, a joke not all of them appreciated. Moss Hart's appointments were just before Herman's, and Herman teased him so mercilessly that Hart moved his appointments.

However, Herman took it seriously enough to spend a few weeks at a psychiatric facility. He had dried out in hotels and hospitals before, but this time he was determined, and he remained in analysis for two or three years. Then he gave up, and despite his inevitable jokes about the process, he was deeply disappointed. Gaining a meaningful understanding of the roots of his behavior had felt like almost a rebirth, and concluding that despite his new insights he was unable to change was heartbreaking.

In February 1938 Herman was the first of ten writers assigned to *The Wizard of Oz*. MGM treated it as an important picture from the beginning, though no one foresaw what a classic it would become. Don and Frank had read all the Oz books, and Herman wrote a lengthy memo urging against making the film. When they proceeded anyway, he had strong ideas about how it should be made, especially that it should be in black and white until Dorothy arrived in Oz. And not sharply contrasting black and white; it should have dully tinted grey tones, "to emphasize the grey nature of the landscape and Dorothy's daily life."

Ordered to proceed, Herman created a Dorothy and Toto who strongly resembled Little Orphan Annie and her dog, Sandy. Then he created an obnoxious dowager, her more obnoxious daughter, and a Pekingese dog named Adolphus Ajax Rittenstaufen III, who was "too valuable to play," not even with Toto, who could "count up to eight." He suggested the cyclone arrive when their limousine left. Once he had that out of his system, Herman started a version closer to Baum's characters and story, but for once he welcomed the news that there were other writers on the assignment, and he was off the picture within a couple of weeks.

Later that year MGM elected not to renew his contract. He stayed on, on a week-to-week basis, almost getting *The Meal Ticket* into production and working his short-lived stint at Columbia. But by September 1939 he had sunk so deeply into debt that he saw no alternative but to beg Mayer for an advance against his salary. Mayer grudgingly agreed to put him back on contract, but only in exchange for Herman's solemn promise to stay out of trouble and, of course, completely stop gambling.

The following day Herman looked up from a poker game in the commissary and saw Mayer looking back at him from across the room. Without a word, he returned to his office to collect his things, plus, as usual, a stack of pads and pencils. Mayer made it official the next day.

CHAPTER 11

Joe's Black Years

JOE AT WORK

Joe called his time as an MGM producer his "black years." He felt "wretchedly unhappy . . . useless, sterile and pretentious," though he was honest enough to admit that much of his misery stemmed from being identified with a group he considered his inferiors, "personalities and types I disliked." In addition to his own friends, like Spencer Tracy, Joe had enjoyed being included in Herman's coterie of intellectual, sophisticated screenwriters like Edwin Justus Mayer, S. N. Behrman, Ben Hecht, and Charles MacArthur, who were also successful playwrights. There were literate and civilized producers, of course, but as a group, they were writers' favorite targets, especially at the so-called producers' studio.

Having an identity that embarrassed him was an unpleasant new experience for a man who had been a star all his life. Herman could laugh at himself. Joe could not. He never lost his prickly self-consciousness, and perhaps those "black years" as a producer also contributed to his growing discomfort with his Jewish background. As one of the few industries that didn't discriminate, Hollywood was full of Jews in its top ranks. Almost all of MGM's producers and many, if not most, of the studios' top executives were Jewish. So were many of the industry's writers, musicians, and other creative types, and even a fair percentage of its actors and actresses. Although the European émigrés obviously understood discrimination and persecution, most of them had little interest in religion. But they generally ignored it as a fact of birth, rather than seeking to escape it, bury it, or ultimately, as Joe did later in life, deny it.

Given the variety of Jews in the industry—Walter Wanger was a Dartmouth alumnus from a wealthy German Jewish family, for example—the vehemence of Joe's reaction puzzled some of his friends. Almost certainly referring to Joe, Herman liked to say that when people said they were half Jewish, they probably meant that their parents were Jewish, but they were not. At college Joe had belonged to a Jewish fraternity as a casual choice, but his aversion seemed to grow over the years. When, in an early-seventies interview, Geist casually referred to his being Jewish, Joe said, practically in one breath, "I don't consider myself a Jew. I have never been confirmed. My father was a rip-snorting atheist. I was raised an atheist. My daughter, as you know, is in the Church. Her grandfather was an archdeacon in the Church and he came over and baptized her in the local church. My sons with Rosa are Catholics because their mother was a Catholic. . . . I've never participated in Jewishness, but I've observed the Jewishness in California and a very unsavory thing it was." Coming from a master of logic, the hodgepodge of protests is telling.

That said, Joe's desire to determine his own identity, no matter what the world considered him, was hardly a unique phenomenon, and his discomfort never interfered with his natural instincts. During the same early 1930s that he became a producer, he also began helping countless refugees (Jewish or not). And beginning in 1937, he served on a Jewish Federation Council of Greater Los Angeles committee overseeing a clandestine operation that monitored and attempted to disrupt Nazi and anti-Semitic activities in the Los Angeles area. (Wanger chaired it.)

Becoming a producer did have its benefits. Along with tripling his $50,000 writer's salary between 1935 and 1938, Joe's status in the outside world rose. A 1938 newspaper story describing the industry's problems quoted studio chiefs, directors, and stars, but the reporter relied most extensively on "twenty-nine year old Metro producer Joe Mankiewicz, hailed as the next Thalberg by the wiseheads of the film city":

> The trouble is, old men, old ideas. They are frightened, frantic they've made the boy-meets-girl formula story 101 times when it can only stand a hundred. The public knows what's coming, yawns and stays away. The studios are overweighted with dead wood—shelved stories and discarded stars—and still think they are making films for twelve year olds, not knowing that the picture public has grown up and started to think.

Being labeled the next Boy Wonder was heady, but it wasn't enough, and Joe sought comfort in the creative opportunities of his job. Producers possessed almost absolute power over their films, including the very power Joe had resented as a writer, the power to change the script, and

Joe took full advantage. Even when he didn't personally rewrite his pictures' scripts, he had no problem ordering writers to keep going until he got what he wanted. (Sam Marx called him a "pencil-picking-up producer.") Still, it wasn't the same. As a producer, he was barred from taking a writing credit unless he wrote the entire script, and he wanted that recognition. To Joe, the producer's credit failed to acknowledge his creative contributions, which he regarded as crucial to his films' success, at least to the pictures that succeeded.

In short, being a producer was often uncomfortable and sometimes even mortifying, but Joe's actual work as a producer was not unalleviated misery, and he was very good at it.

His first assignment was supposed to be a B-picture. MGM wanted a new version of *Three Godfathers,* a western about three outlaws who find a baby in the Mojave Desert. Joe knew that "the one thing . . . they were looking for was someone who could produce good B pictures," and he was determined not to be that someone. So he embellished the script and filmed on location to make it a much more expensive "B" movie than had been planned, and the result was just bad enough to enable Joe to say, "Well, fellows, this ought to convince you I can't make B pictures."

If Joe had to produce, he wanted to produce artistically interesting A-pictures, which turned out to be harder than he had expected. He pitched a musical based on *Drei Walzer,* a new operetta by Austrian composer Oscar Straus, telling Mayer that three acts about a ballerina, her operetta-star daughter, and her film-star granddaughter could be "new, different, enchanting." Like many corporate chiefs, Mayer had no problem with "new" as long as it was exactly like old-but-proven—like Warner Brothers' 1933 hit musical *42nd Street.* "New, different, enchanting," Mayer mocked. "Young man, let me tell you what I want from you. I want *43rd Street, 44th Street, 45th Street.*" Building up steam, Mayer chased Joe down the hall shouting, "Don't come to me with anything new. Give me *46th Street, 47th Street* . . . !"

Finally Joe turned to *He Who Gets Slapped,* Leonid Andreyev's play about a tragic clown, which the studio had adapted in 1924 for its first film. Mayer approved, but in an effort to find work for the studio's European refugees, he assigned Joe an assistant, Leopold Jessner, an eminent producer/director from German expressionist theater and cinema. Joe was embarrassed but gamely asked Jessner, "Of course you know the play?"

"Young man, I knew Andreyev," the Great Man responded. A mortified Joe beat a hasty retreat, thinking, "What's the use. He probably worked with Andreyev on the play and told him what was wrong with the second act."

He turned to an idea he had heard from playwright/screenwriter Norman Krasna. After reading a *Nation* story about lynching, Krasna had wondered what would happen if innocent victims' lynchings were captured by a photographer. Joe expanded on it. Instead of a lynching, what if a newsreel photographer captured a mob setting fire to the jailhouse? And what if the presumably dead innocent man secretly survived and sought revenge on his attackers? He envisioned his good friend Spencer Tracy in the lead.

Tracy loved it. Mayer hated it. "L.B. didn't want me to make that picture," Joe told a reporter a few years after making it. "He said if he kept me from making it, I'd never be any good to the studio. I'd always hold it against him in my heart, feeling I hadn't had my chance. And if he let me make it but cut down on the budget or didn't exploit it like a hit, then again, I'd unconsciously resent it all my life." Or as Joe recounted it in 1980 (his stories got better with age), Mayer said, "All right, Harvard College [Mayer's nickname for Joe]. . . . I promise to spend as much money advertising "Fury" as Irving Thalberg spends on Romeo and Juliet [starring his wife, Norma Shearer] . . . I will give you the greatest advertising campaign. . . . You will get fantastic critiques but it will be a disaster."

Krasna, who was in New York, had practically forgotten about the idea, so after they talked, Joe dictated what he remembered. That telephone conversation earned Krasna $15,000 from MGM and a best original story nomination from the Academy. Joe assigned Bart Cormack to work on the story and wanted the talented, world-renowned Austrian Fritz Lang to direct. David Selznick had hired the creator of the chilling *Metropolis* (1927) and *M* (1931) in 1934, but by 1936, Mayer was ready to fire him. Joe hoped to utilize Lang's expressionist sensibility.

The arrogant, monocled director quickly antagonized the cast and crew, who grew to despise him. Tracy, whom MGM was grooming for stardom, usually got his performance right in one or two takes, but Lang believed in breaking down the actors, so he ordered numerous takes and routinely worked the cast and crew from early morning straight through to the wee hours of the following day. The only lunch break he allowed was his own, when a pill was served to him on a silver tray by his secretary the others called "The Iron Butterfly."

The crew finally appealed to Tracy, who courteously asked, "Mr. Lang, it's one-thirty and the fellows haven't had their lunch yet. Don't you think we ought to break?"

Fritz Lang directed *Fury* (1936), Joe's first A-picture as an MGM producer. It starred Spencer Tracy and, to Louis B. Mayer's dismay, made a profit.

"On my set, Mr. Tracy, I will call lunch when I think it should be called," the Great Director responded, whereupon, Joe recalled, "Spencer took it with that wonderful look, that meek look—and look out when he looked at you meekly." Then he brushed his hand across his face, smearing makeup that would take an hour and half to replace, called "lunch," and walked out.

When Lang's sadistic marathons continued anyway, the crew decided to retaliate by dropping a lamp on Lang's head, but managing it so that no one could be blamed. Joe found out and managed to talk them out of it, so after that they confined themselves to acts of quiet sabotage. Joe was generally pleased with the results, except for a scene that sent preview audiences into fits of laughter: Lang had ghosts chasing Tracy's character, then hiding behind trees when he looked back. When Lang refused to cut that or any other part of the picture, studio boss Eddie Mannix fired Lang and told Joe to cut it himself.

Reviews were almost universally positive. Even the Communists approved. Their New York *Sunday Worker* review ("Hollywood Picture Indicts Lynch Law") deemed it "well worth seeing. . . . [though w]e would have preferred to see a picture in which a Negro is the victim." But when

Joe ran into Lang with Marlene Dietrich at the Brown Derby two days after the film opened to excellent reviews, Lang refused Joe's proffered hand. Snarling, "You destroyed my movie," he turned his back on Joe.

Mayer was also dismayed, because *Fury*, so dark, so angry, so different from MGM's usual rose-colored offerings, actually made money. He solved that problem by neglecting to share the information with Joe. As late as 1938, Joe still believed it had been a flop, though even then, he predicted it eventually would break even.

In 1936 Mayer asked Joe to produce Joan Crawford's films. "You're the only one on the lot who knows what to do with her," Mayer explained, though both knew the prestigious assignment would challenge even Joe. Compared to MGM's other two top stars, Crawford felt ill used. Greta Garbo was revered, and Norma Shearer was protected by her husband, Irving Thalberg, at least until he died that September. Crawford was dismissed as Harry Rapf's former chorus girl and cast in an endless series of love triangles and working-girl dramas. Between 1936 and 1942, Joe produced seven of Crawford's thirteen MGM films and savored the role of rescuer.

Sleeping with the talent was a perquisite of studio powers, and many executives treated actresses like prostitutes, sometimes quite abusively. The main difference between then and now is that in those days, their behavior was so accepted that many felt no need for concealment. That coarseness was probably yet another reason Joe was uncomfortable with his identity as a producer. (Writers, by contrast, were viewed as so powerless that the notion of sleeping with a writer to get to the top was the punchline to a joke.)

Obviously, a number of actors and actresses also pursued relationships for their own ends, of which there were a variety. Crawford famously said, "I need sex for a good complexion but I'd rather do it for love," and for a while, she did it with Joe. Joe was married for most of his adult life, but he was usually in love with at least one actress, sometimes more than one, and despite Hollywood's plentiful supply of pulchritude in both sexes, Joe possessed serious sex appeal. He was an accomplished raconteur whose piercing blue eyes, omnipresent pipe, professorial clothes, and boyish charm were appealing, but what women found irresistible was his intense and genuine interest in their minds (ironic clichés notwithstanding). Joe loved playing amateur psychologist, mentor, and, given the necessity of subterfuge, imaginative intriguer.

Many of the women with whom he had affairs adored him for years afterward. As Crawford recalled, "I was madly in love with him and it was lovely. . . . At one time or another, all the ladies at MGM were in love with him, I'm sure. He had a crooked little smile that was absolutely irresistible to any woman. . . . He gave me such a feeling of security I felt I could do anything in the world once I got on that stage. . . . I didn't have much sense of humor about myself . . . He relaxed me, teaching me to have fun in my work. I'd had joy, not fun. He brought that out of me, frothy or not."

Stars hungering for respect for their acting instead of their star power is also a cliché, but Joe took Crawford seriously enough to try to help her grow, searching for properties with more texture and depth, and rewriting some himself. "Joe was the first producer to let me come into his office, sit in a corner, and listen to the director's idea of my character. I never uttered a word but just sat and knitted or made notes," Crawford recalled. He also discussed her character with her and suggested bits of business as a director would. At the same time, he cautioned her to remember her fan base. Critics might ridicule the designer clothes and fantasy homes of her working-class characters, but he reminded her, "Forget those snobs. We're not making pictures for them. . . . Just remember the shop girl, who sees you in a fantasized version of her own life. She doesn't want to see you in a housedress with armpit stains. She wants you dressed by Adrian, as she would like to be."

Their professional collaboration lasted longer than their affair, but both allowed Joe to play Pygmalion, a role he relished though he was only in his twenties and four or five years younger than this Galatea (Crawford's birthdate moved around). Certainly, Joan Crawford offered an embarrassment of riches to an amateur psychiatrist. Her slavish devotion to her fans as well as to her own stardom fascinated him. "She woke up like a movie star and she went to the john like a movie star. She had a special outfit for answering her fan mail and another for having lunch." Her daily role playing intrigued the lover as well as the producer. An advance call from his secretary hinted at the role of the day—would she arrive at the studio in sports car, a sedan, or a limousine?

> You'd have to watch the way she came in. If Joan was wearing a pair of slacks, that meant you'd go over and slap her right on the ass and say, "Hiya kid. You getting much?" In turn, she'd be as raucous as Billie Cassin [her teenaged self] from Texas at that moment, and you'd have an absolute ball. She could come back the next day wearing black sables and incredible sapphires, and by Jesus, you'd better be on your feet and click your heels, kiss her hand, and talk with the

> best British accent you had, but never in any way indicate she was different in any respect from the way she was yesterday, because the following day she'd come in in a dirndl or a pinafore and you'd be on the floor playing jacks with her. I loved it. You had to be an actor and be adaptive to what she was playing, though the moment she left my office, I went back to what I was before she came in.

Because Crawford wanted a serious costume drama like her rivals', Joe produced *The Gorgeous Hussy* (1936), about an innkeeper's daughter (Crawford) and Andrew Jackson (Lionel Barrymore), with Robert Taylor, Melvyn Douglas, James Stewart, and Franchot Tone as her suitors. Crawford later defended the box office failure as a boost in dramatic prestige, but she and Joe played it safe for her next two pictures.

An inferior copycat of *It Happened One Night, Love on the Run* (1936) costarred Clark Gable and Franchot Tone as two newsmen competing for Crawford's heiress, and it raked in the money. *The Bride Wore Red* (1937) was less successful. Combining a standard Crawford two-suitor, poor-Cinderella, Adrian-gowned vehicle with an Alpine setting and dirndls, it pleased neither critics nor audiences, so they reverted to the original formula with *Mannequin* (1938).

In that picture, Joe risked casting Crawford opposite Spencer Tracy, whose underplaying usually allowed him to steal his scenes and make the other actors look overwrought (hardly difficult with Crawford), but Joe bet Crawford's professional instincts would kick in and they did. Crawford appreciated the lesson in underplaying, and she appreciated Tracy, with whom she began an affair. Their romance lasted only long enough for Tracy to introduce Crawford to polo, for which her enthusiasm was equally short lived, but the picture accomplished the mission. The drama "restores Miss Joan Crawford to her throne as queen of the woiking goils," proclaimed *New York Times* critic Frank S. Nugent. "Joan Crawford Is Herself Again . . ." reported the *Washington Post.*

In May 1938 Crawford was devastated when an exhibitors' trade publication designated Crawford, Katharine Hepburn, Mae West, Greta Garbo, Marlene Dietrich, and a number of others as "box office poison," especially because her MGM contract was about to expire. Mayer assured her that the public and the studio appreciated her and that he, of course, loved her like a daughter (though, as she told Joe, "Somehow his hand always touched my right tit whenever he said the word 'daughter'"). Once she learned Mayer's paternal regard extended only as far as a one-year contract, Crawford became frantic to find a hit.

"No more goddamn shopgirls," she declared, and convinced the studio to buy *The Shining Hour,* a 1934 Broadway play previously considered for Norma Shearer. She also wanted Margaret Sullavan and Fay Bainter for the other female parts, despite Mayer's warning that two superior actresses could steal the picture. "I'd rather be a supporting player in a good picture than the star of a bad one," she insisted. It was not a hit.

The last two Crawford films Joe produced were *Strange Cargo* (1940), the last of her eight pictures with Clark Gable, and *Reunion in France* (1942) a wartime version of her typical vehicle. Joe described *Strange Cargo* as "almost a good film," though it performed poorly, as did *Reunion in France,* in which Crawford played a Frenchwoman in German-occupied Paris. Although Joe hired Marc Connelly to help with the screenplay, Jules Dassin to direct, and John Wayne to co-star, MGM's frivolous treatment of the French situation offended contemporary critics. (Joe clearly contributed to the script—the pilot's hometown is Wilkes-Barre, Pennsylvania.)

Crawford always remained fond of Joe (Joe's last wife thought she still carried a torch), but her favorite MGM films were *The Women* (1939), *Susan and God* (1940), and *A Woman's Face* (1941), all of which she had to fight for, all of which were directed by George Cukor, and none of which were produced by Joe. Cukor, who was gay, was revered as a "women's director," and in later years, when Joe also became admired for his direction of women, he would snort to intimates, "Cukor flattered them. I fucked them."

Around the time he started producing Crawford's pictures, Joe also became a father. Unfortunately, by the time Eric Young Mankiewicz was born on July 1, 1936, Joe had lost interest in Eric's mother. Screenwriter John Lee Mahin recalled a dinner party at the Mankiewiczes' when Crawford and Joe disappeared at the same time and a tearful Elizabeth sent him to retrieve them. Mahin found them in Eric's room, with Crawford kneeling by Eric's crib, saying, "This should have been mine."

Joe moved out in November 1936, and though they reconciled once or twice, the marriage was over. Their divorce became final on May 20, 1937, their third anniversary, and against his lawyer's advice, Joe agreed to fifty months of $1,000-a-month alimony, plus $500 a month in child support. Elizabeth moved to New York and tried to restart her stage career. She was cast in Herman's play *The Meal Ticket,* but fortunately for Elizabeth, the show proceeded without her, because it closed out of town. In June 1938 she married Eugene Reynal, a publisher of art books, who became a loving stepfather to Eric.

When Lionel Barrymore was too ill to play Scrooge, Joe replaced him with Reginald Owen, and *A Christmas Carol* (1938) became a classic.

Besides *Three Godfathers*, *Fury*, and seven Crawford films, Joe produced ten other MGM pictures. Two were based on literary classics; two were World War I dramas starring Margaret Sullavan; one was a semimusical spy spoof starring Jeanette MacDonald in her last MGM picture; and five were comedies. Joe described his MGM producing career as "some hits, some runs, mostly errors." *A Christmas Carol* (1938) turned out to be one of his perennials. At least four film versions already existed when Lionel Barrymore, who had played Scrooge on the radio for many years, asked MGM for his own. When they needed to start shooting in time for the 1938 Christmas season, however, Barrymore was too ill from hip injuries to begin. Joe offered to delay the picture for the following year, but Barrymore insisted they proceed, so Joe moved Reginald Owen from Marley's Ghost to Scrooge and replaced Owen with Leo G. Carroll. He cast Gene Lockhart and his wife, Kathleen, as Bob and Mrs. Cratchit, and when their thirteen-year-old daughter asked him if she could play one of the Cratchit children, Joe gave June Lockhart the first role of her long career. It opened at Radio City Music Hall three days before Christmas and became such an annual fixture on television that Joe liked to imagine the pleasure of owning even a tiny royalty on the picture.

Despite the efforts of Mickey Rooney and Rex Ingram as Huck and Jim, *The Adventures of Huckleberry Finn* (1939) did not fare as well, and Joe's World War I films with Margaret Sullavan were both timid responses to Europe's worsening political situation. In the poignant but comic *Shopworn Angel* (1938), about spoiled Broadway star Daisy Heath (Sullavan), her sophisticated patron (Walter Pidgeon) and a naive soldier about to go to war (James Stewart), Daisy has several songs, including "Pack Up Your Troubles in Your Old Kit Bag and Smile, Smile, Smile." When asked if she could sing, Sullavan assured Joe and composer Franz Waxman that she could, but when Waxman sat down at the piano, out of Sullavan's mouth, Joe recalled, "came the goddamnedest caterwauling you've ever heard in your life. There was nothing approaching a note that was anywhere near true, and Franz and I just stared at her incredulously." Sullavan then explained that demonstrating seemed to be the only way she could convince producers and directors she was not simply being modest: she really, *really* could not sing. A still-undiscovered Mary Martin dubbed her songs.

Joe's other film with Sullavan haunted him for the rest of his life. Based on an Erich Maria Remarque novel, *Three Comrades* (1938) could have been the industry's first major openly anti-Nazi film. The Nazis had already burned Remarque's books, but despite MGM's history of craven pandering, the studio bid determinedly for the film rights. With Herman's efforts on *Mad Dog* a few years in the past, Joe eagerly approached the story of three friends (Robert Taylor, Robert Young, and Franchot Tone) and Taylor's tubercular wife (Sullavan), struggling to survive Germany's grim post–World War I economy and the Nazis' rise to power.

Joe replaced the first screenwriter with F. Scott Fitzgerald, whose work he greatly admired. Although reports of Fitzgerald's drinking had reached the studios, and he had just published a series of self-denigrating, confessional essays in *Esquire*, Fitzgerald was still so respected that MGM paid him $1,000 a week, renewable to $1,250 in six months. That was a very high salary for a screenwriter, especially one with no screen credits, and Fitzgerald had already failed twice in Hollywood. But he needed the job and approached the craft of screenwriting with great seriousness.

Joe considered Fitzgerald's first draft an improvement but far from final, and brought in veteran E. E. Paramore to help with the next. At the very least, he wanted to eliminate some of Fitzgerald's more bizarre ideas, like inserting St. Peter and an angel into Remarque's narrative. Fitzgerald was furious at being forced to collaborate, but he dutifully worked with Paramore, on another six drafts. Along the way, Joe, who was also overseeing MGM's training program, brought in more writers, including Waldo Salt, and eventually he incorporated some of their work as well. Then Joe also started rewriting himself. At that point, Fitzgerald lost it. As much as he desperately needed the work, he castigated his young boss:

> I feel like a good many writers must have felt in the past. I gave you a drawing and you simply took a box of chalk and touched it up. . . . I guess all these years I've been kidding myself about being a good writer . . .
>
> To say I'm disillusioned is putting it mildly. I had an entirely different conception of you. For nineteen years, with two years out for sickness, I've written best-selling entertainment, and my dialogue is supposedly right up at the top. But I learn from the script that you've suddenly decided that it isn't good dialogue and you can take a few hours off and do much better.
>
> I think you now have a flop on your hands—as thoroughly naïve as "The Bride Wore Red" but utterly inexcusable because this time you *had* something and you have arbitrarily and carelessly torn it to pieces. . . . My God, Joe, you must be intelligent enough to see what you've done. . . .
>
> Oh, Joe, can't producers ever be wrong? I'm a good writer—honest. I thought you were going to play fair. Joan Crawford might as well play the part now, for the thing is as groggy with sentimentality as The Bride Wore Red, but the true emotion is gone.

As Fitzgerald acknowledged, his frustration was a cliché. All Hollywood screenwriters, from Herman Mankiewicz to William Faulkner, were routinely rewritten, many by far worse writers than Joe. Unfortunately for Joe, as Fitzgerald's position in the literary canon rose over the years, his letter to Joe was published again and again. Long after Joe escaped his "black years" as a producer, he had to endure periodic resurrections as the stereotypically crass, insensitive, illiterate, cigar-chomping philistine producer that Joe and his writer friends loved to ridicule.

That lay in the future. In 1938 Joe was not only improving Fitzgerald's dialogue, he was fighting off the combined efforts of German consul Georg Gyssling, Louis B. Mayer, MPPDA Production Code censor Joseph Breen, and the Catholic Legion of Decency, all intent on assuaging Nazi sensibilities and protecting the German market. Little by little, they chipped away at the original. Instead of the late 1920s, they pushed the

Instead of gaining admiration for his 1938 success at retaining *Three Comrades*' anti-Nazi message, Joe was condemned for decades as a crass, philistine producer, "the swine who rewrote F. Scott Fitzgerald."

story back to the years just after World War I, when Nazis were not yet a force. Jewish characters were removed. Next came any reference to Jews. Then Catholics. Eventually, Remarque's powerful political drama was reduced to romantic melodrama, but even that did not satisfy Joseph Breen. Aware that audiences would still read the thugs and bullies as Nazis, he wanted the villains turned into Communists.

Then Joe lost it. Slamming his hand on the desk, he threatened to leave the picture and go to the press. Breen gave way and Joe won the battle. Actually, he won more, because the press got the story anyway. When he heard, Fitzgerald threw his arms around Joe in the commissary and kissed him, and Joe had no idea Fitzgerald was still so angry that even during production he was darkly predicting failure: "The thing will be the most colossal disappointment of Metro's year," Fitzgerald to wrote his agent. "The producer wrote it over. The censors hacked at it. Finally, the German Government took a shot. So what we have left has very little to do with the script on which people still congratulate me. However, I get a screen credit out of it, good or bad, and you can always blame a failure on somebody else."

Fitzgerald even took it out on Herman. He had hired a former secretary of Herman's for his outside work, telling her, "I love Mank." But after Joe rewrote his script, Fitzgerald wrote his editor Maxwell Perkins, "Hard times weed out many of the incompetents, but they swarm back—Herman Mankiewicz, a ruined man who hasn't written ten feet of continuity in two years, was finally dropped by Metro, but immediately picked up by Columbia! He is a nice fellow that everybody likes and has been brilliant, but he is being hired because everyone is sorry for his wife—which I think would make him rather an obstacle in the way of making good pictures. Utter toughness toward the helpless, combined with super-sentimentality—Jesus, what a combination!"

In love with Fitzgerald, gossip columnist Sheilah Graham was the first to attack Joe on Fitzgerald's behalf, and she did it subtly. She had started plugging Fitzgerald soon after they met, but once Fitzgerald finished *Three Comrades* and moved on to a Crawford script, Graham ostensibly addressed the need to rescue Joan Crawford's career from "a series of mediocre offerings." Aside from *Rain* ("terrible"), she listed only films produced by Joe: *The Gorgeous Hussy*, "poor"; *The Bride Wore Red*, "bad"; *Mannequin*, "only slightly better." The implication was that unlike Crawford's inept producer, Fitzgerald could write a screenplay that would restore Crawford to her rightful place.

However, aided by Frank Borzage's direction, *Three Comrades* opened to favorable reviews and a strong box office; it made many top ten lists for 1938 and earned Margaret Sullavan her only Academy Award nomination. Fitzgerald's contract was not renewed, but he remained in Hollywood, freelancing and working on a novel about the industry. He modeled an unsavory producer named Jaques La Borwits on Joe, to whom Fitzgerald referred as "an ignorant and vulgar gent," and "Monkeybitch."

In 1940 Fitzgerald, forty-four, died of a heart attack, and in 1945 his friend Edmund Wilson published *The Crack-Up*, a collection of Fitzgerald's writing and letters. Joe talked Wilson out of including Fitzgerald's letter in that book, but starting with Fitzgerald's first biography in 1951, his letter to Joe has remained in print. Graham also kept up the drumbeat in memoir after memoir, reinforcing the image of Fitzgerald as the injured genius and Joe as the unappreciative producer whose insensitive rewrites drove Fitzgerald off the wagon.

In the 1950s Herman's son Don asked Joe for advice about a play he was adapting, and Joe said, "You realize that if you rewrite it and then the playwright kills himself, everyone is going to say it's your fault. That you killed him." Don knew Joe was thinking of Fitzgerald. When Aaron Latham interviewed him for *Crazy Sundays*, his 1971 book about Fitzgerald's experiences in Hollywood, Joe said, "When I rewrote Scott's dialogue, people thought I was spitting on the flag." Latham obviously agreed with them. Conceding that Joe was "sometimes right" in changing Fitzgerald's dialogue, he nevertheless added that Joe "ruined lines which he probably did not even understand," and in case readers missed the point, he accompanied that patronizing assessment with an unflattering portrayal of Joe directing. As if it couldn't get worse, practically every review of Latham's widely reviewed book mentioned or quoted the letter, effectively paying more attention to Joe's supposed travesty than to *The Great Gatsby*.

A few years later other Fitzgerald scholars revisited the scripts and began to agree that, despite Fitzgerald's exquisite short stories and his quintessential great American novel, perhaps Joe knew more about screenwriting. The rehabilitation was gratifying, but too little and way too late for Joe. He had spent too many years as "the swine who rewrote F. Scott Fitzgerald."

Joe's five comedies were a mixed lot. In *Double Wedding* (1937), William Powell plays a vagabond artist romancing Myrna Loy, an uptight businesswoman. Critics ridiculed its obvious imitation of the superior *My Man Godfrey* (1936) and dismissed its slapstick finale, but audiences liked it. Joe hoped that starring Frank Morgan in *The Wild Man of Borneo* (1941) and adding Billie Burke, Donald Meek, Marjorie Main, Bonita Granville, Dan Dailey, and Phil Silvers would compensate for the weaknesses of Herman and Marc Connelly's 1927 theatrical flop. It did not. As for *The Feminine Touch* (1941), the dialogue supplied by poet Ogden Nash and screenwriters George Oppenheimer and Edmund L. Hartmann outshone the plot.

However, Joe's two Katharine Hepburn comedies redeemed all his years as a producer. Hepburn was on the same 1938 box office poison list that upset Joan Crawford, but Hepburn was not as vulnerable as Crawford, whose laborious ascent from poverty resembled many of her onscreen characters'. Instead, Hepburn, whose Bryn Mawr education and privileged family background resembled many of her characters', got mad and got even. She bought out her RKO contract and returned to Broadway to star in *The Philadelphia Story*, which was written specifically for her by her friend Philip Barry. In what would become the quintessential Katharine Hepburn plot—the taming of the shrew—she played Tracy Lord, a Philadelphia society woman about to marry the wrong man.

Once they knew the play was a hit, Hepburn's former lover Howard Hughes bought the film rights so she could retain artistic control. She asked her friend George Cukor to direct and insisted that MGM cast two major male stars for additional box office insurance. Only the reporter's role in the play was meaty enough to attract a star, so Joe suggested combining the parts of Tracy's brother and her former husband, C. K. Dexter Haven, which created a role large enough to attract Cary Grant. As the reporter, James Stewart won a Best Actor Academy Award.

Given the quality of Barry's play, Donald Ogden Stewart claimed his Academy Award–winning adaptation was the "least-deserving-of-praise bit of script writing" he had ever done. Cukor thought Stewart understated his subtle contributions. Joe, who revered Barry as the ideal to which he aspired, annoyed both Stewart and Cukor by recording a live performance of the play so they could hear when audiences laughed, and by repeating the story for years afterward. Cukor always insisted he and Stewart played the recording only after the picture was made, and that the laughs in the film and the play occurred in different places anyway.

Although the film remained generally faithful to the original, Joe created a new opening, in which Tracy throws out Dexter and breaks one of his golf clubs, and he also suggested the closing montage of freeze frames, a technique later used frequently, including by Joe himself in *All About Eve*. It was an enormous critical and popular success, breaking Radio City Music Hall's previous records and receiving another four Oscar nominations: best picture; Hepburn as best actress; Ruth Hussey (the newspaper photographer) as best supporting actress; Cukor as best director.

Joe's second Hepburn picture was historic for another reason. "Be in your office Monday at 3 o'clock," Hepburn wired Joe, then telephoned to say she was sending him an unsigned, unfinished script and giving MGM twenty-four hours to accept or reject her terms. She refused to identify the writers but demanded MGM pay them the hefty sum of $100,000, along with $100,000 for herself, $10,000 for her agent, and $1,000 for her expenses. *Woman of the Year* was a romantic comedy pitting Tess Harding, a foreign affairs newspaper columnist resembling Dorothy Thompson, against Sam Craig, a newspaper sports columnist. Joe, who urged Mayer to buy it, suspected the authors might be under contract elsewhere—perhaps former newspapermen Ben Hecht and Charles MacArthur. Once MGM accepted, Hepburn revealed they were the young, relatively unknown Michael Kanin (brother of Garson) and Ring Lardner Jr., whose sportswriter father was also Dorothy Thompson's lover.

Although she hurt George Cukor's feelings, Hepburn insisted MGM borrow George Stevens from Columbia Pictures to direct; she believed Stevens would be more adept at handling the sports scenes, as well as the visual gags. She wanted Spencer Tracy for Sam Craig, though they had

As a producer, Joe was barred from receiving credit for his contributions to *The Philadelphia Story*'s screenplay (1940). Here, James Stewart, Cary Grant, and Katharine Hepburn are surprised by a photographer.

not met. The day she and Joe encountered him at the studio, Hepburn was wearing the platform shoes she favored (the better to intimidate), and when Joe introduced his old friend, Hepburn said to the future love of her life, "Mr. Tracy, I think you're a little short for me."

"Don't worry, he'll cut you down to size," Joe responded, summing up the stars' next twenty-seven years together, both on and off screen. The script was witty, the cast delightful, and the production all that Hepburn had hoped—except for the ending, which Joe again reshaped. According to Joe, preview audiences disliked the lovers' reconciliation at the end, so he had John Lee Mahin devise a scene in which Tess tries to fix Sam's breakfast and fails abysmally. As her new husband watches with surreptitious amusement, Tess's coffee boils over and her waffles leak out of the waffle iron. It was a long, elaborate, gag-filled scene that Joe believed the "average American housewife" needed. If the superior Tess were taken down a notch, "they could turn to their schmuck husbands and say, 'She may know Batista [Cuba's president at the time], but she can't even make a cup of coffee, you silly bastard.'"

Hepburn, Kanin, and Lardner detested it, and decades later they still resented it. The writers believed they already had structured that particular battle of the sexes to "suit the comedy conventions of the time" and recalled begging Joe to limit the scene to just "a few concessions to orthodox femininity." But, whether or not the director and producer were the "strong exponents of male dominance" that Lardner called them in 1970, Joe was in charge (Stevens disavowed the scene to Geist). Hepburn dutifully played the new scene as instructed, though she considered it "the worst piece of shit I've ever read," and eventually Joe allowed the writers to add a few ameliorating lines, including Sam's telling Tess that abandoning her career would be absurd. However, that message was so overpowered by the visuals that many reviewers mentioned the kitchen scene and noted approvingly that Tess was trading her career for marriage. (Which probably proves that Joe really was more in tune with the times—or, perhaps, with the sympathies of the male critics.)

Joe considered Tracy "the best screen actor that ever lived," and the picture was another enormous hit. It earned Hepburn her fourth Academy Award nomination, and Kanin and Lardner won best original screenplay, though even the Oscar did not assuage their anger. They remained so frustrated that they ignored Joe's outstretched hand on their way to the dais to accept it.

Joe's last two MGM films were Crawford's *Reunion in France* and Jeanette MacDonald's last MGM film, *Cairo* (1942), which was intended as a spoof of spy stories. MacDonald played an American movie star in wartime Cairo, with Robert Young as a befuddled journalist, and Ethel Waters as MacDonald's maid and secretary. Unfortunately, the picture opened in November 1942, just as the British general Montgomery gave the Allies their first major victory over the Nazis—about 150 miles from Cairo. A serious drama or a cleverer spoof might have escaped ridicule, but the stirring war news datelined "Cairo," finished off what was an already unsuccessful hybrid. Only Ethel Waters, the best-known black singer at the time, emerged unscathed, her performance widely praised. Joe's name eventually disappeared from *Cairo*'s credits—he had it removed.

JOE IN LOVE

Joe's years as a producer seemed even bleaker when Herman won an Oscar for cowriting *Citizen Kane* in 1942. For all Joe's hard work, there he was, precociously successful in a profession he despised; and there was

Aboard his eighty-four-foot yacht, *Sartartia*, with Franz Waxman and his captain. Joe found escaping to sea restorative.

Herman, wildly self-destructive and continually requiring rescue from Joe and everyone else, at the pinnacle of the very profession to which Joe yearned to return. The usually disciplined Joe lost himself a bit over those years, gambling for high stakes and spending more money than he could afford, especially on boats, because the sea offered a refuge he could not find elsewhere. He worked his way up from a relatively modest thirty-six-foot motor boat to expensive yachts, one purchased from violinist Jascha Heifetz. At one point he owned three boats, and Billy Wilder told him he had the second-largest fleet in the Pacific. Eventually he entered analysis with Otto Fenichel, an eminent Freudian psychoanalyst, and spent three painful but fruitful years working on his compulsive gambling and overspending.

Boats were intermittently restorative, but Joe's most enduring outlet was romance. Sex was gratifying and pleasurable and to be taken when available, but seduction and the rush of romance were addictive. Married or unmarried, sequentially or concurrently, Joe was always pursuing women, usually a high-profile actress. His affair with Loretta Young followed his divorce from Elizabeth. A professional since the age of three, Young was an ardent Catholic, though her religious scruples were idiosyncratic. She married at seventeen, and after having the marriage annulled a year later, she embarked on a series of affairs with men she

Loretta Young was ready to marry. Joe was not.

could not marry, including Spencer Tracy, a married, observant Catholic himself, and Clark Gable—predecessors who probably enhanced Young's appeal to Joe.

Young so abhorred profanity that on her sets she imposed a graduated scale of fines for cursing, depending on the word. Irritated by her sanctimoniousness, Joe once asked, "How much would it cost me to tell you to go fuck yourself?" Joe was already divorced when they became involved and had no interest in seeking the papal dispensation from his divorce Young hoped he could obtain in order to marry her. In fact, when Loretta Young noticed Elizabeth Young's "Y" monogram on Joe's silverware and casually remarked, "Oh, we won't have to change the silver," that was enough to scare him out of the relationship.

Not that Joe was averse to marriage in general. At the age of thirty, he married Rosa Stradner, a beautiful Austrian Catholic émigré actress, who seemed, like Elizabeth, to be on her way up. The studios were importing

In 1937 MGM imported Viennese actress Rose Stradner on the same ship with fellow countrywoman Hedy Lamarr.

overseas talent in an attempt to discover the next Garbo or Dietrich, and Rosa arrived in 1937, on the same ship as Hedy Lamarr. She had started acting at sixteen and became prominent under the tutelage of Max Reinhardt, playing leading roles all over Europe in works by Shakespeare, Ibsen, Wilde, and even Kaufman and Ferber, in *Dinner at Eight*. She also appeared in a number of Austrian and German films and was married to Karl Heinz Martin, a prominent German leftist theater and film director twenty-seven years her senior, who was known for his expressionist films. When introducing Rosa to the public, MGM expunged both her marriage and her previous film experience, and after she became involved with Joe, Rosa returned to Europe to divorce Martin.

They met when the studio asked Joe to help Rosa with her English as he had with other German-speaking émigrés, a task he enjoyed. Besides his affinity for theater and actresses, Joe revered Europeans, especially German-speakers. Many were his closest friends, including Ernst Lubitsch, musician Franz Waxman, and writer Walter Reisch, who was from Vienna and had worked with Rosa in Europe. More femme fatale than ingénue, Rosa combined an impressive European theatrical pedigree with the mixture of danger and vulnerability that Joe found so appealing in Joan Crawford.

Her beautiful skin and stately carriage enabled Rosa to carry off dramatic clothes with elegance, but MGM first cast her as the mousy, naive, Old World wife of gangster Edward G. Robinson in *The Last Gangster* (1937). Reviews were positive, and the studio floated potential screen names like Andra Marlo and Andrea Marion before allowing Rosa to retain her own (sometimes she was Rose).

Joe did not realize how high-strung she was until they moved in together. Rosa could be physically violent, and when the studio failed to put her into a second picture right away, she began taking out her anxieties on Joe. In 1938 MGM loaned her to RKO for *The Saint in New York,* but RKO replaced her. Joe cabled agent Leland Hayward for help when Rosa was being considered for a New York staging of *Lorelei,* but she didn't get the role. Drifting downward, she moved to Columbia Pictures, and the studio cast her only once, in a sixth-billed role as Ralph Bellamy's character's wife in *Blind Alley* (1939).

When the red flags became impossible to ignore, Joe said he was not going to marry her. Rosa responded by attempting suicide, and instead of leaving, Joe married her on July 28, 1939, at Erna's apartment in New York. Their wedding was covered even more extensively than Joe's first, and when they returned to Los Angeles on Rosa's twenty-sixth birthday, MGM writers and producers surprised them at the railway station with rice and a ten-piece orchestra.

Rosa gave birth to Christopher on October 8, 1940, and Spencer Tracy and Liesl (Mrs. Walter) Reisch were his godparents. Tom followed less than two years later, on June 1, 1942. A few months after Tom's birth, Rosa and Joe joined Alice and Franz Waxman for a vacation at Arrowhead Springs Hotel, a San Bernardino mountain resort favored by celebrities. There, Rosa sank into so severe a catatonic state that she was taken home by ambulance.

Whether by emotional distress, postpartum depression, despair about her career, or mental illness, Rosa was clearly overwhelmed. Some old friends, like Walter Reisch, believed Rosa was high-strung but not necessarily mentally ill (or so Reisch believed, when interviewed in the 1970s). At the time, Joe sent her to the place he considered the best available, the Menninger Clinic in Topeka, Kansas, and Rosa spent the next nine months under treatment by Dr. Karl Menninger, the most respected and influential psychiatrist west of the Mississippi.

Menninger was a doctrinaire Freudian whose views on the psyches and subordinated roles of women were quite clear from his advice columns in women's magazines. He usually admonished wives writing about their husbands' extramarital affairs to examine their own shortcomings for the probable cause and then forgive and forget. Whatever his treatments' theoretical or personal underpinnings, Menninger's cure for whatever ailed Rosa did not seem to do her much good and may have done real harm.

From 1942 on, Rosa was usually medicated. Although she habitually supplemented her prescription drugs with too much alcohol and attempted suicide more than once, Joe was an ardent Freudian, so Rosa spent the rest of her life under the care of Menninger and likeminded psychiatrists. Rosa's doctors undoubtedly cared about her wellbeing (as they defined it), but they were also uniformly captivated by Joe. Rosa's husband was not only brilliant, charming, and important but fascinated by their profession. All of that was immensely flattering but may not have served Rosa's best interests.

While she was at Menninger's clinic, Rosa met Friedrich (Fred) Hacker, a Viennese psychiatrist who moved to Los Angeles shortly afterward. Hacker, who did not treat Rosa at the clinic, already knew Herman and Sara, and over the years, Joe and Rosa became close friends as well, both using Hacker as a confidant to complain to about the other. They both trusted him and valued his friendship and counsel, as he did theirs, and he tried to be helpful.

Menninger also became involved in Joe's dealings with Elizabeth. Shortly after Tom's birth, Joe's lawyer contacted her about reducing Joe's monthly payments, and in February 1943 Elizabeth responded by asking for full custody of Eric. In order to provide Eric, now seven, with "emotional security" and "a sense of 'belonging,'" Elizabeth also wanted to change Eric's surname to Reynal and discontinue his summer visits, though Joe would be welcome to visit him, when and if he came east. Elizabeth explained that these issues had concerned her since Eric turned four (which was when Eric's half-brother was born, though she did not mention that).

Joe was not unsympathetic, but he angrily questioned the timing. If the problems had existed since Eric was four, why was Joe being apprised of them only now, when money was involved? He also worried that if he complied, how might Eric feel about him later on, if he believed his father had traded away his parental rights for financial reasons?

On Joe's behalf, Menninger contacted a New York psychiatrist about evaluating Eric, explaining that he had asked Joe: "(a) How much do you yourself love the child? (b) How does the child himself feel about you, your name, these visits to you, and about his mother's proposed changes in the arrangement?"

According to Menninger, Joe had answered, "I think the child loves me more than I love him," and added, "I should be disappointed not to see him, but I should not be broken-hearted; on the other hand, I should feel guilty all my life if I did something that hurt the boy, even though it were something requested by his mother."

Menninger also noted, "I might add that I told Mr. Mankiewicz my impression was that so possessive and calculating a mother would probably ruin the child, no matter what was done . . ."

Eventually concluding he could not win and might do harm by persisting, Joe acceded to Elizabeth's terms. As he wrote to Menninger, with success seeming impossible, he believed pursuing the matter would only lead to his becoming "once more a beautiful martyr, very pleasing to me neurotically but very stupid as far as my practical responsibilities to Rose, the children and myself are concerned. And so I turned the entire matter over to my lawyer to deal with as he saw fit."

Joe added, "I was surprised when you wrote, 'I know this is one of the serious and deeper anxieties in your life.' I have only one serious and deep anxiety—and that would be my lack of any." It was a brutally honest assessment of his own detachment.

Rosa returned home to formidable challenges. She was turning thirty that summer, and her career was stalled; her almost-three-year-old son had gained a brother and lost a mother in confusingly quick succession; she and her one-year-old were virtual strangers. She desperately wanted to resume acting, but instead she spent the next few years working at being a good mother, studying to become a US citizen and establishing the household she and Joe considered commensurate with their stature. (Herman's family disliked Rosa, considering her snobbish.) They eventually worked their way up from Pacific Palisades to a spacious house at 111 North Mapleton Drive on three acres in Holmby Hills, with a tennis court and swimming pool.

Rosa also returned to a husband who was emotionally engaged elsewhere. As much as Joe loved rescuing women, he was already tired of rescuing Rosa, and while Rosa attempted to rebuild their family, Joe was out and about with Judy Garland. He was working on *The Pirate*, an S. N.

With Judy Garland at the 1942 Academy Awards dinner.

Behrman Broadway hit he considered a good vehicle for Garland, when he began to see in Garland a skilled raconteur with a sardonic sense of humor. Soon "Josephus" and "Miss Sherwood" were rendezvousing at the Beverly Wilshire Hotel, eating at restaurants where they imagined themselves unseen, and openly attending Joe's friends' parties together. To the amusement of guests like James Cagney and John Garfield at a party of Danny and Sylvia Kaye's, Garland played Princess Pitti-Sing to Joe's Princess Yum-Yum in *The Yiddish Mikado*. When she turned twenty-one, Joe and Dore Schary created a record, "The Life of Judy Garland," on which Joe portentously narrated a *March of Time*–style reenactment of her young life.

Garland was mesmerized. Her brilliant, handsome, creative, intellectual producer seemed to possess every quality she had admired in previous crushes, both requited, like Tyrone Power and Johnny Mercer, and unrequited, like Oscar Levant, Artie Shaw, and Mickey Rooney. She was thrilled to follow glamorous predecessors like Joan Crawford and Loretta Young. Joe's way of concentrating his blue eyes and every ounce of his attention on her thoughts and his sensitivity to her feelings made Garland feel so loved, so seen, that she eventually joined other previous lovers of Joe who recalled him as the love of their lives.

Less beautiful but more talented than his previous lovers, Judy Garland was the most extreme example of Joe's preferred type—widely adulated but in need of rescuing—and Joe fell hard. Herman and Joe both sympathized with women and recognized the hurdles they faced, but unlike Herman, Joe was attracted to women for their vulnerability, not their strengths. Joe did not fall for peers.

He advised Garland about her career, though not always wisely (he urged her against doing *Meet Me in St. Louis*), because besides helping her personally, he also wanted to help her fulfill her professional potential. He had seen her perform as a child and had tried unsuccessfully to get her an audition. It was Al Rosen (the same Al Rosen who spent years trying to produce Herman's *Mad Dog of Europe*) who finally signed Garland with MGM in 1935, when she was thirteen. By the time she became involved with Joe at twenty, Judy Garland was one of the studio's most important stars, but she was also deeply troubled.

She had been performing since the age of two, but MGM's process of turning her into a star turned her into a mass of insecurities and self-loathing. Pushed and prodded to change her nose, her teeth, her figure, her weight, and surrounded by beauties like Lana Turner and Elizabeth Taylor, she felt valueless; her personality and talent seemed inconsequential, especially when she was subjected to unceasing comments about how homely she was, which were echoed by her mother and even by Mayer, who called her his "little hunchback."

"Christ almighty, the girl reacted to the slightest bit of kindness as if it were a drug," Joe recalled. To Joe, Judy Garland was an unspoiled innocent who was treated "like a piece of equipment, a money-making device." Directors could be callous and even cruel, and MGM squandered her gifts in formulaic vehicles when she had the potential to be a great actress. "She had a fresh kind of a foresty look, as though there were dew on her," Joe elaborated. "I wasn't in love that way [with marriage in mind]," he told one of Garland's biographers. "I was in love—and I know this is a terrible analogy—the way you love an animal, a pet."

Even before they were involved romantically, Joe urged her to see a psychiatrist. He frequently saw psychoanalysis as the answer, but Garland was an obvious candidate for some kind of intervention. By late 1942 Joe was already so enmeshed with Karl Menninger that when Menninger visited Beverly Hills, Joe was able to arrange a meeting.

Menninger believed Garland could be helped, especially if she would spend a few months to a year at his clinic, but knowing that was impossible, he sent her to Herman's analyst, Ernst Simmel. The Teutonic Simmel (Herman called him the Obermacher—Big Boss) was probably a bad fit for Garland, and she eventually dropped analysis. But she absorbed enough to start defying her mother. So when Ethel Gumm reported her disobedient twenty-one-year-old to Louis B. Mayer, Mayer, who revered mothers and disapproved of analysis, defiant employees, and Joe's relationship with Judy, promised to talk to Joe.

Joe was on his way home aboard the Super Chief when MGM's publicity chief, Howard Strickling, knocked at his compartment and said Mayer wanted to see him. As soon as he entered, Mayer lit into him. Judy was thirteen years his junior. How dare he carry on with her and pretend to be her friend just to have an affair with her? "He talked to me about God and motherhood and wifehood and parenthood and the studio. How when you lie down with dogs, you get up with fleas," Joe recalled. Mayer essentially told Joe to live like a monk when he was not with his wife, but as Joe saw it, Mayer was really saying, "You mustn't mess with our property." He concluded, "I'm not speaking to you like a father. I'm not speaking as a boss. I'm speaking to you as a friend."

"Actually," Joe said, "you've been neither, Mr. Mayer. You're talking like a jealous old man."

"Get him out of here," his infuriated boss screamed, and Joe left.

Joe's instincts were probably more accurate than he realized. Garland had told him about her discomfort at being made to sit on men's laps at sales meetings and sing for them, but, he told Clarke, "I don't think for a minute that she was ever in any way molested by anybody that I know of. I don't think that ever happened." However, in later years, Garland echoed Crawford's and others' experiences, recalling that when Mayer complimented her on singing from the heart, he typically dropped his hand onto her left breast, apparently to remind her of where her heart was located. Al Rosen told an even more damning story.

In late 1939 Rosen dropped in on Garland unexpectedly and, to his horror, saw the seventeen-year-old orally servicing Mayer. Rosen hurried out, praying that Mayer, who was facing the door, had not recognized him without his glasses. However, the next day he was summoned to Mayer's office, where Mayer coldly informed Rosen he was buying out Garland's contract and reassigning it to Frank Orsatti (Mayer's friend, bootlegger, and procurer of women). As Rosen described the interchange, "Without saying a word about what had happened between Judy and himself, he was flexing the biggest biceps in the movie industry. He really was giving me an ultimatum, a silent warning to keep my mouth shut."

Mayer handed Rosen a $40,000 check, and though it was a pittance compared with Garland's value, Rosen knew he would never work in Hollywood again if he talked. So he took the money, kept his mouth shut, and continued to do business with Mayer as if nothing had happened. Given Rosen's account, Mayer's aversion to the prospect of Garland in psychoanalysis could only have been amplified.

When Joe returned to work, Mayer summoned him to his office so Mrs. Gumm could add her own harangue to Mayer's, including her proud assertion that she locked Judy in the closet to discipline her. At that point Joe had had enough. "L.B.," he said, "I don't think this studio is big enough for both of us. One of us has to go." Mayer's production chief, Eddie Mannix, whom Joe so liked and respected that he was Tom's godfather, was at that meeting, and after nearly falling off his chair at Joe's effrontery, he repeated the story all over town.

So Joe left MGM. But he did not leave Judy Garland. When she finally understood that Joe was not going to leave Rosa for her, she made one last attempt to hold him by saying she was pregnant. Aware that she was either fantasizing or lying, Joe considered her too fragile to challenge directly, so he discreetly crossed the country to New York, where they agreed she would have an abortion. They stayed together at the apartment of his friend, agent Mark Hanna, and after Garland shared the "news" that she was not pregnant, the two of them took a four-night, three-day train trip back to Hollywood together. The train was filled with troops, and though Garland and Joe laughed and cried and slept together in Joe's compartment, most of the time she went from car to car, singing and talking with the soldiers, "keeping other people from grief and sorrow, what she had a surfeit of," recalled Joe.

After that, they gently drifted apart. Joe left the studio, and Judy Garland became an icon and a wreck. But she always treasured their intimate journey, and over the years, she periodically reached out to Joe. In June 1961 Joe was in Los Angeles working on *Cleopatra* when he received a call from New York. Garland had just finished the Carnegie Hall concert that, even in the moment, was an obvious artistic and financial triumph. However, in the middle of that night, she needed to talk to her Joe. She needed to talk to Joe again the following night, this time at 1:00

a.m. (4:00 a.m., New York time). And again a few days later, this time at 1:30 a.m. She called him once more, to say she was all right. What they said only the two of them knew, but a few weeks later Garland informed Sid Luft, her husband of ten years, that she wanted a divorce.

As Joe later told one of Garland's biographers, "You must present the even flow of an incredible talent to the tragic destiny of a Stradivarius winding up in a junk heap." Recalling her endless complexity, he said, "You can write down everything Lana Turner ever thought and felt and meant, and then put the pencil down. That's it, a closed book. But I don't think anybody's going to close the book on Judy Garland."

CHAPTER 12

Citizen Kane

BY THE TIME JOE LEFT MGM IN 1943, HERMAN HAD TURNED HIS LIFE AROUND, at least temporarily. And it was all by accident. Literally.

When Mayer fired him in September 1939, Herman decided to use the expulsion as an opportunity for a fresh start. He couldn't replicate his Hollywood salary back east, but perhaps he could return to newspaper work. Sara was skeptical but acquiescent, and Herman even had a free ride east with Tommy Phipps, a young screenwriter (and Lady Astor's nephew). So with cash borrowed from Joe, off he went.

The following morning Joe received a panicked call from Sara: Herman had left behind a mountain of debts. Joe assembled his business manager, his lawyer, Herman's manager, and Sam Jaffe to assess the situation; and once they ruled out bankruptcy, Joe, Jaffe, Sara's relatives, Erna, and even Pop—all of whom had helped before—pooled enough money to bail them out. Joe began searching yet again, for more work for Herman.

Meanwhile, oblivious to the frenzied efforts in his behalf, Herman considered himself the miserable one. As they drove across the desert in Phipps's convertible, he had to listen to Phipps drone on and on about his no-longer-requited love for Ethel Butterworth, an actress nine years his senior (Eddie Sutherland was one of her previous husbands). His ordeal finally ended eighty miles west of Albuquerque, when Phipps lost control of the car in the rain, and they skidded and flipped over. Phipps suffered a concussion, and Herman was pinned down with a leg broken in three places. Herman later swore that as they slid across the road, he saw, "written in letters of fire across Tommy Phipps's forehead, 'She'll be sorry when she hears about this.'"

Herman was transported to Los Angeles, where he spent a month in the hospital in traction, "somewhat in the posture of a lower-class Klondike whore," then went home, not only broke, unemployed, and

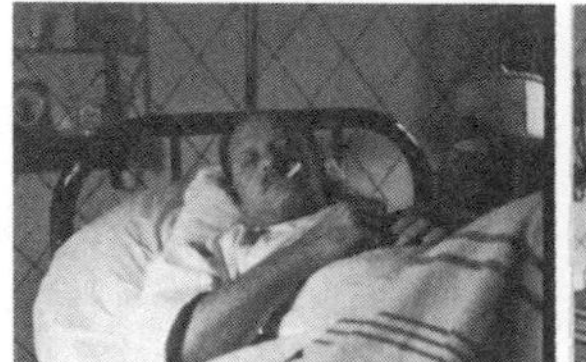
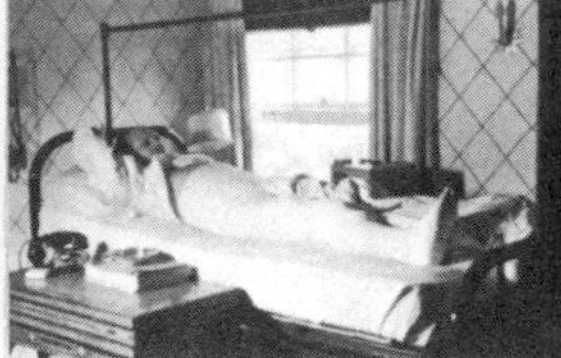
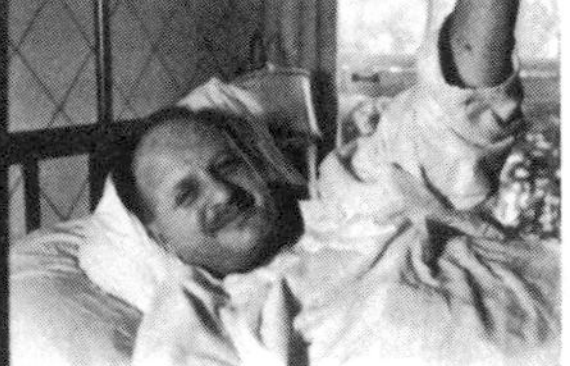

Herman described himself as "somewhat in the posture of a lower-class Klondike whore."

in terrible pain, but also encased in a full body cast that left him itching constantly. He recounted his tale so vividly to his visitors that Alice Duer Miller encouraged him to turn it into a five-thousand-word short story and call it "Free Ride." "Write it in the first person, keep all the first eight hour discussion as it was," she suggested, adding that he should conclude by giving his companion a new love affair with a desirable blonde and leave himself with nothing but a broken leg.

Instead, Herman writhed and smoked and complained incessantly while everyone scurried around trying to make him more comfortable. Margaret Sullavan provided a makeshift air conditioner and long sticks to help him scratch inside his cast (he was grateful); Joe brought his own lap board to help him write (Herman growled); a group of MGM writers brought a silver cigarette box engraved "From Manky's pals" (he cried when they left).

He was also visited by a brilliant young writer/director/actor he had met in New York several years before and taken to immediately. The large, handsome actor barely in his twenties oozed charm and overflowed with ideas he communicated in a remarkable, resonant voice. For his part, Orson Welles found Herman "amazingly civilized and charming."

Welles's life read like a fairy tale. His cultured, affluent midwestern parents educated him at home and exposed him to the worlds of music and theater, then died by the time their son was fifteen. Two mentors took him under their respective wings, Dr. Maurice Bernstein, a family friend, and Roger Hill, headmaster at the boarding school Welles attended after his father died. At Hill's school, Welles became an accomplished magician, performed on the school's radio station, and immersed himself in theater. Immersion for Welles meant writing and designing classical, contemporary, and musical productions; designing the costumes; and usually playing the lead. He was still in his teens when he and Hill co-authored a young people's guide to Shakespeare that remained in print for many years. After high school Welles traveled abroad, and when he returned, Thornton Wilder introduced him to Alexander Woollcott, who led him to Katharine Cornell's repertory theater company in New York. In 1934 producer John Houseman saw Welles playing Tybalt in Cornell's *Romeo and Juliet*, and by December, the two had joined forces. Welles was nineteen.

Houseman's background was also exotic. He was born Jacques Haussmann, in Bucharest, Romania, in 1902, to a Jewish Alsatian father and a British mother. They sent him to England to be educated, but when his father died, he left to help support his mother. He worked as an international grain merchant in Argentina, London, and New York until the 1929 crash, then turned to theater, his longtime passion.

After Houseman was appointed to head the Works Progress Administration's (WPA) Negro Theatre Project in 1935, he and Welles created an all-black production of *Macbeth*, set in nineteenth-century Haiti. Then they left to form Mercury Theatre, a repertory company that staged innovative productions, including a contemporary-dress version of *Julius Caesar* (using Shakespeare's political melodrama as a comment on the rise of fascism); Marc Blitzstein's *The Cradle Will Rock*; and George Bernard Shaw's *Heartbreak House*. They financed Mercury through Welles's work on the radio, where he had become a top performer. Besides playing Lamont Cranston of *The Shadow*, he impersonated a variety of characters on Columbia Broadcasting System's (CBS) *March of Time* news dramatizations, ranging from arms merchant Basil Zaharoff to Italian king Victor Emmanuel, Sigmund Freud, and even the Dionne quintuplets.

Welles also wrote, produced, and directed radio programs of such obvious genius that *Time* dubbed him "Marvelous Boy" and put him on its May 6, 1938, cover (Welles's twenty-third birthday). By the time the *New Yorker* profiled him that October, CBS had given Welles an hour show to create, introduce, and narrate. However, his time slot was Sunday evening, opposite ventriloquist Edgar Bergen and his dummy, Charlie McCarthy, who were so popular that many members of the audience tuned into Bergen and McCarthy first, then switched to Welles's program at the first break. That was why, on October 30, 1938, many listeners tuned into Welles's program twelve minutes late and missed the introduction to his dramatization of H. G. Wells's novel *War of the Worlds*. Some mistook his program for an actual news broadcast about an ongoing hostile Martian landing in New Jersey, and though reports of widespread panic have been greatly exaggerated, the event was enough of a phenomenon to keep Welles on the front page of newspapers for days.

Eventually, even Welles's radio income failed to cover Mercury's expenses, so he and Houseman turned to motion pictures. Studios had been clamoring for Welles, and he was intrigued by the medium—he already had experimented with film footage to incorporate into one of their plays. He held out for artistic control, and in June 1939 RKO studio chief George Schaefer agreed to an unprecedented contract that would pay Mercury Theatre $100,000, plus a portion of the profits, for each of two pictures. Welles would write, produce, direct, and star in each, and, most importantly, there would be no studio interference.

The terms were not as outrageous as they seemed. RKO retained the right to approve his subject and restricted Welles to a budget of $500,000 per picture, which was not huge for an A-picture. But the right to final cut was a shocking concession, and the fact that it was awarded to a twenty-four-year-old neophyte was, to the Hollywood community, the unkindest cut of all. With a few exceptions, they reacted with anger and rudeness to the point of cruelty, and even the trade press taunted and ridiculed the Boy Wonder. When Welles gave a party, no one came.

Herman was one of the exceptions, though he, too, enjoyed repeating, "There but for the grace of God goes God." Welles appreciated Herman's kindness and visited him at the hospital and later at home, which at that point was a small house belonging to actor Laird Cregar (so they could rent out Tower Road). Welles also offered him work. Adapting books into scripts for Welles's radio program at $200 apiece was a comedown, but anything was welcome, including another $500 Welles passed along to Herman for ghostwriting a *Cosmopolitan* magazine article. Altogether, Herman wrote five radio episodes and told the press that Welles's "4-way movie contract—producer-director-writer-actor," was especially impressive compared to his own "2-way contract at Republic Pictures. Producer-janitor."

Even the provider of needed income and welcome stimulation did not completely escape snarls from his grouchy beneficiary, but Welles and Herman complemented each other. Both were usually performing, though their need to entertain stemmed from opposite childhood experiences. Herman's internalized self-hatred remained intense, while Welles had bathed in adult approval. However, because that attention had lasted only as long as he amused, Welles had become adept at reading and engaging older mentors. Both enjoyed slipping in and out of a mentor/disciple relationship and talked far into the night. With no other seating in the small bedroom except Sara's bed, Welles would lie beside Sara and massage her neck while they talked. Even years after relations had soured, Sara recalled Welles's kindness and charm.

When RKO's projection came in over a million dollars, Welles shelved his plan to adapt Joseph Conrad's *Heart of Darkness* and shifted to a less ambitious wartime spy thriller, *The Smiler with the Knife*. Even Herman took a stab at *Smiler*, but by mid-December 1939 that, too, looked impossible, and Welles began to worry seriously about fulfilling his contract. At that point Herman suggested an idea he considered almost impossible to sell to a regular studio.

Years afterward, Herman described their original storyline: "The basic plot conception was the death of a man and an inquiry into what had caused him to be the manner of man he was in the eyes of close friends, strangers . . . and . . . what had caused him to be that, not only in regard to surface happenings, but something that early in life had formed a subconscious compulsion to which he responded, although he didn't know he was responding to it." Herman saw the protagonist as "a whirling pagoda: you look this way and see one side; turn your eyes away, look again and see another side, so that people looking at it from different angles see ostensibly the same man but not the same man at all."

As they tossed around ideas, Welles and Herman had no idea they were brainstorming their way into history, and over the years *Citizen Kane*'s success attracted many parents. Sometimes Welles claimed the plot was his idea, though the concept was hardly unknown. Herman himself had already played with it in his John Dillinger play and used it in *John Meade's Woman*. Searching for a character complicated enough to generate a range of interpretations, they considered a soldier; a businessman; a politician like William Jennings Bryan; and even Alexandre Dumas, whose life included revolutions, successful careers in theater and journalism, and at least forty mistresses.

Finally they settled on William Randolph Hearst. As Don said, "I have always thought of his Hearst idea as a coin Pop carried around in his pocket, and then he finally spent it." In later years when Welles portrayed Herman as an employee he had hired to execute his first draft, he would claim Hearst was his idea. On other occasions he ceded Hearst to Herman. "I suppose I would remember if it had been me," he told Herman's biographer in the 1970s.

Hearst was an irresistible subject to anyone who knew about him. Aside from his grandiose scale of living, there were his monumental building projects; his obsessive collecting; his wrongheaded direction of Marion Davies's career; his shift in the 1930s from left-wing Democratic Party populism to right-wing support of European Fascists; his enormous power over public opinion. Hearst had already inspired several biographies, including Ferdinand Lundberg's scathing 1936 exposé, and he was appearing in fiction as well. John Dos Passos included a section about Hearst in the third volume of his *U.S.A.* trilogy, and Aldous Huxley had just published *After Many a Summer Dies a Swan*, a satirical novel about an eccentric, acquisitive millionaire and his mistress. Though Herman knew Hearst personally, Welles also had connections. His parents' friend, Chicago theater critic Ashton Stevens (uncle of director George Stevens), was also Hearst's former banjo teacher, and Welles liked to think his father and Hearst had known each other as well.

Once they agreed on their protagonist, they turned to structure. They planned from the beginning to introduce their public personage through a parody of the *March of Time* news stories, utilizing its distinctive backward-flowing *Timese* language for both verisimilitude and humor. Herman wanted to combine the Hearst–Davies love story with elements of other powerful men and their mistresses, then construct the plot around the 1924 death of silent film producer/director Thomas Ince. According to rumors, Ince was mistakenly killed on Hearst's yacht instead of Charlie Chaplin, who supposedly was involved with Marion Davies. Herman wanted to portray the events and then have recollections from various sources create a prismatic portrait of the Hearst character. Welles overruled him, but when Hearst later retaliated against the film, Welles speculated that perhaps he should have heeded Herman's argument. Herman's theory was that using the murder would shield them from reprisals, because Hearst would never risk pointing out the similarities.

When they started talking, they were simply searching for a quick way to fulfill Welles's contract. But the more they developed it, the better it sounded, and the more obvious it seemed that Herman should write the first draft. Besides his familiarity with Hearst and his extensive historical and political knowledge, Herman was an experienced screenwriter, which Welles was not. But Welles was an accomplished editor, so it seemed a perfect solution.

Welles offered Herman $1,000 a week to write the draft while he started pre-production—as usual he was already teeming with ideas. But as much as Herman needed the money and wanted the job, he also insisted Welles hire John Houseman to work with him as an editor. Why Herman suddenly wanted a companion or collaborator is a mystery, but he was adamant. Houseman had edited Herman's radio scripts harshly, so perhaps Herman simply respected him. Another possibility is that once more Herman sought to snatch defeat from the jaws of victory.

Houseman was in New York, working with Howard Koch and John Huston on a play about Woodrow Wilson, and after a huge blow-up, he and Welles were not speaking. But Welles flew east, applied a charm offensive that fooled neither of them, and returned to Los Angeles with Houseman in tow.

It took Houseman only a few hours in Herman's bedroom to say he was in, and Welles brought over a magnum of champagne to celebrate. After the three spent a few days refining the concept, Welles formally hired them for twelve weeks. With little time and a complex screenplay, they all agreed that removing Herman from distractions and temptations would be advisable, so they rented a bungalow at a guest ranch called Rancho Verde (later Kemper Campbell Ranch), in the Mojave Desert near Victorville, about eighty miles outside Los Angeles. They embarked in a two-car caravan loaded with a typewriter, reams of blank paper, mounds of research materials, and a box of anti-alcohol pills. Herman lay in the back of a studio limousine, accompanied by two sets of crutches and a German nurse. Houseman and Rita Alexander, an English secretary Sara had found, followed in a convertible.

Alexander, whose loyalty they rewarded by naming Kane's second wife Susan Alexander, also performed several nonsecretarial duties, none of which fazed her. The first was liquor patrol, and as Houseman recalled, "No pair of internal revenue agents could have been more diligent in their daily inspection of Mank's room for intoxicants." Alcohol was banned at the resort, but no one underestimated Herman's ingenuity.

She also administered the bicarbonate of soda that Herman, a champion burper, routinely ingested in enormous quantities—it chased down his Scotches when he was drinking and merely followed a meal when he was not. On their first day at the ranch, Herman explained sheepishly, "Mrs. Alexander, one of your duties is of a kind that I hesitate to ask of you, but we might just as well get down to it from the beginning." He followed each enormous belch with a courtly apology, but Alexander simply laughed them off. She also participated in Herman's frequent work breaks. Once he realized she was an excellent cribbage player, he punctuated his dictation with low-stakes games that he usually lost but tried to recoup by raising the stakes, and long, entertaining stories about his Hollywood and Algonquin days.

Herman typically rose around nine thirty and spent the morning arguing with Houseman over the new material he had written. Still an invalid, he napped in the afternoon. In the evenings he and Houseman drove to the Green Spot, a local café, where they nursed one Scotch apiece and watched the locals play pinball and dance to western music from the jukebox. Afterward, they returned to the ranch, and Herman dictated until midnight or one in the morning. Alexander typed up the new pages and gave them to Herman before she went to bed. In the morning while Herman was still asleep, Houseman went horseback riding and read the new pages.

An astute editor who knew Welles intimately, John Houseman was the perfect collaborator. As he recalled, "(W)e were not working in a vacuum, developing a script for some absent producer; we were—and we never for one instant forgot it—creating a vehicle suited to the personality and creative energy of a man who, at twenty-four, was himself only slightly less fabulous than the mythical hero he would be portraying. And the deeper we penetrated beyond the public events into the heart of Charles Foster Kane, the closer we seemed to come to the identity of Orson Welles." Welles not only recognized the resemblance, "he pushed it even further when he came to shoot the film."

Herman's route to Charles Foster Kane was Hearst; Welles's was Orson Welles. In the 1970s, Welles talked to Meryman about their complementary contributions.

> When we were together in New York, Mank was absolutely beside himself with delight over the banker Richard Whitney, who was sent to Sing Sing, a perfect J.P. Marquand type. The head of the stock exchange with stripes on. . . . I think Kane was a WASP boogeyman to Mank. A suitable topic for jokes. And Mank's spleen was given a marvelous direction by that; it gave energy to his writing.
>
> There is a quality in the film—much more than a vague perfume—that was Mank and that I treasured. It gave a kind of character to the movie which I could never have thought of. It was a kind of controlled, cheerful virulence; we're finally telling the truth about a great WASP institution. I personally liked Kane, but I went with that. And that probably gave the picture a certain tension, the fact that one of the authors hated Kane and one loved him.
>
> . . . [But] I don't think a portrait of a man was ever present in any of Mank's scripts. . . . I felt his knowledge was journalistic, not very close, the point of view of a newspaperman writing about a newspaper boss he despised.
>
> I don't say that Mank didn't see Kane with clarity. He saw everything with clarity. No matter how odd or how right or how

> marvelous his point of view was, it was always diamond white. Nothing muzzy. But the truths of the character, Kane, were not what interested him.
>
> Mank was only interested in very personal terms in the all-devouring egomaniac tycoon. So the easily identifiable, audience identifiable reasons for what happened to Kane were part of Mank's contribution—and what made the picture finally popular. I think if I had been left to my own devices, we would have had to wait another fifty years.
>
> My *Citizen Kane* would have been much more concerned with the interior corruption of Kane. The script is most like me when the central figure on the screen is Kane. And it is most like Mankiewicz when he's being talked about. And I'm not at all sure that the best part isn't when they're talking about Kane. . . . I'm not saying I wrote all of one and Mank wrote the other.

Actually, Herman's view of Hearst was more nuanced. When Harold Ross wrote Herman in 1943 seeking information for a profile of Hearst, he responded:

> I happened to be discussing Our Hero with Orson. With the fair-mindedness that I have always recognized as my outstanding trait, I said to Orson that, despite this and that, Mr. Hearst was, in many ways, a great man. He was, and is, said Orson, a horse's ass, nor more nor less, who has been wrong without exception, on everything he's ever touched. For instance, for fifty years, said Orson, Hearst did nothing but scream about the Yellow Peril, and then he gave up his seat and hopped off that band wagon two months before Pearl Harbor.

Houseman also helped with the other characters. Welles planned to use actors from Mercury productions and his radio work, both because he respected their abilities and because he wanted faces new to moviegoers, and Houseman knew them well. The first draft had too many characters, but the five narrators in the final picture were there from the beginning, many of them named for people in Welles's life. Whitford Kane was an Irish American actor and a beloved acting teacher whom Welles had revered since childhood. He and Welles had clashed in recent years, but as Patrick McGilligan wrote in his Welles biography, "Orson had a way of crawling into people's laps to apologize for his bad behavior," and

Like Herman at the *New York Times* in 1925, Jed Leland (Joseph Cotten) passes out at his typewriter in *Citizen Kane* (1941) before finishing his review of Kane's wife's opera debut.

Kane later enjoyed the honor. Herman had favored "Craig," arguing that Kane was too evocative of Cain and Abel. "Do you suppose anybody's ever thought of that?" Welles asked Meryman.

Kane's Jewish manager, Mr. Bernstein, was named for Welles's friend and guardian Dr. Maurice "Dadda" Bernstein, and for all of Herman's jokes about Jews, Mr. Bernstein (who lacked a first name and always called Kane "Mr. Kane") was his favorite character. Herman modeled Bernstein on Louis Wiley, the *New York Times* business manager who helped Adolph Ochs build his newspaper into an institution. (Hearst had a plausible counterpart, though the austere Solomon Solis [S.S.] Carvalho was nothing like Bernstein.)

Welles wanted to base Kane's aristocratic friend Jedidiah Leland on Ashton Stevens, but he told Herman also to make him a southern gentleman for Joseph Cotten, who would be playing the part. Welles named him for producer Jed Harris and agent Leland Hayward (who was also Cotten's agent, though, Herman assured Cotten, "There all resemblance ceases"). Herman modeled Kane's banker-guardian Walter P. Thatcher on financier J. P. Morgan, and Welles named him for his piano teacher's husband. John Houseman believed Welles modeled Kane's butler, Raymond, after Houseman's Los Angeles butler ("a sinister and idle figure whose only accomplishment was making soggy crêpes Suzette").

Kane's first wife, Emily, was merely a type, and as the drafts evolved, Emily lost her status as a narrator and most of her scenes. Herman clearly based much of Kane's second wife, Susan, on Marion Davies: her relationship with Kane; Kane's attempts to control her career; and Davies's own habits of drinking and working jigsaw puzzles. But he did not give her Davies's warm, self-deprecating humor.

Herman and Welles already had decided to open with their Hearst character intoning a mysterious last word, "Rosebud," as he dies. The *March of Time* parody identifies him as the rich, powerful Charles Foster Kane (its rhythm echoes William Randolph Hearst) and provides an overview of Kane's accomplishments, their controversial nature, and the contradictory opinions he has evoked (like accusations both that he was a communist and a fascist). Then the newsreel's dissatisfied editor turns it off and, complaining that it needs an angle, dispatches the reporter Thompson to uncover the meaning of Kane's dying utterance as the key to Kane.

Welles originally wanted the characters' accounts to conflict, as in the later Japanese film *Rashomon*. Herman thought intertwining Kane's life with actual historical events and the various characters' accounts already made their narrative so dense that the accounts should merely overlap and expand on one another. Fortunately Welles conceded, because Herman and Houseman found that even without conflicting accounts, every new scene added complexity. Because the flashback narratives intersected with one another and echoed the *March of Time* newsreel (they called it *News on the March*), every addition and every change required revisiting every preceding scene and narrative to reconcile conflicts and remove repetition.

Their first draft was long and crowded, but much of it was so polished that some of its original scenes remained, word for word, in the finished film. When he dictated Kane's dying word, Rita Alexander asked who Rosebud was. "It isn't a who, it's an it," Herman said.

"What is a rosebud?" Alexander amended.

"It's a sled," Herman explained.

Herman recycled memories of his childhood grief for his lost bicycle to create Charlie Kane's yearning for his sled, but he named the sled for one of his few successful bets, Old Rosebud, a horse that won the 1914 Kentucky Derby.

None of them loved the Rosebud device, but they liked Welles's idea of a quotation from Samuel Coleridge's "Kubla Khan" even less. They considered Rosebud a somewhat embarrassing piece of "dimestore psychology," but they needed it for the plot. Ultimately, Herman interwove it so skillfully that "Rosebud" became the film's most famous line. One persistent story of its origins is that Rosebud was Hearst's nickname for Marion Davies's genitals. Given Herman's penchant for self-destruction, it is certainly plausible. But Herman explained years ago that he had based the sled motif, meant to symbolize Kane's loss of family, childhood, and love, on recollections of his own childhood anguish when his bicycle was stolen. And he had named the sled after Old Rosebud, a 1914 Kentucky Derby winner he successfully bet on during his first year at Columbia. He even planted a hint in the smoky projection room scene. As the journalists speculate about "Rosebud's" meaning, one man says, "A race horse he bet on once, probably—" Another responds, "Yeah—that didn't come in." Rawlston (the editor) asks, "But what was the race?"

Herman reinforced the motif of nostalgic yearning through Bernstein. When Thompson dismisses Mr. Bernstein's suggestion that Kane's

"Rosebud" might refer to "some girl," Bernstein offers a more sympathetic perspective on Kane by echoing the emotion:

> BERNSTEIN: You're pretty young, Mr.—*(Remembers the name)*—Mr. Thompson. A fellow will remember things you wouldn't think he'd remember. You take me. One day, back in 1896, I was crossing over to Jersey on a ferry and as we pulled out there was another ferry pulling in—*(Slowly)*—and on it there was a girl waiting to get off. A white dress she had on—and she was carrying a white parasol—and I only saw her for one second and she didn't see me at all—but I'll bet a month hasn't gone by since that I haven't thought of that girl. *(Triumphantly)* See what I mean? *(Smiles)*

Welles called that his favorite scene in the film and "the best thing in the movie," and noted to Meryman it was Herman's. Sara later said it was autobiographical and that she was always jealous of that unknown girl.

If Mr. Bernstein's cheery, unwavering loyalty to Kane pushes him to the edge of fatuity, he is also granted perspicacity. Summing up Thatcher, he says, "That man was the biggest darned fool I ever met."

Thompson protests, "He made an awful lot of money."

"It's no trick to make a lot of money, if all you want is to make a lot of money. You take Mr. Kane—it wasn't money he wanted. Mr. Thatcher never did figure him out. Sometimes, even, I couldn't . . ."

And when Thompson informs Bernstein that Jed Leland is alive and living at a hospital, he says, "Nothing in particular the matter with him, they tell me. Just—" Bernstein rescues him from embarrassment.

"Just old age. (Smiles sadly) It's the only disease, Mr. Thompson, you don't look forward to being cured of."

The film's eerily lit opening scene is also in the original Victorville script, spookily propelling the viewer into Kane's mysterious estate ("very much UFA," pronounced George Cukor, referring to its German expressionist roots). The backward-winding newsreel parody, "'Path to Tycoon Glory'" is also there, as well as the snow scene in which young Charles is wrenched away from Rosebud and his mother (Agnes Moorehead).

Other iconic scenes await Welles, especially his montages: the breakneck race that moves from Kane's childhood (Thatcher to Charles the child: "Merry Christmas and") into adulthood (Thatcher to Kane the adult: "a Happy New Year."); the breakfast table sequence depicting the deterioration of Kane and Emily's marriage; Kane's slow progress through a hall of mirrors. And of course Welles's breathtaking pace, his

Creating *Kane*: Orson Welles visits. John Houseman reads. Herman's nurse mops his brow. Rancho Verde, 1940.

visual and aural innovations, and all the devices that made the picture so extraordinary.

Those twelve weeks in the Mojave Desert were a magical interlude, a writer's retreat for two—or actually three, since Rita Alexander was present except for one three-week hiatus. Alexander and Herman became so close that Herman took her along when he worked afterward at Twentieth Century Fox, and Herman, Sara, and Houseman remained close for the rest of their lives. That sojourn became part of *Citizen Kane*'s creation myth, but as encapsulating as it felt, they were not uninterruptedly alone. In addition to Sara, who visited every week and sometimes brought Josie, Welles conferred with them by telephone and visited periodically. Welles's assistant Richard Wilson recalled, "We used to go up to Victorville . . . after the radio show every week and let the prisoners out for . . . a breath of air or something, because there were big pressures on them to get a draft. . . . Now three months, allow me to say as a picture maker, is a remarkably short time for one to get from a long draft like that to a shooting [script]." During the last couple of weeks they stepped up the pace even more, because the war in Europe was heating up, and Herman was eager to get home to keep up with the news.

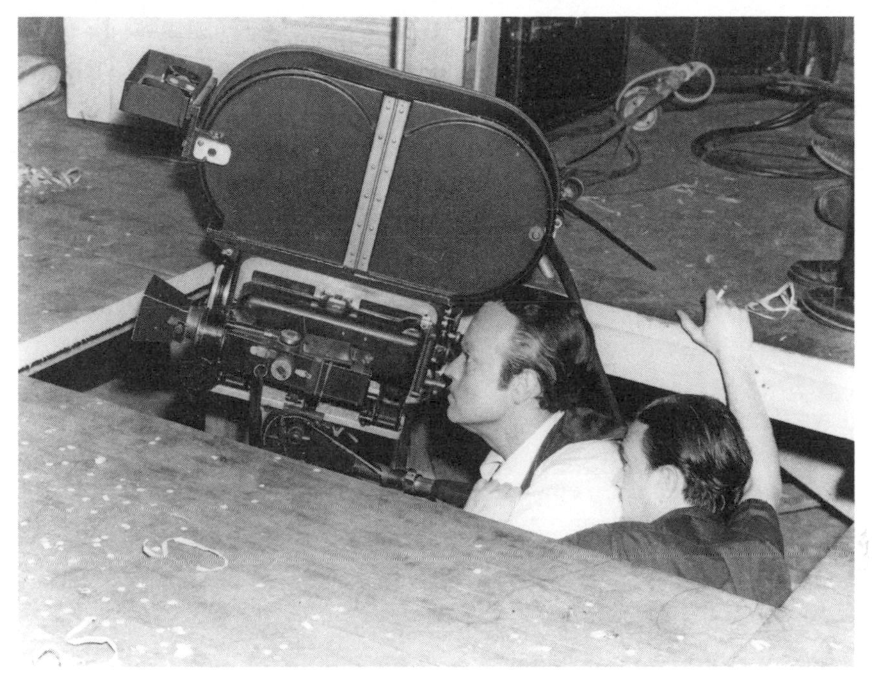

With cinematographer Gregg Toland, Welles explores unusual camera angles.

In late May 1940, they departed in the same two-car procession, detouring at RKO's studio to ceremoniously hand Welles their 325-page manuscript of *The American*. Houseman left for New York a few days later, and Herman went to MGM to work on *Comrade X*, a Hedy Lamarr/Clark Gable picture about an American newspaperman in Moscow secretly filing unflattering articles about Russian Communists.

On June 14, 1940, RKO completed a preliminary budget estimate of $1,081,798, not counting the $150,000 Welles had already spent. Because Welles needed to stay below $1 million, Herman went back on salary and spent the next few weeks rewriting, arguing with Welles, and helping him search for Kane's two wives, the only major roles to be filled from outside Welles's circle. Eventually Welles cast Ruth Warrick as the first Mrs. Kane, but they did not find Dorothy Comingore until late June. After seeing her test, Herman concurred, "She looks precisely like the image of a kitten we have been looking for." Comingore then confessed she was two months pregnant, and Herman wanted to withdraw the offer. Welles overrode him.

With help from Welles and even the actors, Herman kept working to cut the screenplay by half. To evade a rule about uncompensated rehearsing, the cast sometimes gathered at Herman's house, where Sara fed them barbeque and Herman periodically dashed up to his office above the garage to type new lines.

Once actual shooting began, Herman's work was done, but, welcome or not, he visited the set occasionally, and Welles gave him a cameo in the smoky newsreel-room scene. Herman was used to the transformation from page to screen, but he found Welles's innovations so startling that he vacillated among dismay, worry, indignation, and admiration.

Then Louella Parsons quoted Welles saying he had written the film, and Herman called Welles's publicist, Herbert Drake, in a fury. Herman (or rather, "Herman J. Mangel-Wurzel," as Drake called him in his report to Welles), had threatened to "come down" on Welles because he was a "juvenile delinquent credit stealer beginning with the Mars broadcast and carrying on with tremendous consistency." He had Welles "by the _____S," and unless Welles behaved, he was going to take drastic measures like:

1. Take a full page ad in the trade papers.
2. Send a story out on every leased wire in the country. Said story is prepared. [Drake added in pencil, "—sez he!!"]
3. Permit Ben Hecht to write a story for the *Saturday Evening Post.*

Drake added, "Mr. Hecht allegedly is in such a state of moral fervor about your delinquent behavior that he will write this for nothing." Herman had called him because Drake was Welles's "Press Agent and [would therefore] wish to keep my boy's name unbesmirched."

Herman calmed down and called Drake back to offer advice about the rushes: Everett Sloane (Bernstein) was "an unsympathetic looking man," and Welles "shouldn't have two Jews in one scene." (The offending scene included actor William Alland [Thompson] interviewing Bernstein in Bernstein's office.) Herman also worried that with so few close-up and action shots, Welles was not observing "enough standard movie conventions," so the result would seem "too much like a play."

"Mark you,—he thinks the stuff is 'magnificent,'" Drake reported, adding, "If he says it is 'magnificent' I'm beginning to worry. Please understand that he made it a point that he approves very much of what you are doing from the aesthetic point of view, but wonders if the public will understand it." Drake also sent along a couple of Herman's corrections to make the newest versions consistent.

In short, the battle for writing credit on *Citizen Kane* began even before the shooting stopped, and as Herman mentioned, the contretemps was not Welles's first. Earlier that year Welles had heard that Hadley Cantril, a Princeton professor, was writing a book about the *War of the Worlds* broadcast and attributing the script to Howard Koch. Welles had wired him, simultaneously insisting on his own authorship and pleading with Cantril to help protect his reputation. Given Koch's copyright and the evidence provided by the secretary to whom Koch had dictated from his own handwritten manuscript, Cantril stuck to his position, though he tried to placate Welles. He already called it the "Orson Welles Broadcast," on the cover and title page and had hoped Welles and Koch could have settled the matter, but he would strengthen the language "in subsequent printings to state explicitly that you and your associates originally conceived and developed the broadcast."

When *Citizen Kane* later began its ascent to iconhood, Welles usually threw Herman a few crumbs of credit. He always ceded Rosebud, and once it was safe to admit the film was mostly about Hearst, he acknowledged Herman's knowledge and political perspective about Hearst. He usually used phrases like "a few scenes" or mentioned specific pieces of dialogue, like Bernstein's elegiac description of the girl in white on the ferry. But at the time, even after Herman calmed down, his reaction to Parsons's column triggered a general alarm among Welles's coterie. About a week later, Drake reported that Herman understood he had contracted to work for hire: "Mankiewicz says the last thing he wants is for us to write any stories indicating he is the author of CITIZEN KANE, co-author, or had any connection with it. He says he realizes completely that we can't stop the result of a year's four-ply publicity. He will take no action when such things appear. What he wants is simply this. . . . He asks that you don't in a personal interview say that you wrote CITIZEN KANE."

Welles's New York lawyer Arnold Weissberger believed the issue was far from settled and wrote to Welles, "I have reason to believe that Mankiewicz is going to cause trouble in connection with the screen credit for the writing of 'Citizen Kane.'" Weissberger explained that he did not want to say more in writing, but he was still looking into the matter. He had inserted a clause into Herman's contract deeming Mercury the author of anything Herman wrote for Mercury, for the express purpose of denying Herman "any credit whatever," but he had carefully steered clear of the word *credits* to avoid calling Herman's attention to his intention. Not knowing Herman very well (if at all), Weissberger imagined that because Herman had signed the contract, he must not be aware of its implications: "If a man chooses to sell his right to be known as the author of a work, he ought not thereafter to be able to come forward and claim that right, especially in view of the fact that this particular provision in the contract was put in for the very purpose of eliminating that right."

Herman was well aware of the clause—he had worked under similar conditions for his entire career as a studio employee. And as he made clear to Drake, he understood the value to RKO of marketing their Boy Wonder as producer, writer, director, and star of his own picture. But just as Herman was beginning to regret his agreement to the point of searching for a way to circumvent it, Weissberger was beginning to realize that in the motion picture world, copyright ownership, and screen credit were separate issues. He cautioned Welles to say nothing while he checked with the Screen Writers Guild (which at that point was itself embroiled in controversy over that very issue). Once he determined his clause's efficacy, "it will be timely enough to confront Mankiewicz with his contract when he begins to make trouble."

Egged on by Sara, Herman did begin making trouble. Insisting he had written the entire screenplay, he sought full credit, and one of *Citizen Kane*'s most enduring anecdotes is that Herman told Hecht that Welles had offered him $10,000 to forsake his own credit, and asked what he should do. "Take the money and screw the bastard," Hecht supposedly advised. Asked years later if the story was true, Nunnally Johnson said, "I like to believe he did," a response probably prompted more by his affection for Herman than by strong belief in that story's veracity—it sounds more like Herman and Hecht than Welles.

But news of the conflict spread, and it became obvious that despite the number of people he had offended over the years, Herman had many well-wishers in Hollywood. Herman was theirs, warts and all; Welles was the interloper with the outrageous contract. So Herman's indignant rantings about the newcomer's efforts to usurp credit fell on receptive ears, and Hollywood sided with "Mankie." Even the trade press picked up the story.

Arnold Weissberger confirmed that the clause in Herman's contract did allow them to withhold credit, but, he wrote Welles: "I do not suppose that you intend not to give Mankiewicz any credit. On the other hand, the fact that you have the power to exclude him from credit under his agreement can be used by you tactfully to indicate that your allowing him to have credit is a matter of good will on your part."

At first Welles misunderstood, and Richard Baer, another of his assistants (Houseman called them Orson's slaves), wrote Weissberger, "Orson is delighted with the progress made in the Mankiewicz situation," and "delighted to discover that he can say: 'Mankiewicz, you can have this or that credit.'" But he was "anxious to know whether Mankiewicz can make an issue of this which would be brought to the attention of the Screen Writers' Guild so that a public arbitration would be necessary." Not only would that be bad publicity, but Welles himself was a member, and taking it to the extreme might cause the Guild to expel him.

Realizing he had been too subtle, Weissberger wrote, despite their legal rights, "I gather that you feel as I do, that it would be most imprudent to allow a dispute of this sort to be aired. . . . It would be unwise to deny Mankiewicz credit on the screen and have him get credit therefore through the press by publicising his complaint. For that reason, I think it advisable that you make clear to Mankiewicz, as tactfully as possible, the weakness of his legal position without insisting too much upon your intention of enforcing our rights."

Herman eventually did file a protest with the Guild, but then he began to worry about retribution from the Hearst forces. So two days before his hearing, Herman withdrew his complaint. By then Welles had agreed to share credit and even to place Herman's name ahead of his own. Ironically, once that question was resolved, Guild secretary Dore Schary raised another issue: the Guild's prohibition on writing credits for producers unless they had written the entire screenplay. Instituted in response to producers' habit of helping themselves to writing credits, that was the rule that had prevented Joe from taking a writing credit on pictures he produced. Because Schary was an old friend of Herman's, Weissberger worried that Herman might again be inspired to push for sole credit. However, Herman agreed to join Welles in a statement that RKO lawyers drafted for them, and the Guild acquiesced.

RKO and Welles had managed to keep the film's subject under wraps, and once the finished picture emerged from editing, the studio confined it to the lot and banned unauthorized viewing. Hearst had not reacted to other critical portrayals, but no one knew what he would do about a motion picture—movies were a more powerful medium, they reached a much broader audience, and Hearst himself was part of the motion picture community.

Then, in an act of incredible self-sabotage even for Herman, he showed his script to Charles Lederer, Marion Davies's nephew. Herman was no longer welcome at San Simeon, but he remained fond of Marion Davies and did not want her hurt by the Susan Alexander character. Lederer, who assured Herman he saw no resemblance, afterward always insisted he had not shown the script to anyone. But when he returned Herman's script, its pages were filled with pencil lines marking references to Hearst. When Herman saw the marks, he concluded—and continued to believe for the rest of his life—that Hearst had intended to respond to the picture with the same benign neglect he had accorded previous detractors. Louella Parsons confirmed that in her 1961 memoir, writing that Hearst said at the time, "I don't believe in lawsuits. Besides, I have no desire to give the picture any more publicity."

But none of them had thought to worry about potential fallout from competing gossip columnists, and as it turned out, the rivalry between Parsons and Hedda Hopper provoked a battle of intimidation and libel threats that fatally damaged the film's distribution. In July 1941, after *Citizen Kane*'s May 1 New York opening but before its general release, Herman sent an account of the debacle to Alexander Woollcott.

> Harpo ordered me the other day, by phone, to supply you with a report—he was reading from your letter—of the dildos connected with the release of "Citizen Kane." I had already begun some fascinating research in this connection when I happened yesterday to find out it was didoes you were after. With a good deal less enthusiasm, I herewith submit my report:
>
> In the first place, there's the question of how much Mr. Hearst knew about the subject matter of the picture before it was finished. Mr. Lederer, to whom I gave the completed script shortly before it went into production, could probably tell you more accurately whether it reached San Simeon or not. I do know that at a dinner party soon after the picture was completed and was being shown to select audiences in RKO projection rooms, I was bitterly attacked by a lady who had just returned from a week with Marion and Mr. Hearst, on the ground that it was scandalous to have a sequence in which a President of the United States—President Norton, surely you remember President Norton—was assassinated as the culmination of a series of bitter and incendiary attacks upon him by Charles Foster Kane, a publisher. Peculiarly, however, this episode was not

only never shot but was dropped from the script during revisions and was not even included in the script which Mr. Lederer received.

It is my opinion that Mr. Hearst, who is, unberufen, [knock on wood], smart at these things, would have ignored "Citizen Kane," positively and negatively, had he been given the chance. (There are, as you know, two biased and unfavorable "Lives," which he has treated as if they weren't there and which have attracted very little general attention.) But this same behavior was denied him in connection with "Citizen Kane," chiefly, as far as I can find out, because of an idiot named Louella Parsons and a very smart woman named Hedda Hopper.

The general subject matter of "Citizen Kane" was a matter of public knowledge for months to everyone connected with the picture industry, except Miss Parsons, its most comprehensive and authoritative reporter. In fact, just a few weeks before the scandal broke, she had called Orson and asked him to confirm or deny, on his sacred word of honor, her exclusive scoop that "Citizen Kane" was about Communism. Orson denied this.

All during the period of editing the film, Hedda Hopper had begged to be allowed to see the first rough cut. When, for publicity purposes, Orson assembled the picture and arranged to show it, in a very rough form, to "Life" and "Look," Hedda forced her way into the showing. At its conclusion, I am told, she got to her feet, screamed magnificently that this constituted an outrage against a great American, and proceeded to call the great American at San Simeon to tell him what she had just seen. (Hedda has for some time been letting it be known that she would be much better in Louella's job than Louella is, which is true, and it is not impossible that her call was connected with her ambitions.)

Whereupon, Mr. Hearst called Louella and told her about the picture. Louella, every ounce of her suet apoplectic, summoned two Hearst lawyers from down-town Los Angeles, demanded and received an immediate showing of the picture, and at once started telephoning young Bill Hearst, in addition to all the other Hearst executives she could get hold of. She also called George Schaefer, President of RKO, and told him she would run him out of the business.

An immediate order was issued banning all "Citizen Kane" publicity, plus all mention of Welles, myself and others connected with the picture, from the Hearst papers. Mr. Hearst, himself, got in touch with Louis B. Mayer and gave him a calm and unexcited version of the situation as it seemed to him.

To wit: Mr. Hearst had no specific attitude as to whether the picture should be released. He thought this was an attitude the industry should determine. Personally, if he were the motion picture industry and were so beholden to a great friend for past favors and services—almost daily for twenty years there have been requests that some item or other of personal aggrandisement be published in the Hearst columns and frantic cries that some item or other of personal misbehavior be suppressed, the requests and the cries all having been heard and disposed of sympathetically—he would think twice before engaging in behavior that might sour this great friend. Again, any publisher not a great friend of the industry might well consider it his duty to play up the spicy sexual involvements which picture people were always bringing upon themselves. Yet again, the problem of the unduly large extent to which the picture industry is employing refugees, some of whom do not even speak English, was one that a publisher not friendly to the industry might regard it as his duty to present to the American public. One wouldn't have to have at all an unfair presentation in mind. The most objective of stories might bring with it racial and religious connotations, for instance, to a public that isn't as open-minded as it might be.

Mr. Mayer went into action at once. He called Mr. Schaefer and screamed and hollered at him, with no result. (Mr. Schaefer is a hard-headed, unimaginative fellow, whose point was that he had made a picture that was artistically superb, that had cost a lot of money, and that he intended to release it.)

It quickly became difficult, through Mr. Mayer's efforts, for RKO to get bookings for the picture. The Music Hall in New York, for instance, which had the picture scheduled for release on February 14, found that previous bookings made it impossible to keep that date and that there seemed to be little chance to set a new date for months and months and months to come. Harry Warner, who controls an enormous amount of theatres, told RKO he would be delighted to have "Citizen Kane" play his theatres but that, since there were so many rumors about possible law suits, involving many penalties and even jail sentences for local managers, he thought it only a matter of ordinary business precaution

> to ask RKO to provide him with a $5,000,000 indemnity bond. In RKO's present financial situation, a $50.00 indemnity bond would be funny, whereupon this was dropped. The Loewe theatres, controlled by MGM., were obviously out of the question.
>
> The Board of Directors of RKO engaged in a bitter dispute for weeks with themselves and with Mr. Schaefer. I don't know how much authority the Board has over Schaefer, nor do I know what went on, actually, but the final decision of the Board seems to have been to let Schaefer try to release the picture, if he could, without compromising RKO or its theaters. I have an idea this solution was acceptable to Mr. Hearst and Mr. Mayer. For one thing it tended to quiet a sort of public clamor that had sprung up. For another thing, there was a legal obligation in the form of a profit sharing contract that Orson held—he was to receive 20 percent of the profits—which might have become embarrassing were there no release. With a release, however, though it might involve only a handful of theatres, Orson might well have no ground for suit, since the picture <u>had</u> been released and had failed to make a profit. (On the other hand, it's now pretty definite that there will be a general release this Fall.)

After adding that Weissberger might be willing to fill in further, Herman concluded,

> Thanks for your kind words about the writing of the picture. In case you didn't know, I feel it my modest duty to tell you that the conception of the story, the plot, the characters, the manner of telling the story and about 99 per cent of the words are the exclusive creations of
>
> Yours,
>
> HJM[written]

The previous six months that Herman described so entertainingly were actually a nerve-wracking nightmare for everyone connected with the picture. With the acquiescence of other studio heads, Mayer had offered to cover RKO's negative costs if Schaefer would destroy the film, an offer Schaefer withheld from his board for fear they would force him to accept. Hearst encouraged his friend J. Edgar Hoover to put Welles under surveillance and provoke questions about Welles's draft status. His newspapers tried to smear Welles as a communist. Privately, Louella Parsons threatened RKO board members with "fictionized" stories of their lives, and the Rockefellers (who owned Radio City Music Hall) with an exposé of their father, while publicly maintaining a continuous barrage against RKO in her column.

In an effort to create momentum and irresistible demand for its release, RKO ran an advance screening in March for important media, and critics responded enthusiastically, condemning its possible suppression and rhapsodizing about its importance. John O'Hara opened his *Newsweek* review: "It is with exceeding regret that your faithful bystander reports that he has just seen a picture which he thinks must be the best picture he ever saw. With no less regret he reports that he has just seen the best actor in the history of acting. Name of picture: CITIZEN KANE. Name of actor: Orson Welles. Reason for regret: you, my dear, may never see the picture."

Denied a Radio City Music Hall extravaganza on February 14, RKO refurbished its Palace Theatre and opened there on May 1, 1941. Newspaper reviews were equally rapturous. The *New York Tribune*'s Howard Barnes wrote that *Citizen Kane* was "not only a great picture; it is something of a revolutionary screen achievement. From the standpoint of original treatment and technical innovations, one has to go back to "The Birth of a Nation" to find its equal. As a starkly compelling entertainment, using all the tricks and artistry of the cinema, it can only be compared with [John Ford's 1935] 'The Informer.'" Barnes attributed its "fully dimensioned characters" partly to the actors' portrayals but mostly to the "scenario fashioned by the producer-director and Herman J. Mankiewicz, and the brilliant Welles direction." Quoting Herman almost exactly, Barnes applauded the elements Herman had worried about: "Being a daring novice, he has violated many Hollywood conventions—in the grouping of his characters, in his lighting and even in his sets."

The *Times'* Bosley Crowther could not make up his mind. He waxed enthusiastically the morning after the preview, then backpedaled in a Sunday piece a few days later, writing that *Citizen Kane* was "not truly great," because its story relied too much on audience members' relating it to its putative subject. He reversed himself yet again in December, including it in his ten best for the year.

All spring, sympathetic newsmen rallied around Herman. Barnes's colleague Richard Watts Jr., *Tribune* theater critic and former film critic, responded to Barnes's praise of the picture's "so-called innovations" by calling attention to the picture's ability to go "deep into the soul of a singularly unlovely and unlovable man and by its understanding makes him a believable and pathetic human being." He attributed that to the "good, sound dramatic writing, filled with true insight into character," which he considered the picture's "chief virtue," and saluted Herman, who, "I am told . . . is the chief author." In a March *PM* magazine piece, Ben Hecht wrote about Hearst's attempts to suppress the movie, attacked Louis B. Mayer for his part, and tried a bit of preemptive defense: "This movie was not written by Orson Welles. It is the work of Herman J. Mankiewicz, one of the wittiest of the scenario writers. Herman let me read the script before it was shot. 'Do you think,' he asked me, 'that Willie Hearst will figure it's about him? I didn't write it about him but about some of our other mutual friends—a sort of compendium.' I told Herman that it had no more to do with W.R. than with Preston John."

Syndicated columnist Lemuel F. Parton wrote that Herman "seems to have been overlooked—like the soldier who was in the woods cutting down a tree to make himself a wooden leg, while the general was making his victory speech. Reporters, as distinguished from critics, know all about Mr. Mankiewicz as he was a fast and limber leg-man on the New York World in 1922, before he headed into the theater and the movies. . . . He achieved distinction in 1935 when the Nazis barred from the Reich any film that he had anything to do with."

Through it all, Herman and Welles continued what Houseman later called "our long conspiracy of love and hate for Maestro, the Dog-Faced Boy." Two days after the opening, Welles wired Herman,

> DEAR MANKIE. IF YOU HAVEN'T SEEN ALL THE PAPERS I'LL BE GLAD TO SEND THEM ON. IN THE MEANTIME FEEL YOU SHOULD KNOW THAT A LADY NAMED MISS CLOSER HAS BEEN PHONING ME CLAIMING TO BE YOUR ROSEBUD. SHE SAYS SHE HAS WRITTEN HER OWN LIBRETTO THIS IS AN ACTUAL QUOTE AND SOME DAY YOU WILL HAVE TO HEAR HER SING. SHE TELLS ME TO TELL YOU THIS. PLEASE ADVISE. LOVE ORSON

Herman probably wrote the response:

> HERMAN CLAIMS HE'S NEVER HEARD OF THIS MISS CLOSER BUT HE'S MADE SIMILAR CLAIMS BEFORE PERSONALLY AS THE ONLY ORIGINAL AUTHENTIC ROSEBUD I WOULD BE MUCH OBLIGED IF YOU WOULD REPORT DIRECTLY TO ME ON ALL OF HERMAN'S ROSEBUDS YOU MEET GIVING FULL DETAILS INCLUDING WHAT KIND OF SPECTACLES HOW MANY PIMPLES AND SO FORTH STOP ISN'T IT WONDERFUL ABOUT THE PICTURE LOVE SARA

As it turned out, all the well-intentioned efforts to aid Herman or the picture were but puny arrows, bouncing off Hearst's armored juggernaut. Despite ample coverage of Hearst's attacks, the major studios' resistance to exhibiting the film in their theaters so crippled RKO's distribution that despite ecstatic reviews, it barely covered costs.

But even before its release, *Citizen Kane* resurrected Herman from the professional dead, boosting his self-confidence, strengthening his resolve to stay sober, and reinvigorating his career. No longer an alcoholic has-been, he was in demand again. MGM adapted *The Wild Man of Borneo* and based two family pictures (*Keeping Company* [1940] and *This Time for Keeps* [1942]) on one of his short stories. He adapted James Thurber's *My Life and Hard Times* into *Rise and Shine* (1941) for Twentieth Century Fox. At the end of 1941, Samuel Goldwyn hired him to write "The Lou Gehrig Story," which became *Pride of the Yankees* (1942). Paramount started work on *The Good Fellow* (1943). Other assignments never made it to the screen.

Herman and Welles also remained involved. In May 1940 Herman, Welles, and John Houseman had formed United Productions as a West Coast version of the Mercury Theatre, through which they hoped to stage plays in Los Angeles. Instead, United's only production was an adaptation of Richard Wright's novel *Native Son* that Welles directed in New York in 1941. It was a great success, though its combination of Wright's communism (and race) with the story's attack on racism, provided Hearst with additional ammunition in his attempt to paint Welles as a communist.

Despite his understanding RKO's marketing needs, Herman's pleasure in *Citizen Kane*'s success was diminished by its promotion of Welles's quadruple achievements. He continued to assert (as he wrote Pop) that "there isn't one single line in the picture that wasn't in writing—writing from and by me—before ever a camera turned." At forty-three Herman was still on the defensive with his father, especially with his latest bail-out so recent, and both he and Joe still heard Pop's voice in their heads telling them that neither stature in the industry nor financial success could redeem their choice of career. To give Pop his due, he did try to show an interest, dutifully reading the *Hollywood Reporter*, attending their pictures, and even offering professional advice. Find Joan Crawford more substantive roles, he admonished Joe more than once (advice that would have made Crawford yet another of Pop's many fans, had Joe told her).

Hanna generally had more health problems, but in the fall of 1941, Pop felt too ill to teach, so they went to Los Angeles to be near their sons while he recovered his strength. The day after he arrived, Pop collapsed

The power of Pop over his sons lasted their entire lives. Joe wrote on the back of this photograph, "There it is, that look at each other! About something I was not to know—and never did know."

at breakfast. He suffered a cerebral hemorrhage in the hospital a few days later and never recovered consciousness. He died on December 2, two days after his sixty-ninth birthday. Both sons were stunned, and Herman was inconsolable. All hope for absolution, expiation, reconciliation, or any other kind of resolution was lost forever.

The brothers accompanied Pop's body on the train back to New York, and Herman spent the time drinking and talking interminably about his stolen bicycle. He was so drunk when they arrived that a friend had to help Joe manage the coffin. They held a private funeral, but 150 or so friends, relations, and colleagues crowded in to pay tribute and share their memories.

Pop had lived long enough to witness *Citizen Kane*'s glowing reviews and accolades in the *Hollywood Reporter*'s spring poll, but he was gone before it began attracting more meaningful honors. On December 21 the National Board of Review of Motion Pictures named it best picture of 1941. A number of critics put it on their top ten lists. On December 30, the New York Film Critics gave it top honors. On February 8, 1942, *Citizen Kane* was nominated for nine Academy Awards. Welles was

"You can kiss my half," Welles wrote to Herman after their screenplay won *Citizen Kane*'s only Oscar.

nominated for best actor, best director, and, with Herman, best screenplay. (John Ford's *How Green Was My Valley* received ten nominations, and *Sergeant York*, starring Gary Cooper, eleven.)

Because of the war, the Academy tried to tone down the festivities at the Biltmore Hotel, but attendance reached a record sixteen hundred. Neither Welles nor Herman was present. Welles was in Rio de Janeiro, working on a government-sponsored film, and Herman stayed away out of fear of misbehaving. Wearing his bathrobe and slippers, he sat in the bedroom with Sara and Frank, pretending not to listen to the broadcast. When *How Green Was My Valley*—instead of *Citizen Kane*—won the cinematography award, they heard Louella Parsons and her friends cheer loudly. When Preston Sturges announced Herman and Welles for best original screenplay, they heard the same group boo. But they also heard, "Mank! Mank!" and above the general melee, Irene Selznick calling, "Where is he?"

Herman jumped up, grabbed Sara in his arms, and waltzed her around the bedroom, wobbling on the leg he had recently rebroken in an inebriated fall. Sara's mother was visiting the Foxes, and when Olga and Mattie arrived in their nightgowns, Herman danced his mother-in-law around the floor, too. Boos continued every time *Citizen Kane* was mentioned, and by the end of the evening, Herman and Welles had won the film's only award.

Joe was also listening at home, and his joy for Herman was mixed with frustration. "He's got the Oscar and I'm a producer at Metro, goddam it," he thought miserably, telling Rosa, "I don't think I'll ever win an Oscar."

For once, Herman did not bother to hide his pride, and when George Schaefer sent over his statue with "best wishes from a high-priced office boy," Herman happily acceded to Sara's suggestion that they display it in their living room. Welles wrote,

> Here's what I wanted to wire you after the Academy Dinner:
> "You can kiss my half."
> I dare to send it through the mails only now that I find it
> possible to enclose a ready-made retort. I don't presume to write
> your jokes for you, but you ought to like this:
> "Dear Orson: You don't
> know your half from a
> whole in the ground."
> Affectionately

Herman did not live to witness *Citizen Kane*'s enshrinement in the canon—or the development of a canon, for that matter. That probably started with the 1962 poll by British Film Institute's magazine *Sight & Sound*, when critics from all over the world voted *Citizen Kane* the top motion picture of all time. It was number one again in 1972, 1982, 1992, and 2002. Not until 2012 did it slip to second place, behind Alfred Hitchcock's *Vertigo* (1958), which had been gaining on it.

Nor did Herman live to experience his own resurrection, canonization, and demotion, all of which cried out for his mordant comments. In 1971, eighteen years after Herman's death and thirty years after the picture's release, the *New Yorker* published critic Pauline Kael's "Raising Kane," a two-part, fifty-thousand-word polemic disparaging the film and attacking Orson Welles as a credit hog who had unfairly deprived Herman of the recognition he deserved for writing the script. The essay was written to be an introduction to a Bantam Books edition of the screenplay, but the *New Yorker* ran it first in its February 20 and 27 issues, reaching a more diverse audience than the screenplay's potential readers. Most members of the general moviegoing, *New Yorker*–reading public were oblivious to the fact that Kael's story of the film's creation was a tendentious account owing more to her professional disagreements with fellow film critics than to any real desire to set the record straight on that particular film.

Kael had been feuding for years with film critic Andrew Sarris, *Cahiers du cinema*'s Nouvelle Vague filmmakers, and other adherents of the auteur theory, which she rejected with characteristic vehemence. To oversimplify, auteur theory postulated that directors with enough creativity and vision should be respected as their films' actual authors, a prominence that implicitly diminished the importance of the contributions by screenwriters, designers, cinematographers, and musicians, as well as singling out some directors Kael (and other critics) considered less than stellar. A not-inconsiderable aspect of *Citizen Kane*'s appeal to the *Sight & Sound* polls' critics was that Orson Welles was so obviously an auteur, so completely was the picture a product of his individual talents. If Welles had actually written the script, so much the better.

That was what Kael set out to demolish. But her claims on Herman's behalf were so hyperbolic and her dismissal of Welles so patently unfair that Welles's admirers—who were, and are, deservedly, legion—have been punishing Herman, Kael, and John Houseman (a major Kael source) ever since. Kael attributed virtually the entire script to Herman. She also argued that, rather than a masterpiece created by one man in spite of the studio system, the film was an example of the studio system at its best.

Welles had unquestionably minimized Herman's role over the years. "He wrote several important scenes," he told interviewers for *Cahiers du cinema* in 1964. "I was very lucky to work with Mankiewicz: everything concerning Rosebud belongs to him." The meaning of Welles's next few sentences isn't difficult to infer, though the translation is execrable: "As for me, sincerely, he doesn't please me very much; he functions, it is true, but I have never had complete confidence in him. He serves as a hyphen between all the elements." Then he praised Gregg Toland's cinematography and the actors.

However, restoring Herman to the *Citizen Kane* narrative hardly required Kael's over-the-top attacks on Welles. She even chose not to interview him, though Welles was alive and well. Kael's argument on behalf of the studio system was not implausible (though she appalled readers familiar with the mechanics of filmmaking with her ignorance of the process). But as John Houseman said in a 1974 oral history, "The whole thing is idiotic; it's not worth discussing. Herman Mankiewicz wrote it but it's Orson's picture just as *Stage Coach* is John Ford's picture, even though Dudley Nichols wrote it. Orson brings these things on himself by trying to take credit for everything. Pauline Kael got all her facts right but just carried her conclusions too far."

Andrew Sarris responded that spring, with "Citizen Kael vs. Citizen Kane," a defense of film and filmmaker that stretched over several issues of the *Village Voice* and observed that "if we shall always remember Welles from *Citizen Kane*, it is not so much because he created it as because it created him and because also, in some ineffable way, he has never been unworthy of it." The controversy raged on for years. Robert Carringer, a film scholar who studied all the screenplay revisions and wrote extensively on Welles, wrote of Herman in *The Making of Citizen Kane*:

> His principal contributions were the story frame, a cast of characters, various individual scenes, and a good share of the dialogue. . . . Welles added the narrative brilliance. . . . He also transformed Kane from a cardboard fictionalization of Hearst into a figure of mystery and epic magnificence. Citizen Kane is the only major Welles film on which the writing credit is shared. Not coincidentally, it is also the Welles film that has the strongest story, the most fully realized characters, and the most carefully sculpted dialogue. Mankiewicz made the difference. While his efforts may seem plodding next to Welles's flashy touches of genius, they are of fundamental importance, nonetheless.

There is no perfect way to allocate credit, and it shouldn't matter, anyway. At the time the extravagance of Kael's claims embarrassed even Sara. But as ridiculous as she considered Kael's 100 percent, she had her limits. Carringer attributed about 60 percent of the final film's words to Herman, and when Meryman used that figure in his biography of Herman, Sara summoned him to her house. With Herman's Oscar statuette prominently displayed on her mantel and the supportive presence of Mattie Fox at her side, the diminutive octogenarian shook her finger at the biographer. "You may think it's over," she warned, "but it's not." Frank also visited Meryman in New York to protest; he always believed his father wrote the entire screenplay.

Joe rarely spoke publicly about Herman's role, but in 1991, he said,

> My brother, Herman, was the most knowledgeable man I ever knew about the American political scene from, let's say 1850 to the present day. And if anyone knew Hearst, Herman knew Hearst. Knew about him. Had read everything about him. . . . Did Orson Welles write the screenplay or did he not? Orson Welles caught lightning in a bottle with that first deal he made, in which he was the complete boss of everything . . . He did a brilliant job. But he also had the most incredible ego. . . . Now, given this power, do you think that, having written the screenplay, do you think he'd take second billing to a man who was in no other way connected with that film?

CHAPTER 13

Apprentice Director

HERMAN'S OSCAR ONLY MADE JOE HUNGRIER. BUT DESPITE ALL HIS hard work, the best move of Joe's career was, like Herman's, an accident, though Joe's did not involve automotive vehicles. When he ejected out of MGM in 1943, Joe's contract ran another three years, which meant the studio could assign him wherever it chose. MGM allowed Joe's agent, Bert Allenberg, to pursue all possibilities, and Joe went to Twentieth Century Fox (Fox), which had been created in 1935 by a merger between the old Fox Films and the newer Twentieth Century, which was founded by Joseph Schenck, Darryl F. Zanuck, and William Goetz.

Joe considered Schenck ("one of the great poker players of all time") to be "as honest and gentlemanly as his brother [Loew's chairman Nicholas] was devious and dishonest." Zanuck had been so prolific a Warner Brothers writer that he wrote scripts under more than one name and became head of production at twenty-five. William Goetz had contributed $100,000 to the merger, courtesy of his father-in-law, Louis B. Mayer, who wanted to equalize Goetz's stature with David Selznick's. With Zanuck at the helm, and because the studio's only important stars were Shirley Temple and Will Rogers (who died in 1935), Twentieth Century Fox treated its writers relatively well.

Joe negotiated with Schenck because "Darryl was away liberating Africa" and made two requests. Because he was leaving the industry's top studio for a lesser one, he wanted a raise for the sake of his image, and he wanted the opportunity to direct as well as write. Joe's contract allowed him to write, direct and produce, and Fox treated Joe as a catch from the beginning, assigning him a spacious bungalow for an office and assuring him use of the studio's top resources for his pictures.

Just as John Houseman brought out the best in Herman, Joe did his best work under Darryl F. Zanuck. Physically tiny, Zanuck was a metaphorical giant, the prototypical Hollywood executive and real-life tycoon upon whom countless celluloid characters were modeled. Expert in polo and pugilism, he strode through the studio in jodhpurs with a phalanx of yes-men in his wake, goosing stars with his riding crop, and barking out commands between puffs on a giant cigar. His workday began about eleven and ended around four the following morning, interrupted only from four to four thirty in the afternoon, when he retired to a private chamber for sex with a starlet, usually a different one each day. After the war he discontinued only the sex breaks; he was still the same tycoon.

Zanuck oversaw every Fox film through every phase of production, from script and casting through rushes and beyond, monitoring every detail, from makeup and hair to the director's adherence to the schedule and number of takes. He had his weaknesses—casting was not his strong point—but he was the perfect boss for Joe. Most importantly, he forced Joe to streamline. As Nunnally Johnson recalled, "I always thought Zanuck had a Geiger counter in his head. Zanuck would read a script and the minute it got dull or didn't move or went off the track—tick-tick-tick! He'd go back two or three pages and figure out where the movement stopped or went wrong."

Zanuck would negotiate with writers and directors until he approved the final script. Then he allowed no deviation, even if the director was also the writer. Fox writers still had to tolerate screenwriters' lowly status—their credits appeared in smaller letters than producers' and directors'; they were not invited to premieres; directors still received the public credit. But for the first time, Joe had a superior who shared his priorities (up to a point) and whose own strengths complemented his. Joe spent the rest of his years in Hollywood complaining about the industry and chafing under its restraints, but the studio system served him well. The training and opportunities available to him at Fox enabled Joe eventually to make the kind of pictures he wanted (again, up to a point).

Nunnally Johnson had adapted A. J. Cronin's bestselling novel *The Keys of the Kingdom* before leaving Fox, and Zanuck showed his confidence in Joe by assigning him to write and produce what was to be the studio's second-most important film of the year (Zanuck's Woodrow Wilson biopic was first). Joe threw himself into the story of Father Francis Chisholm, a Catholic missionary in China, only to find himself enmeshed in what seemed like endless rewrites. He had endured intense script conferences before, but Zanuck's, which frequently started at ten or eleven at night, were the extreme-sports version. When Zanuck pronounced his first draft too long, Joe tried blaming the excess length on his detailed instructions. Zanuck wasn't buying. He knew scripts, and

Rosa hoped starring in *Keys of the Kingdom* with Gregory Peck would revive her career.

Joe's needed major surgery: "You have done a magnificent job . . . [and] greatly improved the book . . . [but] I am a very good judge of the length of a script and I judge this to be considerably longer than GONE WITH THE WIND."

At the next day's script conference, Zanuck offered concrete suggestions. Don't worry about deviating from the book, he counseled. "In GRAPES OF WRATH we took out one of the most important elements of the book, the starvation, and yet people talked about how true to the novel it was. In HOW GREEN WAS MY VALLEY we left out the strikes, and there was no criticism of the picture on that score."

When Fox cast him as Father Francis, Gregory Peck was already an acclaimed theater actor, but he was shooting only his first film at RKO. Zanuck planned to rely on Ingrid Bergman's proven box office appeal as the haughty Mother Superior. Then Bergman became unavailable, and Fox awarded the role to Rosa, who, according to Hedda Hopper, had gotten the part on her own. That is, Rosa had found a manager and secured the test before Joe knew about it, thus putting "her husband Joe Mankiewicz in a spot." That scenario is so unlikely that the studio probably fed it to Hopper to forestall accusations of nepotism.

Twentieth Century Fox also publicized Rosa as a wife and mother, with "Tommy," Chris, and Lucky.

Then Bergman became available again, and Zanuck wanted to use her. Gregory Peck was generating interest, but he was still a newcomer, and Rosa had not appeared on screen since 1939. To assuage Rosa's disappointment, Zanuck offered her a two-picture contract, which was a generous offer. Rosa resisted, however, so Joe begged him to let her keep the role to help save his marriage. Before Zanuck had to choose between box office insurance and Joe's marriage, Bergman decided she was no longer interested, and Rosa played the part.

Rosa's sensitive performance attracted only praise, but her appearance failed to rescue either her career or her marriage. She received no more offers, and in November 1944 Joe moved out. When she left for the picture's New York opening a few weeks later, however, Joe took her to the train, and eventually they reconciled.

Joe expected sole writing credit, but Nunnally Johnson challenged him, and the Screen Writers Guild determined they should share it. To avoid Oscar competition for *Wilson,* Fox delayed its release until 1945, and though they opened to mixed reviews, the picture earned four Academy Award nominations. One of them was best actor for Gregory Peck, whose career was taking off.

Joe's first directing assignment was based on Anya Seton's gothic thriller, *Dragonwyck,* which he had originally dismissed. "I can imagine no woman preferring the hero to the villain in this case, for either bed or breakfast. The melodrama must inevitably conflict and suffer by comparison with REBECCA and SUSPICION. The politico-economic applications are naïve, over-simple and made unexciting by the times in which we live." However, he added, "The background is new, the opportunities for production are exciting, and the cost will be overwhelming." He later distanced himself from the picture (melodrama was "not exactly my cup of witches' brew"), saying he only wrote and directed it to help Ernst Lubitsch, for whom he "would have written and directed the Pomona telephone book." Lubitsch needed to produce rather than direct while recovering from a heart attack.

Dragonwyck is the estate belonging to Nicholas van Ryn, a powerful mid-nineteenth century patroon (landowner) in New York's Hudson River area. After he brings his beautiful cousin Miranda to live with his family, he poisons his invalid wife and marries Miranda, hoping for a son to carry on his line. When their infant son dies, Nicholas retreats into opium and tries to murder Miranda, who falls in love with the local doctor. The doctor supports Nicholas's tenant farmers, whose confrontation with their patroon ends in Nicholas's violent death. Joe's material about the patroon system, religion and class enriched the melodrama, though, as usual, it made his script much too long: "The characters talk and talk and talk, and incidentally their talk is very good but they talk so much that there are no surprises left and there is no chance for acting left," Zanuck advised.

Zanuck had wanted Gregory Peck and John Hodiak for Nicholas and the doctor but had to settle for Vincent Price and Glenn Langan, with Gene Tierney as Miranda. Lubitsch had badgered Tierney into the performance he sought in *Heaven Can Wait* (1943), but Joe approached her more gently. From the beginning, Joe communicated softly but explicitly, in contrast to the many directors who humiliated actors or called for take after take, sometimes without offering any explanation of what they wanted. Believing that less beautiful actresses like Bette Davis tended to be the most profound, Joe consciously worked to develop the skills to direct actresses like Tierney, who he believed needed more from a director. As Tierney's marriage to designer Oleg Cassini deteriorated during production, she and Joe fell into an affair.

Joe's affairs were usually with the more beautiful, less skilled actresses like Tierney, but it would be inaccurate (and churlish) to imagine he used the relationships solely to get the performances he wanted—he so clearly

Making *Dragonwyck* (1946), Vincent Price watches Gene Tierney and Joe make eyes at each other.

relished the entire process of seduction, romance, intrigue. But it didn't hurt. He was drawn to beautiful leading ladies slightly in distress whom he could rescue and educate. If Herman liked Spencer Tracy–Katharine Hepburn jousting, Joe cast himself as a more traditional romantic hero, though both he and Herman consistently created strong female characters in their scripts.

Tierney's feelings were obvious to those around them, though Price, who believed all the women in the studio were a little in love with Joe, assumed it was merely an actress's crush on her director. He was right. Tierney soon transferred her affections to a visitor to the set; she continued her affair with handsome war veteran John F. Kennedy until Kennedy ended it when he decided to run for office.

Jessica Tandy, who, with her husband, Hume Cronyn, was already a close friend of Joe's, played Miranda's crippled Irish maid. Anne Revere, who had won an Oscar as Elizabeth Taylor's mother in *National Velvet*, played Miranda's mother. Walter Huston was Miranda's father. Surrounded by a seasoned cast along with Lubitsch hovering over his shoulder, Joe became so self-conscious that at one point, he peered into his cameraman's lens finder, merely to look like he knew what he was doing. The cameraman was Arthur Miller, one of the industry's top cinematographers (he already had two Oscars for *How Green Was My Valley*

Directing for the first time among so many seasoned professionals made Joe so nervous that he looked through the wrong end of a lens finder.

and *The Song of Bernadette*), and Miller gently took the lens finder from Joe, turned it the right way around, and handed it back to him, along with some advice that Joe passed along for the rest of his career.

Miller had learned from all the great directors with whom he worked, and Joe should do the same. Try to utilize the knowledge of the veterans around him. Ask his cameraman for advice, which he could take or not. If he took it, he could even pretend that had been his intention all along. Joe not only followed and repeated Miller's counsel, he recycled the humiliating incident a few years later, having Bill, the director in *All About Eve*, say, "Remember when I looked through the wrong end of a lens finder?"

Being sidelined frustrated Lubitsch, who at one point turned to Tierney and moaned, "What have I done? How could I give our picture to this novice? He knows nothing." After Joe shot a scene where Nicholas berates Miranda in their bedroom, Lubitsch sent Joe an angry memo saying the arrogant patroon would have closed the door so the servants could not hear them. Joe contritely acknowledged his error, but by the end of production, Lubitsch and Joe were barely speaking. Eventually they reconciled, remaining close until Lubitsch's death a few years later.

Vincent Price was sufficiently impressed by Joe's first directorial effort to predict that Joe's "insight into character and story" would, "if you want it, make you one of the great directors." Price was already grateful to Joe for giving him the role. He had played the fat Monsignor in *Keys of the Kingdom,* and Joe said he envisioned Nicholas as very thin and commanding. Price lost thirty pounds, and Joe gave him the role, but he also had Price laced into a tight corset to make him look even slimmer and to help him maintain a stiff posture. Just before the scene where Nicholas proposes to Miranda, Joe reminded Price to hold himself erect throughout the scene. Then after demanding complete quiet from the crew, he called out, "Now, Vincent, are you ready? Remember, nice erection!" Cast and crew broke up.

Joe's next assignment was "The Lonely Journey," a film noir so convoluted that Joe gathered screenwriter Howard Dimsdale, director/acting coach Lee Strasberg, W. Somerset Maugham, and their producer, Anderson Lawler, at George Cukor's house to attempt a rewrite. It became *Somewhere in the Night* (1946), which Joe opened with subjective shots of amnesiac war veteran George Taylor (John Hodiak) awakening in a ward where he is healing from his wounds. On a nightmarish quest to recover his identity, Taylor visits menacing Los Angeles neighborhoods, alternately eluding and succumbing to various exotic predators, sometimes assisted by Christy (Nancy Guild), a nightclub singer who seems to know some people from his past.

As an inexperienced former college student, Guild (studio publicity rhymed it with "wild") was extremely self-conscious among the professionals, so Joe decided to build her confidence by eating lunch with her every day. Like a good psychiatrist, he drew out her life story, and his patient developed an intense transference, also known as a "wild mad crush." Joe reciprocated with a therapeutic countertransference of his own.

When Guild refused his advances because he was married, Joe told her, with an uncharacteristic lack of originality, "She doesn't understand me." The sophisticated Guild of later years regretted her naiveté and wished she had had an affair with him, but at the time Joe reminded her too much of her father, telling her what to read and appealing to her intellect instead of her appearance. As Vincent Price had noticed, Guild was only one of the many young women around the studio with crushes on Joe. Several, including John Ford's daughter, even formed a Joe Mankiewicz fan club. They had themselves photographed looking at his picture and, though they allowed Guild to join, they refused Gene Tierney and Peggy Cummins. Basking in his groupies' adulation, Joe gave them photographs and individually chosen presents, and met them for weekly lunches.

Joe enjoyed his roomy bungalow and hefty $175,000 salary, but in February 1946 Bert Allenberg began negotiating with producer Hal Wallis, who had left Warner Brothers to form his own company at Paramount. Although Joe announced publicly in May that he would be leaving, he and Wallis failed to come to terms, so in June he signed a long-term contract with Fox. Over the next eighteen months, he directed three films adapted by Philip Dunne from works by popular authors—John P. Marquand's *The Late George Apley*, R. A. Dick's *The Ghost and Mrs. Muir*, and John Galsworthy's play *Escape*—and consciously used them as a directing apprenticeship to develop his skills.

As he wrote in "Film Author! Film Author!" in the May 1947 issue of the *Screen Writer* (the Guild's magazine), he wanted to direct to protect what he had written. Later in life he again directed screenplays written by others but Joe always considered directing second-best to writing.

> Writing and directing moving pictures . . . should be . . . the two components of an hyphenated entity . . . the direction of a screen play is the second half of the writer's work, or . . . the writing of a screen play is the first half of the director's work . . . a properly written screen play *has already been directed* [emphasis his]. . . . Thus the size of the image, the camera angle, the length of the cut, the tempo of movement and speech, the stage of characterization, the reading of the line, the need and nature of musical background—in short, the film must be before the screen writer's eyes and in his mind as he writes.

Joe assumed most writers shared his desire to direct so that they, too, could be "film authors," and he blamed their lack of opportunities on their own lack of originality. Too few of them wrote screenplays of the quality of *The Great McGinty* or *Citizen Kane*, he wrote, in an interesting selection of examples. Preston Sturges was an obvious choice of writer/director, but what to make of Joe's reference to *Citizen Kane*?

Joe respected Philip Dunne, and *The Late George Apley* (1947) was a gentle period piece, more congenial to Joe's sensibility than his two previous projects, and a prestige production for Fox. Every studio competing

Joe thought working with Rex Harrison in *The Ghost and Mrs. Muir* (1947) improved Gene Tierney's acting.

for Marquand's 1938 Pulitzer Prize–winning portrait of Boston's turn-of-the-century ruling class had courted Ronald Colman, who waited two years for the right script.

In *The Ghost and Mrs. Muir*, Joe directed Gene Tierney for the second time and Rex Harrison for the first time. Harrison could be difficult, but Joe, who often described him as a Stradivarius, appreciated his dedication and talent, and they eventually made four pictures together. Harrison, who was adept at handling Joe's dialogue-rich scripts, appreciated Joe, too, even in his earliest days as a director. "Actors have the advantage of comparing directors," he reflected years later, whereas "directors have no chance of comparing themselves to other directors." He respected Joe's ability to recognize actors' vulnerability and put them at ease, and as a perfectionist himself, he valued Joe's meticulous preparation.

Joe always arrived on the set with every move planned. He knew how he wanted every line delivered, including at what rhythm and with what inflection. He usually asked actors if they found his choice comfortable and would adapt if necessary, but only up to a point. His tactful practice of whispering to each actor rather than publicly critiquing their work was uncommon when he started, and Harrison applauded it, because actors are "always either inwardly or outwardly nervous." Soon, Joe also stopped declaring, "Action!" and let the actors start themselves when they felt ready. Reasoning that they could hear the camera whirring, he felt they had enough to deal with, and that once they became used to it, they liked the freedom.

Harrison played the ghost of a salty sea captain in turn of the century England who tries unsuccessfully to scare away Lucy Muir, a spunky young widow who has rented his house. The story's combination of fantasy and earthy humor was so appealing that it became the basis of a 1960s television series. Critics, who were generally positive, were unsurprised by Harrison's skill, and they damned Tierney with faint praise. However, John Ford, who had directed Tierney in *Tobacco Road*, wrote to congratulate Joe on his "pure unaffected direction" and called Tierney's performance "superb." A thrilled Joe responded that he had just seen an old diary entry in which he had despaired of ever coming "within even hailing distance of you as a director," so Ford's note was "the highest award I could have asked for, and I shall always treasure it with great pride. Because to me you are the master, and praise from the master is praise indeed."

At Rex Harrison's request, Fox purchased the rights to *Escape*, a 1930 film starring Gerald du Maurier and Edna Best that had been adapted a from a nine-episode, 1926 John Galsworthy play about an escapee from Dartmoor prison. Joe hesitated when Zanuck offered him the picture, but eventually he accepted and went to England to film it. *Escape* was the first postwar American picture shot entirely in Britain in order to take advantage of a US–British agreement intended to revitalize the British film industry. While Joe was filming interiors at Denham Studios and on location at Dartmoor prison and environs, Zanuck wired to ask about his next assignment. "I REALIZE THAT YOU ARE OCCUPIED WITH ESCAPE BUT IT IS IMPORTANT THAT I KNOW HOW MUCH PROGRESS YOU HAVE MADE ON LETTER TO FIVE WIVES YOU GAVE ME THE IMPRESSION YOU WERE GOING TO. . . . PROBABLY HAVE THE FIRST SCRIPT COMPLETED BEFORE YOU STARTED SHOOTING ESCAPE."

Joe had not, but struggling with recalcitrant British crews, he responded, "Your use of the word 'occupied' in connection with 'ESCAPE' shows a talent for understatement I didn't know you had. Unless you meant it in its military sense . . ." As he later complained to his producer, William Perlberg, "J. Arthur [Rank] and his cohorts are really slipping us the finger, Bill. We have a crew and staff of over a hundred people, of whom perhaps six show any signs of having been connected with the making of a picture at some previous time. . . . They don't want to work, and they don't know how to work."

When they returned to Denham, Joe unwound by taking walks at night with twenty-year-old Sam Goldwyn Junior and talking about the power their fathers still held over them (Goldwyn Senior was still alive). Once he saw *Escape*'s rushes, Zanuck sent praise and let Joe keep the Five Wives assignment. A new phase of his career was about to begin.

CHAPTER 14

Promised Land

WHILE THEY WERE WORKING ON *ESCAPE*, JOE TOLD REX HARRISON HE hoped never again to direct pictures he had not written, and from the moment he read John Klempner's *Letter to Five Wives*, Joe wanted to write and direct it. Klempner had expanded his 1945 *Cosmopolitan* story into a 1946 novel that examined five marriages in an affluent, postwar American suburb, and after several Fox writers, including Joe, tried unsuccessfully failed to transform it into a workable film property, producer Sol Siegel hired novelist Vera Caspary.

Klempner had written little more than portraits of five mediocre marriages as recalled by each wife when each receives a sexy divorcee's letter saying she is eloping with one of their husbands. Siegel and Caspary removed one of the wives and made the divorcée an unseen narrator. After Caspary fashioned eight spouses and four marriages that were less generic and more individual, Zanuck tried to assign it to Ernst Lubitsch, but Siegel fended him off. Not only was Lubitsch in ill health, but Siegel wanted Joe. And Joe wanted Four Wives: "I knew I had looked upon the Promised Land," he later recollected.

Zanuck, however, did not want Joe. "For Chrissake, that arrogant bastard," he complained to Siegel. "I can't get along with him now, after four flops. If he gets a hit with this, he'll be unlivable." Like Herman, Joe often made it obvious that he considered himself the smartest one in the room, and at the moment his lack of humility was exacerbated by the fact that Nicholas Schenck and Louis B. Mayer had approached him about taking over Irving Thalberg's old job (they also tried Walter Wanger and David Selznick).

Although Zanuck wanted to start production before Joe would be available, he acceded to Siegel, and Joe promised to finish the screenplay before he left to shoot in England. Joe failed and while he was abroad, Schenck pressured Zanuck to fire Joe, because, despite his pictures' good reviews, his box office receipts were disappointing. Zanuck resisted but sent Joe a stern reprimand about his tardy screenplay, accompanied by a list of Joe's failings, past and present.

Joe was stung.

> In view of what appears to be a pretty disheartening financial record, I must be considered a rather expensive luxury at the present time . . .
>
> How can a director control costs? By finishing on schedule? I finished "The Late George Apley" seven days ahead of schedule—and over budget! Nor was it I who broke Gene Tierney's foot during "The Ghost and Mrs. Muir." Should a director have his work laid out in advance? My cameraman has always known every set-up in a scene before we started it. I have to date never changed a set-up. I don't believe in lengthy rehearsals. I am about average in the number of takes I make. You have mentioned over-shooting to me only once—in the Ghost's farewell scene. You will find that every angle I shot was in the final cut. . . . I'm not trying to whitewash myself, Darryl, . . . I would appreciate some realistic constructive advice in the matter. Merely to point out that my last two films cost too much money and were box-office flops, doesn't necessarily mean that I am an expensive director. It may mean that I am a bad director—which is always a frightening possibility.

But Zanuck's point was taken, and after Joe returned, he worked at a rented house in Malibu, and on Saturday, April 17, recorded, "FADE OUT, THE END at 11 P.M. 9 weeks and 1 day . . ." He created even more distinctive individuals, with more interesting homes and home lives and more complex marital problems. His dialogue turned soap opera into high comedy, and he added characters and satirical situations that commented on social mores and contemporary issues. He removed the wives' internecine bitchiness, consigning all bitchiness to the unseen, husband-stealing narrator, Addie Ross. Zanuck wrote Siegel that Joe's script was "magnificent, one of the best scripts of its type I have ever read. It looks like at long last Mr. Mankiewicz is going to be associated with a very big picture."

With what Joe admiringly called an "almost bloodless operation," Zanuck then shortened it by suggesting Joe eliminate the least interesting of the four couples. In Joe's final version, the wives receive Addie's telegram just as they embark on a boat to take underprivileged children on

In *A Letter to Three Wives* (1948), Lora Mae Hollingsway (Linda Darnell), Rita Phipps (Ann Sothern), and Deborah Bishop (Jeanne Crain) receive the fateful letter from Addie Ross (Celeste Holm).

a daylong trip. Unable to reach their husbands, each wife recalls scenes from her marriage as she wonders if her husband is the one eloping with Addie (Celeste Holm).

Deborah Bishop (Jeanne Crain) is a former farm girl who met Brad (Jeffrey Lynn), the town catch, when both were in uniform during the war. Out of her depth at her first country club dance, she recalls, she was so nervous about her dowdy, out-of-style dress that she drank too much and popped her seams on the dance floor.

In an unusually sympathetic portrayal of a middle-class professional woman trying to juggle husband, children, and household, Rita Phipps (Ann Sothern) writes radio soap operas and makes more money than her husband, George (Kirk Douglas), a high school English teacher. Rita flashes back to a dinner party she gave in hopes that her boss, Mrs. Manleigh (note the name), would hire George, so he could make more money. Channeling Joe, who started including mouthpiece characters in his films when he could, George kills that scheme with complaints about underpaid and underappreciated educators, grammar, the inanities of radio programming, the ills of modern advertising, and the debasement of the culture in general.

One of Joe's earliest mouthpieces, high school teacher George Phipps (Kirk Douglas), holds forth on the regrettably low status of teachers and the inanities of radio programs, during the Phipps's disastrous dinner party.

> GEORGE: "I'm a school teacher. That's even worse than being an intellectual. Schoolteachers are not only comic, they're often cold and hungry in this richest land on earth . . ."

Joe gave the Phipps a wisecracking maid named Sadie (Thelma Ritter), whose damning compliment of radio—"I can understand it even when I'm not listenin'"—sets up one of the few double entendres he was able to slip in.

> MRS. MANLEIGH: Sadie may not realize it, but whether or not she thinks she's listening, she's being penetrated.
> GEORGE: It's a good thing she didn't hear you say that.
> MRS. MANLEIGH: After penetration comes saturation, and when she's saturated, she'll find herself recommending products to her employers.
> LORA MAE HOLLINGSWAY: Not Sadie. I've seen her when she was saturated to the eyes.

Issues of class permeate all three marriages but are most explicit in the story of Lora Mae (Linda Darnell) and Porter Hollingsway (Paul Douglas). Porter is a self-made chain store owner who aspires to "class"—as embodied by Addie Ross—though he marries Lora Mae Finney, one of his employees. Porter's lavish living room is full of bookshelves devoid of books. Before her marriage Lora Mae Finney lived not merely on the wrong side of the tracks but right next to them: every time a train rattles by, the Finneys pause mid-sentence and bounce during its noisy passage, then resume talking where they left off (as Joe and his family had, when they lived next to New York's Third Avenue El). Porter resents Lora Mae for using sex appeal to marry him for his money and fails to realize Lora Mae genuinely loves him. Their segment is the most poignant as well as the most comedic.

Joe added other touches as well. Deborah's torn dress and George's broken record are physical manifestations of the threat to one of their marriages, a motif he rounds out with Lora Mae tearing her own stocking as an excuse to show off her legs to Porter, and a breaking cocktail glass at the end.

Siegel and Joe convinced Zanuck that shooting exteriors in the East would add authenticity, but when rain kept them indoors for nine straight days, Joe and Linda Darnell used the time to begin an affair that lasted, on and off, for the next six years. Fox had signed Monetta Eloyse Darnell as a fifteen-year-old Dallas sophomore, and she had eloped at nineteen with a forty-two-year-old cameraman. When she tried to leave him to marry Howard Hughes, Hughes jilted her. By the time she became involved with Joe, Linda Darnell was a twenty-four-year-old veteran of twenty-four pictures who faked sophistication with drinking, smoking, and excessive swearing.

Their affair became an open secret when they returned to Los Angeles, and Joe spent lunch hours in Darnell's dressing room. When they finished shooting, Darnell tried to repair her marriage by taking a vacation with her husband, but she spent much of the trip drinking heavily and living for Joe's telegrams, which often included an outlaw alias ("Dillinger has a sunburned nose and looks like a banana split," arrived in New Orleans). With her distorted childhood and overbearing stage mother, Linda Darnell was Judy Garland lite, and as usual Joe urged her to go into therapy. Also like Garland, Darnell knew Joe had no intention of leaving Rosa but considered him the love of her life.

In October 1948 Joe was back in New York to shoot exteriors for his next film, and with both Rosa and Darnell there, he was busy juggling his needy mistress and his even needier wife. Rosa had been cast in *Bravo!* a play about a Hungarian playwright modeled on Ferenc Molnár (Oscar Homolka), living with a group of European refugees in a US rooming house. It was written by George S. Kaufman and Edna Ferber, and Max Gordon was producing. In Boston for Rosa's rehearsals, Joe fended off Darnell's attempts to join him: "Darling . . . I haven't slept. I am just as eager as you and love you for wanting to try to come, but I can't let you take so many chances with so much at stake for both of us."

Still under pressure in New Haven, where he went to surprise Rosa at the opening, Joe wrote Darnell, "Everything under control, but I can't call. Think I can spend most of Sunday in New York. Will try to call tomorrow."

Rosa's long-awaited opportunity became a nightmare. She looked so beautiful that when she appeared onstage for the last act, the audience gasped audibly. Joe recorded, "Rosa's opening. Play stinks. She's wonderful." His opinion of the play apparently was shared by everyone except Kaufman, who was also directing. Joe's old friend Sam Marx and Marx's wife took Joe and Rosa with them to Kaufman's opening-night party, all of them assuming Joe had not been invited, because no one knew he was coming. But when Kaufman, Gordon, and Ferber ignored Joe and spent the evening talking to other writers about the show's problems, the four finally left, confused and offended.

The next day the coolness made sense. Kaufman wanted Rosa fired, though he made Gordon do it. Telling the press Rosa looked too young for the part, they replaced her with Lili Darvas (Mrs. Ferenc Molnár); it didn't help. Although it was scant comfort to Rosa, *Bravo!* closed after forty-four performances.

As Joe frantically worked to find her another part, Rosa seemed oblivious to the challenges she faced. She was a skilled actress of great beauty, but she was also thirty-five with an Austrian accent in a crowded, competitive profession. Furthermore, as a conscientious and genuinely devoted mother, she was unwilling to take just any part. Reinforcing her choosiness were her memories of her stature in Europe and her sense of herself as the wife of an important Hollywood director. In short, Rosa was arrogant and elitist when a more accommodating attitude might have opened the way to more opportunities. Rosa saw none of that. The only impediments to her career that Rosa perceived were her obligations as wife and mother, and for those she resented Joe. As Joe's stature rose, Rosa's professional jealousy increased concomitantly, and Joe's affairs with women who had what she wanted but could not have only added to the pain.

As *A Letter to Three Wives'* release drew near, Joe looked forward to finally seeing "Written and Directed by Joseph L. Mankiewicz" on the screen. When a Fox lawyer reminded him that Vera Caspary merited an adaptation credit, he agreed to settle for "Screenplay and Direction By." Then Caspary sought co-credit for the script as well. Joe contested the claim with Fox's backing, and the Screen Writers Guild ruled in his favor.

They opened at Radio City Music Hall in January 1949 to rave reviews, and both the *New York Times* and *Herald Tribune* devoted Sunday-section pieces almost entirely to Joe's contributions. In praise more revealing of himself than the picture, *Times* critic Bosley Crowther hailed Joe: "He has made a film in which women are acknowledged to be fallible and in which, at the final showdown, the pants are worn by the men." He concluded approvingly, "In a fresh and sophisticated fashion, as writer and director of this film, he has candidly called the females to witness against themselves. He has cautioned, at last, that women should never over-estimate their powers—from which ladies can profit and we men can draw relief."

Private congratulations poured in. "YOU'VE SET TELEVISION BACK ANOTHER SIX MONTHS," wired Charles Brackett and Billy Wilder. Vera Caspary and John Klempner sent praise, as did Richard Rodgers. A San Diego school official wrote that Joe's "honest and realistic characterization . . . did more to improve the status of teachers than many of us in school public relations can do in a year." A fraternity brother recalled Camp Wayne's owners firing Joe as a drama counselor for lacking "interest, ability, humor and imagination," adding, "It's always good to see improvement."

On MGM letterhead, playwright Paul Osborn wrote that the picture made "all the other movies I can think of look pretty juvenile. My God, if I could write a movie like that I'd really get interested in writing movies." Gene Kelly sent a "fan letter" calling it "one of the best things ever done in the American cinema. The 'shack-shaking' scenes were hilarious in the best kind of Capra, McCarey, etc. tradition, and the characterizations were poignantly real. But through it all, the overtones and undertones that make your picture such a terrific commentary on the mores of our generation, also make it as compelling a social document as has come our way in many a celluloid moon."

Joe gloried in his newfound recognition as a social critic, telling the *Los Angeles Times* that once he finished "The East Side Story" (*House of*

Strangers), he hoped to return to social criticism, especially "the women's clubs, our phony approach to culture and, most of all—mom!"

> Because a woman performs a perfectly natural function, she is thereby supposed to become endowed with all the virtues she did not possess five minutes before the news got around! There's no reason—ipso facto—why a child should love a mother who doesn't earn the love of that child. Too many sniveling, hypocritical women hide behind that label of "mom"! That's Philip Wylie's concept, of course [from Wylie's 1942 *Generation of Vipers*], but I'm proud to be known as a disciple. And the first picture that defies the phony movie idea of every mother as Mickey Rooney's "ma" will have such a success as has never been dreamed of! The American male will benefit by it, too—in the exact degree that it helps him escape from "momism"!

Given Rosa's situation, his attack on mothers seems insensitive to the point of cruelty. But despite his propensity for creating spunky heroines whose lives were not necessarily limited to a conventional husband-and-children (*Dragonwyck*'s Miranda, Lucy Muir, and his latest three wives), Joe also strongly believed that women could not find fulfillment in career alone—that to women, love and family were more important, no matter how engaging or successful their work might be. Perhaps he was sending a message.

At a weekend of discussions on the state of the motion picture industry convened by *Life* magazine, Joe was equally outspoken about the business in general. With movie attendance sagging, *Life* editors sought explanations other than the rise of television. Drawing from a group that included MGM production chief Dore Schary, Alistair Cooke from the *Manchester Guardian*, and writer/director John Huston, *Life*'s June 27, 1949, piece "A Round Table on the Movies" quoted Joe more than any of the others. He was "violently opposed to the concept of the motion pictures only as a business" and opined that the influx of so many genuinely creative people had given the industry a certain "schizophrenia of effort." In other words, creative people wanted to make art as well as money.

When Cooke observed that publishers addressed a similar problem by publishing a few high-quality books a year that they did not expect to be profitable, Joe ignited a minor firestorm. The publishers were not owned by the bookstores, Joe pointed out.

> We're different. Are we selling to an audience or do we make pictures for theaters? There's a hell of a difference. . . . *Who controls the movies?* Here at this table are people who *make* movies. We would like to make good movies. . . . But isn't it true that a real estate operator whose chief concern should be taking gum off carpets and checking adolescent love-making in the balcony—isn't it true that this man is in control?

Theater owners responded angrily, but by then Joe's point was essentially irrelevant. Audiences were indeed diminishing, but in May 1948 a Supreme Court decision ordering motion picture companies to divest themselves of their movie theaters had already dealt the studio system a death blow. Severing studios from theaters not only deprived the parent companies of a huge revenue stream, it removed the studios' guaranteed outlet for whatever they produced. The system was already on the wane. Even so, Joe would continue to earn handsome sums from the motion picture industry, and he never did stop biting the hand that fed him so well.

By the time the *Life* piece appeared, honors were pouring in for *A Letter to Three Wives*. In May 1949 the Screen Directors Guild gave Joe its first annual award, and Academy Award nominations for both directing and writing followed in February 1950. It was also nominated as best picture, which was a rare honor for a comedy, and though Joe always disparaged awards and insisted they meant nothing to him, they actually meant a great deal to him, and he was thrilled. "Things are working out for me," he admitted to himself. "All those years of cotton-picking under this damn sun; my coming to Fox; my analysis; my growing up. I guess things are working out."

Joe followed his comedy of suburban manners with *House of Strangers* (1949), a film noir that combined *King Lear*, the Old Testament's Joseph, and Bank of America's founding Giannini family. Philip Yordan, a playwright and specialist in gangster and other B-pictures, had turned a Jewish family in Jerome Weidman's 1941 novel, *I'll Never Go There Any More*, into an Italian family whose patriarch founded a bank. After seeing Yordan's first seventy-five pages, producer Sol Siegel fired Yordan and asked for Joe, who rewrote much of the story and all of the dialogue.

The story follows lawyer Max Monetti (Richard Conte), the favorite son of a powerful Italian American immigrant banker Gino Monetti (Edward G. Robinson). After spending seven years in jail for jury tampering to save his father from conviction for banking infractions, Max is obsessed with punishing his brothers for betraying him to the police. His lover, society woman Irene Bennett (Susan Hayward), wants him to forget the vendetta and move on.

Despite a few weaknesses in the script, the picture's atmosphere and the actors' performances were powerfully effective. Robinson's performance earned him Cannes Film Festival's best acting prize, and though Joe walked off the set at one point to force Robinson to play a scene the way Joe wanted, Robinson later said he would work with Joe anytime. Zanuck was so impressed with Susan Hayward's performance that he signed her to a seven-year contract.

House of Strangers is interesting in the context of Joe's other work. The sparring between Max and Irene echoes the verbal foreplay between Lora Mae and Porter and anticipates his later films intertwining sex and power, like *All About Eve* and *Five Fingers*. In the background of a bar scene, he put an older man at a table with a young woman who is weeping, and liked it so much that he used it again in *The Barefoot Contessa*.

Siegel and Joe again talked Zanuck into allowing them to shoot exteriors in New York, and this time, the urban moodiness they captured seemed to justify the expense. The film is in black and white but the Monetti mansion's lavish interiors, and touches like Gino's predilection for a favorite aria and the family's uncomfortable dinners, capture the same combination of loyalty and oppressiveness among first-generation Italian American families that *The Godfather* evoked so memorably in 1972. Siegel believed *House of Strangers* would have been much stronger with John Garfield, his original choice for Max ("he walked out on me"), but he thought *House of Strangers* had some of Joe's best direction.

Fox's chief, Spyros Skouras, dampened revenues when he decided the story was really about his own Greek family, disguised as Italians, and refused to distribute the picture well. Joe again sought sole screenplay credit, and when Yordan appealed the Guild awarded Yordan both story credit and screenplay co-credit. Joe suspected they were either punishing him or trying to make amends for the previous decision against Caspary, and instead of accepting co-credit with Yordan, he angrily refused to take any writing credit. Siegel complained that the Guild "obstinately ignore producers' descriptions of who deserves it and were probably influenced by Joe's acid tongue."

Despite its disappointing performance, Siegel considered the story so strong that a few years later, he recycled it into *Broken Lance* (1954), a western starring Spencer Tracy, Robert Wagner, and Richard Widmark, and to Siegel's and Joe's extreme irritation, it earned Yordan an Academy

Award for best original story. Yordan was not untalented, but he was predatory, eventually amassing more than a hundred writing credits by delegating assignments to other writers, many of them blacklisted, and taking credit for their work. After winning the Oscar, he took out a two-page advertisement in *Variety* saying, "Thank you, Sol Siegel."

Siegel wired *Variety* that Yordan had nothing to do with *Broken Lance*, only *House of Strangers*, but his wire was never printed; and Yordan, no stranger to fiction, later told reporters, "Joe Mankiewicz tried to put his name on my screenplay as the co-author and Sol struck it off."

Joe tangled again with Yordan on his next picture, *No Way Out*, which was based on a story by Lesser Samuels about an encounter between a black doctor and a white racist. Fox paid Samuels $87,500, which was a steep price for a story at that time, but the competition was fierce. Several Fox producers wanted it, but Zanuck kept it for himself and hired Yordan to develop it, perhaps because Yordan's successful 1944 play *Anna Lucasta* had been adapted on Broadway for an entirely black cast.

Fox had already tackled race with *Pinky* (1949), and Zanuck took great pride in the studio's other social-problem pictures—*Gentleman's Agreement* (1947) dealt with anti-Semitism, and *The Snake Pit* (1948) depicted treatment of the mentally ill. Writing Samuels and Yordan, Zanuck explained, "We must conscientiously avoid propaganda, but . . . the final result . . . should be a picture which is actually powerful propaganda against intolerance." Unusually for the times, Zanuck also thought in terms of transcending stereotypes. He wanted to "go into Luther's home. I would like to see how real Negroes in a metropolitan city live. I would like to see them as human beings. Perhaps Luther has a mother, and a father, he is part of a family."

One of Zanuck's strengths was his ability to balance doing good with doing well. He wanted to include the story's race riot but suggested they downgrade it to a barroom brawl or street corner fight, because

> even in certain so-called white cities, such as Detroit, Omaha, St. Louis and Philadelphia, we are apt to have the picture banned totally by the Police Commission. We already know that we will lose about 3000 accounts in the South who will not play the picture under any circumstances. But it would be a terrible thing if we have something in the picture which would give the so-called white cities a chance to turn us down. . . . It is fine for us to be courageous, but we must also be sensible, and not too courageous with other people's money.

Joe rewrote Yordan's screenplay in about six weeks, juggling it with work on "The Wisdom of Eve" (*All About Eve*—see the following chapter). For once using no flashbacks, he concentrated on creating psychologically complex characters and convincing dialogue. Dr. Luther Brooks (Sidney Poitier), a city hospital's first black intern, has to treat a pair of criminal brothers, Johnny (Dick Paxton) and Ray (Richard Widmark) Biddle when they arrive in the emergency room. Suspecting that Johnny has a brain tumor, Luther administers a spinal tap, and when Johnny dies shortly afterward, his viciously racist brother accuses Luther of killing Johnny. Luther asks for an autopsy to clear himself, but Ray refuses, so Luther and his boss, Dr. Wharton (Stephen McNally), visit Johnny's widow, Edie (Linda Darnell), to ask for her permission. Because Edie and Johnny are divorced, she cannot grant it, but Edie visits the hospital to suggest Ray authorize the autopsy. Instead, Ray convinces Edie the doctors have duped her and enlists her help in getting even. Ray's white friends plan an attack on the black community, but the blacks hear of it and attack first. An autopsy finally reveals Luther was correct, but Ray is so consumed with hatred that he tries to kill Luther anyway. Edie, who regrets her actions, aids Luther, then watches incredulously as Luther saves Ray, who is about to die.

When scheduling problems kept Anne Baxter from playing Edie, Linda Darnell was thrilled to get the assignment. Darnell had been asking for more complex roles, and, even better, Joe was directing. As Joe wrote the script during the summer of 1949, they appeared together in public so often that when the film was released the following summer, a *Los Angeles Times* reporter felt free to comment, "Linda's admiration for Joseph L. Mankiewicz, who collaborated on the script as well as directed the picture, is, I gathered, as personal as it is professional."

The only actor Zanuck insisted on was Richard Widmark for Ray Biddle. Although Widmark was personally very kind, he was so effective as the fiendishly giggling psychopath in *Kiss of Death,* his first screen appearance, that he earned an Oscar nomination and a stream of villainous roles for years afterward. Zanuck scheduled production around him and even postponed starting for an extra week so that Widmark, who had just lost fifteen pounds shooting *Night and the City* in England, could return by ship instead of air to give himself time to gain some weight. (Zanuck and Joe had already worried that the solid Darnell might outweigh the slight Widmark.)

Aside from some army short films, *No Way Out* was Sidney Poitier's film debut. He had toured in *Anna Lucasta,* and when Joe went to Harlem

Starring as Dr. Luther Brooks in *No Way Out* (1950) launched Sidney Poitier's career. He laughed off Richard Widmark's continual apologies for his racist lines, and the two became lifelong friends. Linda Darnell welcomed her meaty role.

to scout for African American actors, Poitier was acting on stage but supporting himself as a janitor. Poitier always credited Joe with launching his film career and appreciated his sensitivity throughout production. When they finished shooting, Joe sent Poitier to Zoltan Korda, who gave him his second big part in *Cry the Beloved Country*. The picture also began a lifelong friendship between Poitier and Richard Widmark, who was the first person in Hollywood to invite Poitier into his home. During filming, Widmark was so embarrassed by his character's racism that he kept apologizing after every line until Poitier finally told him, "Hey, we're actors. It's just lines."

No Way Out was also Ossie Davis's film debut, and the first time Davis and Ruby Dee, who were married by then, appeared together on the screen. The African American cast members were pleased to be in a picture that avoided their usual depiction as "tap dancing, superstitious, crap-shooting lackey[s]," as a member of the black press put it, but they still had to deal with Fox's completely white staff, who tried to be helpful but lacked experience with African American hair or makeup. Finally, Dee, a lifelong activist who had been picketing since she could walk, approached Joe to ask if they could have a black hairdresser. She later said she hadn't realized one did not approach one's director about such things, but Joe took care of it sensitively, and from then on, the actors generally applied their own makeup.

In spite of Zanuck's concerns and Joseph Breen's admonition that the race riot scenes, in particular, possessed "a kind of inflammatory flavor," Joe directed some of the most visually arresting, dramatically lit scenes he ever shot. The expressionistic sequences depicted blacks from "Niggertown" attacking the whites just before the whites came after them. Breen did not object to the language, though the prevalence of "nigger" and other epithets was, and is, still so shocking that the film rarely appears on television. Breen objected only to the phrase "to suck around a white man" as "coarse." He reminded the studio to cover women's breasts; to conceal Luther's jabbing the needle into Johnny; and to exclude "passionate, prolonged, lustful or open-mouth kissing." He also suggested that while the deputy might be hit once with a blackjack, a second slugging was "uncalled for and unnecessarily brutal."

Again, Philip Yordan sought co-screenplay credit, and again, Joe fought back. In a two-page letter to the Guild, he wrote that Yordan's "obvious, unimaginative and crude" effort "vacillated between pasting the pages of the original story into script form and wandering off into gratuitous, pointless violence." Calling Yordan's characterization "nonexistent," his structure "baseless," and his dialogue lacking "either impact or meaning," he concluded, "The script structure is mine, the script characters are mine and certainly, with the exception of technical phrases and street addresses and perhaps a dozen odd lines, the dialogue is all mine. If ever I wrote a screenplay, gentlemen, I wrote the screenplay of NO WAY OUT."

He was proud of the script (which holds up well, despite its age), and the arbitration committee unanimously awarded writing credit to Joe and Lesser Samuels. The following year, almost unnoticed among *All About Eve*'s record-breaking fourteen Academy Award nominations, was Joe and Samuels's nomination for best story and screenplay. The National Board of Review of Motion Pictures also named it one of 1950's best films.

Marketing was tricky, and after they failed to find a line as effective as *Pinky*'s "I passed for white," Fox publicists gave up and ran advertisements that said nothing about race: "Adult motion picture which challenges one's ability to experience the emotions of others." When it opened in August 1950, New York critics were impressed, but as Zanuck had feared, commissions in Chicago, Philadelphia, and Boston banned the film. Joe told *Life*, "I find it highly commendable for the city fathers to be keeping Chicago, with its high cultural standards, isolated from any violence." Eventually Fox removed some of the riot footage for Chicago and Philadelphia, and the Boston authorities allowed it to run, but never on Sunday.

Reaction from the black community was mostly positive. The Negro Newspaper Publisher Association condemned its language, but National Association for the Advancement of Colored People (NAACP) head Walter White disagreed. So did other civil rights leaders, who organized a tribute at the Ritz-Carlton Hotel to honor Fox for its courage. Other awards followed, and Joe accepted them in person when he could.

By then, however, he had one foot out the door. Joe continued to despise Hollywood and wanted his sons educated outside the "intellectual fog belt." He hoped moving to New York would allow him to combine work as an independent movie writer/director with writing plays and even books. But first he owed Fox a few more pictures.

CHAPTER 15

All About Eve

ACTRESSES HAD ALWAYS FASCINATED JOE. SO HAD AWARDS. FOR years he had imagined opening a picture with an Academy Awards ceremony, then flashing back to show how the actress got there. So when Joe saw Mary Orr's 1946 *Cosmopolitan* story about Margola Cranston, a famous theater actress, and Eve Harrington, her ruthless understudy, he pounced. As he wrote Zanuck in April 1949, Susan Hayward could star in "a very funny and penetrating high comedy about the theatre" that could also allow them to "show up some of the weaknesses of our longhaired brethren of the theatre which they fondly keep describing as 'Hollywood.'"

Once Zanuck approved, Joe poured his ideas into an eighty-two-page treatment so fully realized that right in the middle, on page 41, Margola warns her guests, "Fasten your seatbelts. It's going to be a bumpy night." Aside from a week off to write and direct additional scenes for *No Way Out,* he finished the screenplay in six weeks, this time sequestering himself in Santa Barbara. Instead of Oscars, he created a fictitious Sarah Siddons Society that honors theatrical actresses and opened the picture at its awards dinner. As Eve Harrington receives the award, the screen freezes and three of the characters recall Eve's climb to the top in flashback. The three narrators' differing perspectives enrich the story with complex, sometimes inadvertent, self-portraits.

Foremost is Margo Cranston (later, Channing), the famous actress Eve understudies. Margo worries about turning forty, the "big four-oh," with all it implies for her career as an actress, as well as her personal life. To heighten her concerns about aging, Joe gave Margo a lover instead of a husband, and made him eight years younger.

The second is Margo's best friend, Karen Richards, who is married to Lloyd Richards, the playwright responsible for many of Margo's successful plays.

The third narrator, critic Addison DeWitt, speaks first. Joe always enjoyed naming his characters, and besides echoing the name of Eve's biblical mate, Addison's adder-like character is venomous. Like the original serpent, Addison opens this Eve's eyes in a climactic scene. Outwardly, Addison resembles the acidulous theater critic George Jean Nathan, an old friend of Herman's who could be malicious, used a cigarette holder, and surrounded himself with beautiful, young protégées. His name is a double pun, because Mr. DeWitt also serves as Joe's mouthpiece in commenting on the world of theater.

Joe lavished care on his characters as well as his dialogue. Orr referred in passing to Margola's maid; Joe created Birdie Coonan, a former vaudevillian, especially for Thelma Ritter, whom he adored. Birdie provides a withering counterpoint to the other characters' rosy views of Eve, and of themselves as Eve's benefactors. The dyspeptic Max Fabian (Gregory Ratoff) transcends the generic producer. Claudia Casswell, the quintessential starlet and "graduate of the Copacabana school of acting," has unusually good lines (and unintended retrospective importance, because she was played by then-starlet Marilyn Monroe). Eve's young fan Phoebe (Barbara Bates) represents the world's infinite supply of Eves and adds yet another sinister touch to the comedy.

Joe had lofty ambitions from the beginning. If he was going to write movies, he wanted them to say something, not just entertain, and though he often irritated his boss, Zanuck respected him. As Joe finished work on *Eve*, Zanuck asked him to comment on an adaptation of Ernest Hemingway's "The Snows of Kilimanjaro" he had commissioned. Joe described the element he considered crucial to any screenplay's success: characters with whom audiences could identify. Drawing on his efforts with *Eve*, he wrote that he consciously worked toward audience "participation" in his characters' "subjective, internal, emotional existence," because if a screenplay could achieve "[d]epth and—above all else—universality of characterization," the picture could tell "a truly magnificent story . . . of potentially profound characters."

> If ALL ABOUT EVE were nothing more than a story about an ambitious young actress, an aging actress, and a woman married to a playwright, we would have on hand a highly esoteric film with a very special appeal and of dubious interest to the audiences of the world. But we were particularly careful, in telling our story, never to let the external characteristics of our chief protagonists cover the universal applications of what they were as people—a young

> girl obsessed by ambition and a compulsion to realize that ambition whatever the means and cost; a woman who is undergoing the most frightening transition in a woman's life—from youth to middle age—with all of the anxiety and fear that accompanies it; and finally the stay-at-home wife, whose husband spends his professional life in contact with attractive young women—her realization that she may lose him at any time, her inability to combat her inevitable fate. Here we dealt with the emotional stuff of which all women are made—and to which all women react and recognize, whether the symbols are actresses, nurses, queens, or whores.

Rarely inhibited by false modesty, Joe compared them to Arthur Miller's characters in his Pulitzer Prize–winning *Death of a Salesman*. The magnificence of Miller's writing was that it was "not necessarily about a salesman. It is to each man in the audience—himself. The death of his dreams, his ambitions, his pride, his love. In lesser hands than Arthur Miller's, and written without that tremendous depth of emotional application, it would have been a play about a salesman and his particular problems. . . . a play of restricted interest and restricted audience participation."

In his quest for universality, Joe did not disregard specificity. He later said he could not write an unmotivated character, and in common with good literature, Joe wanted his plots to grow out of character. He took pride in his ability to tailor dialogue to each character, so that Birdie Coonan used the vocabulary of a former vaudevillian and sounded nothing like Radcliffe-educated Karen Richards, whose vocabulary and sophisticated syntax sounded nothing like Margo's.

They started casting before the script was ready. Zanuck liked Claudette Colbert or Barbara Stanwyck for Margo, John Garfield or Gary Merrill for Margo's lover, Bill, and Jeanne Crain for Eve. Crain was very popular with the public and would shortly be nominated for an Academy Award for her title role in Fox's *Pinky*, but fresh from his *Three Wives* experience, Joe resisted.

> I know Jeanne to be a sincere, honest, young actress who performs her chores in a sincere and honest fashion. Those aspects of EVE are obvious in her—but also, they <u>are</u> her. And there lies the rub. Crain, to my mind, is incapable of understanding—much less portraying—the burning, ruthless, driving and at times evil force that is the core of EVE. And which, we ultimately determine, <u>is</u> EVE.

> I can see Jeanne Crain rise to receive an award—but not as EVE. I cannot see her "lay it on the line" for Bill; I cannot see her in an instinctive, petty, vicious reaction to her rejection. I cannot see her cold, hard, and unyielding opposite Karen in the Stork Club encounter. Most importantly, I cannot see her fence and parry with Jose Ferrer [the original Addison DeWitt] in their great clash—certainly not where she lies exposed and whipped on the bed, fighting back desperately as he strikes at her . . . nor can I see her suddenly tired, empty and old before her time at the end.

Joe actually had someone in mind who both resembled Claudette Colbert (the presumptive Margo) and could deliver the range he envisioned. "Perhaps you could spare a few minutes to canvas other possibilities with me. One of these, by the way is Anne Baxter. She could look the 22 or 23 that EVE should look [Baxter was twenty-six], she could supply the earnestness and sincerity of EVE's assumed character without ever tipping her mitt—and she could certainly kick hell out of the fireworks."

Fox had announced Crain for the role, but Zanuck yielded—the fact that Baxter was also under contract probably helped. Joe understood the economics of using Fox contract players Gary Merrill for Margo's lover, Bill Sampson, and Hugh Marlowe as Lloyd Richards, and his focus was the female characters anyway. Joe had approved of Jose Ferrer but was not displeased with George Sanders, when Ferrer was unavailable.

For Karen, Zanuck wanted Jane Wyatt, but Joe urged him to hire an actress "as close to Irene Dunne as money and availability permit," like Ruth Hussey or Margaret Sullavan. Eventually they revisited the idea of Celeste Holm, despite Zanuck's and Holm's mutual animus. Fox had suspended her once, and she had just bought out her contract because she couldn't stand the roles Fox offered her: "Mr. Zanuck only knew about virgins or whores. There was nothing in between. Jeanne Crain was a virgin, though she had five children . . . she was a lady . . . [whereas] any woman with a sense of humor was a whore. He as much as said so. I found he didn't have a clue what I was."

However, Holm and Zanuck were nothing if not expedient, and Holm was extremely talented. She had played *Oklahoma*'s original Ado Annie on Broadway before winning an Oscar for Fox's *Gentleman's Agreement* and a nomination for playing a nun in its *Come to the Stable*. "I never thought I'd live to see the day when I hoped we could work out a deal to get Celeste Holm," Joe wrote Zanuck. "But she would be perfect for the part, and the combination of the three will be an exciting one—in more ways than one."

Before signing Colbert, they had considered other possibilities for Margo, including stage actress Gertrude Lawrence, whom Joe favored. After Colbert signed in early February, she injured her back and had to drop out, and Zanuck wanted Marlene Dietrich. Joe pushed for Lawrence, though she was over fifty and best known as a stage actress, until Lawrence's lawyer/manager informed him she wanted neither to smoke nor drink in the picture and instead of a pianist's playing "Liebestraum" at Margo's cocktail party, she wanted to sing a torch song about Bill Sampson. That took her out of the running. Shortly afterward Lawrence bought the rights to *Anna and the King of Siam* and starred to great acclaim in *The King and I,* but she remained upset about losing the role of Margo.

At that point, Bette Davis was forty-one and privately agreed with the Hollywood columnists who were declaring her finished. After making more than fifty Warner Brothers films in eighteen years, Davis had left the studio in 1949 by mutual consent. The coup de grâce was *Beyond the Forest,* a picture so bad that Hedda Hopper wrote that if Davis "deliberately wanted to ruin her career, she couldn't have chosen a better vehicle." (In the picture's defense, it went on to become a cult classic and provided Davis with "What a dump," one of her most famous lines.)

Furthermore, Davis and Zanuck hadn't spoken for years. He had backed her in 1941 as the Academy's first woman president, but once she took office, she encountered such intransigent resistance every time she made a suggestion that she finally resigned. "You'll never work in this town again," a furious Zanuck told her, and they hadn't talked since. So when Zanuck called to offer her Margo, Davis thought someone was playing a telephone trick. She played along until she suddenly realized it actually was Zanuck.

Once word got out that Bette Davis had the part, a number of directors called Joe to warn him how difficult she would be; one said she would show up with a yellow legal pad and a script marked with changes in every line. Davis's reputation for being difficult actually came from years of fighting to get the roles she deserved, but Joe was so apprehensive that when they met for dinner at Davis's request, he asked her agent, Lew Wasserman, to come as well, "in case [Joe wrote Zanuck] she gives any indications of an intention to be either the writer or the director of the picture."

Instead, Davis told him she loved the script. She asked about her character, and when Joe said Margo was "the kind of dame who would treat her mink coat like a poncho," Davis felt that was all she needed to begin. Shortly afterward, William Wyler, who had directed her in *Jezebel*, *The Letter*, and *The Little Foxes* (and with whom Davis had been in love) called to tell Joe, "She is the perfect actress for the part, and whatever you expect from her, she'll give you more. She's the hardest worker you'll ever find, and you couldn't find a finer actress." But even Joe, who had become increasingly confident as a director, worried about the chemistry among three actresses of such temperament and stature. (Marilyn Monroe was not an issue—she was an interchangeable starlet, hired mostly as a favor to her mentor/lover, William Morris agent Johnny Hyde.)

Fox had reserved San Francisco's Curran Theatre for the theater scenes, and because the theater could not move the date later, Davis had no time to rest between films. Furthermore, she had to shoot *Payment on Demand* all day at RKO and go for wardrobe fittings at night. Fox designer Charles LeMaire was designing the costumes, but Davis wanted Edith Head to design hers, and LeMaire, who was friendly with Head and engaged on another project as well, didn't mind. Although Head consciously channeled Tallulah Bankhead in her designs, Davis and Joe always insisted the hoarse voice Davis used to play Margo was not due to a Bankhead imitation (which Bankhead claimed), but rather to a sore throat (from screaming at her soon-to-be-ex-husband). With Claudette Colbert as his original choice and Joe's insistence that he had modeled Margo on eighteenth-century English actress Peg Wolfington, there is little reason to disbelieve him.

On March 23, 1950, Joe accepted his two Academy Awards for writing and directing *A Letter to Three Wives*, which followed his February Screen Writers Guild award for best American comedy. When shooting began in April, someone put two Kewpie dolls on Joe's lectern to honor him and bring them all good luck. The production was charged with excitement from the beginning. They stayed at San Francisco's Fairmont Hotel and gathered on the first night for drinks at the bar. Joe acted as genial host, puffing on his pipe and watching "the interrelationship of the children," as Celeste Holm put it, the actress in her discerning Joe's tendency to observe other people as if they were characters.

Bette Davis recalled the entire experience as a magical interlude: "*Eve* was the only picture, the only one, where everybody working on it was in seventh heaven, and it all came out right. I've made many films where everybody had so much fun but the results were so terrible. . . . Another *death* thing that can happen on the set is when everybody sits down to see the rushes and you start saying, oh, isn't this *marvelous*? That's *death*.

You can't tell what's going to happen till it's all put together. But in *Eve* there was just a smell about it—you just *knew* it had to be great and that it would be great for all of us."

Besides reviving her career, *Eve* changed Davis's life. When shooting began Davis and Gary Merrill were both married, but they fell in love the first week and shed their spouses so quickly that they married in July, even before the picture premiered. The picture outlasted their ten-year marriage in which, according to both parties, life imitated art. They even named their adopted daughter Margot (they added a "t").

MARGO: What about Bill?

KAREN: He's in love with you.

MARGO: More than anything in this world, I love Bill. And I want Bill. I want him to want me. But me. Not Margo Channing. And if I can't tell them apart—how can he?

KAREN: Why should he—and why should you?

MARGO: Bill's in love with Margo Channing. He's fought with her, worked with her, loved her . . . but ten years from now—Margo Channing will have ceased to exist. And what's left will be . . . what?

When they met, Davis was forty-one, and Merrill thirty-seven. As Davis recalled, Merrill married Margo Channing but got Bette Davis. "For three years I was solely a wife and mother and Gary fell out of love with me," she wrote shortly after they divorced.

"Why couldn't I be just a wife?" she wondered. Merrill said, "I don't want you in the kitchen all the time. . . . You're not Mrs. Craig; you're Bette Davis," and Davis pondered, "I rather thought I was Mrs. Merrill."

At the time, their passion sparked their performances, even to the extent of excluding the rest of the cast. Holm, who did not get along with Davis, recalled them as a sort of cabal, "like two kids who'd learned to spell a dirty word . . . two rebels against the world." But neither the lovers' rapture nor Davis's antagonism toward Holm interfered with the performances, and cast members often stayed around to watch, even when they were not in a scene. Besides enriching their own characterizations, they liked watching Joe direct. Anne Baxter recalled Joe's brilliance as he created "all the nuances" at Margo's party.

Davis told Joe she needed more to do, to get through the talky scene when Margo argued with Bill, so he told her, "As you get angry, you want a piece of candy. The angrier you get, the more desperately you want candy. You look toward the candy jar on the piano."

Bette Davis, Anne Baxter, and Celeste Holm take a break while shooting the Sarah Siddons Society scenes. Inspired by Joe's creation, a group of Chicago women established a real Sarah Siddons Society in 1952, and when they honored Celeste Holm in 1968, Holm was offended by Joe's amusement.

There was no candy jar on the piano.

"There *will* be. And then, finally, passionately, you *eat* the candy," her director said.

And, with a memorable Bette Davis chomp, Margo ate.

They all admired both the script's richness of "skullduggery and bitchcraft," and Joe's insightfulness. "Joe knows more about women than any man I've met. We're all just made of glass—he knows what makes us tick and it makes him a superb director because he knows what is deep in us," explained Anne Baxter, adding, "It'd be tough to be involved with Joe as a woman with a man because he'd know everything. You trust him."

Joe considered Anne Baxter's performance so impressive that he assumed she would steal the film and worried that Bette Davis would be hurt that she had the lesser part. (Once he started putting the film together, he saw it was Davis's.) For the scene between Eve and Addison in Eve's New Haven hotel room, he worked hard to synchronize Baxter, who called herself a "horse that runs all out on the first take," with George Sanders, who could be lazy and usually slept in his dressing room until he was needed. Joe tried to relax Baxter with jokes while he repeated the scene to push Sanders up to the energy level he wanted. (Perhaps Sanders really was exhausted—at the time, he was married to Zsa Zsa Gabor, who was so jealous of Marilyn Monroe that she ordered Sanders to get her a part in the film. He did not, but she appeared on the set one day, insisting that Sanders leave to go shopping with her. "We're making a fucking picture, honey," Joe told her.)

During her previous contract with Fox, executives had used Marilyn Monroe more for sexual services than acting and she presented Joe with another challenge. She was so intimidated by the rest of the cast and so anxious to do well in a scene with Bette Davis that she ruined take after take. One day when she arrived an hour late, Gregory Ratoff, who was a director as well as an actor, said, "That girl is going to be a very big star."

Celeste Holm was skeptical. "Why? Because she kept us waiting for an hour? It takes more than that." Holm saw only a "sweet but terribly dumb chorus girl who had been cast because she was someone's girl."

The stories about Monroe during the shoot, even her own, are unreliable, precisely because she was so obscure then and so famous soon afterward. Joe recalled asking what she was doing with a copy of Rainer Maria Rilke's *Letters to a Dead Poet,* and her response that she knew nothing about the German poet but had bought the book because it looked interesting. Joe told her a bit about Rilke, and the next day, she gave him a copy of the book. Actually, Monroe had been given the Rilke book by Natasha Lytess, a Columbia Pictures drama coach with whom she lived before she became involved with Johnny Hyde. Joe also recalled her as "the loneliest person I had ever known." Whenever cast members gathered to eat or drink together in San Francisco, Monroe never joined them unless specifically invited. "She was not a loner. She was just plain *alone*."

Ten years later, when Monroe was a star but not yet a myth, George Sanders, whose sense of humor was not unlike Addison DeWitt's, recalled her with more sympathy than Holm and more humor than Joe:

> Even then she struck me as a character in search of an author and I am delighted she found Mr. Miller eventually. . . . I lunched with her once or twice during the making of the film and found her conversation had unexpected depths. She showed an interest in intellectual subjects which was, to say the least, disconcerting. In her presence it was hard to concentrate.

The studio certainly played its part in the creation of Marilyn Monroe—Fox publicists lopped two years off her age and circulated the supposed twenty-two-year-old's height and weight. Accompanying sexy photos referred to her appearances in *Eve* and *The Asphalt Jungle* with descriptions like, "She was 'discovered' in army training films," and "When Marilyn called crooked Lawyer Louis Calhern 'Uncle' in 'The Asphalt Jungle,' there wasn't a male within miles who didn't find himself hankering for a nice 'niece' like her."

While the publicity machine fueled anticipation, Joe addressed details like the score, sending Zanuck and music director Alfred Newman a five-page memo on the subject. He wanted "the narrated, or unreal, portions" underscored but not the "real" portions, and he envisioned an Eve theme, with "three very distinct variations," each colored by the "three very distinct characterizations of Addison, Karen, and Margo." The basic Eve theme would be played at the end of the picture "when Eve is fully disclosed and when the audience sees her not through any one else's eyes but its own. The very finish, for instance, should be pure EVE." At that point Eve's theme, "out in the open, for the first time," would dramatize "the emptiness and bitterness of her life." Beginning right after the last line of dialogue, the music "should build constantly, underscoring and underlining the cumulative steps by which the little girl from Brooklyn assumes Eve's character—and promises us that she will be another Eve—and finally the full realization, dramatically and musically, that the world is filled with Eves and that they will be with us always."

For Margo's party, Joe instructed, "Please, please do not have one pop tune—whether out of our catalogue or public domain—follow another, without variation in tempo or style or without thought as to content and application to the film it underscores." Furthermore, when the pianist tried to shift away from "Liebestraum," Joe wanted something other than what had been recorded, "Don't Blame Me," which he considered more appropriate to "Shirley Temple's playroom than Margo Channing's living room." He got "Stormy Weather."

The film was a smash from the beginning. Leo Rosten praised Joe's oeuvre (*A Letter to Three Wives, No Way Out*) as an attempt at social commentary and compared him to Preston Sturges. Joe appreciated tributes from friends in the business. Arthur Hornblow wrote, "I want to read your script. I want to read and re-read it, and savor the whole dish privately. This has never happened to me before out here, so I feel like a virgin about the whole thing. I don't even like to read my own scripts, either before or after making a picture!"

Addison DeWitt (George Sanders) introduces his protégée, Miss Claudia Casswell (Marilyn Monroe), "graduate of the Copacabana School of Acting," to wide-eyed Eve (Anne Baxter) and amused Margo (Bette Davis) at Margo's "bumpy night" party.

"In the thirty odd years that I've been in the picture business, I think I've written about three fan letters—this may be the fourth. . . . I am proud of you because if you hark back, you will remember me as the 'dirty bastard' who made you start at $50.00 per week instead of $75.00, the amount you wanted. . . ." wrote M. C. Levee, former Paramount executive.

Fresh from her *Sunset Boulevard* triumph, Gloria Swanson wrote, "So, now I join the parade of actresses who would give their souls to be in one or your pictures."

Months later, he heard from Robert Sherwood. As a favor, Sherwood had taken over working with Clive Brook to revise Philip Barry's *Second Threshold* after Barry died. Because it wasn't Sherwood's play and because Brook was "so obviously right for it," Sherwood had "resisted frequent temptations to tell him to go take a jump in the lake." So when Ellin and Irving Berlin screened *Eve* for Slim and Leland Hayward, and Sherwood and his wife, "I was absolutely amazed to hear my name mentioned from the screen together with those of Arthur Miller and Beaumont and Fletcher. When Lloyd, the playwright, was storming out of the theatre he turned and shouted at Bette Davis something about, 'Would Miller, Sherwood, Beaumont and Fletcher stand for any nonsense' from a star? At that point, I whispered to Slim, 'I can't speak for Miller, Beaumont or Fletcher—but Sherwood would and does.'"

Honors poured in. *Eve* appeared prominently on ten-best film lists for 1950. *Holiday* magazine named Joe Hollywood's Man of the Year for *Eve* and *No Way Out*. The New York Film Critics Circle named it best film, Joe best director, and Bette Davis best actress. On February 3, 1951, Random House published *Eve*'s screenplay in book form. On February 9, Joe accepted a scroll from the thousand-member Books & Authors, Inc., for writing the film of greatest literary excellence. Later that month the Screen Writers Guild named Joe and Mary Orr creators of the year's best written comedy. At the *Look* Magazine Motion Picture Achievement Awards, Bob Hope handed Bette Davis her best actress plaque and named Joe best writer. The British Film Academy voted it best picture over all. The Hollywood Foreign Press Correspondents gave the top acting award to Gloria Swanson but gave Joe its Golden Globe for best screen play. On March 15, the Screen Directors Guild gave Joe, its president, its quarterly award for best director and later in the year deemed him best director for the entire year. The film buyers named him 1950's best director. The Cannes Film Festival named Bette Davis best actress and gave the film the special jury prize.

Life and *Collier's* ran long profiles. In *Life*, Robert Coughlan wrote "Fifteen Authors in search of a character named J. L. Mankiewicz," evoking Pirandello's *Six Characters in Search of an Author* while parodying Joe's (and Herman's) propensity for multiple narrators. He quoted Herman and Erna, Celeste Holm and Linda Darnell, Darryl Zanuck, and anonymous sources designated only as Psychiatrist (Fred Hacker), Friend, Critic, and Producer.

Herman openly acknowledged the brothers' opposite trajectories. Their father had been such a powerful influence, Herman said, that his sons would be either "very ambitious or very despairing. You could end up by saying, 'Stick it, I'll never live up to that and I'm not going to try.' That's what happened eventually with me." As for his quasi-paternal relationship with Joe, "I've been an influence in Joe's life, but it's mostly been negative. Like Shaw said, 'Parents should be a warning to their children instead of an example.' Nobody can deny I've been a good bad example . . . I helped him at first, but he learned fast."

In *Collier's*, former critic Frank Nugent predicted that Joe had a good chance of winning Academy Awards for both directing and writing twice

A night of triumph. Holding his record-setting, second-in-a-row pair of screenwriting and directing Oscars, Joe is flanked by Fred Astaire (host); Nobel Prize–winning Ralph Bunche (speaker); Darryl Zanuck, holding both his third Irving Thalberg Award and *All About Eve*'s Best Picture Oscar; and Academy president Charles Brackett, holding his Oscar for co-writing *Sunset Boulevard* (with Billy Wilder).

in a row. One critic prophesied he would become "the Scott Fitzgerald of his medium." A *New York Times* crossword puzzle included a clue, "One of Joseph Mankiewicz's talents." The answer was directing.

Eve's fourteen Academy Award nominations set a record that remained unequaled until *Titanic* tied it in 1997, and *La La Land* in 2017. In addition to one for best picture and, to Joe, for writing and directing, best actress nominations went to both Davis and Baxter, because Baxter had insisted Fox submit her as a lead rather than a supporting role. She later considered that a mistake, though Thelma Ritter and Celeste Holm were both nominated as supporting actresses.

Edith Head and Charles LeMaire were nominated for best costume design in black and white. Film editor Barbara McLean received the last of her seven nominations (she won for Zanuck's *Wilson* and held the nominations record until 2012). The other nominees were George Sanders for best supporting actor; W. D. Flick and Roger Heman for sound; Alfred Newman for score; Lyle Wheeler, George W. Davis, Thomas Little, and Walter M. Scott for black-and-white art direction; and Milton Krasner for black-and-white cinematography.

At the ceremony, *Eve*'s cast were a tearful lot. Finding her dress torn, Marilyn Monroe burst into tears backstage; seamstresses patched it up in time for her to appear on stage, eyes downcast and voice barely audible, to present the sound recording Oscar to *Eve*'s team. After accepting his best supporting actor award, George Sanders retired backstage where he, too, began to cry. In addition, the film won the black-and-white costume design category. (Edith Head also won the color costume design Oscar for Cecil B. DeMille's *Samson and Delilah*, but she did not return to the podium, saying later, "I always had to do what that conceited old goat wanted, whether it was correct or not.")

After Joe accepted his writing award from actress-turned-novelist Ruth Chatterton and his director's award from another two-time best director, Leo McCarey, he and the other 122 million listeners around the world had to sit through an interminable speech by Nobel Peace Prize winner Ralph Bunche before learning that *All About Eve* was the Academy's best picture for 1950.

Joe was the man of the hour, and his record of back-to-back Oscars for both writing and directing is still unbroken. *Eve* was not a huge moneymaker, but it was profitable and popular. There was no way of knowing it was the peak of Joe's career. Nor could anyone have imagined the extent to which *All About Eve* would permeate popular culture. The film eventually inspired books, a Broadway musical, a London West End adaptation, and countless imitators. Its Wildean dialogue is quoted, paraphrased, and parodied. It became an icon of gay culture, and Margo Channing a drag queen staple. Credit for its endurance has to go beyond Joe's obvious wit to his aspirations to "universality of characterization." If Margo Channing and Eve Harrington are caricatures, they are also so authentic that they have joined fictional creations like Miss Havisham and Ebenezer Scrooge, and even Hamlet and Othello, in becoming archetypes. Just as one can be a Candide or a Frankenstein monster or a Willy Loman, one can be a Margo or an Eve.

CHAPTER 16

Breaking Away

ALL ABOUT EVE ALREADY HAD THE SMELL OF SUCCESS IN JULY 1950, when Joe and Rosa sent the boys to camp back east and left for Europe. Under Cecil B. DeMille's sponsorship, Joe had been elected president of the Screen Directors Guild (SDG), and he planned to meet with some of his European counterparts while he was abroad. The plan was not without risk. Quiescent during the war years, anticommunist sentiment had come roaring back, and in 1950, any engagement with foreigners could be suspect. With movies' outsize influence on American culture; studios' abundance of liberals, intellectuals, foreigners, and Jews; and a rich supply of household names and famous faces guaranteed to elicit publicity, the motion picture industry offered an irresistible hunting ground for subversives. The House Un-American Activities Committee (HUAC) had already pushed the film industry into maintaining both a blacklist and a gray list that had ruined countless careers and lives.

For an intellectual, anti-racist Jew, Joe was unusually immune from guilt by association. He was a Republican who had written radio advertisements to help defeat Upton Sinclair in the 1934 California governor's race, and he had supported Wendell Wilkie over Franklin Roosevelt in 1940. Furthermore, because he considered Herman "as politically knowledgeable as I was politically illiterate," Joe had always heeded Herman's counsel to avoid communist-front organizations no matter how worthy their goals (Pop did the same for Don when he was at Columbia University in the 1930s).

As a result, Joe's only public quasi-political affiliation was heading Hollywood's chapter of the Finnish Relief Fund, a humanitarian group Herbert Hoover had founded in 1939 to aid Finnish victims of the Soviets' early World War II invasion, which may even have helped, because it shielded Joe from accusations of being a "premature anti-Fascist," a label applied to many supporters of the Hollywood Anti-Nazi League in the 1930s. He had also served as the Screen Writers Guild's first secretary, but that didn't seem to matter. Nor would his membership on the executive committee of the Hollywood Branch, Los Angeles Jewish Community Committee, a clandestine operation to monitor and foil local Nazi activities, if it were known.

Joe was disgusted by the anticommunist witch hunts, but he was as cautious as Herman was intemperate and kept his head down. By contrast, DeMille was so ardent that he volunteered to help the government expose film industry subversives. While Joe was on his way home from Europe and incommunicado, DeMille took the opportunity to convene an "emergency meeting" of the Guild's board to pass a motion requiring all members to take a loyalty oath, swearing they neither were Communists nor belonged to any other organization that advocated governmental overthrow. The members of the board were already required by law to take such an oath, but general members were not. Once the board approved it, they mailed out open, presigned ballots. Guild members were instructed to vote for or against imposing a mandatory loyalty oath on themselves and mail it back. The open ballots would allow DeMille to report the names of the Guild members who objected to the oath to the FBI, which he did. Not surprisingly, the motion carried, 547–14.

Joe arrived in New York five days later to a flurry of inquiries from reporters and angry telegrams from Guild members. He responded cautiously, submitting a statement to the board for prior approval before releasing it: "In response to telegrams and telephone calls regarding the recent action of SDG on non-Communist affidavits, I had no knowledge of the action taken until my arrival in NY last night. I was not consulted nor informed of the pending action, but will have a statement to make on arrival in Hollywood, at which time I'll ascertain what prompted the move and I'll get a complete picture."

The topic was so inflammatory that Louella Parsons's assistant followed up, telephoning Joe to ask exactly what he needed to know. Joe answered, "I cannot understand why it was deemed an emergency meeting since the Screen Directors Guild is in no way entrusted with war secrets, and I cannot understand why members, on a matter as vital as this, were not given the right of a secret ballot before it came up for a vote." He tipped his hand a bit more during a speech in New York shortly afterward. Accepting a B'nai B'rith award for his work on *No Way Out*, he deplored the existing political climate, citing the persecution of American liberals by groups setting themselves up as tribunals.

That started DeMille moving against him. Searching for signs that he might be soft on communism, DeMille scoured Joe's movies, his organizational allegiances, and even his ideological heritage (Pop had supported a socialist candidate decades before). The lack of evidence did not prevent him from planting hints in the press, which not surprisingly, only pushed Joe closer toward open disapproval of the mandatory oath. Whatever Joe's initial hesitations, Rosa, who was impelled less by politics than a firm sense of morality, urged him forward.

Joe was back in Hollywood for the Guild's October 9 board meeting, when DeMille and his supporters went further, proposing that they send producers the names of any members not signing the oath. That idea appalled even the reliably conservative John Ford, one of the Guild's founders, who asked why directors would create their own blacklist for potential employers. DeMille had the votes, however, so the motion passed.

Joe was so dismayed that he proposed they convene a general meeting. He would present his opposition to the open ballot the board had sent out, and the general membership could express their views. Then if Joe found himself out of step with the general members, he would resign. Board members talked him out of it, and Joe and DeMille parted on an amicable note.

However, two days later, *Daily Variety* ran an article reporting the board had had a "bitter debate" over the oath and that Joe had refused to sign it. DeMille assumed Joe had leaked the item as a first step toward attacking his faction. Joe, who had not leaked it and had already signed the oath as a board member, had no idea DeMille suspected him and said nothing to DeMille or anyone else about the article.

Determined to defend themselves from Joe's apparent rebellion, DeMille and his supporters gathered by six that evening to organize a recall of Joe as Guild president. They created a ballot that read, in full, "This is a ballot to recall Joe Mankiewicz. Sign here [Box] Yes." There was no box for "No." Although the recall required approval by 60 percent of the membership, before they sent out ballots they removed the names of about fifty members they suspected would support Joe or inform him of the plan.

Believing speed and stealth were essential, they had their ballots hand-delivered to members' houses by motorcycle courier, echoing the plot of Frank Capra's *Mr. Smith Goes to Washington* (1939). Capra, who, despite his films supporting the common man, was a staunch Republican and sometime FBI informer himself, originally belonged to DeMille's group. Eventually he found the group's tactics so appalling that he began trying to reconcile the two factions. But that was later.

About eleven o'clock the night the ballots were delivered, Joe was in Fox's screening room watching Henry and Phoebe Ephron's *Jackpot* when he received a call from Herman. "What do you have in common with Andrew Johnson?" Herman bellowed.

Joe, who figured his brother had had a few too many, asked, "Herman, are you drunk?"

"You are about to be impeached," Herman told him. There is "a fucking recall action on against you. . . . Johnny Farrow said some guy just drove up on a motorcycle to his house to get him to sign the petition."

The attempt to cull potential Joe-supporters had been so disorganized that even Joe himself received a recall ballot, and the DeMille group began receiving reports that members were confused about why Joe was being recalled. In response, they followed the ballots with a telegram intended to clarify their reason:

Joe had "pitted himself against the . . . Board of Directors."

"He repudiates the democratic vote of its membership. He stands with 14 against 547." The telegram was signed by fifteen names, the exact number of directors on the Guild's board, making it appear to have been sent by a unanimous board. In actuality, only eleven board members supported the recall. So, being movie directors, they thought like directors and devised an illusion. In order to create the impression that the Guild's entire board of directors wanted Joe recalled, they added the names of four regular Guild members who supported the recall and hoped the recipients wouldn't notice.

With more than his Guild presidency at stake, Joe knew he had to defend himself. Aided by his attorney, Martin Gang, he gathered a group of friendly directors in a back room at Chasen's restaurant the following evening, where Gang explained that a recall would probably end Joe's career. Once the group agreed to help, Gang suggested they pursue two actions. First, they should seek an injunction to stop the balloting. At the same time, they should petition for a general meeting so Joe could explain his side of the issue.

John Huston volunteered to sponsor the injunction and was the first to sign the petition. The group then fanned out all over town to accumulate the twenty-five directors' signatures they needed for the petition. Directors who eventually signed ranged across the political spectrum, from John Farrow and Don Hartman on the right, to Joseph Losey, who was later blacklisted. Each understood that even signing such a petition was dangerous, especially for the emigrés, and at Gang's insistence, every director who signed the petition also signed the loyalty oath.

When the board reconvened a few days later, Ford, Capra, and others pleaded with DeMille to rescind the recall motion and tried to talk Joe into canceling the general meeting. Once DeMille refused to yield on the recall, Joe hardened his position on convening a general meeting. Capra, who had tried to draft a joint statement acceptable to both sides, resigned from the board. Joe told the press he hoped to wrest control away from DeMille's group. The meeting was set for Sunday evening, October 22, 1950.

Almost the entire Screen Directors Guild membership gathered at the Beverly Hills for the six-hour meeting that Joe later called "the most dramatic evening in my life." Joe had brought along Elia Kazan for moral support, but before Kazan even got out of the car, he rattled Joe by refusing to go inside. DeMille knew he had belonged to the Communist Party, Kazan explained, so he was at risk, and his presence would damage Joe. (In 1952, Kazan named names at a HUAC hearing.)

Once the meeting began, Joe conquered his nervousness and delivered the speech he had written with help from John Huston, George Seaton, Kazan, and others. DeMille followed Joe. He started conciliatorily but quickly descended into naming organizations with which the twenty-five signers of Joe's petition were associated. Although the audience began to turn on him, DeMille kept going, even throwing in references to the *Daily Worker* and *Pravda*. Then he reversed course. He concluded by saying that he, too, favored rescinding the recall and having the ballots destroyed.

By then it was too little, too late. Directors across the political spectrum rose to speak, most of them to denounce DeMille. John Huston said, "In your tabulation of the twenty-five at the restaurant the other night. . . . how many were in uniform when you were wrapping yourself in the flag?" George Stevens, a past president, announced that he, like Capra, was resigning from the board and after summarizing the deceptive maneuvers in which the board members had engaged, he called it a conspiracy. DeMille continued the smearing anyway. Finally, one of the conservative directors called for him to resign from the board, and another begged him to apologize. DeMille refused and continued his invective.

Then John Ford rose and announced, "My name is John Ford. I am a director of Westerns." After the laughter at the revered director's modest description of himself died down, Ford spoke in defense of both Joe and

DeMille, clearly trying to save the Guild. Eventually, the entire board resigned, and once the tenor of the room calmed, a small interim group took over, with Joe as president, Ford and Capra as vice presidents, and Stevens as secretary.

When they met three days later, their first act was to adopt a voluntary loyalty oath. But the day after that meeting, *Variety* ran an open letter from Joe, asserting that he had never opposed a loyalty oath and urging Guild members to sign one voluntarily. Frank Capra was furious. He resigned from the board for the second time, accusing Joe of "vindication and sanctification for himself and his disciples, and consignment to hell for the opposition. His idea of meeting you half way is to pay for half the expenses of your funeral."

Joe protested (accurately) that he supported a voluntary but not a mandatory oath and that he deplored the open ballot that had been used to extort approval from the members. He remained in office for the next six months but declined to run for reelection. The following year, the board made the oath mandatory for all members.

Thus ended Joe's political career. His bravery during those perilous times needed no embellishment, but over ensuing years, his accounts of the events shifted leftward, following the zeitgeist of the 1960s, 1970s, 1980s. In Joe's revisionist versions, Joe became a Democrat instead of a Republican. He implied that he had totally opposed a loyalty oath rather than its mandatory imposition. DeMille's speeches became cruder and more derogatory. For example, recounting the episode in 1980, he imitated DeMille, "The twenty-five who wish to stop the will of the majority: 'Mr. Villiam Vyler, Mr. Fred Ssinnemann, Mr. Billy Vilder'" and said DeMille "pronounced every name in an anti-Semitic way." In his retellings, Ford supported only Joe. He also liked including his quip that DeMille "had his finger up the pulse of America."

In November 1950, right after the meeting, the *Los Angeles Times* reported that Joe was leaving Hollywood. That was not in response to the turmoil; Joe had been moving toward the goal for some time. Now it was public. With his newest Fox contract scheduled to start in May 1951, he announced that he planned to divide his time between New York and Hollywood (or the Ivory Ghetto, as he sometimes called it), so he could write plays as well as films, and maybe even books. His writing was clearly suitable for theater, where audiences were used to longer speeches, but there were skeptics. Phoebe Ephron, a playwright as well as a screenwriter, observed to her husband that Joe had never written anything from scratch and bet him $200 Joe would never get a play produced.

About six weeks after that, Zanuck sent Joe an extraordinary memo. Zanuck expected to continue to function on Joe's pictures as he had with *All About Eve* and *No Way Out*, but he planned to stop taking a producer's credit.

> When you are both the writer and director on a film the producer is inevitably subjected to a forgotten or completely secondary role. I am experiencing this now on ALL ABOUT EVE and it is the first time. . . . Usually I give a director a finished script to work with. That script is the result of my collaboration with the writers. It is my job. PINKY was handed to Kazan when the script was completed. The same was true with GENTLEMEN'S AGREEMENT. I worked it out with Moss and then we called in Gadg. As a matter of fact it has always been true, including TWELVE O'CLOCK HIGH, HOW GREEN WAS MY VALLEY, GRAPES OF WRATH, etc. . . .
>
> I am saying this to you now because I don't want you to feel that later on I am ducking out. You completely deserve all of the credit you are getting on ALL ABOUT EVE. By the same token, when I put my name on a picture as the producer I have my own conscience as well as my own reputation to consider. In DR. PRAETORIUS [later *People Will Talk*] you will again make the major contribution and if the picture is a hit you will get the major share of the credit since you will serve in two capacities.
>
> . . . Both my conscience and reputation will survive or fall on the result of my work and good or bad I will not be lost in the shuffle.

Zanuck took the producer's credit on *People Will Talk* (1951) anyway, and despite its flaws and poor box office performance, it remained one of Joe's favorites. As Joe later recalled, "the picture was essentially the second or third of my films against certain pomposities . . . a miniscule attempt to do what Moliere did as a work of genius." Always intrigued by psychiatry as well as medicine, Joe used Curt Goetz's German play and film *Dr. Praetorius* to comment on issues that interested him, including (but not limited to) the medical profession, the relationship between mental and physical health, the virtues of writers and educators, and the evils of farm subsidies. Not surprisingly, the film's genuine wit sank a bit beneath the weight of its ideological burden and lengthy speeches.

Despite all Joe's interesting sociological themes, the film is political. Goetz's Germany of 1932 transplanted easily into the 1950s climate of intimidation in the United States, and in addition to the satisfaction of

After battling Cecil B. DeMille in the Screen Directors Guild, Joe enjoyed seeing Cary Grant play Dr. Noah Praetorius, his alter-ego/mouthpiece in *People Will Talk* (1951), especially when the noble young doctor triumphs over a malevolent older rival seeking to destroy him.

pitting a Joe-like hero against a malevolent DeMille-esque villain, Joe had the pleasure of having his alter-ego/mouthpiece played by Cary Grant. When Dr. Noah Praetorius (Grant) is not teaching or treating gynecologic patients in his modern, patient-centered clinic, he conducts the medical school orchestra and plays with electric trains. His combination of unorthodox ideas, popularity, and financial success provokes the animosity of Dr. Ellwell (the reliably vindictive Hume Cronyn), who searches Praetorius's past for evidence of wrongdoing. In a hearing reminiscent of HUAC's, Ellwell grills Praetorius about his silent, hulking companion, Shunderson (Finlay Currie). After Praetorius refuses to answer questions about anyone except himself, Shunderson breaks into the meeting and recounts his own tragicomic history, revealing Praetorius's kindness and shaming his inquisitors.

Threaded through the political plot is a romance between Praetorius and Deborah Higgins (Jeanne Crain), a medical student who tries to commit suicide when she learns she is pregnant. To prevent future attempts, Noah tells Deborah that she is not really pregnant, then marries her and brings her father Arthur (Sidney Blackmer) to live with them. Joe took pride in the fact that he had managed a rare, if not unique, achievement in American 1950s film, portraying an unmarried pregnant woman who was allowed to go unpunished. Walter Slezak, who played Praetorius's bass-fiddle-playing atomic scientist friend, so enjoyed the break from playing villains that he used his $10,000 salary to add a "Praetorius Pasture" to his Bucks County, Pennsylvania, farm, which he planned to populate with a Mankiewicz Herd of cows.

Joe's last film under his Fox contract was based on *Operation Cicero*, the true story of a World War II spy in Turkey, written by the spy's German contact, L. C. Moyzisch. Codenamed "Cicero" by the Nazis, the spy was the Albanian valet to the British ambassador to Turkey. Cicero provided documents of such value (including minutes of the Moscow, Cairo, Tehran, and Casablanca conferences and D-Day invasion plans) that the Germans decided he must be a British plant and refused to act on what they assumed was false information. Doubling the irony, Cicero insisted the Germans pay him for selling out the British in British pounds. Tripling the irony, after their initial payment of £20,000, the Nazis paid him another £300,000 in custom-made counterfeits, courtesy of master German forgers.

Zanuck had assigned Michael Wilson to write the script and Henry Hathaway to direct, but when Joe saw Wilson's script, he asked to take over, provided he be allowed to tighten the action a bit and add "humor, sex and excitement" to the dialogue. Zanuck consented if Joe would agree to forgo a writer's credit and to accept Otto Lang, Zanuck's former ski instructor, as his producer.

Wilson had added a fictitious love interest, Anna Staviska, an impoverished Polish countess whose late husband had employed Cicero as his valet while he served as Poland's ambassador to Britain, and Joe used that relationship to comment on sex and class. Recycling the sexually charged power struggle from *Eve*, even down to the slap, he created some very un-English, Lubitschean skirmishes between Anna (Danielle Darrieux) and her former employee, Ulysses Diello/Cicero (James Mason). In a reference to class, the diplomats' myopic assumptions about the aristocratic Anna and the servant Ulysses enabled the pair to manipulate their British and German dupes, adding to the film's subtle humor.

When Joe went to Turkey in 1951 to scout locations, he also indulged in a bit of intrigue. He met with Elyesa Bazna, the actual Cicero, whom he described as "the most obvious-looking villain I've ever met . . . almost bald, with wisps of hair across his head, gold teeth, and two

In *Five Fingers* (1951), Joe created some very Lubitschean skirmishes for his spy, Cicero (James Mason), and Cicero's accomplice, Anna Staviska (Danielle Darrieux).

different color eyes," but refused Bazna's request that he be paid as a "technical advisor." Without money, the former spy declined to help, but Joe had arranged for concealed photographers to capture their meeting and passed along the photographs to *Life,* which used them in a three-page piece promoting the picture.

The British had warned Fox that even exterior shots of the British embassy would be considered an unfriendly act, and admission to its actual grounds was out of the question. Joe spent seven weeks in Turkey anyway, shooting thirty-three thousand feet of film, though he used very little. After contending with traffic jams and crowds, he wired Linda Darnell, "Airmail in Turkish means get lost. Leave tomorrow for Rome. Then to Los Angeles, flea-bitten, exhausted, but always your boy and all love. Pancho Villa." The cable was still in her wallet in 1965, when Darnell died in a fire at the age of forty-one.

Joe did not care for *Five Fingers* as a title, but Zanuck feared audiences would associate "Cicero" with that summer's highly publicized race riots in Cicero, Illinois, and he considered titles with numbers lucky. The reviews were mostly positive, though at least one critic allowed himself the phrase "no man is a hero to his valet." *Saturday Review* put Joe on its cover, and Bosley Crowther named the picture one of his best ten for 1952.

Wilson won the Golden Globe and Edgar Allan Poe Awards for the screenplay, and the Screen Directors Guild gave Joe one of its quarterly awards. Wilson and Joe received Oscar nominations for screenplay and direction respectively, though by then, Wilson had been blacklisted for refusing to cooperate with HUAC. He had won the previous year's Oscar for *A Place in the Sun*, and though *Five Fingers* was not his last nomination (*Bridge on the River Kwai*, *Lawrence of Arabia*), Wilson's name disappeared for the next twenty years while he struggled to support himself and his family.

As usual, Joe smarted at forgoing credit for his work. He had retained Wilson's continuity, but many of his touches are obvious, as is the witty dialogue. More than fifty years later, critic Dave Kehr recalled *Five Fingers* as his favorite Mankiewicz film and asked if, despite the fact that Joe took no writing credit, there could be a more "Mankiewiczian moment" than Countess Anna's explanation of her flight from Poland: "Bombs were falling. I felt I was in the way."

In October 1951, before directing *Five Fingers*, Joe moved his family into a fourteen-room Park Avenue apartment, directly above that of Richard Rodgers. At first the boys' heavy feet and loud voices disturbed the composer, but Joe sent a disarming apology, and all was quickly resolved. Joe's long-desired move also generated a devastating loss. As much as he had yearned to start over in New York, he had hardly planned to eradicate his past. But before it even left Los Angeles, the Bekins moving van carrying his records, files, letters, journals, and keepsakes caught fire, which destroyed most of the contents. There was nothing Joe could do besides carefully preserve the few singed documents that survived, and he mourned that loss for the rest of his life.

Forgoing a $4,000-a-week salary and the support of a studio was a big gamble, but Joe's timing was astute. The studio system was declining, and other producer-directors were jumping ship. Joe had talked publicly about going independent as early as 1946, and in 1951 he was the man of the hour. Envisioning independence as the opportunity to restrict himself to quality projects and execute them free of studio constraints, he signed a contract with Dore Schary, who had replaced Mayer at MGM, to write, direct, and produce three MGM pictures within a five-year period. At $250,000 a picture, he calculated, he could provide for his family while branching out into the riskier and less remunerative theatrical world of his and Herman's dreams.

Anticipating the leave taking, Joe made a point of seeing Herman more often and tried to help him. Recording one "long, evasive talk" with Herman, he sighed, "He will not or cannot accept the concept of first work, then pay." By 1951 Herman was a sick man. But despite Joe's clear preeminence, Joe was still competing with him. Even in Herman's perennial disgrace, a number of Old Hollywood giants like David Selznick regarded Herman as the superior intellect and consigned to Joe the role of cold, calculating younger brother who had to compensate with hard work what he lacked in Herman's brilliance. There was no way to prove relative brilliance, of course, and it was a comforting myth for those who chose to believe it, a group that certainly included Sara.

That group did not necessarily include Herman. He almost surely enjoyed the comparisons at Joe's expense, but his sense of competition was simply less intense. Herman had never defined himself in relation to Joe to the extent that Joe had in relation to Herman. Joe spent his entire childhood and early adulthood following in Herman's footsteps; Herman went to high school the year Joe was born. David Thomson, who interviewed Joe near the end of his life for a biography of David Selznick, recalled Joe stressing the importance of the sibling rivalry between David and his brother Myron. By then, Joe saw it as a lifelong dynamic and told Thomson "it was only possible to understand his [own] life by grasping the ceaseless rivalry he had felt with his beloved brother Herman."

Not that Herman was completely uncompetitive. Nunnally Johnson fondly recalled that "one of Herman's few gentle emotions was his pride in the accomplishments of his younger brother," but both Herman and Joe understood that at some level, the burdens Herman's failures inflicted on Joe were a bit of payback for Joe's success. The pleasure of punishing Joe through his own self-destruction (otherwise known as cutting off one's nose to spite one's face) obviously had its limitations. But with Herman and Joe, it also had a neat complementarity.

Because if Joe had to pay for Herman's failures, he also benefited from Herman's successes. Joe's lifetime habit of disciplined application owed at least something to his determination to emulate his brother's accomplishments. Brilliance has its downside: easy accomplishments can breed poor work habits, and Pop never could get Herman to care much about those other eight points on the test. Joe cared. Even if he was just as brilliant (there is no reason to imagine he wasn't), he had something to prove, a model to emulate. And later, a name of his own to earn. Sibling rivalry benefited Joe.

Even when Joe succeeded in fulfilling Herman's dream of returning to New York, he couldn't completely shake Herman. Herman had established himself in New York's theatrical and newspaper worlds before becoming a reluctant Hollywood fixture, and he was still beloved in those circles. Joe was a creature of Hollywood. But he had timing on his side. If some of the old guard still thought of him as Herman's brother, it mattered less and less as he made his own friends, his own place.

He consciously set out to conquer New York, and he succeeded because there was no reason why he shouldn't. He arrived as a celebrated writer/director, but Joe was also genuinely good company, a stimulating thinker and a witty companion. He had the means to entertain beautifully, and he and Rosa were polished hosts. They plunged in, blending worlds of wealth (Lasker, Warburg, Loeb, Vanderbilt), publishing (Guinzburg, Cerf), theater (Hart), and media (Paley), with selected Hollywood friends like Irene Selznick.

In the beginning Rosa was an asset. Besides her obvious beauty, she could be charming and interesting and took pains to create an appealing setting for their frequent entertaining. They enrolled Chris and Tom in two of Manhattan's top private boys' schools, and for the first few years, their strife remained behind the closed doors of the elegant Mankiewicz apartment, invisible to the outside world. Within, Rosa was unpredictable, alternately warm, loving, and parental, or terrifying in her rages, especially when she drank. Like his father, Joe had to win every argument, though in contrast to Pop (and Rosa), his style was coldly withering. However, as parents, they generally operated as a team, and at least during the first few years, they kept their own fights out of their social lives.

By the time Fox released *Five Fingers* in February 1952, Joe was juggling four projects. He was reading *Jefferson Selleck*, a novel MGM had sent him about a middle-aged man's review of his middle-class life; writing *Contessa with Bare Feet*, a Hollywood Cinderella story he planned to write, direct, and produce himself; considering an offer to direct the Metropolitan Opera's new production of *La Bohème*; and negotiating with Dore Schary about directing Shakespeare's *Julius Caesar*, in addition to his three-film contract.

The opportunity to direct MGM's first Shakespearean production since its 1936 *Romeo and Juliet* seemed like an auspicious beginning for his new professional life. The producer was the literate, imaginative John Houseman, whose 1937 contemporary-dress version with Orson Welles had clearly related the play to Mussolini and the rise of fascism. The Cold War offered a new crop of demagogues, though that designation seemed to depend on the eye of the beholder. To the enthusiastic anticommunists at *Time*, lean and hungry Cassius was the revolutionary, duping Brutus, a hapless liberal. Joe and Houseman actually admired Cassius and sympathized with Brutus, whom Houseman saw as the "tragic figure in our times, the liberal man, torn between his principles and the need to vindicate them with bloodshed. Brutus is Shakespeare's first draft for Hamlet."

Joe moved the family into Norma Shearer's luxurious Santa Monica beach house while he shot the picture, but Rosa's violent mood swings turned their summer into a nightmare. Fueled by jealousy, Rosa's drinking seemed to escalate in tandem with the demands of Joe's schedule, and she kept him up at night with draining fights that left him exhausted when he most needed the energy to direct. One night she came at him with a knife. Tom had suffered from asthma for years, but that summer Chris began coughing as well. The attacks abated when they sent him to sleep at Herman and Sara's.

It was a vicious circle. The more they fought, the more Joe escaped into work, though this project was a great pleasure anyway. Joe and Houseman wanted to enhance, rather than overwhelm, Shakespeare's tale of Julius Caesar's assassination, so they decided to use only Shakespeare's words, but fewer of them, and to treat the play as a political thriller. Each adapted the play separately, and Joe combined their versions (though uncredited—Joe demurred at the idea of sharing a credit with Shakespeare).

Casting was gratifying, with many American and British actors volunteering to work for a fraction of their salaries. Interested actors included Brian Aherne, Michael Redgrave, Trevor Howard, Alec Guinness, Maurice Evans, Richard Burton, Emlyn Williams, Richard Widmark, Anthony Quinn, John Carradine, Anthony Newley, Martin Gabel, Margaret Rutherford, and even Petula Clark. Joe went to England to meet with some, but despite the plethora of supplicants, he worked hard to convince John Gielgud to be their Cassius. Gielgud had already played Cassius in two important stage productions, but he generally avoided film. They cast Louis Calhern as Julius Caesar, Joe's close friend James Mason as Brutus, and two British MGM contract stars, Greer Garson and Deborah Kerr, as Calpurnia and Portia. American Edmond O'Brien was Casca, a character similar to the hardboiled roles he often played.

Their most radical choice was Marlon Brando for Mark Antony (as they spelled it). Fresh from *A Streetcar Named Desire* (1951) and *Viva Zapata!* (1952), Brando was the most acclaimed American actor of the

Covering his nervous eczema with a glove, Joe prepares Marlon Brando for his "Friends, Romans, countrymen" speech in *Julius Caesar* (1953).

moment and a guaranteed box office draw, though his prominence also made him a highly visible gamble. Brando's natural acting style was very different from the others', and the press conflated his roles with his abilities. *Time* speculated he would deliver his funeral oration "muttering and grumbling his lines in a Polish accent," and Hedda Hopper was downright hostile.

Brando shared their doubts, but he was not without experience. He had memorized long Shakespearean passages before and had played Sebastian in a New School production of *Twelfth Night*. However, he labored for a month before even daring to play Joe a tape recording, only to be told, "You sound exactly like June Allyson." So the two worked together intensively, and then Joe convinced Dore Schary with another tape. During shooting, Brando continued to work hard, both with Joe and with Gielgud, who devoted many hours to helping both Brando and James Mason, who had become rusty after so many films. Joe was thrilled with the results and talked about Brando's "Friends, Romans, countrymen" speech for the rest of his life.

Over studio objections, they filmed in black and white. Houseman wanted to remind viewers of newsreels of demagogues like Mussolini, and Joe believed the film would look more serious. They also hoped the black and white would disguise the fact that they were using sets recycled from *Quo Vadis*. (The sets look fake anyway, but color would have been worse.) The production was unusually austere for MGM, but despite its parsimonious $1.8 million budget, the studio allowed Joe to spend three weeks rehearsing the actors on the sets in costume, and to film in continuity as much as possible.

Adding to the challenges, Joe and Houseman wanted to avoid looping (dubbing dialogue where extraneous sounds or other recording problems interfered). Dubbing was not difficult to intercut with ordinary speech, but Shakespearean dialogue, delivered whole and intact, was much trickier. Because it had to be spoken over a storm, they knew they had to loop Cassius's monologue in which he plots to pull Brutus into his assassination conspiracy, but Gielgud was so intimidated by the looping mechanism that Joe considered hiring an imitator. Gielgud asked to try it himself, first. Without watching himself on film, he listened twice to the audio of the take they were using and then recorded it twice. He matched his original performance perfectly both times.

After Joe returned to New York, the studio continued cutting the film, and when Joe began hearing details, he begged Houseman to restore at least some of the cuts. Houseman sympathized but refused. Then, to take advantage of the novelty of the new wide screens, MGM opened the picture in New York with a shorter, wider version that cut off feet and heads—or parts of heads—in a number of shots. Joe pleaded with Nicholas Schenck to restore the original aspect ratio, and when Schenck refused, Joe escalated. They finally had a "screaming fight worse than any [he] had had with Mayer" that ended with Schenck throwing Joe out of his office and threatening, "You will never work in this business again!"

MGM marketed the film as a prestige production, at first running it only twice a day at the legitimate Booth Theatre, with reserved seats. Despite the peculiar semidecapitations, reviews were positive and attendance enthusiastic, with first-week revenues surpassing the wildly successful *Quo Vadis*. Joe continued to push them to restore its original proportions, at least for the British version, and studio executives eventually relented. When they moved it to another New York theater, the studio supplied an original-aspect version, and *New York Herald Tribune* critic Otis Guernsey Jr. noted the improvement: "Caesar's statue broods over the conspiring Brutus and Cassius without having the top of its skull cut off," and "when Cassius circles Brutus, stinging Brutus' conscience . . . you do not have to follow Cassius across a wide screen like a spectator at a tennis match."

Guernsey also praised Joe's "fascinating compositions of actors and masonry in different depths and levels to give his dialogue scenes a visual life." Later critics derided his camera work as boring and unimaginative, but as a product of his time, Joe generally believed in directorial invisibility: "I have no style or technique. My material dictates the style and technique," he averred in the 1970s. In 1980 he told a film festival audience he used the camera "to punctuate dramatically what I want the audience to receive, to feel, to participate in" and regarded noticeable camera movements as self-indulgent attempts to draw critics' attention to the director instead of the story. For Joe, a perfect film "would appear not to have been directed at all." He wanted to give viewers "the experience of having lived through something—funny, tragic, horrifying, whatever—but not having been manipulated."

Of course, Joe's pictures were never really devoid of visual interest or imagery, and he took great pains with sets and sound design. But he did not compose shots for the sake of aesthetics or to test the boundaries of the medium; they always served the narrative. He commented on the action in ways he found comfortable, such as close-ups of grotesque faces in the crowd in *Julius Caesar* to emphasize the dangers of demagoguery. However, as even Joe conceded at times, not only did words always predominate in his films, but sometimes he loved too many of them too well.

Julius Caesar's English reviews were stronger than the Americans', which surprised even the English. "Those who came to mock," reported the *Manchester Guardian*, "remained to be stirred by a fine account of a brave tragedy." It received Oscar nominations for best picture, black and white cinematography, and musical scoring and won for best art direction. Brando was nominated as best actor for the third year in a row. The British Academy (BAFTA) also nominated it for best picture and selected John Gielgud as best British actor and Marlon Brando as best foreign actor. The National Board of Review named it best picture and James Mason as best actor.

After Shakespeare, Puccini's *La Bohème* at the Metropolitan Opera seemed a fitting sequel, though unlike the $100,000 Joe earned for directing *Julius Caesar*, the nation's foremost opera company paid him $2,000. The prestigious new production employed painter and set designer Rolf Gérard to design new sets; MGM publicity chief and part-time lyricist Howard Dietz to write a new English libretto; and Joe to stage both English and Italian versions (his fee covered both). They were all beneficiaries of Met general manager Rudolf Bing's effort to boost box office sales by debuting new singers, expanding the number of productions in English, and hiring luminaries from the outside world, like Tyrone Guthrie (*Carmen*) and Garson Kanin (*Die Fledermaus*). Bing had approached Joe in 1950 about directing *Die Fledermaus*, and in 1951 about Mozart's *Cosi fan tutte*.

After studying the libretto and playing the record nonstop, Joe decided to eliminate some oversentimental staging and sharpen the bohemian raffishness of the Latin Quarter. He had only ten rehearsals to work with the leads and one for the chorus, so, well aware of the limitations of singers compared to actors, he confined himself to simple changes. He gave the four bohemians bits of business—sort of "fake D'Artagnan horseplay," which he thought they appreciated "because they usually ad lib . . . it gave them something to do so they weren't making horses' asses of themselves."

He also changed the end of Act I, and to his delight the conductor, Alberto Erede, who had actually known the composer, told him Puccini "would have loved my idea of having Mimi [Nadine Conner] and Rodolfo [Richard Tucker] stay there and fuck before they went out . . . instead of going out hand in hand" as they usually did. In public, Joe described his alteration more demurely as "they fall into each other's arms." Euphemism or not, Joe's modification was short lived. Besides the obvious objection, some critics considered the unseen Mimi's and Rodolfo's voices floating back to the audience more poetical.

In Act II his decision to set Musetta (Patrice Munsel) and Marcello (Robert Merrill) back to back instead of across the stage from each other as was traditional, also evoked mixed reactions. Only Joe's attempt to make the crowds behave more realistically was universally applauded. Crowds in operas usually reminded Joe of "a glee club," so he asked if they had to "walk across the stage in a kind of crablike walk, facing the conductor, or could they actually look upstage? Or offstage? Or at each other?" When the answer was yes, Joe reblocked accordingly.

For Mimi's death at the end of the last act, Joe wanted the consumptive heroine sitting in a chair instead of lying in a bed, and he wanted her muff to roll dramatically onto the floor when she died. Upright Mimi was controversial, too, but she lasted a few more years, except for those occasions "when Mimi [had] no lap." A more rotund Mimi was supposed to hold the muff in front of her, and when she died, as Joe later wrote, the muff might be "flung into the air, much like a football."

If critical responses to Joe's direction varied, Howard Dietz's English libretto was slaughtered. A literal translation of practically any opera's libretto is laughably banal (as supertitles later proved), but Dietz's injections of wit and rhyme evoked scornful comparisons to Gilbert and Sullivan and, from Virgil Thomson, accusations of "commercial show-business" and "appalling" taste. Perversely, it was also criticized as unintelligible. So despite an enthusiastic response from broadcast listeners in the hinterlands, Dietz's version lasted only about six performances.

Joe's version, bowdlerized though it was, lasted about a quarter of a century, though little by little, the company chipped away at the touches he considered his most important contributions. At the time, however, Joe enjoyed the prestige and savored the experience. Aware of the respectful treatment foreign film directors enjoyed, Joe found the traditional world of opera even more hierarchical than the European motion picture world, and he loved it. "I came through the stage door and people started saying 'Maestro.' Maestro Mank-i-e-vich," Joe later recalled with pleasure. "And I purrrrred."

CHAPTER 17

Exit Herman

BY THE TIME JOE MOVED TO FOX IN 1943, HERMAN WAS ALREADY struggling to maintain his post–*Citizen Kane* momentum, and over the ensuing decade, Joe rose to the top of their profession while Herman drifted gently downhill.

The movie business generally thrived during World War II, but some films conceived before the United States entered the action seemed off-key once US soldiers were actually in harm's way. *Rise and Shine* (1941) was one of the disappointing wartime casualties. Though it was supposedly based on James Thurber's 1933 deadpan memoir, *My Life and Hard Times*, Herman constructed the entire story around a football player Thurber described only briefly: "At that time Ohio State University had one of the best football teams in the country, and Bolenciecwcz was one of its outstanding stars. In order to be eligible to play it was necessary for him to keep up in his studies, a very difficult matter, for while he was not dumber than an ox he was not any smarter."

Herman's manic screenplay combined a Marx Brothers sensibility with liberal borrowing from football films, college musicals, gangster comedies, and Kaufman and Hart's *You Can't Take It with You*. It was Mark Hellinger's first film as a Fox producer, and he assigned Allan Dwan to direct, Hermes Pan to choreograph zany musical numbers, and Jack Oakie to play a sleepy Bolenciecwcz who periodically bursts into song. Casting thirty-seven-year-old Oakie was part of the joke—he had played football players several times, but not for the past ten years, and he was decidedly chubby as well as long in the tooth. Linda Darnell, who turned eighteen on the final day of shooting, was more age-appropriately cast as a cheerleader, though her suitor, George Murphy, whose role as a nightclub singer allowed him to show off his tap dancing, was thirty-nine. The cast also included Donald Meek as Darnell's magic-crazed professor father; Sheldon Leonard and Milton Berle as gangsters Menace and Seabiscuit

(Berle made horse noises); and Walter Brennan as Darnell's lecherous Civil War–veteran grandfather (he stole every scene he was in). Critics and audiences found it delightful, but when the Japanese bombed Pearl Harbor two days after its release, the national mood changed.

At that point Herman didn't care. He was drinking his way east on a train with Pop's body. He was still desolate in February, writing an old friend:

> I seem to become more and more of a rat in a trap of my own construction, a trap that I regularly repair whenever there seems to be danger of some opening that will enable me to escape. I haven't decided yet about making it bomb proof. It would seem to involve a lot of unnecessary labor and expense. And then every now and then, after all, people put such shiny new silken bows on the sides of the trap and re-furnish and air-condition the whole thing so charmingly and efficiently—how do I know I would like it in the great world anyhow?

One of those silken bows was his contract with Samuel Goldwyn to write a biopic about Lou Gehrig. The baseball hero had succumbed to amyotrophic lateral sclerosis (ALS, sometimes called Lou Gehrig's disease) only the previous June 1941, so his story was still fresh with the public. Herman knew Goldwyn well enough to have lost thousands of dollars to him in the early 1930s, playing poker, bridge, backgammon, and even acey-deucey. Goldwyn once had borrowed him for a few days' work in 1931, but according to the *Hollywood Reporter*, the rumor around the United Artists lot was that "Sam wanted a bridge game and, with all the good players working, he had to pay Paramount for the loan of 'Mank.'"

One of Hollywood's original moguls, Samuel Goldwyn was so astute that he had cofounded both Paramount and Metro-Goldwyn-Mayer, and so difficult that he had been pushed out of both. As a successful independent producer, he was known for the high quality of his polished productions and his Goldwynisms—Yogi Berra–esque malapropisms, most of which he never said. Some were created for him by press agents, and others were invented by people in the business to see if they could get them attributed to Goldwyn. Goldwyn considered baseball movies box office poison, and he knew nothing about the game anyway, but after watching footage of Gehrig's Yankee Stadium farewell speech (twice), he burst into tears, then bought the rights to Gehrig's story from Gehrig's

Herman and Jo Swerling's screenplay earned them one of *Pride of the Yankees'* (1942) ten Academy Award nominations. Shown here with the real Babe Ruth, right-handed Gary Cooper learned to bat and catch left-handed like the real Lou Gehrig, but he threw "like an old woman tossing a hot biscuit." So the editor reversed Cooper's throwing shots and won the picture's only Oscar.

widow. He told the press the film was "not a baseball picture," but rather "one of the most inspiring, and at the same time, tragic stories I have ever known." However, he hired sportswriter-turned-novelist Paul Gallico to write the story, and Herman and Richard Maibaum, a screenwriter around Joe's age, to turn it into a screenplay.

Herman was drinking so heavily that he failed to show up for work, so Maibaum wrote it by himself, and when he heard, Goldwyn castigated Herman: "You ought to be ashamed of yourself. I only hired you this time because I like your wife very much. . . . I'll never forgive you, and you'll never work for me again." But once he read Maibaum's script, the pragmatic producer fired Maibaum, kept Herman, and hired Jo Swerling, who excelled at construction, to work with Herman, whose forte was dialogue. The final picture has less baseball footage than many fans would have preferred, but it does include Babe Ruth and other Yankee stars playing themselves.

The choice to minimize the playing scenes owed something to Goldwyn's resistance but also to Gary Cooper's athletic ineptitude. He had no baseball experience and, in contrast to Gehrig, was right handed. Professional coaching by batting champion Lefty O'Doul and Cooper's own hard work enabled him to bat and catch on camera as a lefty, but according to O'Doul, he threw "like an old woman tossing a hot biscuit." They used stand-ins for some shots, but the editor, Daniel Mandell (who won the film's only Oscar), suggested they print Cooper's jersey backward and have him throw right-handed, and he would reverse the shot. The studio put out the word that all of Cooper's playing sequences were reversed, that Yankee lettering on all the players' jerseys was backward, and that Cooper ran to third base instead of first. That story lasted until 2013 when Tom Shieber, senior curator at the National Baseball Hall of Fame, debunked it.

Besides having a love for baseball, Herman related to Gehrig as the first-generation son of German immigrants, and Gehrig's parents' apartment in the film reminded his son Don of his grandparents' home. *The Pride of the Yankees* opened to great acclaim in July 1942, resonating with both critics and audiences, and earning Goldwyn more money than any of his previous films. It was nominated for eleven Academy Awards, including one for the screenplay. Herman again stayed away from the dinner, telling his family that going looked like preening. This time his low expectations were fulfilled.

That same summer of 1942, Herman visited George and Beatrice Kaufman's Bucks County, Pennsylvania, farm to collaborate with Kaufman on a screenplay for Warner Brothers. Beatrice had always adored Herman, but by then, she told her friends, he was in such ill health that he was "emitting sounds from every orifice" and she would have preferred to enjoy his witticisms secondhand. Herman and Kaufman wrote *Sleeper Jump*, about a troupe of actors traveling on a train across the country, including a self-destructive alcoholic who, despite a revived career, is unable to stay sober. They copyrighted it in July 1943, but after David Selznick told Kaufman he thought it too slight, Kaufman set it aside.

The character certainly hit close to home. Columnists were still running Herman's witticisms, but items about his drinking appeared with increasing frequency. Leonard Lyons reported that when Nunnally Johnson invited Herman, "who never could qualify for membership in the Anti-Saloon League," to a preview of *The Lost Weekend* (about an alcoholic's four-day bender), Herman refused, asking, "Would you invite Admiral Halsey to come and play with the boats in your baby's bathtub?"

A couple of months later, an Earl Wilson column headed, "Be Calm, Mrs. Mankiewicz, This Piece Isn't Too Nice," quoted Herman complaining that people were scaring Sara: "They saw me and it seems I wasn't drinking. I appeared to be working hard. This new character of mine unsettled her. It's not normal for me." Less than two weeks after that item, Leonard Lyons reported that during a visit to Helen Hayes and Charles MacArthur in Nyack, New York, Herman suddenly interrupted his telephone conversation with Sara about "the pattern of sober, gentlemanly behavior to which he firmly adheres," to exclaim that a donkey had just walked by. Naturally, Sara asked to speak to MacArthur and naturally, MacArthur denied their pet donkey's existence. By then, Herman was forty-eight and MacArthur fifty, long past the age when getting drunk could be considered naughty or amusing. But like many in their group, both men seemed stuck in the prolonged adolescence of the Prohibition Era.

Perhaps Herman craved attention so much that he resigned himself to embracing the image, especially after the national coverage of his drunk-driving trials, courtesy of Hearst. Aside from its salutary effects on his professional life, Herman had assumed he was through with *Citizen Kane*, but as it turned out, the model for *Citizen Kane* was not through with Herman. When Hearst attempted to smear Orson Welles as a communist, he left Herman alone, even though Herman was the former guest who had enjoyed his hospitality. Then, on March 11, 1943, Herman was driving home after a few drinks at Romanoff's when he veered to the wrong side of the road and collided, head-on, with a station wagon. As he leapt out to apologize, he recognized his old friend and neighbor, Lee (Mrs. Ira) Gershwin.

Aside from banged knees and a head cut requiring three stitches, Gershwin was unharmed; her secretary and her laundress were uninjured. But Herman had the incredible bad luck to crash right in front of Marion Davies's bungalow. Davies had moved her former dressing room to her Benedict Canyon Road estate, and at the very moment Herman hit Gershwin's car, Hearst was inside, entertaining William Curley, the publisher of his New York *Journal-American*. Hearing the noise, Curley went outside to investigate and stayed on to observe the police arrive and book Herman for drunk driving.

According to Hearst's Los Angeles *Examiner*, Herman confessed, "I am drunk. This is all my fault." The *Examiner* also reported that the police detected alcohol on his breath, that "he stumbled and nearly fell, that his "gait was staggering, his speech was slurred. . . . His eyes and pupils were dilated." Furthermore, he was "insulting, sarcastic, impolite and talkative." Back at the police station, Herman complained about being held: "I am Mr. Mankiewicz. I have no right to be here. This is an injustice. I want out of here." The account did not report that the police kept Herman at the station for five hours without allowing him to call a lawyer, a relative, or even his dinner date, before finally releasing him about eleven thirty that night, on a $500 bond, though they managed to dredge up a 1931 citation of Herman for "allegedly failing to make a boulevard stop."

Given Gershwin's and Herman's prominence, local coverage was inevitable, and both the *Los Angeles Times* and the *Daily News* ran brief items. But Hearst's *Examiner* and *Herald-Express* ran lengthy articles day after day, often on the front page beneath headlines like "Felony Charge Filed against Mankiewicz." Accompanying the police descriptions of Herman's condition in gory detail were a variety of visuals, like photographs of a disreputable-looking Herman and a crashed car, or diagrams explaining the accident. In nine days, the *Examiner* ran 253 inches and fifteen photographs; the *Herald-Express* piled on with 205 inches and nine photographs. Hearst maintained such a drumbeat that eventually trade papers, newspapers all over the country, and even *Time* magazine ran stories about his excessive coverage.

In the glare of Hearst's unwavering attention, the court arraigned Herman on felony charges that carried possible jail time and assigned him to trial by jury. The *Examiner* covered his two-week trial with lurid photos and headlines like "Mankiewicz Intoxicated, Police Charge," followed by the subhead, "Four Officers Testifying Screen Writer Was Drunk When His Auto Injured Two Women." Herman hired attorneys-to-the-stars Jerry Giesler and Norman Lyre, who instructed Don and Frank, both in the army by then, to attend the trial in uniform whenever possible. Frank was in basic training at Camp Roberts, two hundred miles away, but during his only break, he ran more than a mile to the Post Exchange (PX), bought all five copies of Hearst's paper, thrust them into the trash, then ran back for more exercises.

Mildred and Sam Jaffe attended every day of the trial; Saul Fox testified that his office had been ransacked and Herman's file left out in the debris; the ordeal frightened all of them. After Herman's attorneys attributed his tottering walk on the night in question to a limp rather than alcohol, Orson Welles testified as a character witness and confirmed that Herman had walked with a rolling gait ever since he broke his leg for the second time. Herman's attorneys earned their fees: the jury deadlocked, seven to five, against conviction, so Herman was acquitted.

Once the criminal trial ended, Gershwin and her secretary sued Herman for $51,275, though they eventually settled for $3,216.27—$1,285 to Gershwin for her contusions, bruises, and three stitches, and $1,931.27 to her secretary, who reported sixty-five visits to a psychiatrist. Herman then got to work milking the ordeal. "Tell Mrs. Gershwin to stay the hell off the street for the next twenty minutes. Herman Mankiewicz is on his way home," he bellowed one night as he left Romanoff's. To Harold Ross he reported that he "had been dragged from the obscurity of the police blotter and—a middle-aged, flat-footed, stylish-stout scenario writer—been promoted by the INS [Hearst's International News Service] into Cary Grant, who, with a tank, had just drunkenly ploughed into a baby carriage, occupied by the Dionne quintuplets, the Duchess of Kent, Mrs. Franklin D. Roosevelt (the President's wife), and the favorite niece of the Pope, with retouched art combining the more unflattering features of Goerung [*sic*] and Dillinger."

He did not mend his ways. Between the 1943 criminal trial and the 1944 civil trial, he was fired from Universal for drinking while writing *Christmas Holiday* for Felix Jackson, an émigré producer whom Herman actually liked and respected. Jackson rehired him soon afterward (the regard was mutual), and Herman sobered up enough to finish the assignment and even take some pride in it. Directed by Robert Siodmak, another German émigré, the film noir was based on a 1939 W. Somerset Maugham novel of the same name, about a Russian prostitute in Paris who debases herself to atone for the sins of her murderous husband.

Herman set the story in New Orleans, and the prostitute, thinly disguised for the censors as a jaded singer, was played by Deanna Durbin, the former child star whose pictures had saved Universal from bankruptcy (she married Jackson in 1945). In the film's lurid conclusion, the husband (Gene Kelly, also cast against type) escapes from prison and tries to kill his wife before police shoot him instead. With Gale Sondergaard as his malevolent mother, critical reaction was mixed. Some viewers were shocked at the decadence of Durbin's first truly adult role. But the picture was a huge moneymaker. It was the most successful to date of Durbin's films, and subsequent noir enthusiasts came to admire it. (In a weird connection, in it Durbin sings Irving Berlin's "Always," which was also featured in *Pride of the Yankees*, because it was Gehrig's favorite.)

Herman accumulated three more credits during the rest of the 1940s, all at RKO. Arthur Pinero originally wrote his play *The Enchanted Cottage* (1922), as a morale booster for disfigured World War I veterans (it was also a 1924 silent film). When a homely woman and a man who has been disfigured in the war meet at a cottage in the woods, they fall in love and are physically transformed. They believe the cottage has magical powers until outsiders cruelly disabuse them of their fantasy. Eventually they realize reality doesn't matter; their love made them beautiful in each other's eyes. The supposedly hideous versions of Dorothy Maguire and Robert Young were not terribly different from their magically beautiful selves, but Herman liked it, as did reviewers. The producer was Harriet Parsons, daughter of Louella and one of the industry's few female contract producers, and though DeWitt Bodeen wrote the original adaptation, the director, John Cromwell, wanted Herman to rewrite it. Parsons consented, though she joked, "I'll never dare go to the Hearst office again!"

The Spanish Main (1945) was a swashbuckling pirate adventure, hardly a typical Herman story, brought to him by Paul Henreid, who was hardly a typical pirate. Henreid was so tired of playing ladies' men—his Warner Brothers contract even stipulated that he get the girl—that he wrote a treatment about a Dutch pirate who defies both Spain and England to fight for freedom of the seas. He contracts to deliver a bride to the governor of Tortuga but falls in love with her on the way, so the governor imprisons both the pirate and his crew. The thrilling adventure story concludes with a slave rebellion that enables the lovers to escape amidst a city on fire.

"When I want a pirate, I'll get Errol Flynn," Jack Warner told Henreid. So Henreid took his idea to RKO's production chief, Charles Koerner, who liked it enough to assign the picture a $2 million budget, Technicolor, Maureen O'Hara and Walter Slezak as the bride and governor, and Frank Borzage to direct. Henreid loved everything except RKO's script, which he loathed. So he waited until the picture's sets and models were almost finished, then threatened to take a suspension unless they allowed him to bring in another writer.

Once Koerner agreed, Henreid armed himself with a bottle of Scotch and went to see Herman, whom he considered the best writer on the lot. "Forget it!" said Herman. "I don't do pirate pictures."

However, all those years of onscreen seductions had left Henreid a master of the art. As he plied Herman with Scotch, he wooed him with descriptions of "a different kind of story," and by the time they had exhaustively discussed Henreid's freedom-of-the-seas angle, the Scotch was almost gone and so was Herman's resistance. Now he appreciated the concept of a political yarn about "a pirate as a freedom fighter" and delivered a good-humored, exuberant swashbuckler.

Henreid loved it, especially its spectacular conclusion. However, near the end of shooting, Koerner (who clearly also knew how to play chicken) regretfully informed Henreid that the slave revolt and the burning of Tortuga would increase their original $2 million budget by another $200,000, which they simply could not afford. Henreid was so upset he had to be talked out of financing them himself. Once he resigned himself to shooting a diminished conclusion, he had to face Herman.

As consistently as Herman disparaged screenwriting over the years, he just as predictably became incensed if asked to alter any of his creations. "I gave you a terrific script," he stormed at Henreid and refused to "butcher" his ending. Another writer had to do it instead, but even without the original conflagration, the final picture was another healthy contributor to RKO's bottom line.

When Dore Schary, whom Herman had helped more than once, became head of RKO's production, he assigned Herman to produce as well as write *A Woman's Secret.* It was to be directed by Nicholas Ray, whom Herman had met in New York when Ray worked as John Houseman's assistant. In February 1946 Herman, Houseman, and Ray drove across country to California together, and the companions Houseman described as "two of the most violently self-destructive men I have ever known" bonded immediately. Long after Ray became revered for directing *Rebel Without a Cause,* he continued to describe Herman as the man who taught him everything he knew about screenwriting.

Houseman and Herman were trying to collaborate on a western love story, but both were so unenthusiastic about it that, in an effort to recapture the magic of *Citizen Kane,* Herman returned to the Campbell Ranch, this time with Ray as his "companion and guardian." He finished the script in five weeks but Houseman was unable to interest any actors in the picture. Then Howard Hughes took over RKO, and the project was shelved anyway. (After Hughes cut three-quarters of the studio's production, Herman said RKO under Hughes was like the Los Angeles Country Club: they wouldn't admit movie people.)

A Woman's Secret, which was based on Vicki Baum's 1946 novel, *Mortgage on Life,* failed to generate much enthusiasm either. Maureen O'Hara and Melvyn Douglas agreed to star only because each owed RKO a picture. Schary convinced O'Hara to take the part by giving her husband a director-producer contract (ironically, his film was *Strange Bargain*). Douglas's main recollection of the film was that it was the only occasion in his career that he became aroused during a love scene. Actually, the real heat was generated behind the camera, from the steamy affair between Gloria Grahame, who played O'Hara's character's protégée, and Ray, who married her shortly after she became pregnant.

As the screenwriter, Herman injected some welcome humor in the form of the police inspector's amateur-detective wife, who meddles enough to solve the mystery. As the producer, Herman collected $33,000 in addition to his $80,000 for the script, making his compensation second only to Melvin Douglas's. Although Herman the producer succeeded in finishing ahead of time and under budget, he left Ray mostly to his own devices, and the reviews were poor, especially for the screenplay by Herman the writer, and the picture lost money.

In between, Herman pieced work together. In 1944 he, Ben Hecht, and Czenzi Ormonde (who was working her way up from being Hecht's—and later Hitchcock's—secretary) sold a story, "Cornered," to RKO for $50,000. In 1945 he wrote a new treatment of George Kaufman and Moss Hart's *Fabulous Invalid*. In 1946 he tried to turn a series of John Cheever's *New Yorker* stories into a play. In 1948 he convinced Margaret Sullavan and Joseph Cotten to star in *The Man with a Load of Mischief*, a 1925 English comedy he wanted to produce. He also spent a few weeks in New York, researching the life of Johnny Broderick, a larger-than-life police detective, for an RKO picture. Hughes killed it when he took over the studio and pushed out Dore Schary as well as Herman.

Shortly after Don sold his first story to the *New Yorker* in 1945, Herman started sending in satirical pieces of his own. When Herman's were rejected, he wrote to Harold Ross, complaining that Ross's secretary must have made a mistake. After that Ross rejected them himself. *Saturday Review of Literature* eventually ran one, "A Monograph on Mr. Tomlinson," that was so facetious that either the magazine's editors considered Herman's byline prestigious enough to justify anything, or they ran it out of pity. "Heartbreak, heartbreak," Sara recalled years later. "I saw it in his face almost every day the last ten years."

In one of Herman's idiosyncratic political twists and turns, in 1946, just when anticommunist forces were gearing up again to pursue leftists (including "premature anti-Fascists"), Herman joined an effort to establish a writers' equivalent of the American Society of Composers and Publishers (ASCAP), to protect copyrights and collect royalties. Under the leadership of James M. Cain, a group including Ring Lardner

Jr., George Kaufman, Henry Myers, composer Sigmund Romberg, and lawyer Martin Gang sought to consolidate power among the four guilds (screenwriters, authors, radio, and dramatists) by creating a closed shop that would exclude publishers (unlike ASCAP). That effort provoked an opposing group, American Writers Association (AWA), led by Herman's old Screen Playwrights ally Rupert Hughes. AWA outlasted Herman's group and even participated in the 1947 HUAC witch hunts, though they left Herman alone.

Herman abhorred the blacklist, but he also considered some of its victims undeserving of the level of sympathy they attracted. One day he opened the door to a man soliciting donations to help Lester Cole, a blacklisted screenwriter having trouble getting work. Herman, who was living in yet another small house in order that they live off Tower Road rental income, asked, "Lester didn't seem to get much work before he was blacklisted. I certainly don't think he should be blacklisted—I'm opposed to that—but I was just wondering. I don't seem to get any work either. Is there any thought of raising a committee for me?"

When told no, because his problem wasn't political, Herman said, "You're telling me you would organize a committee for him but not for me because he is a subversive?"

"I wouldn't put it that way," said Cole's hapless advocate.

"Well I just did," Herman said. "And let me tell you something, young man. If you could see into my heart of hearts, you would think Lester was a patriot."

At that point Herman was working on a screenplay he hoped might be the work of lasting value he still longed to leave behind, based on the life of Aimee Semple McPherson, a, world-famous evangelist whose megachurch had millions of followers worldwide. The controversial McPherson was a faith healer who spoke in tongues. She supported ecumenism and opposed evolution. She had married three times and had numerous lovers. She mysteriously disappeared and then insisted, despite overwhelming evidence to the contrary, that she had been kidnapped. Herman based his 1950 screenplay on *Woman of the Rock*, a 1949 novelization of her life by Hector Chevigny, and it was in immediate demand. Both MGM and Fox were interested. Robert Aldrich wanted to work on it with Joseph Losey. William Wyler, Otto Preminger, and even Joe wanted it. Mercedes McCambridge, who had just won a best supporting actress Oscar for *All the King's Men*, wanted the part, as did Evelyn Keyes.

Then Herman sabotaged it exactly as he had *Citizen Kane*. Despite having based it on a work of fiction, he showed the script to McPherson's daughter. The daughter showed it to McPherson's son, who was also the leader of his mother's church, and the son threatened to sue Herman for libel and invasion of privacy. Herman hired Greg Bautzer, a high-powered entertainment lawyer, but the threats drove away the studios. Orson Welles turned him down, as did Bennett Cerf, when Herman suggested publishing it as a book. Eventually, Samuel Goldwyn Jr. optioned it and held the rights even after Herman's death, but he never produced it.

By then Don and Frank were grown. In 1946 Don had married Ilene Korsen, who seemed to meet with Sara's approval, and in 1951 he published *See How They Run,* a novel about the world of horseracing. Despite his pride in Don's accomplishment, Herman scoffed at the subject matter and teased him about his efforts to make it a best seller. "Don't try to get the Baltimore relatives to buy it," he advised. "Buy copies and send them." He did not live to see Don's second novel, *Trial,* a political and social commentary that won the prestigious Harper Prize.

Frank graduated at the top of his class at UCLA and went on to both law school and journalism school. In 1952 he married Holly Jolley, a UCLA graduate student and lapsed Mormon whom Sara patronized so unkindly that Herman interceded. He told Holly that Sara, whom he respected and sometimes feared, was both an intellectual and an intellectual snob, and sometimes, just a snob. "There are actually two Saras," he said. "One is a very conventional Jewish girl from Baltimore with very narrow vision. There is also the very worldly Sara, who knows as much about classical music as anyone and is very sophisticated in many areas; who reads widely and has an enormous store of knowledge. I never know which of the two Saras I'm going to find—Worldly Sara or the Baltimore Sara. It's very confusing and you'll have to figure it out."

Herman teased Holly because he was fond of her, and Holly loved Herman. She felt that she learned something from him in every encounter—he always enlarged her perspective. Herman was particularly intrigued by Holly's resignation from the Mormon church, periodically asking, "How did you do that? You actually wrote a letter? Where can I do that to resign?" (When Joe became Episcopalian years later, he told Holly, then added, "Don't tell Sara.")

Only Johanna, also known as Josie, was still at home with Herman and Sara, providing Herman with material when he wrote her brothers. ("Johanna is rapidly becoming blonde and the long, broad nose that characterized her is now scarcely noticeable the way we dress her hair.") In fact, he was in awe of his beautiful, bright daughter, leaving Sara to

Born when Herman and Sara were forty, Johanna (Josie) was an unexpected joy. She was only fifteen when Herman died.

set and enforce standards—which she did, with Josie's friends as well as Josie. She grew up with friends like Jill Schary (Dore's daughter), Susan Kohner (agent Paul's daughter), Louisa Wallace (director Richard's daughter), Sharon Disney, and Jane Fonda. In her memoir Jill Schary Robinson described Josie as their group's "arbiter." She made national news as a high school sophomore, when she wrote to Albert Einstein seeking help for a geometry problem, and Einstein answered. Almost certainly alerted by Herman, all the wire services ran the story.

In 1947 Ferdinand Lundberg, author of the 1936 biography *Imperial Hearst: A Social Biography*, sued Herman, Welles, and RKO for copyright infringement, accusing them of plagiarism. Hoping to exhaust the journalist's funds, RKO stalled for several years, but Lundberg hung on, so in 1950 the case went to trial in New York. Lundberg's attorney had to chase down Welles in Morocco to depose him, but RKO sent Herman and Houseman to testify. Herman admitted reading Lundberg's book but called it "a tendentious, one dimensional tract" and insisted he already

"I don't know how it is that you start working at something you don't like, and before you know it, you're an old man."

knew everything it included. The case ended in a hung jury, and RKO settled out of court in 1951.

Herman was barely in his fifties by then, but his health was declining along with his prospects. The laudatory 1951 *Life* piece on Joe had made the unsayable explicit and public, quoting an anonymous friend that "someplace along the way . . . the two brothers passed each other, one going up, the other going down." Herman was as irascible as ever, but his friends stuck by him, enjoying his company and finding him work when they could.

When he wasn't employed by a studio, Herman wrote at home. Suffering from liver infection as well as failing kidneys and an enlarged heart, the previously chunky Herman became wizened. "I don't know how it is that you start working at something you don't like, and before you know it, you're an old man," he said, and he looked it. When he was awake, he was usually in his study, wearing his beloved faded bathrobe and slippers, a cigarette dangling from his mouth, engrossed in a book or the *New York Times,* to which he subscribed by mail, along with every other newspaper he could obtain. Josie remained in awe of Herman, tiptoeing around with her friends to avoid disturbing him.

Joe helped get Herman his last completed picture, *The Pride of St. Louis* (1952), an amiable biopic about baseball player/sportscaster Dizzy Dean. It was slight but well received, and a number of reviewers singled out Herman's script. Praising "old hand" Herman's "nice mixture of humor and sentiment," *Saturday Review of Literature* critic Hollis Alpert also noted that actor Dan Dailey (as Dean) "easily outshines, with his playing ability, former major leaguers like Jimmy Stewart, Gary Cooper, and William Bendix." (They had played respectively Monte Stratton, Lou Gehrig, and Babe Ruth.) It was a fitting bookend to *The Pride of the Yankees* a decade before.

In the fall of 1952, Frank started law school at Berkeley, but he and Holly visited almost every weekend because Herman had become so frail. By early 1953 he was too ill to drink, but he continued to work. In addition to adapting *The Number,* a play about a bookie that George Abbott had staged on Broadway, he had an assignment from Fox (ironically, it was "Mock the Midnight Bell," based on a line from Shakespeare's *Antony and Cleopatra*). He also was negotiating on a third with Sam Jaffe. Even when none existed, Jaffe loyally manufactured assignments to help Herman emotionally as well as financially.

On February 26, 1953, Joe and Rosa stopped on their way to Palm Springs to visit Herman in Cedars of Lebanon Hospital. He had been hospitalized before, and though his condition had been defined as somewhere between "tolerable" and "bad," Sara had discouraged Don from flying out with them. Joe found him in an oxygen tent (though still smoking), and the brothers talked for hours. Herman alternated between contemplating his death and discussing his new RKO assignment. At one point, apropos of nothing, he said, "You know, I've never had a bad steak. Some weren't great, but none were bad." He assured Joe he had his affairs in order so that if he had to, he was ready to meet his maker. "Or, in my case, should I say co-maker?" he joked. Joe had spent his entire adult life serving as Herman's "co-maker," or co-signer, on a seemingly endless stream of Morris Plan (high-interest) loans that Joe often had to pay off.

Herman's nights were miserable, but his days were tolerable, so when his doctors anticipated no imminent crisis, Joe and Rosa left on March 1 for the La Quinta Hotel. But Don flew out the next day, and by March 3, Herman had deteriorated so much that Joe and Rosa returned. Frank and Holly flew down from San Francisco, though neither really believed Herman was dying, even after visiting him in the hospital. When Herman apologized for being a bad father, Frank burst into tears.

The Mankiewiczes, Foxes, and Jaffes gathered at the hospital, and Joe later sent Erna an account of Herman's last day of life:

> Wednesday, the 4th, was, in many ways, almost a replica of pop's last hours. The spectacle of an unyielding, unconquerable, spirit and mind, to all intents and purposes disembodied, seemingly existing apart from a body that was already dead, but refusing to give up. We all spoke with him that afternoon. With Sam Jaffe, he actually discussed details of the RKO deal and corrected Sam when he mis-stated some of the terms. Alone with him, I had a long and warm and intimate talk. . . . Importantly, among other things, he spoke of his imminent death—this right after his conversation with Jaffe!—and he talked about pop and Joe Stenbuck, your Joe. Herman told me that what he wanted, more than anything, after death, if and when, was to follow pop and Joe: to be cremated. He doubted that his wish would be granted; he told me that he had been over and over it with Sara, that she had begged him not to demand that of her—and that he could understand her feelings. . . . As you can imagine, I answered mostly in noises. Knowing that he was dying, I had to assure him that he wasn't, and, at the same time, promise to do everything possible to have him die as he wanted to.

Along with Don, Frank, Holly, Josie, the Jaffes, and a few other relatives, Joe and Rosa remained at the hospital all day and almost through the night. Joe promised Herman he would pay for Johanna's college education. Sara ran interference against "a particularly unctuous rabbi, who hovered about Herman's door like a compassionate vulture" (Joe wrote Erna). Herman comforted Frank and Johanna and gave Don instructions for his funeral. Clergy were welcome but only in mufti. Don was to run a newspaper notice saying, "In lieu of flowers, contributions may be given to plant trees in the Arab section of Palestine." Furthermore, Don was to order that no one could keep his hat on (a là Orthodox Jews), and if Dore Schary wore his anyway, Don was to tap him on the shoulder and say, "Dore, I have a message for you from the deceased: Take off your hat, you're in the house." Don agreed to all of Herman's orders and obeyed none of them.

That night they could hear Herman crying out in his room, "Let it all end," and shortly after Sara and their children returned in the morning, he gave up, dying of uremic poisoning. Sara remained in his room, practically keening, and when they led her to an unoccupied wheelchair in the hall, she stopped crying for a moment, looked up at the heavens, shook her fist, and in a threatening voice, declared, "I will never forgive you as long as I live!" She clearly did not mean Herman.

Eventually, Sara regained her composure and impressed Joe with her dignity and refusal to countenance "self-perpetuating semitic wailing" (Joe to Erna). On the way home from the hospital, Joe gingerly broached the subject of cremation. Everything should be as Herman wanted, Sara told him without hesitation, including cremation. She hoped Joe would arrange everything.

Despite Herman's ban, the Hollywood Cemetery Chapel overflowed with flowers and a crowd of more than three hundred, encompassing Hollywood history, from silent pictures stars to young writers from Fox and MGM who knew Herman only vaguely. Sara earned fifteen-year-old Josie's lifelong resentment for keeping her away—many of her friends attended and were puzzled by her absence. Nunnally Johnson was terrified of speaking in public but acceded to Joe's request that he deliver the eulogy. "It was a chore that was painful to him," Joe wrote Erna, "emotionally as well as psychologically. Yet he did it—simply, awkwardly, movingly and beautifully." Johnson articulated what so many felt: great joy in Herman's gifts and great regret at their waste.

> When a friend leaves you forever . . . you can't help wondering how great really is this loss. . . .
>
> . . . Now that I must look ahead to a life without him, I can very well see what a vital part of it he was, and how much he contributed not only to my pleasure but to the actual formation of my belief and opinions. In effect, to the kind of person I am. And if you must have a friend of such influence, you would be lucky to have one like Mank. Or better still, Mank himself. . . .
>
> I have never known the like of his wild wit and imagination—in which there was also, always, natural wisdom—and the kind of bloodcurdling perceptiveness that disposed of all nonsense and confusion and laid bare the bones of truth clear enough for anyone to see. After that, of course, he might very well blow up a new storm of confusion and a new kind of nonsense, but now it was entertaining—and we all knew where we stood on the matter.

> . . . I don't think anyone could have been with Mank for five minutes without remembering—sometimes uneasily—that there are standards of quality and behavior that are immutable—in which respect he was often like a skylarking preacher—and no one could be with him long without reappraising his own scale of values.
>
> . . . I don't think I'll ever be able to forgive . . . that he should so recklessly squander on a few what he should have made available for everybody. He was a profligate by nature—and not the least of what he threw away without thought was the contents of a brilliant mind.
>
> . . . next to being with Mank has always been the fun of talking about him when he was not there. The simple mention of his name was enough to set off stories and arguments good for three-quarters of the night.

As they left the chapel, everyone seemed reluctant to leave and stood around talking, partly about the simplicity, "the Herman-ness" of the service, as Joe put it to Erna. "It was as if they had all had one last opportunity to lunch with Herman, to sit with him for awhile, and—as Nunnally put it—Herman picked up the check."

While visitors thronged in all weekend to exchange Herman stories and console one another, Joe investigated Herman's finances and, to his relief, found them less dire than he had anticipated. Herman had brought his affairs up to date, leaving enough insurance to cover his debts and "a modest nest egg" for Sara, though she would have to sell the house and move with Johanna to a smaller apartment. She also sold Herman's library, and her sons always remembered that the library and the house each fetched the same amount, $80,000.

Sara had never doubted Herman's superiority, but after his death, she heard from many others who shared her regard. From Fred Hacker: "By writing one makes an attempt to close the gap that has been opened by the loss . . . but . . . I do not think one should 'get over' Herman in any sense of the word. . . . It may sound strange to consider a man so vital, so impulsive, so uncontrollable and often so unrealistic, the representative of a predominantly moral force, but it is as such that I experienced him. . . . What I loved in him particularly was his seeming negativism which really was but the steadfast refusal to come to terms with glibness, complacency, and 'the laziness of the heart' which compromises when it ought to fight."

Ben Hecht wrote, "I gave up trying to think of him as dead a week after his funeral, and I'm reconciled now to living a fair part of my time through with my snorting old friend at my side. So help me, Manky dead, is three times a livelier companion than most of the living I know."

From John Houseman, "You and Herman were my family—yours the house to which I regularly returned from the East—and Herman (supposedly irascible, unstable Herman), my ever-sympathetic, ever-understanding, always patient and infallible advisor and benefactor, on personal decisions, on business matters and in all the more intangible problems of life and people, Herman's was the voice (through all the yellings and exaggerations and perversities) which always made sense, moral and intellectual and practical sense—and the sense of the heart."

Charles Brackett wrote, "I feel impoverished. . . . I loved him."

From George Kaufman:

> I have resented all the Mank stories in print, because they have not done him justice . . . badly told, always—disgracefully, sometimes. I have been telling them a lot myself—but picking my audience with

care, because Herman had a rare mind and a wit so razor-sharp and subtle that it was not meant for everyone. (Subconsciously I flatter myself by implying that I was one of the rare spirits that appreciated him to the full, but damn it! I was.)

Memories of our working together—a play, a movie, The Times . . . gorgeous memories, some of them, and a few exasperating ones, too. . . . That's all, and little enough. But I just want you to know that I will think of him for a long, long time.

Then there was the letter Sara did not see.

I shouldn't write this letter since you're in the middle of finals and all, but I have to.

. . . Frank, I miss him so much. You don't know what it's like . . . having to pretend a nonchalance, an indifference about the whole thing and holding back the tears when Mother cries & muffling your own every night in the pillow so she won't hear. . . . I only had 15 years of that tenderness and wisdom and insight. . . . he won't know my husband and he won't see me get married & he won't see me graduate & he won't see my annual and he won't see me go to Wellesley and he won't be there for any of it, and I want him there. . . .

Maybe I'm selfish but it's not fair to me . . . I want him to straighten out my life, to differentiate between right and wrong, to tell me what to do.

. . . I keep remembering how awful I was to him—sometimes on purpose . . . there were times when I would deliberately not answer him because I knew it irritated him—

And he died before I could tell him how much he meant to me and how very much I loved him.

JOE

CHAPTER 18

Hollywood Cinderella: A Cautionary Fairy Tale

HERMAN'S DEATH WAS A RELIEF AS WELL AS A LOSS, BUT JOE DID NOT handle death well. Not even his dogs', and certainly not his beloved brother's. As usual, he coped by compartmentalizing, erecting walls—in his own way, almost literally. As was his custom, Joe printed Herman's name in tiny letters on the March 5th page of his diary and drew a small box around it.

Then he moved on. He kept in touch with Sara and the Foxes and saw them when he was in California, but he rarely mentioned his brother in conversation or even in his diaries. At that point Joe was absorbed in founding his own independent production company, Figaro, Inc. He named it for the barber in Mozart's opera *Le nozze di Figaro,* because Figaro did "a little bit of everything." On May 12, 1953, the *New York Times* reported that Figaro had entered a two-picture deal with United Artists, with their first undertaking to be *The Barefoot Contessa,* based on a story Joe "originally had planned on doing as a novel."

By then motion picture studios were reducing staffs and renting their sound stages and backlots to television production. Movies were often shot on location, often produced by companies like United Artists, which financed and distributed films by independent companies like Joe's without maintaining a costly studio of their own. Besides movies, he wanted Figaro to produce plays and books, by others as well as himself, and he convinced the courtly, German-born Robby Lantz, his sometimes agent and longtime friend, to run the operation. Bert Allenberg, Joe's Hollywood agent, agreed to serve as Figaro's West Coast vice president in addition to his regular job.

Joe loosely based his first completely original screenplay on the life of Rita Hayworth. She had been a dancer before she became a movie star; left Hollywood to marry Prince Ali Aga Khan; and definitely did not live happily ever after. He planned to use Hayworth's unhappy experiences to debunk what he regarded as the detrimental romanticism of the Hollywood Cinderella story. Besides taking on Hollywood as he had the theater in *All About Eve,* he wanted to discredit the international jet set as worthless parasites. He relied yet again on flashbacks, not only to enrich the story through multiple points of view, but also as a way of demonstrating the impact of the past on the present.

After opening on the funeral of Maria Vargas, three male characters tell her story in flashback. Harry Dawes, a burnt-out director, and Oscar Muldoon, a sweaty, anxious press agent, accompany their employer, Kirk Edwards, a ruthless financier Joe modeled on Howard Hughes, to see Maria dancing in a Madrid café. At Edwards's orders, Dawes builds Maria into an international film star, but Maria cares less about her stardom than for finding a storybook prince. She leaves Hollywood with a South American playboy, and when he mistreats her, she is rescued by Count Vincenzo Torlato-Favrini, the last member of an Italian aristocratic family.

Maria adores her fairytale Prince Charming and does not learn until their wedding night that Vincenzo cannot consummate their marriage because of a war injury. Naively eager to provide Vincenzo with an heir, Maria has an affair with Vincenzo's chauffeur. When she tells Harry, he warns her against telling Vincenzo, but he is too late. Vincenzo shoots her for her infidelity, then erects a statue in her memory.

To accentuate the deception and heartbreak behind the notion of marrying a prince and living happily ever after, Joe wanted to make the count a closeted homosexual. Knowing that would never be approved by the censors, he settled for impotence based on a war wound, as with Jake Barnes in Ernest Hemingway's *The Sun Also Rises*. He wanted James Mason as Vincenzo, and to interest Gary Cooper in playing Dawes, he sent a lengthy summary of the story, along with pictures and descriptions of some of the characters.

> The character [Harry Dawes] is that of a motion picture director. If you want to visualize him, superimpose your fondest memories of Vic Fleming upon your fondest memories of Greg LaCava and Bill Wellman and Jack Ford, etc. . . . He's unsentimental, incredibly wise and instinctive about people, bitter because his life has been bitter, cynical because his life has been cynical. He speaks with wit because he is unafraid—and he is unafraid because he's

been down to a bench in Griffith Park and up to a bungalow at the Ambassador.

He . . . is the voice of wisdom and reality and truth—whether the truth be pleasant or unpleasant, reassuring or shocking.

Needless to say, Harry Dawes was also the voice of Joe, and he had a great deal to say about Hollywood. Joe described two of the other characters to Cooper:

Kirk Edwards is

a girl-crazy delinquent, who was born with half of Texas in his mouth. His occupation, preoccupation, and sole ambition was to go to bed with all the women in the world. So he decided to produce movies, as a means to that end. . . . In the entire relationship between Harry and Kirk, I want to dramatize something very important. The hatred of the man who has nothing but money, toward the man who has talent and sensitivity and humanity. . . .

Alberto Bravano [is] a South American replica of Kirk Edwards. With one major difference—where Kirk disguises his behavior by an outward appearance of piety and Good Clean Americanism, Bravano is openly a playboy. (I also intend to satirize, and hold up to some well-deserved scorn, the whole international riff-raff set which congregates annually on the French Riviera. . . .)

. . . the contessa may be an unknown if you play Harry Dawes . . .

Joe reported to Bert Allenberg: "I spoke to Gary Cooper, from Paris yesterday morning . . . I didn't understand a goddam word he said."

Linda Darnell expected to play Maria and was heartbroken when Joe failed to offer her the part. Allenberg suggested Jean Simmons, whom he represented, but Joe had an earthier candidate in mind. Unfortunately, at that point Ava Gardner was one of MGM's hottest stars, and Loews chairman Nicholas Schenck was still furious at Joe over *Julius Caesar*. Allenberg was surprised to find that Dore Schary, who had replaced Mayer, opposed the idea as well (unbeknownst to Allenberg, Gardner was probably Schary's favorite female star). However, Benny Thau, the executive in charge of MGM's talent, gave Allenberg some encouragement.

Gary Cooper showed no interest, so Joe cast Humphrey Bogart as Dawes, as well as Edmond O'Brien as Oscar Muldoon. For his first color film, he hired Jack Cardiff, the world's top Technicolor cinematographer, and planned to save money by shooting at Italy's Cinecittà studio outside Rome. He asked Polish director Michael Waszynski to cast many of the parts in Europe, but by the time he sailed for Europe on October 12, Joe still lacked a Maria. Jennifer Jones (by then Mrs. David O. Selznick) was angling for the part, and Allenberg wrote that she was looking "very sultry, very sexy looking. You could do worse, in a pinch."

However, by then Joe had become so obsessed with getting Gardner that on October 27 Allenberg wrote Joe to stop pestering him, "Don't you know, dear boy, how much I realize this urgency . . . ? Mr. Haggiag [head of Cinecittà] telephoned me all out of breath at the club on Sunday, to tell me that he had just talked to you and how important it was to you to know about Ava Gardner as soon as possible. For crying out loud, am I a moron? Don't answer that!"

Allenberg added, "I had Ava in here this afternoon and she and Frankie [Sinatra] are now splitting officially. It looks like a divorce. Because of this, she now would like to get the hell out of town and really wants me to press on the Metro thing, even more than she indicated to me when she first agreed to do the picture. Her additional support and backbone in this will also be helpful."

By October 30 Gardner was even more determined:

> Ava has now become so violently rabid to do it that she said she would tear down the walls in the studio if it could not be arranged. . . . Krim [head of United Artists] just phoned us today that he had met with Schenck this morning and Schenck was violent in his refusal. Schenck told Krim that not only did they have a picture for her, if she wanted to go abroad, but that for certain personal reasons which he would not discuss, he would not loan her to you, even if she had nothing else to do. . . . I have reported all this to Ava, who is livid and we are making a date to see Schenck on Monday. . . . That's all, Joey. Love, Bert

Eventually Schenck capitulated, but only after extracting punishing terms. On November 17, Allenberg wrote:

> I know you like everything explained to you from "hello" onwards, but I am not going to drag you through the entire conversations, just a brief resume. . . . First, Ava saw Dore who was quite

> adamant. Prior to that I had sent a long wire to Nick Schenck over her signature, to which he replied that he would see her but that it was useless insofar as a loanout was concerned. When Nick got here she saw him and put on a helluva performance of pleading, begging, getting angry, crying, etc., and Nick was absolutely adamant, swearing that it had nothing to do with personal grounds, but that they could not loan [her] to an independent from whom they could not get anybody in return, whereas in loaning her to a major they could get some star back. . . . Ava came out of the meeting absolutely sunk, and decided that it was hopeless.

After painstaking negotiations with Benny Thau, Dore Schary (who, Thau told Allenberg, was actually more opposed to the deal than Schenck), and eventually Schenck himself, it finally came down to money. Allenberg agreed to $200,000 plus 10 percent of the gross. Although it was "a rough deal," Allenberg believed Gardner's presence could "add a million dollars to the gross of the picture." Furthermore,

> Ava is thrilled about the fact that it is now going to be done in Technicolor and that you have gotten Jack Cardiff as the photographer; she thinks he is great. [When Cardiff filmed her in *Pandora and the Flying Dutchman* (1950), Gardner told him, "You must light me carefully when I'm having my period."]
>
> P.S. I forgot to tell you that on Friday when the deal was practically closed, Benny Thau got a long exhorting wire from Elizabeth Taylor, begging for permission to do the picture and saying that you had given her the script in Rome. . . . Benny got mad as hell and thought you used poor judgment in doing this because if the company refused to loan Ava, why in God's name would they loan you Taylor. He said it put him in a terribly embarrassing position with Taylor to have to tell her that they were loaning Ava. Unfortunately, Schenck saw the wire too, and he hit the ceiling and got so damn mad that they almost called the deal off. In fact, Schenck said if it wasn't for the fact that he didn't want to upset me and because of the fact that he had given his word, he would not go through with it.

November 23 *Los Angeles Daily News*:

AVA GARDNER ITALY BOUND SANS FRANKIE

Smokey-eyed actress Ava Gardner was packing for Rome, and one of the things she did not slip into her suitcase was down-to-118 pound Frank Sinatra.

November 25 Joe to Allenberg:

I'M NOT AN IDIOT. IT WAS SHE [TAYLOR] WHO APPROACHED ME IN ROME. I ASSURED HER THAT METRO WOULD NOT LOAN HER TO ME, AND THE CABLE SHE SENT WAS HER OWN IDEA.

Jane Ellen Wayne, *The Leading Men of MGM*:

Sinatra insisted Ava's place was with him, but Ava wanted to get as far as from Frank as possible. She flew to Rome to film The Barefoot Contessa. Frank attempted suicide by cutting his wrists and was hospitalized with a nervous breakdown. . . .

December 8 Wire, Allenberg to Joe:

. . . FRANKIE TELLS ME AVA QUITE DISTURBED LACK OF ACTIVITY AND WONDERS WHY SHE RUSHED OVER AND CANNOT UNDERSTAND YOUR NOT TAKING ADVANTAGE HER PRESENCE FOR REHEARSALS TRAINING ETC LOVE BERT

December 8 Wire, Joe to Allenberg:

. . . EVER SO GRATEFUL BEING INFORMED SINATRAS CONCERN ABOUT GARDNERS INACTIVITY . . . JOE

December 14 Wire, Joe to Allenberg:

ANSWER SOONEST POSSIBLE TWO CONFIDENTIAL ITEMS . . . WHAT EXACTLY MUST WE PAY FOR EXAMPLE DO LIVING EXPENSES INCLUDE PHONE CALLS TO SINATRA IN CALIFORNIA ETCETERA . . . LOVE JOE

December 15 Letter, Joe to Bertie:

The following is a breakdown of the hotel bill of your mistreated and anxious-to-be-cooperative Miss Gardner for the period of November 30th through December 9th:

Rental of suite	192,200
Meals	56,390
[Coffee, Laundry, Liquor	67,570]
Telephone	218,680
Cables	50,873
[Radio rental, magazines & newspapers, Drug store, Stamps, Opera tickets, Flowers	70,379]

I have omitted about 61,000 lire additional. . . . In addition . . . she received 250,000 lire in cash—of which 100,000 was stolen out of her pocketbook in a nightclub. In addition, we have paid 77,275 lire for nine days rental of an Alfa Romeo which remained in front of her hotel for most of that period because she was bedded with a cold for part of the time. In addition, she has hired a secretary who receives 45,000 lire a week.

On the 10th of December, Ava moved out of the hotel and into an apartment . . . rental . . . 400,000 lire a month. She insisted upon having heat 24 hours a day, for which there is an additional charge of 3,000 lire a day. . . . I assume that her telephone use will be in proportion to what it was in the hotel. . . .

In addition to the secretary, Ava has engaged five servants. We have not yet been informed as to their salaries. Among other extraneous items, I understand she purchased 26,000 lire worth of tube roses the day she moved into the apartment.

. . . Quite simply, Bertie—what the hell do we do about it?

. . . Exactly where do living expenses end and infantile insanities begin? Is our commitment to M-G-M or to Ava Gardner?

. . . As to her being lonely and forlorn. From the moment of her arrival, our entire staff has been put at her disposal. . . .Arthur Krim, himself, and Robert Haggiag were her personal escorts available at all times during my five day absence in London. She had a girl friend fly in from Madrid the second day she was in Rome. . . . In addition to her girl friend and secretary, I put my entire production unit at her disposal when she moved. We rented furniture for her, which is being charged to the production. Our Unit Manager has devoted all of his time for the past week in getting her apartment straightened out.

There are 623 lire to the dollar. Long before we have finished with Ava, she will have spent more than $30,000 to satisfy her personal whims. Our lire budget—and, believe it or not, we have had to sacrifice in production needs because of Ava and the approaching demands of Mr. Bogart—simply cannot absorb it. . . .

If ever I needed you to act immediately, and your immediate advice, this is it. . . .

December 22 Letter, Bert to Joe:

I immediately went over to Metro. . . . make up a bill of the following items . . . Liquor, Telephone, Cables, Drug Store, Opera Tickets, Flowers; also the 250,000 lira in cash . . . the salary of the secretary . . . the 26,000 lira worth of tuberoses. Have Johnny Johnston [the production manager] present this bill to her, in person, and ask her how she wants to handle it—does she wish to make out a check for it, or just how does she wish it handled. She may yell and scream but you must insist on payment. Then, thereafter, each week, whatever items there are beyond normal living expenses. . . . you are to present her with a bill for them. . . .

She tried this stunt with Metro and they insisted upon, and finally got, repayment of the so-called personal items. . . . Johnny Johnston must likewise tell her that five servants is an unreasonable item of first class living expenses and that you will not permit more than one or two. . . .

Jane Ellen Wayne, *The Leading Men of MGM*:

Ava had been planning to spend the Christmas holidays in Madrid with Luis Dominguin until Frank showed up with a bad head cold. The Sinatras went into seclusion for a few days before he quietly boarded a plane for New York.

In January 1954 Joe, Rosa, and Tom settled into an elegant Rome apartment, where they had Tom, eleven, privately tutored, to keep up with school. Now boarding at Lawrenceville, Chris joined them during school vacations. Rosa's episodes escalated, and they fought constantly. Tom suffered such severe asthma attacks that they kept an oxygen tent by his bedside, and Rosa's mother came from Austria to help out.

By the time shooting began on January 11, 1954, production manager Johnny Johnston had hired almost the entire crew and even many of the same extras, from an unfinished movie about William Tell that Errol

A cheery moment for Ava Gardner and Humphrey Bogart, of which there were too few.

Flynn had been producing in the Italian Alps. Jack Cardiff had finally realized his dream of directing, but when Flynn ran out of money, they had to shut down. Among the crew members was Rosemary Matthews, a young English production assistant so fluent in Italian that Johnston assigned her to coach Rossano Brazzi in his dialogue (Brazzi was now playing Vincenzo, because Mason had become unavailable). Though she was barely twenty-four, Rosemary was so efficient that soon she was driving Tom on outings, taking Rosa to designer collections, and helping with the household's bills and servants.

Joe found conditions at Cinecittà frustratingly primitive, but more disappointing and ultimately more important to the picture, he found himself unable to develop a good rapport with Ava Gardner. His attempts to relax her by teasing just intimidated and antagonized her. Bogart added to her nervousness by openly dismissing her as an actress and behaving badly in general. When he thought a scene wasn't going his way, Bogart found a way to ruin it, and he coughed so frequently that Joe sometimes used a take simply because it had enough dialogue. (Bogart died of lung cancer three years later.)

In addition to his day-to-day concerns, Joe worried about his next project. Without a salary, he had to generate new projects to maintain his income. Even so, he could not resist writing Lantz about "a simply wonderful opera singer by the name of Maria Meneghini Callas." Metropolitan Opera compensation was laughable, but Callas whetted Joe's appetite to return: "Her voice is sensational, she is lovely to look at, and she is the best actress I have yet seen on the operatic stage. . . . There is every chance that I would be available to do a new TOSCA with her, to open the Metropolitan season next winter. . . . You might query Bing about it."

Lantz reported that Bing's plans were already set for the following year, but he hoped Joe might return for the season after that. As for Maria Callas, Bing had been negotiating with her for three years but was unwilling to pay the $2,000 a night she demanded.

Allenberg chimed in to urge patience. "I do wish you didn't feel so strongly about HAVING to actually direct a picture this summer. I don't wish to be boring, but it does throw off our long range thinking. . . . I still adhere to what I have always said—to wit, write your own scripts and direct them. Anything else is a step backwards."

In February, the cast and crew moved to the Italian coast to shoot exteriors, and on February 11, sixteen gathered for a sumptuous Italian dinner to celebrate Joe's forty-fifth birthday. With Rosa still in Rome, Joe and Rosemary began an affair. Rosemary was already besotted with the magnetic, world-famous director and awed by his work (she had trained as an actress), but she knew it was only a fling, which she expected to last, at most, for the duration of production.

While Joe was in post-production, Howard Hughes (another of Gardner's former lovers) contacted Joe about the Kirk Edwards character. His lawyer, Greg Bautzer, told Joe, "Howard likes you, and it's a marvelous script, but you're cutting a little too close to the bone, and Howard doesn't like that." Joe changed "Texas tycoon" to "Wall Street lion" and made a few other alterations that satisfied Hughes, but the resemblance was still obvious, and the press picked it up anyway.

Despite its structural similarities to *All About Eve*, reviewers found Joe's cautionary Cinderella story less than enchanting. Without Zanuck to rein him in, Joe's prolixity overwhelmed his story, and life loused up the script even outside the picture. Joe had his Contessa die at the hand of her long-awaited Prince Charming, but after his costly courtship Ava

Gardner failed to give him the performance he had envisioned. So despite the complete control for which he had so long yearned—writing his first completely original story, directing and producing it himself—his angry picture lacked *Eve*'s sparkle. Even so, his screenplay received an Academy Award nomination, and Edmond O'Brien won as best supporting actor.

Preparing for foreign markets turned out to be trickier than they had anticipated. The first French translator turned down the job, explaining that French audience members would find Vincenzo's wedding-night explanation of his war wounds so unrealistic that they would "snicker and laugh." The second echoed his concern but took the job anyway. French Canadians, on the other hand, were even more prudish than Americans. Quebec officials considered a married woman's adultery and pregnancy more sinful than an unmarried woman's, and United Artists' protestation that Maria's adultery was actually an unselfish sacrifice fell on deaf ears.

Vincenzo's war wounds notwithstanding, French critics loved it. Ever since his down-and-out days in Paris, Joe had disparaged the French. However, when the Nouvelle Vague (New Wave) critics began praising his work in the 1950s, he developed great respect for their discernment. Jean-Luc Godard's first published review, in Éric Rohmer's *Gazette du cinéma* in 1950, had praised *Dragonwyck* and called Joe "one of the most brilliant of American directors." In *Cahiers du cinéma* in 1955, François Truffaut, Claude Chabrol, Rohmer, and others chose *The Barefoot Contessa* as one of the year's best films. Joe especially enjoyed Truffaut's "It is a daring, novel, and most satisfying venture, and Mankiewicz uses it to settle scores with the Hollywood which condemned him to polishing furniture when he had dreamed of breaking down walls." Applauding Joe's emphasis on ideas, dialogue, and character, even at the expense of utilizing cinema's unique properties, the French later defined his work as *théâtre filmé*, and Federico Fellini credited *Barefoot Contessa* as an inspiration for his 1960 *La dolce vita*.

CHAPTER 19

New York Crooks and Showgirls: An American Fairy Tale

DURING THE SUMMER OF 1954, JOE BEGAN TALKING TO SAMUEL GOLDwyn about adapting and directing *Guys and Dolls*. Goldwyn had spent a record-breaking million dollars for the rights to the long-running 1950 Broadway smash, and Joe, who had never worked on a musical, was eager to try. Abe Burrows had based the show's book on the crooks, showgirls, and Salvation Army workers in Damon Runyon's stories, and George Kaufman had directed it. The Pulitzer Prize judges had chosen it as the year's best play, but Columbia University's trustees overrode them, because Burrows had been forced to appear before the House Un-American Activities Committee.

Bert Allenberg worried that Joe would find Goldwyn's micromanaging intolerable, but Joe was confident he could handle the producer: "Mr. Goldwyn and I have been exchanging little notes and cables evidencing our mutual passion—we could not be more in love were we Tony Curtis and Janet Leigh. Or even Louella Parsons and Jimmy McHugh."

Allenberg conceded, at least at the moment: "The old boy is real pleased about the love notes and cables . . . and keeps saying to me, 'Dot's a fine fella, and I vill like woiking wit him.'" Eventually Goldwyn did drive Joe crazy, but by then it was too late. Joe was in love with the project. He hired the show's composer, Frank Loesser, to provide additional songs, and its choreographer, Michael Kidd, for the dances, but he envisioned a highly stylized production for the movie. "GUYS AND DOLLS is, *in its concept*, an American Fairy Tale of our times," he wrote to Goldwyn. "The fact that the story we tell *within* that concept is real, warm and human, does not alter the concept." He wanted fanciful sets to enhance the fantasy of Damon Runyon's world of endearing, lovable criminals who lived by their own peculiar honor code and spoke in carefully enunciated, grammatically reprehensible sentences, and he speculated about framing the story as a kind of anthropological adventure. Maybe he could use a commentator like Edward R. Murrow "or perhaps the guide on a fanciful sightseeing bus" to describe the world of the 'guys' and 'dolls' and "establish Times Square as a not-quite-civilized area of New York City."

The sequence was ironic. Joe followed an angry Cinderella story intended to expose the dark side of Hollywood, that sunniest of fantasylands, with a cheerful fairy tale about tough denizens in gritty New York. Once Goldwyn approved, they hired designer Oliver Smith to design bright, cartoonlike sets that would embody the concept of New York as a Neverland locale. Even the exterior scenes would be shot on soundstages. The wedding finale eventually cost about $250,000, partly because they had to pave a sound stage to accommodate real automobiles (the entire picture cost about $5 million). To help recoup what he already knew would be a considerable investment, Goldwyn wanted four stars for the leads. After failing to get Gene Kelly for Sky Masterson (the singing, dancing, romantic lead) or Audrey Hepburn for Sarah Brown (the Salvation Army "doll" who is Sky's love interest), Goldwyn began peppering Joe with casting suggestions, some of which Joe considered disasters—like Dean Martin and Jerry Lewis for Sky and Nathan Detroit. Eventually Goldwyn proposed Marlon Brando, and Joe loved the idea. Brando was a stellar actor, and his box office appeal was tremendous; Brando had even taken singing lessons, but they knew they could always dub his songs.

Brando was intrigued but apprehensive, so at Goldwyn's suggestion, Joe wired him, "PRACTICALLY CERTAIN I WILL WRITE AND DIRECT GUYS AND DOLLS STOP WANT VERY MUCH HAVE YOU PLAY SKY MASTERSON STOP IN ITS OWN WAY ROLE AS I WOULD WRITE IT FOR YOU OFFERS CHALLENGE ALMOST EQUAL OF MARC ANTHONY STOP YOU HAVE NEVER DONE MUSICAL NEITHER HAVE I STOP WE NEVER DID SHAKESPEARE EITHER STOP I AM CONFIDENT THIS WOULD BE EXCITING GRATIFYING REWARDING EXPERIENCE FOR BOTH OF US STOP."

Meanwhile, Allenberg tried to convince Goldwyn he should hire Frank Sinatra if Brando refused. "Of course, he's never seen him perform and, therefore, not aware of the 'warmth and charmth' [a famous Goldwynism] and the appeal to women which this boy has," Allenberg wrote Joe. But once Brando agreed to take the singing role that would have been a natural for Sinatra, Sinatra started campaigning to play Nathan Detroit, the comic lead, even though the play's Nathan had only one song, "Sue Me." Sam Levene, the original Nathan, was so tone deaf that

Joe and Jean Simmons enjoy a moment.

he was not even allowed to sing along in group numbers—they made him mouth the words. Sinatra even went to Joe's hotel to plead for the part and against his better judgment, Joe finally acquiesced.

Actresses were also vying for parts. Deborah Kerr lobbied for the role of Sarah, though Joe considered her about ten years too old for the part. To his relief, Kerr discovered she had a scheduling conflict, so he could pretend to be heartbroken. Allenberg again proposed Jean Simmons, and this time, Joe liked the idea. He considered Simmons a more talented actress than many of her more famous contemporaries and (not merely because they had a fling during shooting) always wondered why she failed to achieve the stardom he thought she deserved.

Among the actresses eager to play Miss Adelaide, the nightclub singer who has been engaged to Nathan Detroit for fourteen years, were Lauren Bacall, Ann Miller, and Betty Grable. Marilyn Monroe sent him a telegram, but Joe joked that he couldn't imagine her waiting fourteen years for a guy. Goldwyn finally agreed to hire Vivian Blaine, the show's original Adelaide, even though she was not a star, and several other strong members of the Broadway cast, including Stubby Kaye as Nicely

Marlon Brando thought he sounded like "the mating call of a yak."

Nicely and B. S. Pully as Big Jule. (Pully, a former foul-mouthed nightclub comedian, told a reporter, "I got the only contract on the lot says I can't even gargle my trote. I guess this verce is my charm.")

Joe expanded the screenplay, though he retained the basic plot. Nathan Detroit searches for a location for his floating craps game while fending off Adelaide's entreaties to get married. To win a bet with Nathan, Sky Masterson takes Sarah Brown to dinner in Havana, Cuba, and the unlikely pair fall in love. After their return, Sarah lies to the police to protect the gamblers, Sky lies to protect Sarah, Nicely Nicely finds religion, the police are thwarted, and the two sets of lovers marry in a double wedding at the end.

Brando and Simmons assumed their songs would be dubbed, but when Goldwyn heard them rehearse, he decided their own voices were adequate and that having them sing their own songs would sound more authentic. After they were coached extensively, they recorded their songs a number of times, and engineers patched together the best notes from their numerous takes. As Brando later wrote, they stitched them together so compactly that in one song, "I nearly asphyxiated myself

Frank Sinatra sang it his way.

because I couldn't breathe while trying to synchronize my lips." At the time, he told the press he thought his voice sounded like "the mating call of a yak."

Only Sinatra was difficult. Jean Simmons was naturally easygoing and had been acting since she was fourteen. Vivian Blaine had film experience and could perform Adelaide on autopilot (some observers thought she did). After his initial nervousness, Brando, as usual, impressed everyone with his dedication and hard work. But despite pushing his way into the cast, Sinatra was moody and belligerent, especially toward Brando. He not only resented Brando's playing the singing lead, he was still so angry about Brando's Oscar-winning performance as Terry Malloy in *On the Waterfront* that he was suing *Waterfront*'s producer for casting Brando after promising the part to him. Furthermore, Sinatra liked to capture his scenes in one take, both to save himself the effort and because he genuinely—and sometimes correctly—believed he lost spontaneity in repetition. Brando, whom Sinatra called Mumbles behind his back, irritated him with his painstaking Method approach to building his character through multiple takes.

More important to the finished film, Sinatra, out of personal pique and professional pride, refused to perform his songs in character, which upset Brando and Joe, and enraged Frank Loesser. Although Loesser had hoped the film would stay as true as possible to his and Abe Burrows's vision, he had reconciled himself to the fact that Joe's script and direction and the casting already had shifted the balance. Nor did Loesser object to Nathan Detroit's getting more songs than he had in the play. However, Nathan Detroit was supposed to be the comic character, not the romantic one, and Sinatra sang his songs as a crooning, romantic Frank Sinatra rather than a nervously rough Nathan Detroit. When Loesser offered to give him some ideas for singing "Sue Me," to convey his character, Sinatra told him, "We'll do it my way or you can fuck off." Brando, who also resented the addition of a rival romantic hero, asked Joe to intervene. But even Joe, who did not disagree and who jealously protected his directorial authority, balked at the prospect of telling Frank Sinatra how to sing.

Whatever its shortcomings, the film was an immediate smash, grossing $4.2 million in the last two months of 1955 and becoming the following year's top grosser as well, generating $9 million in domestic market rentals. Critics differed in their responses to the musical performances and to Joe's expansion—the finished product was two and a half hours, which even Joe later admitted was overlong. Orson Welles, who saw the film before Abe Burrows, told him, "Abe, they put a tiny turd on every one of your lines." Burrows did not like Joe's version, but he was hardly surprised. Studios rarely trusted a work's original creator, and at the same time that Joe was adapting *Guys and Dolls* for Goldwyn, Burrows was adapting George Kaufman's *The Solid Gold Cadillac* for Harry Cohn at Columbia.

The film's most historically interesting review was written by a young composer who aspired to Broadway success himself. In the December 1955 issue of *Films in Review*, Steve Sondheim, twenty-five, identified "two major flaws" in Joe's first and only musical. He believed Oliver Smith's sets vacillated too much between realistic and stylized; and he regretted that "Sinatra ambles through his role . . . as though he were about to laugh at the jokes in the script." Mostly, the composer applauded. The ballads were "weak," but most of the score and lyrics were "inventive" and "funny as ever," and aside from Sinatra's, most of the performances were laudable. He considered Brando "too young" for the character but conceded "he acts with personality and conviction (almost too much conviction for a musical) and sings pleasantly." He considered Jean Simmons's Havana dance "a high point of the picture." And though Simmons and Brando were "unpleasantly off-pitch in their first duet," Simmons's "charm is immense. Both Simmons and Brando could give lessons to most of the more polished voices in Hollywood on how to *act* a lyric."

CHAPTER 20

Joe Rewrites Graham Greene

AFTER *GUYS AND DOLLS*, JOE RETURNED TO HIS FAVORITE SUBJECT, HIS characters' psyches, this time through Graham Greene's novel *The Quiet American* (US publication, 1956). Greene had covered France's Indochinese War from 1951 to 1954, reporting from Saigon for the *London Times* and *Le Figaro*, during which he had witnessed the growing American presence. The fact that the United States was sending money, military advisors, and quasi-independent aid workers into France's former colony was not widely known, but the general American public was reflexively anticommunist and supported the Cold War to contain the spread of communism abroad.

Greene portrayed the situation through the story of Alden Pyle, a youthful, idealistic American official implicitly backed by the CIA, who arrives in Indochina reflecting his nation, well funded and arrogantly certain he knows what is best for the rest of the world. He meets Thomas Fowler, a burnt-out, middle-aged English journalist who regards the French as interlopers and respects the Viet Minh (Vietnamese communists) as indigenous nationalists, and Phuong, Fowler's beautiful, young Vietnamese mistress, whom Greene clearly intended to represent Vietnam.

To rescue Indochina from both the Old World French colonialists and the communists, the Harvard-educated, naive Pyle supports the idea of a third force of indigenous, anticommunist nationalists (the actual goal of the American apparatus), and he tries to rescue Phuong by offering to marry her and take her to the United States. Although Fowler spends much of his time in an opium haze, after a group Pyle has supported is implicated in an explosion that kills a group of women and children, Fowler rouses himself to help the Vietnamese by assisting a group that assassinates Pyle. After Pyle's death, Phuong resignedly returns to Fowler, and Greene's irony-filled novel concludes with Fowler's reflection

"Everything had gone right with me since he had died, but how I wished there were someone to whom I could say I was sorry."

Like the novel's American reviewers who deplored the anticommunist Right but supported the cold war in general, Joe considered Greene's novel a "petty, snide little . . . polemic" about Americans. But he admired Greene's writing and saw Fowler as an excellent vehicle to demonstrate his belief that personal lives influenced political beliefs, even among intellectuals: Fowler believed his complicity in Pyle's death was a disinterested choice, but actually he was an "aging man [giving himself] a noble motive" for acting on his emotions. He wanted Laurence Olivier to play Fowler, and though Olivier was intrigued, he wanted to see Joe's screenplay before committing. He did not want to star in a film that was either anti-American or anti-British.

He planned to write neither, Joe assured Olivier: "Greene's inability to keep what must be an uncontrollably deep and bitter and consuming, but nonetheless child-like, rage (and an equally child-like Catholicism) from permeating his work—much like a chef who will insist upon spraying his finest dishes with insecticide before serving—is a major frustration in the literary world. . . . Fortunately . . . the story . . . can be wonderfully realized on film—and the insecticide removed—without damage to either."

Robby Lantz was able to coordinate arrangements with no less a personage than CIA chief Allen Dulles, who clearly recognized Joe's usefulness. Joe was courted by Angier Biddle Duke, head of the CIA-linked International Rescue Committee, before he visited Vietnam in January to scout locations and search for an Asian actress to play Phuong. Once he was in Saigon, the Americans saw to it that he was wined and dined in the highest Vietnamese and American diplomatic circles. He socialized with the American ambassador, various generals, and even the US-backed South Vietnamese premier, Ngo Dinh Diem (whom Joe considered "charming, empty").

Although Greene's book had been banned in Vietnam, Joe's description of his own anticommunist, pro-American script gained him assurances of police cooperation, which, given the continued sporadic fighting, was no small consideration. He was also coopted by undercover CIA operative Colonel Edward Lansdale, who reported to the agency that he had suggested Joe give Pyle a more benign occupation than American government employee and had encouraged him to reassign blame for the explosion from the Vietnamese nationalists to the communists (the nationalists were responsible for the actual incident).

Joe's interest in politics was minimal, his political acumen superficial, and his experience with the Directors Guild loyalty oath controversy had left its mark. But like many highly intelligent people, he could be oblivious to his own limitations. The CIA's anticommunist-Left position seemed like the logical, thinking man's response to the cold war, and Joe followed the trail that had been laid for him. Herman might have provided Joe with a more nuanced understanding of the situation's complexities, but Herman was not around. Consequently, Joe retained Greene's portrait of the self-deluding Fowler but turned him into a communist dupe and made Pyle the unblemished hero. Greene's warning about the perils of American interference was reversed to an embrace of American policy, and Joe dedicated the film to American-backed Premier Diem (the same Diem whose assassination the Americans facilitated in 1963). He ended his picture with Phuong refusing to return to Fowler instead of acquiescing, and in a coup de grâce, neatly excised the ironic first half of Fowler's final statement ("Everything had gone right with me since he had died"), leaving only the now-unironic, "How I wish there were someone to whom I could say I was sorry."

An appalled Olivier turned down the role: "I find that in exonerating Pyle to a large extent, you have [made] Fowler . . . the mental case, so to speak (or is it Greene you are after?) instead of Pyle, who now becomes relatively innocent and rather characterless and Fowler a completely twisted degenerate . . . the central character is no longer as seen through the author's eyes, but has become the author as seen through your own . . . and frankly I don't like the part!"

After trying for William Holden, Joe cast James Mason as Fowler and Montgomery Clift as Pyle. When Mason had to drop out, he hired Michael Redgrave, and in May 1956 Clift was severely injured in an automobile accident. So instead of one of Hollywood's finest actors, Joe hired World War II's most decorated soldier. Audie Murphy, who had parlayed his celebrity into a career in westerns, was well aware of his lack of training and technique, so the prospect of starring in a Mankiewicz film, especially opposite the polished, experienced, classically trained Redgrave, alternately attracted and terrified him. Joe was still searching for Phuong when he left for Saigon in January 1957, and eventually he gave up on finding an Asian actress with sufficient English and hired Georgia Moll, an inexperienced young Italian actress.

For the first Western film shot in Saigon, everything was a challenge. The temperature was often over one hundred; the noonday sun was too bright to shoot; the smoky air often reeked of the human excrement commonly used as fertilizer. The Majestic Hotel was the best in town, but its windows lacked glass, so the fifty or so cast and crew members slept as best they could under netting. Rosemary Matthews, now a Figaro employee, smoothed the way wherever she could. They were shorthanded on translators, both to communicate with the Vietnamese and to interpret among the crew's eight nationalities.

Sporadic violence among Vietnamese factions posed real danger. When the crew set off fireworks during a rehearsal for the story's explosion, they so frightened the local population that the police arrested Joe for lacking the proper permits. Joe, who was known as "Frog Face with Pipe," was the target of so many communist plots that he was urged to stay off ladders because they made him too vulnerable to snipers. When he refused to change his methods, his Vietnamese assistant producer, the respected director Vinh Noan, hired an extensive plainclothes network to protect the entire group.

Their most important objective was recording the Vietnamese New Year (Tet) celebrations at the end of January 1957, and for three nights in a row, they filmed tens of thousands of celebrants in Saigon's streets, including acrobats, dancers, fire-eaters, and even an eighty-foot paper dragon. Ultimately, they used very little of the footage, but that turned out to be the most successful accomplishment of a very costly two months' sojourn.

Audie Murphy arrived late and armed with pistols and five hundred rounds of ammunition, in case the communists followed through on their threats against him. His marksmanship exceeded his acting prowess, but his ubiquitous Colt 45's, combined with his explosive temper, kept the already nervous Figaro group even more on edge. About a week after he arrived, Murphy had to be flown to Hong Kong for an emergency appendectomy, which Joe concealed from the rest of the cast, especially after Murphy's doctors estimated Murphy's recovery might take six weeks because of his extensive war injuries.

A lengthy delay threatened to destroy their budget, and frenzied cables flew among Saigon, Hong Kong, and New York. At the same time Joe was assuring Murphy they would not dream of replacing him, Lantz was frantically exploring alternatives. Replacing Murphy would raise costs but offered them an opportunity to utilize a better actor, maybe even Montgomery Clift, who was eager to be rehired. Murphy himself vacillated between hoping for recovery and yearning to escape a role he knew was over his head. As Joe cabled Lantz, "MY FINGER IN DIKE BUT PRETTY SOON NO FINGER LOVE JOE."

Saigon was hot and volatile. Audie Murphy was out of his league. Shooting *The Quiet American* (1958) was a frustrating experience.

While they waited, Joe dragged a jetlagged Michael Redgrave to Tay Ninh, a city sixty miles outside Saigon, to shoot a Cao Dai festival. A home-grown religion combining Confucianism, Taoism, Buddhism, and Catholicism, the Cao Dai had a hierarchy that included a pope exiled to Cambodia by Premier Diem, cardinals of both sexes, and an army that Diem had disbanded. As Joe filmed their colorful procession, the forty-thousand-strong members reversed their banners to reveal antigovernment messages calling for the return of their banished pope. Figuring, "What the hell? No one will know what they mean," Joe kept the cameras rolling.

The police thought the action was part of the film and did not interfere. However, the next day Joe sent an actor dressed as a Buddhist leader into the group, and the Cao Dai, thinking he was installing a rival pope, rioted again. Then they banned filming inside their cathedral. When the government realized Joe had shot a genuine political demonstration, officials pressured him to destroy or hand over the film. He refused, insisting no one would understand the signs anyway, and used the footage in the finished film.

In addition to the physical dangers of their Asian theater of operations, Figaro also became embroiled in what Joe called *l'affair Times* in London. In a January 9, 1957, article, the *London Times'* Saigon correspondent recounted a wildly inaccurate version of Joe's screenplay and called the film a "travesty" of Greene's novel. Greene wrote a letter to the editor, predicting that if the changes were as described, "they will make only the more obvious the discrepancy between what the State Department would like the world to believe and what in fact happened in Viet Nam. In that case, I can imagine some happy evenings of laughter not only in Paris but in the cinemas of Saigon."

Worried that London critics would forget Greene's actual book but remember the word "travesty," Figaro's publicist convinced them to sue the newspaper. The *Times* refused to back down, so the parties spent the next few months trading communiques drafted by expensive counsels, and in the end, Figaro lost anyway. Their legal team considered them fortunate to escape with only their own costs.

To the great relief of cast and crew, on March 7 Joe decided that it was time "to wrap up and fuck off to Italy," where he was again shooting at Cinecittà. Rosa met them in Rome, and after spending his days shooting interior scenes at the studio, Joe spent most of his nights fighting with Rosa. The pattern was familiar, but it seemed to be worsening. As Rosa neared the age when her father had left her mother for a younger woman, she felt even more threatened by Joe's serial philandering. Fueled by alcohol and pills, Rosa confronted Joe about Rosemary, and his repeated patronizing denials of an affair only intensified her rage and humiliation. They sometimes fought all night, ordeals that ended only when Joe stormed out to go to Rosemary's or walk the streets alone or simply return to the studio.

Joe's days were only marginally better. Audie Murphy and Georgia Moll were such weak actors that Joe tried to compensate by leaning on French actor Claude Dauphin (who played the French inspector) and Michael Redgrave. Redgrave, who was also fighting a terrible cold, found that onerous. "I feel like telling him it's one thing to get a performance out of an amateur, another thing to give a performance with one," he complained in his diary. Then, professional that he was, Redgrave tried to harness his anger to fuel his scenes.

They finished shooting in June 1957, and as they moved into editing, Chris and Tom arrived for summer vacation. The fights continued despite the boys' presence, until Joe asked Erna, who lived in Rome, to spend a few nights with them. When the boys left for Vienna to visit Rosa's mother (Grossmutter or, affectionately, Gross), Joe contacted both Rosa's New York psychiatrist, Lawrence Kubie, and their old friend psychiatrist Fred Hacker, who was in Vienna, for advice. Rosa liked the Italian doctor they suggested, and after sedation did not seem to calm her, she agreed to be hospitalized.

A few days later and against her doctors' wishes, Rosa checked herself out and flew to Vienna, leaving Joe to stew nervously for several days until Hacker let him know she had entered a clinic for a "sleep cure." By then the boys were back, and when Hacker also informed Joe that Rosa had told the boys she might not be coming back to him, Joe sat down with Chris, now close to seventeen, and Tom, just fifteen, for their first, ever, frank discussion about their family. He told them he had considered divorce over the years, but when the boys were younger, he had feared that unless he challenged her in court, their mother would be awarded custody. He had not wanted to risk a public airing of Rosa's problems. Now that Rosa was older, he felt an obligation to take care of her. She had no one but him—he was already supporting her mother as well.

In what Joe considered a "long, incredibly revealing, touching talk," Chris and Tom poured out their own stories of abuse, as well as their complete awareness of his and Rosa's fights over the years. They too, especially during the past five years, had experienced Rosa's frightening rages. They, too, had been awakened at night to bring her drinks and listen to her harangues. They described their own insecurity about which mother they would find. Chris referred to Jekyll and Hyde. Tom connected his asthma to her episodes.

Joe later described himself as "shocked" by their revelations. When they also told him Rosa had said she hoped Rosemary would be a good mother to them, Joe dismissed the very idea as yet more evidence of Rosa's tortured imagination. Whether or not they believed him, the boys did not contradict their father's dismissal of such a notion.

Rosa returned to New York about a week later, and after another episode Kubie sent her to the New York Neurological Institute and dispatched Robby Lantz to their apartment to search for hidden liquor and narcotics. Kubie also asked Joe to reconstruct a history of the events leading up to the latest breakdown, a miserable task Joe postponed as long as he could. He already felt overwhelmed. At night, his "duties and responsibilities" threatened to crush him "like so many crumbling walls." During the day, he felt "like a Samson in reverse . . . holding them up."

Eventually, Joe devoted many hours to Kubie's depressing assignment, recounting the painful day-by-day, outburst-by-outburst description of their time in Rome, but despite all that effort, when Kubie asked him directly about the affair, he denied it emphatically. He wrote that though his analysis was incomplete, he had managed to "eliminate two destructive outlets that had or could seriously affect my life with Rosa." One was "compulsive gambling." The other was "not so easy always but still fully accomplished in recent years, my forming childish and neurotically-emotional involvements. I recognize the sign-posts, I am aware of the dangers, and increasingly find less difficulty in avoiding them." Mimicking the loathsome anticommunist loyalty oath, Joe averred, "Let me state directly—and I hope this helps to remove this spot of fog from the windshield—I am not having, I have not been having, I will not be having an affair with Miss Rosemary Matthews. Basta."

In later years, Chris described his father's treatment of Rosa as "gas lighting." Tom believed his experience with his mother's problems triggered his own lifelong pattern of gravitating toward troubled women, usually actresses, in an effort to save them, as he had not been able save his mother. At the time, they were relieved to have a frank conversation with their father, even if it had taken five years for him to take their situation into account and was based on a falsehood.

Chris and Tom remained in Rome, accompanying Joe to work and touring the area with Rosemary, and at the end of July, Joe took them on vacation. After a few days in Austria with Grossmutter, they toured Germany, Switzerland, and northern Italy. To Joe's and Chris's amusement, when they arrived in Bologna, Tom at first refused to leave their Mercedes; he was terrified they would be attacked by the Communists who dominated the city. Eventually the sight of the many luxurious shops surrounding their hotel quieted his fears.

They returned to Rome to find "wonderful letters from Rosa." To Joe's great joy, Eric Reynal, his son from his first marriage, was touring Europe with a college friend and joined them for a few days in Rome. Joe was touched by Eric's "dogged perseverance in referring to Eugene Reynal as 'my father,'" and appreciated that in "this time of depression and unhappiness," he had "the opportunity to be with my sons, to know them, and to love them."

He was still editing when top United Artist executives arrived to check on his progress, and he reluctantly showed them the still-uncompleted film. As he reported to Lantz, Allenberg, and Abe Bienstock,

> They sat through it in stony silence, except for occasional buttock shifting. When it was over, there was a tense lull. [Robert] Haggiag and Winnikus disappeared wordlessly. [Charles] Smadja's first reaction, as far as I can remember, was that the picture was anti-French and pro-French. [UA chief Arthur] Krim wondered whether it was anti-British. . . . Picker suggested that they all go to their hotels and clean up. . . . This suggestion was climbed upon, as if it were a life raft. Turning back from the door Krim congratulated me. The best "film of ideas" in the last ten years, he said.

After dinner his visitors spoke more freely. "They were unanimous in their feeling that a 'film of ideas' was practically unsalable. The phrase "potential disaster was used, as well as a comparison to ST JOAN" (a 1957 Otto Preminger film whose screenplay Graham Greene had adapted from George Bernard Shaw's play). Joe's picture needed drastic cuts—"chunks," they told him—and as he continued editing, Joe dutifully complied.

When he returned to the, United States in September, they continued to press for more cuts and Joe became convinced UA was trying to cut costs by shortchanging the picture's marketing plans. He wrote Krim an impassioned six-page plea: "You are reported as feeling that all 'polemics' should be out. This, Arthur, is the equivalent of asking DeMille to give up bad taste. Polemics are my stock-in-trade. They attract whatever audience and kudos my films have managed to acquire over the years. Remove my polemics and—just to quote a couple—ALL ABOUT EVE and LETTER TO THREE WIVES would have consisted of main and end-titles." As for its box office potential,

> I will never make as commercially successful a film as [AROUND THE WORLD IN] EIGHTY DAYS—nor as bad a film as ST. JOAN.
>
> Whatever my other frivolities are, I am serious in my work . . . my reputation as a creator of good films was, and is in curious excess of my reputation as a maker of box-office block-busters. Yet I had, and have, the . . . distinction of never having written-and-directed a film that did not show a profit. That there were other "profits" in those films of mine, of benefit to Fox and to Metro and to you, which cannot be translated into dollars, is a point which I know you understand and which with I hope you agree.
>
> At any rate, I do not think I warrant having a film of mine either regarded or classified as a flop, until it has flopped.

Interviewed before the film's release, Joe unabashedly acknowledged his reversal of Greene's intentions. Despite becoming a director explicitly to protect what he had written, he had no problem asserting the "inalienable right of the screen-writer to do what he will with any characters at hand"—especially when Greene's American was "a cardboard, stupid, weak-kneed idiot," and Fowler's "lack of any real moral fiber made him far more dangerous than the stupid, idealistic American." Utilizing a doctrine of art as payback, he added that Greene's novel "made me so mad I was determined to make a picture out of it"—it was so "insulting to America and Americans."

In more nuanced circles, Joe repeated the anticommunist-liberal line promoted by CIA-linked organizations like Angier Biddle Duke's IRC, whose board he joined, and the American Friends of Vietnam, another Duke-led organization for whose benefit the picture's glittery premier was held in Washington, D.C. The occasion drew senators and generals, and Joe briefed the press on Vietnam's political situation: "Americans stationed abroad live in a red, white and blue ghetto," never interacting with anyone but Americans, while "the Commie operator sits down in his home with Vietnamese." Americans needed to combat the spread of communism with more people-to-people contact like the American hero of his film.

Most American reviewers acknowledged Joe's complete reversal of Greene's intentions but praised the film. Not surprisingly, most British reviewers found the transformation reprehensible—the word "assassination" was used in the *London Times*—though some were amused. Recognizing the book's anti-Americanism, David Robinson (later, a *London Times* critic) wrote in *Sight and Sound* that the "audacious manner [of Joe's reversal] must elicit a kind of admiration. It seems a much more clever way to impose an ideology to redirect the writings of its critics rather than to suppress them directly, as is the custom of Catholics or Communists, for example."

The French, intensely interested in their former colony, were the most laudatory. Both Jean-Luc Godard and Éric Rohmer ranked *The Quiet American* as their favorite film of 1958. Although he observed that "what is missing from *The Quiet American* is cinema," Godard decided the explanation was that Joe was "too perfect a writer to be a perfect director as well" and speculated, "Mankiewicz probably got so much enjoyment from the writing that there was little enough left for filming it." Nevertheless, he considered it "the most interesting film for this moment" and proclaimed Joe "the most intelligent man in all contemporary cinema." Joe later quipped, "Apparently my films gain something in translation."

Graham Greene, who disliked almost all films made from his stories, later singled out *The Quiet American* as "the most extreme" in its deviation from the book. Describing his disillusionment with a medium he had once loved, he speculated in a 1958 essay that "one can almost believe that the film was made deliberately to attack the book and the author." Then he shrugged. "I am vain enough to believe that the book will survive a few years longer than Mr. Mankiewicz's picture," he wrote, adding that the novel's sale served its purpose so "why should I complain? He has enabled to me to go on writing."

As for the picture's sales, *The Quiet American* was indeed the commercial flop UA executives had feared. Embarrassed in later years by its politics and its confusing plot, Joe usually described it as "a very bad film I made during a very unhappy time in my life." The drain on Joe's personal life was undeniable, but aside from his Production Code concessions (like omitting Fowler's opium addiction), Joe wrote and directed the film he wanted to write and direct. He made his point about emotions' effect on intellect, and the picture's politics were his politics. It was not without merit, and its aesthetic shortcomings were essentially due to his own reluctance to slim it down.

CHAPTER 21

Exit Rosa

BY THE FIRST WEEK OF OCTOBER 1957, ROSA SEEMED STABILIZED, AND Joe plunged into Figaro business, juggling exploitation for *Quiet American*, script development for *I Want to Live*!, and rescue of the project most in need of his help, *The Square Root of Wonderful*, a Carson McCullers play Figaro was coproducing with Saint Subber. Joe considered the script "a mess," and after struggling unsuccessfully to revise it, he replaced director Jose Quintero and a few members of the cast. Even with the changes, the play seemed hopeless, but they brought it to Broadway anyway, with Anne Baxter in the lead, and the results were as disastrous as they had feared. Joe and Rosa's opening night party was more like a wake, and Carson McCullers was so distraught that Tennessee Williams took her away before she could hear the radio reviews. The aftermath was worse. They had such huge advance and theater party sales that they had to run it eight times a week for eight weeks before they could close. Even years later, Baxter still shuddered at the recollection.

Joe spent much of that winter turning *Jefferson Selleck* into a play in which he hoped to star Henry Fonda. Despite the *Square Root* debacle, Subber was interested, as were David Merrick and Leland Hayward, so Joe took it along when he and Rosa left for Palm Springs in February. Although Joe's theatrical aspirations were undiminished, they were becoming a bit of a joke. While they were away, George Kaufman collapsed at the opening of John Osborne's *The Entertainer*, and when Moss Hart visited him in the hospital, Kaufman opened an eye and said to Hart, "Don't worry, Moss. I'm not going until Joe Mankiewicz writes a play." The story made the rounds, and when the Ephrons heard it, Henry Ephron paid off his wife's November 1950 bet. (Joe, understandably hurt, told his sons, "George would never say something like that.")

Rosemary was working for Figaro in Los Angeles, so Joe sometimes saw her when he came in to work. Rosa returned to New York in March, a few days before Joe, who spent his last evening in Los Angeles with Sara and the Foxes. Joe still consulted Saul medically (for uppers) as well as socially, and helped Sara when he could, having his office staff assist with airline tickets and letting her use his Screen Directors Guild card to attend Academy screenings. Joe planned to fly back with producer Mike Todd later that night, but with inclement weather, Sara became so upset at the prospect of Joe's riding in Todd's small, private plane that he finally took an overnight commercial flight instead. Chris and Tom met him at the airport the following morning with the news that Todd's plane had crashed. Joe had canceled so close to departure time that some newspapers listed him among the dead passengers, and the premature reports of his death bothered Joe less than the papers' describing him as a producer.

I Want to Live! was the only Figaro film Joe did not direct. In 1956 Figaro had contracted to pay Walter Wanger $25,000 for every Figaro picture he produced. He would not share in the sales or profits, but Wanger appreciated the arrangement—he had been working since 1952 to rebuild his career after spending three months in jail for shooting his wife's lover in the crotch. Among his many suggestions was the story of Barbara Graham, a suspected murderer who had been executed, which he hoped could become an indictment of capital punishment. Susan Hayward, to whom Wanger had given her first break, was eager to star in it and help him in any way she could. She was so loyal that she later convinced Joe and United Artists to join her in giving Wanger 1 percent of their share in the film's profits.

With Robert Wise directing, the picture was a huge hit, earning hefty profits for Figaro and United Artists and praise from critics as diverse as Albert Camus, Eleanor Roosevelt, and Clifton Webb, who sent Wanger a bill for the fifth of Scotch he said he needed after seeing the film. It also earned six Academy Award nominations. Besides Wise and Hayward, who finally won after four best actress nominations, Don Mankiewicz and Nelson Giddings were nominated for the screenplay.

In June 1958 Erna and Sara joined Rosa and Joe for Josie's graduation from Wellesley College and Chris's from preparatory school at Lawrenceville. In the five years since Herman's death, Josie had become a beloved older sister to both boys, who idolized her, and a surrogate daughter to Joe, who had gone far beyond his promise to Herman to send Josie to college. He wrote her regularly, flew up for Wellesley's Fathers' Day, and gave her a trip to Europe for graduation.

While at Wellesley, Josie had visited frequently. She enjoyed the luxury of their household, of arising to servants quietly opening her draperies and bringing her the breakfast of her choice, and she was very fond of Chris and Tom. But as much as Josie appreciated Joe's generosity, her uncle, like her father, had a way of stepping on his own good deeds. On more than one occasion, Joe told her he considered it important to shatter myths and that she should know the "real facts of life" about her father. These were that Herman had been deeply unhappy and that his drinking and gambling had been extraordinarily destructive. To make sure Josie understood the gravity of her father's indebtedness, he would then produce a charred sheet of IOUs he had preserved from the moving-van fire.

Josie had been fifteen when her father died, so she could hardly have missed the necessity of selling their house and Herman's books, and moving with Sara to a small apartment. She was under no illusion that her parents were free from problems, and in her thirties she wrote a roman à clef in which the screenwriter father plays off his daughter against her admirable but controlling mother. But Josie had no desire to listen to what Herman had said when he was drinking. Nor did she want to hear her father characterized as a hopeless Victorian because he was too inhibited to sleep around. (Perhaps Joe considered Herman's failure to have affairs yet another example of his squandering opportunities.) Josie already had her own issues with Sara, but she did not appreciate hearing her mother portrayed as a pathetic, naive Orthodox Jewish wife, standing by her man.

Joe's kindness and generosity had already earned him Josie's gratitude and affection, but just as he needed to win every argument with Rosa and the boys, he seemed powerless to resist attempting to annihilate what was left of Herman. Needless to say, it backfired. When Joe took Josie to lunch at Romanoff's for her sixteenth birthday, she was nonplussed when he said on their way in, "The kind of woman I want you to be is a woman with shoulders back, proud of your body. . . . Walk into a room as if you are better than anyone in it." He added, "There isn't a woman I have ever slept with who couldn't walk into this restaurant right now and I would be proud and pleased to see her."

"Why keep saying that?" Josie wondered later, to Geist. "And he said that a lot." Her uncle resembled her father in many good ways. "He's terribly funny. He is terribly bright. He can be terribly warm. It's only when you take the big picture that you realize that the warmth comes out of the faucet. He seeks adulation." Joe's insecurity pained and, to a certain extent, embarrassed Josie, and she saw in him a crassness that Herman lacked. "My father could be very vulgar, but it was always with the sense that he knew he was being." Joe seemed oblivious. When Tom was in his early twenties and dating a minor actress, Josie heard Joe tell his son, only half-mockingly, "Never fuck a starlet when you can fuck a star."

Josie found the family's dynamics oppressive, sometimes even frightening, and she observed the relationship between Joe and Rosa with horror and pity. Rosa was "really terrific" but also "*deeply* miserable. God. It was hopeless . . . they set each other off. . . . They would just go at each other . . . and they fed each other. Even as young as I was, I saw that." Eager to do the right thing, Rosa ran a ritualized household, with finger bowls at dinner and elegant parties. Over the years Joe had respected her judgment about his scripts, often arguing about her advice but then taking it. However, by the late 1950s, Rosa was drinking more and became prone to outrageous tirades that made her an object of ridicule.

Although Josie and her friends experienced Rosa as intimidating grande dame, when Joe told Josie one day that Rosa didn't like her and wanted her out of the house, she did not believe him. She did find it plausible, however, that Rosa had come at him with knives. "Perhaps she did, but boy, was she provoked." Watching Joe revisit some of Pop's patterns onto his own sons was upsetting, too, even if she hadn't witnessed them the first time around. Despite believing Pop had severely damaged Herman, Joe seemed unable to resist competing with his sons as well.

"What would you know about that?" he would sneer at Rosa or Chris or Tom, just as Pop had. When one of them wrote with good news about an academic achievement, Joe routinely pointed out spelling errors before delivering the praise. Chris responded by barely scraping by at school, getting by on his charm and considerable verbal skills, which, consciously or not, punished Joe in one of the few avenues available to a boy. Once he was older, Chris defied him more openly. Intimidating though Joe was—"Addison DeWitt in spades"—Chris recalled his angry young self as "a permanent war machine."

If Chris chose fight, Tom reacted with flight. He, too, was brilliant, charming, and witty, but Tom was also an academic star, pleasing his parents and everyone else. Tom kept it all inside. But by fifteen he smoked so heavily that his parents worried he was exacerbating his asthma. Joe and Rosa sent them to separate day schools and separate boarding schools, but both returned home with the identical mixture of eagerness and dread.

During the summer of 1958, Joe and Rosa rented financier Gilbert Kahn's house in Mt. Kisco, New York, near Bennett and Phyllis Cerf. Joe, who was working on both "Jefferson Selleck" and *I Want to Live!*

commuted back and forth, while Chris and Tom spent the summer taking driving lessons and working at summer jobs. Rosa seemed no worse than usual, though the sudden death in August of their friend Mark Hanna was a blow. Hanna, an agent whose clients had ranged from Eleanor Roosevelt to Gypsy Rose Lee, had become a close friend of Rosa's as well as Joe's.

By the last Saturday in September, the family had dispersed—Rosa to Mt. Kisco after a party at the Cerfs' the night before, Joe to the city apartment, Tom back at Phillips Exeter Academy for his senior year, and Chris starting his freshman year at Columbia University. Josie was just back from Europe when Joe called to say he was worried about Rosa. He couldn't reach her on the telephone. Would Josie call? When Josie also failed to reach her, Joe asked her to come over so they could telephone together. When Rosa still failed to answer Joe, who hated to use the phone, asked Josie to call the caretaker.

The caretaker assured them Rosa was sleeping and was fine, but Joe told him to try to wake her up. Then he asked Josie to drive up to the house with him. By the time they arrived, Josie recalled, "The feeling was that she was dead. Nobody had seen her. At any rate, Uncle Joe had not seen her." When they saw Bennett Cerf's car, Joe turned to Josie and said, "You go up."

Joe's twenty-one-year-old niece did as she was told and found her aunt's body with an indecipherable note by her side. Josie could make out only that Rosa was "tired." Rosa had attempted suicide before, and everyone who knew Rosa had worried about the danger of accidental death from her habit of mixing drugs and alcohol. Josie never knew if something had transpired the night before, but she came to believe Joe had had a strong notion of what she would find, and she always resented his sending her to find Rosa's body instead of going himself.

As for the note, Geist wrote, "Mankiewicz says the note was written to Dr. Kubie, Rosa's psychiatrist, but he will not disclose its contents." In the margin of his galleys, Joe wrote, "I didn't read it. If I had—I wouldn't have told." He was certainly under no obligation to share the information with Geist, but the idea that he would not read his wife's suicide note is simply not plausible. Pending an autopsy, the police ruled Rosa's death 'natural,' which allowed her, as a practicing Catholic, to be buried within the church. Two months later the report was revised to suicide. Rosa was forty-five years old.

Josie moved back to the apartment to help with Chris and Tom. Joe sent them to psychiatrists and resumed therapy himself, several times a week with Dr. Edmund Bergler, another orthodox Viennese Freudian. Bergler was a much-published psychoanalyst, best known for treating writer's block and trying to cure homosexuality, though, according to Fred Hacker, Bergler's major contribution to the field was his "description of how people destroy themselves by too much guilt and self-blame."

Joe's marriage had often been a nightmare, but Rosa's death left Joe feeling simultaneously free and bereft. He decided to lose himself in Europe for a while, though before he left he engaged in a frenzy of activity. He conducted business; he downsized Figaro, including letting Rosemary go after five years. He flew down to Washington to see the Cronyns' play. He went out with old friends. He started dating Jeanne Vanderbilt, a vivacious socialite with whom he and Rosa had socialized when she was married to racehorse breeder Alfred Vanderbilt. He sold his apartment, though he had no idea where he was going to live. On his way home from the barber the day he was to sail, he strolled into a showroom and completely on impulse bought a Jaguar, "the entire proceeding taking both the salesman and me by surprise and requiring no more than 5 minutes." Then Joe departed, leaving his sons in the care of Josie, his secretary, Adelaide (Addie) Wallace, and their therapists.

Between his November 19 departure for Europe and his homecoming a few days before Christmas, Joe kept the most detailed journal of his life. Lonely and bewildered, he struggled to make sense of his situation. The writer in him observed and instinctively took notes, but the entries are unusually unreflective for Joe: he felt, he observed, he recorded. For the most part he did not attempt to analyze his reactions or feelings; he simply existed in the moment. But his mental state over that six-week period progressed so linearly from depression to what reads like mania that his record becomes unintentionally comical.

Joe had suffered from insomnia for years, but during this period he found even increasing his medication was ineffectual, at least at first. He ate and drank too much, which left him groggy. His fellow passengers irritated him. He was constantly anxious.

November 19, 1958: "LIFE, one is urged to contemplate, can begin at 49 years, 9 months and 8 days. <u>Ce vidiamo [see you]."</u>

November 20 was Joe's first day at sea: "I find myself curiously unable to relax properly. None—literally not one of the passengers—seem to provide any area of mutual conversation much less intimacy."

On November 21, Joe tried and failed to work on *Jefferson Selleck*. "When will it click? When will I start again?"

November 23: "Should it sink. . . . I can think of no one aboard this dreary vessel who will leave the world emptier. . . . We sit around like a group of removed appendixes . . . Some sun today, and greeted as if it were Winston Churchill."

By Day Five, Joe actually found himself enjoying *Passionate Playgoer*, George Oppenheimer's collection of theatrical writings, though he noted, "My opinion of Woollcott as vomit finally solidified. Ugh."

On Day Six, a cable from Bert Allenberg offering Stephen Benét's *John Brown's Body* prompted him to muse about the story's lack of a meaningful female character. "There is an important inference to be made from the ever-increasing preoccupation of American Theatre and Film with the male to the exclusion of the female. Woman is not only feared, but unknown to our writers today—and not 'box-office,' apparently, even to women."

He played solitaire, wrote postcards, and worried about gaining weight. On his last day at sea, he wrote, "Solitaire, solitaire, restless, restless, fantasies, fantasies."

He arrived in Rome on November 27 to learn that Bert Allenberg had died. It was another terrible loss that he resolutely put out of his mind. He shopped for clothes and Christmas gifts, enjoyed Italian coffee, visited friends and business associates. He forced himself to write to Chris and Josie and received a cheery letter from Josie: "Your point has been made. You are more than essential and necessary and integral. . . . Your two little boys miss you. Eleanor, Hildegard, and Margerita miss you. Adelaide is frantic. Anne [Josie's friend] is pale and sullen. The doormen are jumpy and on edge. I'm not kidding; get home."

After instructing Abe Bienstock to dismiss William Morris as his agency, he lost interest in the rest of his affairs, though he helped with a December 3 press conference and cocktail party for *I Want to Live!* He thought Susan Hayward handled it well and noted, "In her case, her talent surprises me—and her, I think—As if she were in charge of it for somebody else. As a person, she doesn't respect it or even deserve it." He had made the same observation in his diary when he directed Hayward in *House of Strangers*, and he would make it again, a few years later, when he directed her in *The Honey Pot*.

On December 4 he flew to Germany, and the cloud lifted, suddenly and almost literally: "The effect of taking off in Italy and landing in Germany—that of a fuzzy picture coming sharply into focus." The United Artists representative was efficient, the chauffeur was competent, the ride all the way to Salzburg was comfortable. Although the Austrian hotel was "everything an Austrian hotel should not be," he spent a couple of surprisingly pleasant days with Erna and Rosa's mother before leaving for Paris on the Orient Express.

Aboard the train, the acute observer poked back up his head: "The fascinating cars from Bucharest and Warsaw—the provisions and families spread out in the vestibules—the coal burning stoves . . . the literal gamut of economic status from the red-handed peasant women to the white gloved gentlemen in the Wagon Lits."

By the time he reached Hotel Plaza Athénée, Joe was positively buoyant: "a nice suite, fine breakfast, to bath. . . . My spirits awakening for the first time."

Suddenly, all was amusing, even longwinded bores. "Gregory Ratoff to visit me at 3. Tales of his heart attack, his Swiss Clinic, of Zanuck and Juliette Greco, of Zanuck, of Maria Callas, of Charlie Feldman—his own old fat pimping self. How he keeps alive, I cannot guess—Physically, or financially. Probably, as Irwin Shaw suggests, off Zanuck."

At the Irwin Shaws for dinner on December 7, he enjoyed the company, the food, and the Shaws. "Lively conversation and good fun. . . . Home and comfortably to bed."

After talking to his lawyers and shopping, he dined alone at Lê Fouquet's and entertained himself by observing an old woman who fell asleep right after her soup "and was awakened most discreetly—by having the violinist play a lively gavotte in her ear!"

Aboard an American ship bound for home, "the Gentile equivalent of a Catskill hotel—afloat," he took promenades "through good clean American family groups." Daily massages were usually a reliable shipboard pleasure, but even an inadequate masseur, "Texas" (or "Cowboy") Jack Willis, amused rather than irritated him. Willis was "formerly a lousy middleweight fighter, now a lousy masseur. But talkative. And a poet. A student of the subconscious. He recited his poems to me, shilled me for a 5th Avenue health club and almost murdered me with a Scotch Douche. The U.S. Lines must search far and wide for its personnel."

The miserable dinners were partially explained when he learned the chef was English. Playing bingo on December 11, he wondered, "Why very old ladies invariably win at Bingo."

December 14: "Goody. Bingo after dinner. Won nothing."

December 15: "My face breaking out in bumps and blotches—new for me, and unhappy over it. I may fantasize in my 20s, but I look 50. Face it."

At cocktails with the captain, he met several army officers and a US Congressman from upstate New York, whom he pronounced

"Frightening." His wife: "a lush. He, almost a caricature of the 'I'm just a l'il ol' country boy' type politician." After dinner Joe chatted with a colonel, a paratrooper in his early forties who was covered with ribbons and, "like so many of his ilk, just this side of an idiot socially but brilliant and incisive when the subject of talk approaches his work."

December 16, his last day at sea: "'Solitaired' the morning away, it beats masturbation—or does it?—and I found I had won the daily poll at long last."

December 17: "New York harbor at dawn on a clear cold morning—the sky-line against the blood red of the early day as beautiful a sign as there is to see."

Met by Josie and Addie, Joe launched into business dealings before going home to their apartment to be with his sons: "Tom home with happy news about Yale. Chris home, looking fine. Both boys and Josie to dinner. Plans for the holidays and bridge."

With the city's newspapers on strike, Joe noted that it was "difficult to start a day without benefit of newspapers. Query: the effect of the newspaper strike upon the regularity of New York City bowel movements."

Picking up his Jaguar gave him "great delight." He enjoyed Chris and Tom. He became increasingly interested in *John Brown's Body*.

On December 20 he wondered, "Where to live? What to work on?" Life seemed full of possibilities.

Sunday, December 21: "A happy day. Josie brought Myra (Fox) to brunch with Chris, Tom and me. Fires going—the Los Angeles Times and Examiner—much fun. Dozing and listening to a "pro" football game throughout the afternoon. Later, some more of the younger set. I forgot my date at the Alan Lerners'. Peter Davis . . . for cold cuts and cake and games—happy times. It felt good. Slept soundly—without sedation."

CHAPTER 22

Southern Gothic Horror Story

ONCE JOE RETURNED, JOSIE MOVED OUT OF HIS APARTMENT AND SOON afterward became engaged to Peter Davis, whose parents, Frank Davis and the late Tess Slesinger, were also screenwriters. George Cukor gave them an elaborate pre-wedding dinner dance, and they married in the Jaffes' backyard that summer. Joe bought Josie's wedding dress and walked her down the aisle. He also upended tradition by suggesting Josie and Peter face their guests during the ceremony, which afforded Josie the pleasure of telling people Joe Mankiewicz had directed her wedding.

As for Joe, he wasn't sure where he was headed, but he kept moving. Among agents circling him after Bert Allenberg's death was Jules Stein, founder of MCA, Inc. Joe declined to sign with the powerful agency, and when MCA's president Lew Wasserman ran into him one day, he cornered Joe to ask why. "Frankly, Lew, I don't think I should be represented by an agent who calls me Herman," Joe explained. Not that he had corrected Stein. By then he found it endearing.

Buying the Jaguar had been such fun that in January 1959 Joe bought an enormous townhouse with an elevator and fireplaces in every room. Then he flew to Los Angeles to talk to Fox about *John Brown's Body* and to independent producer Sam Spiegel about directing a film version of Tennessee Williams's one-act play *Suddenly Last Summer*. Spiegel, who had just won his second Best Picture Oscar for *The Bridge on the River Kwai*, was at the top of his game. So was Williams, who had won Pulitzer Prizes for both *A Streetcar Named Desire* and *Cat on a Hot Tin Roof*. Elizabeth Taylor, who had been shooting the film version of *Cat on a Hot Tin Roof* when Mike Todd died, agreed to star in it as her first film after her MGM contract ended. She would collect $500,000, against 10 percent of the film's gross profit, making her Hollywood's highest-paid actress.

Williams's southern gothic horror story (it was often described as "Grand Guignol") was considered a masterpiece. It portrayed the struggle between Violet Venable, an eccentric, wealthy widow mourning the death of her beloved poet son, Sebastian, and her niece, Catherine Holly. Catherine is so traumatized from witnessing Sebastian's death that Violet has had her locked in a mental institution so no one can hear her story. Amidst her lush but menacing garden, Violet tells Dr. Cukrowicz, a psychiatrist/neurosurgeon who specializes in lobotomies, that once he lobotomizes Catherine, she will memorialize Sebastian with a million-dollar donation to his hospital. In short, Violet wants the story of Sebastian's death literally cut out of Catherine's brain.

Unwilling to operate without judging Catherine's sanity for himself, Dr. Cukrowicz uses truth serum to draw out the real story: for years Sebastian traveled with his mother, using her beauty as bait to attract young men for himself. When Violet became too old, he invited Catherine and forced her to wear a white bathing suit so revealing that, as Catherine says, it would be "a scandal to the jay birds." Something went wrong when they were in Spain, and the peasant boys on the beach chased and ultimately "devoured" Sebastian. Williams's story, whose creation Williams attributed to his ongoing psychoanalysis with Lawrence Kubie, was grimly autobiographical: his mentally ill sister was violent and had uttered such embarrassing, sexually explicit charges against his parents that their mother eventually had her lobotomized.

Spiegel's plan to obtain Production Code Authority approval for a story that combined cannibalism, homosexuality, an Oedipal mother-son-young woman triangle, and a prefrontal lobotomy would have seemed optimistic to the point of hubris, except that Sam Spiegel, who embodied the caricature of a cigar-chomping, high-living Hollywood producer even more than Darryl Zanuck, was an irresistible force. A refugee from the Nazis, Spiegel was charming, intelligent and completely ruthless. He had worked in the European and English film industries, done time in both English and American prisons, and spent thirteen years using the name S. P. Eagle. (Hearing that, Herman suggested Zanuck become Z. A. Nook and Lubitsch, L.U.Bitch, and when he ran into Spiegel after the release of his 1946 film, *The Stranger*, asked him how *St. Ranger* was doing.) Fellow émigré Billy Wilder called him a modern Robin Hood—"who steals from the rich and steals from the poor." Although he was known for legendary New Year's Eve parties, an impressive art collection, and a continual supply of nubile young women he shared with friends, Spiegel detested Hollywood's lack of culture as much as Joe and left as soon as he could set up elsewhere.

In a deal that pleased both men, Spiegel bought Williams's screen rights for $50,000 up front, plus 20 percent of the net profits, and $300,000 upon completion of the film. Williams later wrote that "the profits were as good as the movie was bad," though he had liked the original screenplay. After an initial try himself, he had recommended Gore Vidal, who retained both the play's menacing opulence and much of its dialogue.

Naturally, once Joe agreed to direct, he wanted to work a bit on the screenplay, so he met Vidal at Spiegel's Lombardy Hotel suite. Spiegel proudly showed them his newest Cezanne, Manet, and Soutine paintings, and after they left, Joe ridiculed their employer: "Isn't it interesting that Sam has the worst picture by each of those famous painters? He has the name but not the game."

Vidal, who thought Joe underestimated Spiegel, admired the producer's "truffle nose," his ability to hire first-rate creative people on the cheap when their careers were in a lull, like Elia Kazan for *On the Waterfront*. Vidal suspected Spiegel had calculated that Joe was due for another hit, especially if he had a strong producer to control his excesses. In fact, Joe's $300,000 fee was hardly niggardly, and since he threw himself into research anyway, he particularly enjoyed being paid to study topics he usually followed on his own, like medical and psychological disorders. He visited a psychiatric hospital; combed photographic files of the National Association for Mental Health for art, wardrobe, and makeup ideas; and asked Spiegel to hire a neurosurgeon for technical advice on frontal lobotomies.

Elizabeth Taylor convinced Spiegel to cast Montgomery Clift as Dr. Cukrowicz, though Clift's substance abuse had made him uninsurable (Spiegel had wanted William Holden). She also insisted on filming overseas for tax reasons, so Spiegel hired production designer Oliver Messel to create a New Orleans garden at Shepperton Studios outside of London. Rosemary Matthews, who was in Hollywood working at Paramount for Carlo Ponti and his producing partner, dropped persistent hints about joining the production, and even offered to pay her own way, but Joe did not respond.

Violet was still not cast by the time Joe arrived in England, but he reported to Josie, Chris, and Tom (or, rather, "(J)ohanna: (C)hris: (T)om") on their progress so far:

> Montgomery Clift has arrived. He flew alongside the jet for a while, but otherwise made the crossing without incident. Mrs. Eddie Fisher, in the best-kept secret since Elizabeth's Coronation, is flying under an assumed name to Barcelona. (She is calling herself Elizabeth Taylor—a very common-place nom-de-voyage). Accompanied by

> 19 bags—just travelling essentials, the trunks are being swum over by Hawaiian beach-boys—3 children, one maid, one secretary, one governess, one husband and a stand-by rabbi. At Barcelona, the whole schmier gets put on Spiegel's yacht (The H.M.S. Spiegel). . . . My relations with Cardinal Spiegel are proper, but tensing. He finds it difficult to part with either a dollar or a decision—and his megalomania more than makes up for the departure from our midst of L. B. Mayer plus C. B. DeMille. He makes Goldwyn look like Grandma Moses.

Taylor, who had just married Eddie Fisher, was attacked by a hostile London press for stealing Debbie Reynolds's husband, an action she herself already regretted. What she and Fisher seemed to have most in common was their love for Mike Todd, so Taylor diverted herself with an affair with journalist Max Lerner and, according to Tom, another with Joe. Rosemary and Chris disagree, and given the complicated setup, their opinion seems more plausible. Not only had Joe brought along Jeanne Vanderbilt, her daughter Heidi, eleven, and her son Alfred, nine, but he had gotten Vanderbilt a nominal assignment overseeing Taylor's children. Joe's eczema, an intermittent nervous condition, had also flared up so severely that he spent much of the time wearing white cotton gloves. A liaison between Joe and Elizabeth Taylor was certainly possible, but given Fisher, Lerner, three Vanderbilts, and Joe's gloves, the prospect seems farcical

Joe did become Taylor's diet coach, however. When the picture's publicity director met her at the airport, he called Spiegel on his yacht. "You better get over here. I warned you about the press, but you have a greater problem—she's fat." The petite star had the beginnings of a double chin, and when Joe saw her, he shook her upper arm and told her it looked like "a bag of dead mice." Taylor promptly began a crash diet, but Louella Parsons, who was still punishing Taylor for husband-stealing, wrote about the production's problems, including Taylor's plumpness. Joe sent Parsons an angry denial that ended, "SORRY TO DISAPPOINT YOUR INFORMANT BUT NOBODY IS MAD AT ANYBODY AND IF ELIZABETH TAYLOR IS OVERWEIGHT I FOR ONE AM AT A LOSS TO SUGGEST WHAT THERE SHOULD BE LESS OF."

Actually, everyone was mad at someone, but each was unhappy in his or her own way. Three years after his disfiguring accident, Clift was still trying to resurrect his career, but with his nonstop consumption of alcohol and drugs, he was a "bog of tics and tremors" and had trouble remembering his lines. He flubbed so many takes that Joe had to piece together his speeches, bit by bit. When he wasn't falling apart, he was behaving like a stubborn child, recalcitrant and habitually late to the set. Joe and Taylor did what they could to pull him through, but to some viewers Clift's deadpan performance made him seem more deranged than the lunatics in the asylum. (Others thought him excellent.)

Katharine Hepburn regretted her decision to play Violet almost as soon as she accepted. She was reluctant to shoot overseas, because Spencer Tracy was ill in Hollywood, and she quickly came to detest both the story and her character. Hepburn wanted to play Violet as obviously mad from her entrance, when she descends in an open elevator and, talking all the while, walks into her menacing garden and feeds flies to her Venus flytraps. Joe disagreed. He wanted Violet to start at "haughty eccentricity" and descend into madness, and when Hepburn objected, Joe simply thought she was being stubborn and trying to direct herself. He had no idea Hepburn was struggling with painful parallels between Catherine's experience and her own youthful trauma at finding her adored brother's body after he had hanged himself.

At the end of the shoot, Joe wanted to emphasize Violet's deterioration by making her suddenly appear old, so he instructed Jack Hildyard, the cinematographer, to use harsh lighting on her face and hands. Hepburn understood what they were doing and was so upset that once shooting was finished, she approached Joe and shocked the cast and crew by spitting in his face. Then she found Sam Spiegel in his office, and after spitting on his floor and telling him, "You're just a pig in a silk suit who sends flowers," she stalked out. The spitting became an oft-repeated story that usually portrayed Joe as an insensitive bully who treated Montgomery Clift with such cruelty that Hepburn spat at him in retribution. In fact Joe had worked hard and sympathetically to coax out Clift's performance; Hepburn was angry about the manipulative way Joe and Hildyard aged her without being honest about it. It wasn't about Clift; it was about herself.

But Joe did prefer Taylor's feminine wiles to Hepburn's androgynous independence and complained to Jeanne Vanderbilt and her children about Hepburn's preference for slacks, not to mention her attempts to mold her character to her own vision. The Vanderbilt children were relatively worldly, but to them Joe seemed large and intimidating, and a bit of a bully—he ridiculed Spiegel behind his back and dominated every gathering.

In the end, Joe was proud of both Hepburn's and Taylor's performances. Each had a long set piece—Williams's speeches were so prolonged

Joking here with Sam Spiegel, Katharine Hepburn later spat on the floor of his office and called him "a pig in a silk suit who sends flowers."

and poetic that Joe called them arias—and Joe considered Taylor's Catherine the best performance of her career. He correctly predicted that both Taylor and Hepburn would be nominated for Academy Awards and that, like Bette Davis and Anne Baxter for *Eve*, they would cancel each other out. Both were also nominated for Golden Globes, which Taylor won, along with the Motion Picture Exhibitors' Laurel Award.

Reactions to the film were mixed. Williams, who considered the adaptation too sensational and too literal with his allegories, told a *Village Voice* reporter years later, "It made me throw up," and privately called it an "abortion." As usual, the negative reviewers had more fun, though *Saturday Review*'s critic entitled his positive review, "Eating People Is Wrong." *Time*'s review called it "the only movie that has ever offered the paying public, for a single admission, a practicing homosexual, a psychotic heroine, a procuress-mother, a cannibalistic orgy and a sadistic nun." *Time* also marveled at Spiegel's success in gaining approval from both the PCA and the Legion of Decency by deeming it "'an adult horror picture' about a woman 'who is suddenly too old to procure boys for her

Suddenly, Last Summer (1959), something terrible happened to Elizabeth Taylor and a cast of thousands.

son'" and quoted Spiegel's response: "Why it's a theme the masses can identify themselves with."

When Joe wasn't engaged in his usual disparagement of the business—"a structure which should never have been built—the creation of the motion picture as an industry"—or Hollywood itself—an "intellectual fog belt"—he also defended the picture, telling the press, "I never thought about homosexuality or cannibalism when I was directing it—only its basic humanity."

Spiegel ran advertisements featuring Taylor in her transparent-when-wet bathing suit with the proclamation "Suddenly last summer . . . Cathy knew she was being used for something evil!" and audiences poured in. The $2.5 million production grossed about six times its costs. By 1966 revisionist critics were beginning to laud the picture, and Joe was still trying to force Spiegel to comply with the terms of his contract that required Spiegel to include Joe's name in his advertisements.

CHAPTER 23

The Toughest Three Pictures I Ever Made

Cleopatra was conceived in a state of emergency,
shot in hysteria, and wound up in blind panic.

—JOSEPH L. MANKIEWICZ, OCTOBER 30, 1962

IF *CLEOPATRA'S* COMBINATION OF GRAND OPERA, SHAKESPEAREAN comedy, Greek tragedy, and Keystone Kops seems farcical in retrospect, it should be remembered that the most costly film in history up to that point also ruined lives, ended careers, and almost took down a public corporation. Joe never really recovered.

"EMERGENCY"

In 1958 Walter Wanger tried to convince Figaro to adapt Carlo Maria Franzero's *The Life and Times of Cleopatra* into a $5 million picture starring Cary Grant as Julius Caesar, Burt Lancaster as Mark Antony, and either Sophia Loren or Audrey Hepburn as Cleopatra. When Figaro passed, he sold the idea to Twentieth Century Fox.

By that time, Fox was not the same company Joe had left in 1951. It was one of the last major studios to maintain its traditional operations, but Fox, too, was downsizing. With the company hemorrhaging red ink, its president, Spyros Skouras, was selling about two-thirds of the studio's 260-acre lot (the future Century City). Darryl Zanuck had decamped to Paris, where he produced films intended to turn his succession of European mistresses into stars, and Skouras, along with Buddy Adler, an amiable but weak producer, struggled to shape Fox's films and control costs.

They assigned *Cleopatra* a $1.2 million budget and a sixty-four-day shooting schedule, starring either Joan Fontaine or another Fox contract actress. Wanger continued to fight for a lavish, Cecil B. DeMille–esque spectacle starring Elizabeth Taylor, and eventually Skouras capitulated. Taylor agreed, but only if they paid her a million dollars and filmed overseas. Taylor's agent, Kurt Frings, negotiated a contract that paid her $125,000 a week for the first sixteen weeks' work; a $3,000-a-week expense allowance on top of hotel rooms; 10 percent of the film's gross income; and a number of other perquisites, including two days off per month for her menstrual period. If shooting went into overtime, Taylor would receive $50,000 a week.

Despite having only an incomplete script that satisfied no one, Skouras insisted they start shooting as soon as Taylor's contract began. So on September 28, 1960, director Rouben Mamoulian started production at Pinewood Studios outside of London, with Peter Finch as Caesar and Stephen Boyd as Antony. They were beset by complications from the beginning, including Taylor's chronic respiratory problems—she was always vulnerable to damp and cold, and her liberal self-medicating with pills and alcohol did not help. Mamoulian was so frustrated that he quit several times. To his surprise, on January 19, 1961, Skouras accepted his resignation.

On January 17, 1961, Joe was contentedly relaxing in the Bahamas, on Hume Cronyn and Jessica Tandy's private island, Children's Bay Cay. He was in a calm relationship with Jeanne Vanderbilt and since mid-December had been fishing, sleeping, swimming, reading, and happily working on *Justine*, a screenplay adaptation of Lawrence Durrell's Alexandria Quartet that Wanger had commissioned for Twentieth Century Fox.

On January 18 he interrupted his idyll to fly to New York for a dinner with his agent, Charles Feldman, and Spyros Skouras, where Skouras begged him to set aside *Justine* and take over *Cleopatra*. Convinced that Joe was the man to save Twentieth Century Fox by saving *Cleopatra*, he promised Joe whatever resources he wanted. He also promised that Fox would make it well worth Joe's while: they would structure a deal that would give Joe real money. Maybe a villa in the south of France. Or a yacht.

Joe was torn. *Justine* was a dream project, and Feldman had negotiated a generous $8,000 weekly salary while he wrote it. Lavish spectacles were not his kind of picture. On the other hand, the prospect of financial independence was enticing. He stayed up almost all night agonizing over the decision and even discussed it with his therapist the next day.

Feldman had no doubts. "Hold your nose for fifteen weeks and get it over with," he urged. Eventually Joe accepted, and Feldman, Joe, and Joe's lawyers gathered in his living room to hammer out a deal.

Feldman, who lived like a prince himself, liked the idea of a yacht, but Abe Bienstock squelched that. "I think it would be a wonderful gift because I enjoy cruising on yachts," he told the group, "and I would love to be Joe's guest. But it wouldn't be as much fun to be a yacht-party guest if Joe wasn't there, and he won't be, because he'll be in a federal penitentiary for income-tax evasion. That is the last I want to hear of tax-free gifts under any circumstances whatsoever." Instead, Fox bought Joe out of Figaro for $1.47 million, plus salary and expenses, and because NBC owned the other half of Figaro, Fox had to pay NBC an equal amount. Hiring Joe cost Fox almost $3 million before he started.

Skouras and Joe flew to London on February 1, 1961, and Skouras exhausted Joe on the way over, trying to convince him to take over as Fox's production chief—Buddy Adler had died the previous summer. Neither Wanger nor Skouras seemed as concerned as Joe about the cost of scrapping everything: the script; the enormous, expensive sets, which Joe considered "bloodcurdling"; Mamoulian's "dreadful," "catastrophic and unusable" footage–a mere ten and a half minutes to show for ten weeks' work; and many members of the cast. Removing Peter Finch alone cost Fox $150,000. They were already up to $5 million.

All that was fine with Skouras, but he insisted that script, sets, costumes, and cast all be ready to resume shooting on March 15, which was only six weeks away. Joe argued that even with Taylor's enormous salary, it would be far more economical to shut down production until they were ready. How could they construct sets or order costumes without a script to tell them what they would need? Skouras was adamant. He was fending off a board of directors who insisted on action.

Before tackling the script, Joe wanted to placate Elizabeth Taylor, who he believed was angry out of loyalty to Mamoulian. Entering Taylor and Fisher's two Dorchester Hotel penthouses, he threaded his way through children, servants, hangers-on, animals, and animal feces, to reach Taylor and Fisher, where he summoned all his charm to win them over. Then he sent them on vacation for a couple of weeks. Taylor returned with such a bad case of Asian flu that she was still bedridden on February 27, her twenty-ninth birthday.

The script already had a long history of contributors, and Joe tried Paddy Chayefsky, Sidney Buchman, Paul Jarrico, Peter Shaffer, and Lawrence Durrell before tackling it himself. By then he had hired Johnny Johnston as production manager and Rosemary Matthews as a production assistant, so he began dictating to Rosemary. Just as Herman's Kane came to resemble Orson Welles, Joe drew on Elizabeth Taylor for his Cleopatra: Taylor had grown up as a pampered studio princess who, despite being sheltered from hardship, had had to fight her own battles with the powerful men surrounding her.

They planned to resume shooting at Pinewood, then shoot exteriors in Egypt, at least if they were allowed. Egypt had barred the newly Jewish Taylor, who had converted when she married Fisher. However, by March 3 Taylor had pneumonia. Despite the ministrations of eleven doctors, including Queen Elizabeth's personal physician, she slipped into a coma and, after an emergency tracheotomy, hovered between life and death. The hospital issued bulletins every fifteen minutes to the surrounding reporters and cameramen, and support poured in from all over the world. When she finally recovered enough to leave the clinic, fans practically tore the door off her Rolls-Royce. Apparently, Taylor's near-death experience had eradicated the public's animosity, and at dinner one night Joe bet William Holden a hundred dollars that public sympathy would get Taylor an Oscar for her role in *Butterfield 8*. (It did.)

Taylor's pneumonia finally convinced Skouras to abandon cold, damp London. He and Joe both favored shooting in Italy for its warm weather and lower production costs, but Fisher and Taylor now insisted on Hollywood, to be near her doctors, so Skouras agreed to film almost everything on the Fox lot. They dismantled the gigantic sets and shipped them back, and started construction in Hollywood a few months later. Then, prodded by Wanger and Joe, Skouras changed his mind again. They would not shoot at the studio that summer; instead, they would shoot in Italy to take advantage of the six-day Italian workweek, move to Egypt in September and October, then film interiors back at Fox. Wanger hired Broadway designer Irene Sharaff to design Taylor's costumes; writer Ranald MacDougall to fashion a script out of Joe's screenplay outline; and three-time Oscar winner Leon Shamroy as cinematographer.

Fox's board continued to pepper Skouras with unrealistic orders, which Skouras passed along to placate them. He even ordered Joe to resume shooting in June, though it was clearly impossible. Taylor still had to recover from her tracheotomy, undergo plastic surgery on the scar in July, then recover from the second operation. The board also started involving itself in casting. Joe wanted Laurence Olivier for Caesar and Richard Burton for Mark Antony. Pushing Joe to retain Stephen Boyd, who was under contract, Skouras argued that Burton lacked mass appeal. Joe dismissed the notion as a foolish economy:

> WHAT IS OBVIOUS TO EVERY COMPETENT FILMMAKER IN THE WORLD . . . [IS] . . . THAT IN FOUR SIMPLE WORDS—ELIZABETH TAYLOR IN CLEOPATRA—THIS STUDIO POSSESSES EASILY THE GREATEST PRE-SOLD ATTRACTION FOR MASS APPEAL IN THE HISTORY OF ENTERTAINMENT. WHETHER BURTON OR BOYD OR YOU OR I OR ELSA MAXWELL PLAYS ANY OF THE OTHER ROLES WILL NEITHER SUPPLY NOR DETRACT FIVE CENTS IN TERMS OF THAT MASS APPEAL. THE ONLY THING THAT CAN POSSIBLY DETRACT FROM THE GROSSES OF CLEOPATRA WILL BE AUDIENCE DISAPPOINTMENT IN THE PICTURE ITSELF.

Fox paid Richard Burton $250,000 in salary and spent another $50,000 buying out his *Camelot* contract.

"HYSTERIA"

Reversing himself yet again, Skouras announced on June 30 that despite all the completed work on *Cleopatra* sets in Hollywood, they would not film interiors in the studio. They would shoot entirely overseas. Fox needed all the space not already promised to television production to shoot George Stevens's biblical film *The Greatest Story Ever Told.*

Joe left for Rome on July 22 with only six of the approximately forty principal roles filled. Production was so short-staffed in Italy that Joe had to help find housing for Taylor and Fisher, who required a villa large enough for three children, five dogs, two cats, and assorted employees. Joe again begged Skouras to prevent waste by postponing production until they were ready. Again, Skouras refused. "For God's sake, get something on film," he insisted. They signed Rex Harrison to play Caesar a mere two weeks before shooting began.

Taylor and Fisher's retinue now included Taylor's personal physician, whose $25,000 fee Fox had agreed to pay, and they hoped the villa's large gardens would maintain their privacy. However, paparazzi immediately swarmed in, disguising themselves as priests, masquerading as servants, and trying to bribe anyone connected with the production. Fox had to pay for additional police protection.

Skouras arrived the day after Taylor and Fisher, looking exhausted. The board had canceled *The Greatest Story Ever Told,* which had been important to Skouras. Now Hollywood studio space would sit idle while they spent millions in Rome, constructing elaborate sets for the third time.

As rehearsals began, men drilled for battle scenes, and Hermes Pan prepared hundreds of dancing girls for Cleopatra's procession into Rome.

Directing a spectacle.

Slave girls and handmaidens went on strike to protest the skimpiness of their costumes.

Construction proceeded on an enormous scale. The sets for the Roman Forum and Cleopatra's Alexandria Palace were larger than the original Forum and Palace and cost $6 million. The Forum covered twelve acres of Cinecittá's backlot and included more than thirty buildings. Fox paid the Borghese family $150,000 to rent land near the beach at Anzio, forty miles south of Rome, to construct Alexandria and build the giant barges and ships they planned to sink during the Battle of Actium. Because Prince Borghese neglected to mention either the unexploded World War II land mines on the property or the NATO firing range next door, Fox had to hire demolition workers to remove the mines and coordinate film schedules with NATO firing practice.

They started shooting on September 25, 1961, and after directing all day, Joe wrote at night, striving to keep his script ahead of shooting. The problems seemed endless. Rex Harrison's wardrobe and makeup made him look like a Martian. The Italians kept finding new ways to squeeze more money out of them. Johnny Johnston, who was ill, tried to quit. Joe became so ill that he had to take a day off, then wondered why none of his "wake-up" pills seemed to work. When he was awakened at five-thirty or six in the morning, he took a Dexedrine. He had a shot after lunch to keep directing, and another at night so he could write. Then he took something to make him sleep. One night he recorded, "Stimulants don't stimulate anymore." Six nights later, he couldn't get to sleep: "too much amphetamine and coffee."

In October they began rehearsing Cleopatra's procession into Rome, which required six thousand extras and hundreds of animals. The Italian elephants were so wild that they had to be replaced with more docile English elephants; the Italian elephants' owner sued, both for slandering his elephants and for not using them. Food and sanitary facilities for the extras were inadequate. Corruption was so pervasive that some extras picked up togas in the morning, hid them, sneaked out to their day jobs, then retrieved them at the end of the day, and collected their ten-dollar wages.

The scale daunted even Rex Harrison. In his first major scene, Caesar was to address the Roman senate just before Cleopatra and her procession entered Rome. The scene was so vast that a rocket had to be fired to cue Harrison to speak, and Harrison uncharacteristically muffed his lines. Before they could start again, all the animals and the six thousand extras had to return to their starting places and "huge cannonball pats of elephants' dung" had to be cleaned up.

Harrison continued flubbing his lines until daylight faded, and they had to stop and start over the following day. "Harrison squeezed through, one line at a time," Joe recorded after they finally finished. Later Harrison asked Joe what had happened to the zebras they had planned for the parade. They weren't going to use zebras, Joe told him, just donkeys painted with stripes. "They forgot their lines," Joe deadpanned.

Several scenes later, Harrison was still forgetting his lines, and though Joe tried "every psychiatric approach this side of shock treatment," they both knew the real reason was Elizabeth Taylor's chronic tardiness. Harrison was notoriously difficult, but he was a dedicated professional, and

Taylor's no-shows made him feel like a "very well-trained sprinter, waiting in the starting position for the gun to go off." Furthermore, he had to sprint in a very uncomfortable toga, and sometimes the wait was several hours. Once Taylor finally showed up, they all had to jump into the scene.

In November, shortly before Skouras and Peter Levathes, his board-appointed heir-apparent, arrived on a cost-control mission, Walter Wanger was approached by Nicolas Reisini, president of Cinerama, Inc. Reisini offered to reimburse Fox for its entire investment in *Cleopatra* and relieve Fox of the project that was supposedly ruining the studio. He would convert the existing Todd-AO footage to Cinerama film and finish it elsewhere. Skouras and Levathes were appalled. "It's not for sale," Skouras told Wanger, insisting that if such an idea ever got out, it would ruin the company.

Instead, Skouras and Levathes ordered Sid Rogell, Fox's man in Rome, to institute new economies. Most of the crew were to commute to the studio in buses instead of cars, even though that made the trip an hour and a half instead of thirty minutes. While Rex Harrison was out of town, Rogell exchanged his trailer for a small dressing room and refused to pay Harrison's driver, whom he suspected of trumping up mileage. When Harrison found out, he summoned Rogell to his newly diminished quarters and, dressed in street clothes instead of his costume, gave Rogell the full Rex Harrison treatment. "I treat my servants very well and you are my servant," he proclaimed. He followed with a profanity-laced tirade and a declaration that he would not be returning to work until all was restored. Then he pointed imperiously at Rogell and declared, "You are now dismissed." When he returned to the set, Harrison received a huge ovation. "He's never been so popular," observed Joe.

After Thanksgiving, Johnny Johnston told Joe he had to quit, adding, "Dr. Pennington is more worried about you than me." The uppers, downers, and every other medication were obviously taking their toll. On December 6 Joe wrote Abe Bienstock, "I will not go into details; it would be a little like going into detail about the invasion of Normandy. Suffice it to say that for the first time in my life I have periods during which my brain simply does not function—and during which my body will not go to sleep because of the stimulants I have been taking." He blamed Skouras, who "makes and unmakes decisions from one moment to the next . . . driven by nothing but a frenzy to maintain, at all costs, a title of President."

When Skouras called to castigate him twice in one night, Joe lost his temper and quit: he would finish the script, and then Skouras could

Calm before the storm. Soon, Joe will lose his health. Walter Wanger will lose his job. Eddie Fisher will lose his wife.

get another director to finish the film more quickly and cheaply. When Skouras said that Levathes was returning to Rome in five days, Joe agreed to stay until "matters are straightened out." Then he cabled his agent, Charles Feldman:

> ANY CONCEIVABLE CHANCE YOU COMING TO ROME NEAREST POSSIBLE FUTURE STOP SORRY BUT CAN NO LONGER COPE WITH ABYSMAL LACK EXECUTIVE UNDERSTANDING OR GUIDANCE ON ONE HAND PLUS CONTINUOUS IRRATIONAL DISTORTED HYSTERICAL REPROACHES AND PRESSURES ON OTHER STOP HAVING WORKED LITERALLY REPEAT LITERALLY SEVEN DAYS WEEKLY FOR MANY MONTHS WITHOUT LETUP AND AGAINST URGENT MEDICAL ADVICE TIME IS NEAR WHEN I MUST CHOOSE BETWEEN MY OWN HEALTH AND CORPORATE WELFARE OF TWENTIETH CENTURY FOX STOP BADLY IN NEED SOMEBODY IN MY CORNER CHARLIE HAPPY NEW YEAR JOE.

Feldman was already on his way to Nairobi, so he stopped in Rome long enough to have dinner with Joe and advise him to "be adamant and unrelenting." Otherwise, tell them they could "get another boy."

"Easier advised than done—especially for me. But I shall do my best," Joe pledged manfully on December 30.

The following night Joe took Chris, now working as an assistant director, and Tom, who was in from Yale for the holidays, to Sybil and Richard Burton's New Year's Eve party at a popular Rome nightclub. The masculine, intellectual, moody Burton, thirty-six, was renowned for his theatrical ability, his capacity for alcohol, and his incorrigible philandering. Although long married and the father of two daughters (including three-year-old future actress Kate Burton), he was reputed to have slept with all his leading ladies except Julie Andrews.

Before shooting began, Burton had seemed determined to take Taylor down a peg, telling friends, "I've got to don my breastplate once more to play opposite Miss Tits." But the first day they actually worked together, Burton was so drunk he was literally quivering, and when he asked for a cup of coffee, Taylor had to help him drink it. Inadvertently, Burton had found the way to Taylor's heart. She was intimidated by his Shakespearean background but charmed by his vulnerability. By the time he blew a line, she was completely smitten.

So when Fisher suggested leaving the Burtons' New Year's Eve party, Taylor resisted, and Burton immediately joined forces. "She hasn't even finished her champagne," he said, and spent the next hour switching his full glass for Taylor's empty one. Fisher noticed the two giggling as he and she used to do, but he had no idea they were holding hands under the table.

An affair between the two would have surprised no one except Eddie Fisher, but at the moment, Joe had too much on his mind to pay attention. On January 3, 1962, he recorded four "crises," but still in the dark, he added, "Miss Taylor's 'after-lunch' behavior mystifying. Tremendous sleepiness, forgetting of lines, then great euphoria and can't wait for the vodka and grapefruit juice . . . (Demerol? Empirin & codeine?)."

Taylor called him that night to apologize for "her embarrassment at the scene today, therefore her giggling—and don't be angry with her. Also, does she have to learn the whole scene for tomorrow?"

"Christ. How long, O Lord?" he wondered, after hanging up.

He soon would find out.

On Friday, January 26, 1962, Elizabeth Taylor summoned Joe to her dressing room. Rumors had been flying, and she wanted Joe to know the truth: she was in love with Richard Burton. From the vantage of long experience, Joe urged her to keep her marriage separate from her affair. It was too late. She had already told Fisher. When she failed to show up

They are not acting.

for rehearsal after lunch, Joe rehearsed Harrison alone for a while then left, hoping he could at least get more writing done.

Instead, a miserable Eddie Fisher called to say he was leaving for New York. Don't go, Joe counseled in a call that lasted two hours. Go back to the villa and stay there.

The next day was Saturday, and Joe was pleasantly surprised to find writing going so well, especially, he noted, considering "the amount of telephonic therapy I was required to furnish Mr. Fisher." After Burton called, looking for Taylor, Fisher called to thank him for advice. Then Taylor's assistant called to report that Taylor was with him. Joe decided it was time to acquaint Walter Wanger with the facts.

"Liz and Burton are not just playing Antony and Cleopatra," he announced to his old friend. Given Burton's reputation, the stars' behavior, and Joe's and Wanger's crowded romantic histories, neither man was completely surprised. But with millions of dollars and hundreds of lives depending on the emotional wellbeing of one volatile twenty-nine-year-old actress, they knew they were sitting on "a potential powder keg."

On Sunday, Joe returned from a walk to learn Eddie Fisher had called. Then Burton appeared for three hours of drinking and talking until Joe called Roddy McDowall to take him home. McDowall, who was playing Caesar's adopted son, Octavian, had been close to Taylor since they starred together as children in *Lassie Come Home*, and now that he was sharing a house with the Burtons, he had become close to Richard and Sybil as well.

Sybil Burton called to see if her husband was on his way home. Fisher called to tell him Burton and McDowall were with Taylor. "Tragic," Joe recorded. "To bed exhausted—by 'Cleopatra'—but not by writing or directing it."

On Monday they were back at work. Burton was "a bit the worse for wear but his sense of responsibility to his craft utterly admirable," Joe observed. On Wednesday, Fisher called to tell Joe that after staying out with Burton the previous evening, Taylor had brought him home to confront Fisher, and Burton had humiliated them both.

"Hope your second year is as happy as your first," Wanger told Joe the following day as he presented him with cake on the set. February 1, 1962, marked Joe's first full year with *Cleopatra*.

Appropriately, it was a day of intrigue: "Burton keeping—or being kept—from Taylor. Roddy on and off the phone. Fisher's calls to me: 'What should I say—and not say?' Taylor insisting Burton come to see her before she returns to the villa and Fisher." Despite—or perhaps because of—the excitement, they made fairly good progress. Basking in his role as the virtuous one, for a change, Harrison began behaving beautifully, and Joe prophesied an Academy Award for his performance.

By February 12 Joe was sick again—genuinely ill, but also sick of his new job as love counselor. That afternoon Burton and Taylor had the incredible effrontery to ask, would Joe, "as a genius, tell them where they can 'piss off' together?"

His answer—"Nowhere"—did not stop them, and Eddie Fisher called at nine thirty that night to tell Joe his wife was still not home. The following day Taylor told him the rest of the story: arriving at midnight, she found her husband sexually aroused and submitted to his wishes. Knowing how much Elizabeth Taylor thrived on conflict and enjoyed having her lovers try to dominate her, her therapist-director suspected his star had not been as "corpse-like" as she described.

On February 14 shooting went so smoothly that Joe dared to believe they might have a good day. Then Taylor arrived at the set to watch Burton. Knowing that Eddie Fisher had brought Sybil up to date on the affair she had believed finished, Burton had barely convinced Taylor to leave before Sybil arrived to spend the rest of that day on the set. Then Martin Landau, who played the loyal soldier Rufio, and who had just come out of the hospital, collapsed after one take. Work ground to a standstill.

Wanger asked Joe to help compose a letter to Taylor and Burton, reminding them of their contractual obligations. Joe, who doubted he could convince them, told Wanger and McDowall the same thing: "The situation cannot be cured—but it must be lived with as rationally as possible. Taylor is a very sick woman." In his diary he noted, "Afraid no one believes me, really. They think—and hope–she just needs 'talking to' or 'a regime' or 'should be frightened' or 'made to realize.' Ignorance. They can never believe how deeply she wants disaster—particularly to herself." By then Joe was very sick, too, but he suffered from fever and a sore throat.

On Saturday, February 17, Burton told Taylor he did not intend to leave his wife, and she swallowed enough sleeping pills to land in the hospital. When Joe found she had taken fourteen, he sighed, "If she can count them, she'll be fine." Taylor reinforced a pet theory of Joe's, which was that if sleeping pills were suppositories, that would eliminate 75 percent of the world's accidental suicides.

Fox's publicity team convinced the press Taylor had food poisoning and begged Burton to say nothing publicly. Once he said something, the press would be able print rumors about the affair without fearing libel charges. But Burton and his press agent just could not resist and issued a statement denying a relationship. After a scolding from Fox, Burton issued another statement, denying the denial, but it was too late. Overnight, the press went berserk, and Richard Burton became a superstar. Many (including Joe) who had suspected Burton of less than pure motives felt confirmed in their misgivings. Taylor was certainly alluring, and Burton an aggressive philanderer (Rosemary had fended him off while working on *Alexander the Great*, 1956), but a liaison with Elizabeth Taylor was also a shot to the reputation.

Paparazzi literally stormed the walls of the Fisher villa, and intruders at the Burtons' so frightened their two-year-old autistic daughter that she screamed for hours. Despite Taylor's affinity for Sturm und Drang, she retreated, pining for Burton but feeling guilty about hurting Sybil. Everyone except Eddie Fisher realized that Fisher's marriage was over.

Always a player, Burton added a Copacabana dancer to his entourage on the set, infuriating Taylor. Taylor and Burton both drank heavily throughout the days and nights, but somehow also managed to perform. Joe maintained a calm facade, belied only by the white gloves shielding his eczema. "When you're in a cage with tigers you never let them know you're afraid of them or they'll eat you," he told Fox's young publicist Jack Brodsky.

While Joe was coaxing performances from alcohol-soaked, love-besotted actors, Twentieth Century Fox shareholders and executives focused on the company's straits. Dissident shareholders sued Fox's management, and the board of directors elected a new board chairman. Judge Samuel Rosenman was a respected jurist and presidential advisor, but his only entertainment experience was writing speeches for Franklin Roosevelt. Skouras flew over to remonstrate with Taylor, Fisher, and Burton and to berate Wanger for bringing Burton into the film. "He will never be a big box office star," Skouras predicted. Then he saw the rushes and offered Burton starring roles in two more Fox pictures.

Back in the US, Skouras shook off Burton's spell and wrote to ask him and Taylor to be more circumspect. The lovers were furious, and Taylor's agent told Wanger that if Taylor received a similar letter, she would quit. Fox's managers spent more than $200,000 in premiums to increase their life insurance on Taylor to $10 million.

Even as Elizabeth and Eddie and Richard and Sybil steadfastly continued to deny any marital problems, the lovers were losing patience—and inhibitions. On March 26 an Italian newspaper printed a photograph of them kissing. Fox's Rome publicist Jack Brodsky wired his New York colleague Nat Weiss:

> March 29: FISHER BOUNCED SYBIL FLYING BURTON TAYLOR GOING OUT IN PUBLIC FOR FIRST TIME STOP GET UNDER THE DESK STOP AM TERRIFIED STOP BRODSKY

Weiss responded:

> March 30: PAPERS ARE FILLED TAYLOR BURTON ON TOWN STOP ANGRY LETTERS POURING IN STOP EXECS UPSET BECAUSE AFFAIR NOW PUBLIC THOUGHT YOU SHOULD KNOW WEISS

> March 31, 1962 *Los Angeles Times*, Rome, Page One:
> Liz, Richard Go Night-Clubbing; Eddie Denies Marriage Is on Rocks
> March 31, 1962 *Los Angeles Times*, New York, Page Two:
> Liz Rebuffs Eddie; She Won't Deny Rift Rumor

March 31, 1962 *New York Daily News*, Page One:
LIZ AND BURTON FIRST PHOTOS, Eddie Talks of Love, But Burton Gets Liz' Lip Service

April 1 Letter, Brodsky to Weiss:

> It gets more incredible every day. . . . Burton says to me, "Jack, love, I've had affairs before. How did I know the woman was so fucking famous? She knocks Khrushchev off the front page." So I say, "Rich, it's none of my business, but you can't very well deny everything in print and then go out on the Via Veneto till three in the morning." So he says, "I just got fed up with everyone telling us to be discreet. I said to Liz, 'Fuck it, let's go out to fucking Alfredo's and have some fucking fettuccine.'" . . . Up until a couple of days ago, everyone thought Burton was giving a great performance offstage. Now he seems like a different person, so caught up in Taylor's web. Anyway RB told JLM that "I fall more in love with her each day."

On April 3 Taylor and Fisher announced plans to divorce. On April 4 newspapers revealed that Burton had cabled his wife he still loved her—he sent the cable in Welsh, apparently under the impression no one could translate it.

Telesera, a Roman newspaper, announced that Richard Burton was actually a decoy and that Taylor was really in love with Joe. When an Associated Press reporter insisted Brodsky ask Joe for a comment, Joe said, "The real truth is that I am in love with Burton and Miss Taylor is the cover-up for us." Then he kissed Burton on the mouth.

The Vatican's weekly *Osservatore della domenica* reprimanded "Madam," for her "erotic vagrancy." Italian politicians denounced them, with the Americans not far behind. Urging Attorney General Robert Kennedy to bar their reentry into the United States, Representative Iris Blitch (D–Ga.) scolded the couple on the floor of Congress for defiling not only American womanhood but the capitalist system itself: "Communists chuckle because the Roman spectacle seems to prove their theses that capitalists are unscrupulous, depraved, wanton and decadent and that capitalism breeds these undesirable traits."

Spyros Skouras was not amused; he was panic-stricken. In a four-page, single-spaced letter quoting angry newspapers from all over the world, he implored Joe to convince the lovers their behavior was jeopardizing their careers. Convincing Burton he was harming himself would have been difficult. In Paris with Sybil to finish a shoot for Zanuck's *The Longest Day*, he was almost as besieged as Taylor.

Back in Italy, Burton took Taylor to the beach for the weekend. Taylor swallowed yet another handful of sleeping pills and landed in the hospital yet again, this time with a bruised nose they blamed on a car accident. Burton's fee for a picture doubled from $250,000 to $500,000, and he bought Taylor a piece of jewelry from Bulgari. At her suggestion, he bought another piece for Sybil, though it cost about one quarter the price of Taylor's. Joe noticed Taylor's diction improving and told the pair that just because Taylor was beginning to sound like Burton was no reason for Burton to start sounding like Eddie Fisher.

Even before the affair, visitors had streamed onto the set. Congressmen. Maria Callas. Isaac Stern. The king and queen of Greece. The infanta of Spain. President Sukarno of Indonesia. Journalists like Max Lerner and Art Buchwald, who reported in his column, "It used to be that one couldn't leave Rome without having seen the Colosseum and the Roman forum. Now you can add having been on the set of Cleopatra." The romance only increased the traffic.

Fox screenwriter Philip Dunne visited and was shocked at the changes in his old friends. Joe looked "wan and haggard." Leon Shamroy "appeared to have aged ten years." When Dunne and his wife joined Antony and Cleopatra for lunch at the studio, paparazzi and gossip writers circled their table, and the screenwriter could not resist recording the bon mots that passed for wit among the Beautiful People:

CLEOPATRA: Well, you sure were a mess last night! Boy, what a mess!
ANTONY: You were a bit of a mess yourself, old girl.
CLEOPATRA: Boy, I mean you were a *mess*!
ANTONY: Could you unhook this armor? It's killing my back.

So it went. La dolce vita.

"BLIND PANIC"

On May 28, 1962, Cleopatra finally expired, and Fox shareholders rejoiced. Running through more than $30 million, twenty-one months of filming, four international relocations, three suicide attempts, two life-threatening illnesses, and one gigantic adulterous affair, Twentieth Century Fox's survival had depended on the physically fragile, emotionally labile, thirty-year-old Elizabeth Taylor. At Fox's May 16 annual meeting, one shareholder even nominated her to the board of directors. The end seemed in sight at last.

Taylor had not completely finished her scenes, but two board representatives and production chief Peter Levathes arrived in Rome to shut down filming. On June 1 the Three Wise Men (as Walter Wanger dubbed them) fired Wanger and ordered Taylor off salary by June 9. All shooting in Italy was to cease by June 30, at which time funds would be cut off. Film, equipment, and personnel were to be sent home. Any remaining scenes would be shot in Hollywood.

Two days later they ordered Wanger—still nominally in charge though no longer paid—to cancel shooting the Battle of Pharsalia. Eliminating the battle scene needed to open the picture so upset Rex Harrison that he offered to pay for it himself. Joe predicted "the first indoor movie in Todd-AO."

On June 5 they summoned Wanger, Rogell, Joe, and production manager Doc Merman to sign a memorandum binding themselves to the new terms. Wanger and Rogell signed reluctantly. Merman walked out. After telling them what they could do with it, Joe left, too.

The board later extended *Cleopatra*'s shooting deadlines, but Fox was on a roll. The following week in Hollywood, Levathes fired Marilyn Monroe for repeated absences from *Something's Got to Give*, telling the press that studios no longer could afford to allow the "whims" of stars to control production schedules. Actually, the seismic shift of power had already occurred in the opposite direction, from studios to stars. Levathes just didn't know it.

In New York the board fired Skouras from the presidency, effective September 30. While they searched for his successor, they also canceled shooting for the Philippi battle.

That was the last straw for Joe. He cabled Judge Rosenman, with copies to Skouras, Levathes, and Feldman:

PHILIPPI CONSISTS OF SOME TENTS ON CINECITTA BACK LOT THREE OR FOUR SETUPS ONE NIGHT SHOOTING STOP WITHOUT PHARSALIA IN MY OPINION OPENING OF FILM AND FOLLOWING SEQUENCES SEVERELY DAMAGED STOP BUT WITHOUT PHILIPPI THERE IS LITERALLY NO OPENING FOR SECOND HALF SINCE INTERIOR TENT SCENES ALREADY SHOT SIMPLY CANNOT BE INTELLIGIBLY PUT TOGETHER STOP MOST IMPORTANTLY IT IS ARBITRARY AND COMPLETELY INCOMPREHENSIBLE

ELIMINATION OF COMPARATIVELY MOST INEXPENSIVE AND MOST VITAL BIT OF FILM LEADS ME TO RELUCTANT CONCLUSION THAT THESE DECISIONS CANNOT REFLECT FINANCIAL EXIGENCY SO MUCH AS BLIND PANIC AND EITHER FRIGHTENING UNCONCERN FOR ASSET CALLED CLEOPATRA OR SHOCKING UNAWARENESS OF FILM MAKING STOP FOR MY PART I HAVE EXHAUSTED SUCH ENERGIES AND TALENT AS I POSSESS AND THE PROSPECT OF A FLOW OF SIMILAR PRONUNCIAMENTOS IN THE MONTH AHEAD IS ONE I CANNOT FACE STOP NOR WOULD I WANT TO FACE THE FILM I COULD NOT ASSEMBLE PROPERLY MUCH LESS TURN OVER WITH PRIDE STOP WITH MUTUAL APPRECIATION OF RESPONSIBILITIES AND SUGGESTING THAT MINE TOWARD THE STOCKHOLDERS IS NO LESS THAN YOURS I SUGGEST THAT YOU REPLACE ME SOONEST POSSIBLE BY SOMEONE LESS CRITICAL OF YOUR DIRECTIVES AND LESS DEDICATED TO THE EVENTUAL SUCCESS OF CLEOPATRA.
JOSEPH L MANKIEWICZ

Originally the board said no. Then they said yes, but on a limited basis.

While Joe, Wanger, Caesar, Antony, and Cleopatra struggled in Italy to complete the picture, Zanuck joined the battle for control of Twentieth Century Fox from Paris. On June 30 he publicly defended Skouras and accused the board of directors of interfering in a process about which they knew nothing. Suddenly Skouras, who had been ridiculed for his lack of production knowledge and blamed for the company's cumulative $35 million in operating losses, was being acclaimed throughout the industry for his showmanship. Zanuck, whose independent productions were all failures, was hailed as the corporation's savior. They were the heroes. The villain was "Wall Street."

Like Napoleon's march on Paris from Elba, Zanuck's return to Twentieth Century Fox attracted more supporters every day. "I do not believe that stockbrokers or their attorneys are qualified to endorse or annul film proposals any more than I am qualified to plead a case in court or sell stock," he told the press, and eventually Zanuck's logic, his forceful personality, and his position as Fox's largest shareholder swayed the board. They elected Zanuck president and Skouras chairman, and the dissident directors resigned in defeat.

Shooting in Egypt had been canceled and reinstated twice by the time the cast and crew arrived in the unbearable July heat to encounter production problems dwarfing those in Italy. On July 23 the nurse administering one of Joe's many daily shots hit his sciatic nerve, forcing him to direct from a wheelchair for the rest of their stay. He was still in a wheelchair in early August, when he flew from Rome to New York and on to Los Angeles, to begin cutting the film.

In September, just when Joe assumed his only remaining struggle would be wrestling the voluminous footage down to a manageable length, he learned that Ranald MacDougall was contesting his writing credit on behalf of himself and Sidney Buchman, who was still unofficially blacklisted. MacDougall felt Joe had exploited their work, and he resented the "slight edge of contempt" with which Joe had treated him and Buchman. At first Joe refused even to submit a statement, but Wanger and a Screen Writers Guild representative convinced him to advocate on his own behalf. After a somewhat hostile hearing, the Guild awarded both MacDougall and Buchman co-credit.

Joe was slightly mollified the following May 1963, when the Guild voted him their annual Laurel Award, given to the member "who has advanced the literature of the motion pictures and made outstanding contributions to the profession of screen writer." But by then, Joe had been flattened by a much more powerful adversary than Ranald MacDougall.

After closing much of Fox's studio and firing about half of its six hundred employees, Zanuck spent the rest of the summer of 1962 in Europe, finishing *The Longest Day*. On August 31 he wrote Joe that he wanted to see a completed first cut and a progress report of expected completion dates no later than the first week of October. In addition to expenses like Joe's and twenty-eight other Fox employees' salaries, he reminded Joe, interest alone was costing Fox $7,000 a day. He added, "I have been told that you have expressed the 'fear' that I will take over the project and edit it myself." That would happen only if he thought Joe had not made enough progress.

Joe replied that his ordeal had been "an experience which violated almost every rule of proper filmmaking, a panic-driven operation which found me working literally seven days and seven nights a week for almost fourteen months—and which left me physically and mentally depleted." He took the opportunity to urge making two films instead of one: "[O]ur objective was to put into one film the material that Mr. Shaw and Mr. Shakespeare put into two full length plays." And reports of his fears had been greatly "exaggerated. I have never been afraid to show you either a rough draft . . or a first cut . . . I still know of no one to whom I would rather present either. My only apprehension has been that I would not have the opportunity of properly acquainting you with what I have set out to do. . . . our most intimate collaboration always took place on the <u>concept</u> of the film. Once you and I knew where we were going, I can recall few if any apprehension, much less 'fears' that were felt along the way."

On October 11 Joe flew to Paris to begin dubbing with Taylor, Harrison, and Burton and to meet with Zanuck. Joe found his former boss at "the peak of megalomania," talking mostly of *The Longest Day*, and apparently uninterested in *Cleopatra* except for its costs. Zanuck approved a four-and-a-half-hour length but rejected the notion of two separate films. After they watched the first half of the four-and-a-half-hour rough cut, Zanuck said only, "Beautifully written and directed." He suggested they save the second half for the following day, but when Joe urged him to continue after dinner, he acquiesced. Joe found even their dinner conversation disquieting. Zanuck completely skirted *Cleopatra*, talking only of *The Longest Day* and theater equipment.

They finished watching the second half at 2:15 on Sunday morning, October 14, and Zanuck repeated his previous comment, word for word, adding that he wanted to spend the next day thinking about it, "particularly the battle scenes," which he found "disappointing." Then he would dictate some notes and meet with them to view the picture again. Later, Edward Leggewie, one of Zanuck's secretaries, called Joe to cancel the meeting, which left him so anxious he cabled Wanger, Feldman, and Rosemary.

Joe returned to dubbing on Monday. and Zanuck again refused to see him, but he sent Joe notes on what he thought the battle scenes needed. It was "almost exactly what the script called for—but what the Board of Directors had decreed was unnecessary to do!" Joe noted.

After his attempts to arrange another meeting were repeatedly rebuffed, Joe received a call from Leggewie. Zanuck would not see Joe and his editor, Dorothy Spencer, because he had a cold. However, the following day Joe learned that Zanuck and his editor, Elmo Williams, actually had gone to Spencer's hotel to discuss the footage she and Joe had eliminated.

Joe tried to arrange to view the film himself, only to be told that the film would not be available to him. Williams and/or Zanuck planned to run parts of it with Spencer.

Didn't they want Joe as well? They did not.

Stunned, Joe asked Leggewie if Zanuck wanted him to leave Paris. Do not leave, he was told. Zanuck was only "crystallizing" his thoughts; he would discuss them with Joe once the crystallizing was done. They were not cutting; they were merely checking the film and looking at the material Joe and Spencer had cut. In the meantime, Joe should stay and finish the dubbing.

Held off for six days, Joe could hardly avoid the obvious conclusion. Yet he hesitated. "I mistrust the entire situation. . . . I still think Z intends to take over but only after I have finished with the three stars—so that he will be safe from their resentment at his treatment of me. In addition to their quite understandable apprehension about what will become of their performances under his editing. Instinctively I feel I should force his hand. But we'll wait and see. It cannot be long, now . . ."

Actually, it was worse than Joe imagined. Zanuck already had Williams cutting and restructuring.

Saturday, October 20, marked a week since Zanuck had seen the rough cut, and Joe decided he had to act. He sent Zanuck a three-page letter demanding to know where he and the film stood, and Leggewie called back within an hour. Zanuck was still "crystallizing his thoughts," but he would definitely meet with Joe on Sunday or Monday before leaving for New York on Tuesday. Then Zanuck's own letter arrived, and Joe predicted, "Unmistakably, he intends to take over the film. The megalomania dripped from the pages as I read them."

Joe responded immediately that he refused to be ignored and insisted on "an honest and unequivocal statement of where I stand"—not that he harbored any illusions. "I do not doubt that I will receive it—between the eyes—but will he have the guts to do it himself? And before I have finished the dubbing?"

The following afternoon he received Zanuck's nine-page answer. After a lengthy discussion of his own plans for the film, Zanuck blamed Joe for the picture's extravagant costs and fired him upon completion of the dubbing. Among Zanuck's charges:

"It was not the fault of the 'Administration' (Heaven knows I have no desire to vindicate them) that you wrote the script during production (or at least re-wrote it)."

"The production was moved to Rome on your recommendation."

"I am not going to ask you why the script was not completed prior to production, but it is only reasonable to point out that this caused you to shoot the major part of the picture in continuity."

"Sets were built on overtime and then left idle for weeks and months."

"Liz was ill a number of times, but the production report shows that she was not 'called' more than 30% of the time . . ."

The injustice of Zanuck's accusations left Joe beside himself. Exacerbating his fury at being blamed for what he had worked so hard to prevent was his "frustration at being completely alone to combat this act of piracy." He spent the night "mentally addressing Zanuck, the Board of Directors, the stockholders and the world . . ." But when he responded, he carefully left the door open:

> I am, I suppose, an old whore on this beat, Darryl, and it takes quite a bit to shock me. And I know that the untalented and parasitical hangers-on in this business, when frightened, will say and do almost anything to avoid taking an honest rap for an honest fuck-up—but never could I imagine the phantasmagoria of frantic lies and frenzied phony buck-passing that you report. . . . They go beyond a mere avoidance of guilt; I consider them slanderous, libelous and damaging to me. I intend to answer, in detail, every assertion made—with names, dates, and proof. Let me hasten to say that my anger is not directed at you; you merely saw fit to throw up to me what you, in good faith, assumed to be the truth.

When Zanuck left the next day without responding, Joe decided it was time to go public. *New York Tribune* columnist John Crosby happened to call, so Joe gave him the scoop, and Crosby in turn helped Joe get his statement to the *New York Times*. Joe spent that evening with Taylor, Burton, and the Harrisons, who all assured him they were eager to help, and the following day, the news appeared on page 1 of the Paris *Tribune*. After calls poured in from *Variety*, *London Evening Standard*, *Reuters*, *Associated Press*, *United Press*, *London Daily Mirror*, and *Le Figaro*, Joe received a call from Zanuck's secretary. Could Zanuck borrow his last letter in order to send copies to Taylor and Burton? "Of course," Joe told him.

Joe first heard about Zanuck's public response when a *Variety* reporter called at 1:30 a.m. and read him Zanuck's statement blaming Joe for the cost overruns. Too sleepy to reply properly, Joe simply read him a prepared statement of his own. The media battle for the public's—and the stars'—allegiance had begun.

On October 25, Joe asked himself, "Why don't I just get out of a way of life I obviously cannot cope with? Ave atque fade-out to the movies." But he spent his last day in Paris conscientiously working with Taylor while Burton looked on. The pair's remote manner puzzled him until he learned the following day that Zanuck had shown them only the portion of Joe's angriest letter that would convince Taylor that Joe intended to blame her for the film's excessive cost. "After all my public defense of her, previously, to the contrary, knowing that there was nothing the bastards would like more." By then almost as angry at Taylor, Joe showed his entire letter to Taylor's agent, Kurt Frings, and at Frings's urging, talked to Taylor and Burton as well. He thought he succeeded in calming down Burton, but not Taylor.

When he arrived back in New York later that day, Chris and Tom met him at the airport, waving American flags and blowing horns. On his front door, they posted a sign, "Mankiewicz, si! Zanuck, no! Go- Joe- go!"

"Wonderful to wake in my wonderful house to tackle the wonderful Sunday papers over a wonderful Sunday brunch with my wonderful sons," Joe rhapsodized the next morning. Then he hunkered down to strategize. Fielding offers of help, he found Feldman annoying and Bienstock invaluable. Brodsky and Weiss called to offer assistance, as well as "a man named Canby from *Variety,*" who actually did provide valuable assistance. Vincent Canby (*Variety's* film critic, who moved to the *New York Times* in 1965) gave Joe a transcript of Zanuck's press conference, which was "more frightening" than he had thought but "full of good material for counterpunches."

At his standing-room-only press conference, Zanuck had said he fired Joe because Joe had demanded "complete control," which Zanuck could not allow. He had refused Joe's unreasonable demand but had "left the door open—wide open—and offered to meet with him at any time, hour by hour." When asked why Joe had been so power-hungry, Zanuck said, "I think that after a year and a half of directing Caesar and Cleopatra and Mark Antony, some of the tinsel must have rubbed off on him." Zanuck quickly softened that, but went on to blame Joe for shooting without a completed script and described Joe's earnings from the film as $1.5 million in capital gains, $260,000 in salary and over $60,000 in expenses. Then he distributed copies of his correspondence with Joe.

That is why, on October 30, 1962, Joseph L. Mankiewicz, who always insisted that he despised publicity, that he had never employed a press agent, and that he believed his work should speak for itself, convened a press conference of his own.

He emphatically denied ever seeking control or final approval for the film: "I'm much too old a cotton picker not to know the score. I know what 'Old Marse' will do with the cotton in the end." He had wanted only the opportunity to discuss the film with Zanuck. He had no plans to sue for his contractual rights. Even if he won in the Supreme Court, "I'd feel self-conscious being escorted into a cutting room by 36 U.S. marshalls."

As for driving up the costs by writing as he filmed and filming in continuity, he explained that he had asked for three things: Rex Harrison, Richard Burton, and a delay until he could write the script. He was granted the first two and refused the third. Without the time to write it beforehand, he had had no choice but to write as he filmed and to shoot in continuity, which he agreed was a terribly costly and wasteful process.

He resented Zanuck's use of correspondence marked "Personal and Confidential" and pointed out that the Fox president had edited them into "Zanuckized" versions that belied their actual contents but served Zanuck's purposes.

He objected to Zanuck's public discussion of his compensation, not to mention his overstating it.

Joe's press conference attracted only about twenty reporters, but all the major general news and trade publications ran lengthy accounts. Joe had carefully avoided ruling out the prospect of directing additional scenes, and that was how the impasse was ultimately resolved. Eventually Charles Feldman, Abe Bienstock, and William Wyler, who was also a Fox board member, negotiated enough of a truce for Zanuck and Joe to meet on December 5 and begin to reconcile. Joe agreed not only to direct additional scenes for *Cleopatra* but to write them as well.

On November 18, he took time out to appear as the mystery guest on *What's My Line?* Hoping Bennett Cerf would not recognize his voice, Joe disguised it, but once Arlene Francis guessed his identity, Cerf asked, "How long were you on *Cleopatra*? Was it two years?"

"I don't think I've ever been on anything else," Joe replied. "I can't remember when I wasn't on *Cleopatra* and *Cleopatra* wasn't on me."

That was the lighthearted facade. Privately, he was shattered. But amidst his broken health, broken spirits, continued drug dependence, and public humiliation, Joe did come to one decision he never regretted. He and Rosemary Matthews had been involved on and off since *Barefoot Contessa* production in 1954. Rosemary's brother-in-law, Caesare Danova, was in *Cleopatra*'s cast, and Joe had hired Rosemary's sister, Pamela, to work with Taylor as an acting coach. The more debilitated Joe became during production, the more he had depended on Rosemary.

"I guess we might as well get married," the master of words said one night in November, as they sat in his living room. Rosemary, who had just turned thirty-three, responded to Joe's less than romantic proposal by jumping up and down, while her new fiancé smiled and puffed on his pipe. The match was hardly inevitable, but marriage had been in the air, with friends like Jessica Tandy, Hume Cronyn, and the Hornblows egging Joe on. Rosemary had trained as an actress, but she was neither an extrovert like Elizabeth nor a forceful personality like Rosa; she was young and attractive, but she was not beautiful. Rosemary shared Joe's world, but she was content to function behind the scenes.

Ever prickly about his image, Joe was aware he would be a cliché, a middle-aged man marrying the younger woman who effectively had been taking care of him for the past two years. He had come to rely on her more and more, but marriage? When he told Chris and Tom, they reacted with snobbish shock. Rosemary? Knowing of their father's affairs, they were surprised he would choose to marry someone so lacking in glamour and worldly stature. But the choice was obviously his, and they were fond of her. The engagement was announced in newspapers around the world.

Only Erna was openly dismayed. Joe and Rosemary suspected she entertained visions of acting as Joe's hostess herself, but Erna risked alienating him by writing what she really thought, because "you're the only living human being I give a damn about and my greatest wish is that you should get out of life everything you want and hope for." With little hope Joe would heed her, she nevertheless urged him to heal a bit first before taking the plunge. She added that under the circumstances, Joe should cancel her monthly allowance. "You know that I have never felt that I should take it—but now I can't. I wish that there were some way I could pay you back . . . but that is obviously impossible."

Actually, Erna was not wrong. Joe made the right decision for the wrong reason. He lacked the strength to heal alone and married Rosemary out of weakness. But Joe's third try at marriage succeeded. After they announced their engagement, Joe spent the next few weeks battling Zanuck and sorting through job proposals with Charles Feldman, while Rosemary quickly arranged their wedding. Her father was a Church of England archdeacon who had served as King George VI's chaplain, and her mother was an ophthalmologic surgeon. Rosemary made sure they joined Joe's family and friends for the occasion.

They married at Joe's house on December 14, and when the judge asked Rosemary if she took Joe to be her lawful wife, Rosemary calmly corrected him. Good wishes poured in, including notes from Joan Crawford, Linda Darnell, and Howard Dietz, who called Rosemary "that fiendish golfer, dark-eyed and a handicap of eight, as P. G. Wodehouse would describe her." Writing from Peru, Frank sent congratulations and a report on Sara's matrimonial prospects: "Apparently, she is holding out for a nice wealthy Jewish man, loaded, with superb taste in music, art and drama, who will leave her largely alone, do occasional shopping at the Farmers market, keep the garden in shape, mix drinks, and permit her to keep her name."

Newlyweds in Spain, 1963.

They left on January 8, 1963, for a honeymoon cruise in the Bahamas, but Zanuck summoned them back almost immediately. By January 14 they were in Los Angeles so Joe could shoot at the studio. and a few weeks after that, Joe joined Zanuck in Spain to film battle scenes. On his flight over, he read Wanger's partially finished manuscript for *My Life with Cleopatra* (1963) and decided to keep his actual opinion ("ass-kissing, self-serving crap") to himself.

Soon after he arrived, Joe sent for Rosemary (wiring, HOW SOON CAN YOU GET HERE?), and once Zanuck left the newlyweds enjoyed time together in Spain. Afterward, in London, Joe finished the last few scenes while they caught up on the latest *Cleopatra* gossip. Jean Marsh, who played Antony's wife, Octavia, told Joe how much she despised Rex Harrison, especially for making a pass at her two days before he married Rachel

Roberts, and joked, "Being in the cast of *Cleopatra* is like being in the army reserve—you are called up every now and then." On March 4, 1963, Joe shot the last *Cleopatra* scenes at Pinewood Studios, back where it had all begun, two years earlier.

In Los Angeles to cut the final picture, Joe faced 120 miles of film. He already knew Richard Burton's scenes were doomed to evisceration after Zanuck said of Cleopatra's treatment of Antony, "If any woman ever acted to me like this, I'd cut her balls off." Joe and Barbara McLean, who headed Fox's editing department, did what they could. "The picture was a very good movie at four hours and five minutes," McLean recalled, but under pressure from exhibitors, Fox continued cutting even after the premieres, to three and a quarter hours and eventually, down to two and a half hours. Different theaters had different versions. "The picture was actually cut so people could make a train to go home," McLean said. It was "stupid." Theaters also chopped it up to get more shows.

In early June, Chris graduated from Columbia, and Tom from Yale, and later that month Chris married Bruna Caruso, an Italian actress who had played one of Cleopatra's handmaidens.

Publicizing the film, Joe described *Cleopatra* as "the toughest three pictures I ever made." For its June 12, 1963, premiere, over one hundred policemen surrounded the Rivoli Theatre to deal with a crowd that, even without the presence of Elizabeth Taylor and Richard Burton, was estimated at ten thousand. Joe was so upset by the mutilating cuts that he could hardly bring himself to say anything positive, and critical reaction was mixed but frequently negative. *New York Times* critic Bosley Crowther called it "one of the great epic films of our day," but Judith Crist concluded, "The mountain of notoriety has produced a mouse."

Individual performances were lambasted, which did not surprise Joe, given what was left for them to see. *Time* said Burton "staggers around looking ghastly and spouting irrelevance, like a man who suddenly realizes that he has lost his script and is really reading some old sides from *King of Kings*." Alistair Cooke wrote in the *Guardian* that Taylor had kept her "common touch. She may be billed as the Queen of Egypt, but she is the universal working girl who dreamed she played Cleopatra in her 'Maidenform' bra."

Rex Harrison fared better. *National Review*'s Francis Russell wrote that the "old war horse" made a "superb Caesar," at least as modern audiences "feel Caesar ought to have been, even if the original Julius was probably more like Mussolini in his private habits and manners." Although much of his footage had been removed, only Harrison received an Oscar nomination. Overall, *Cleopatra* received nine nominations, only one less than *Tom Jones*'s ten. It was nominated for best picture, but Joe was nominated for neither screenwriting nor directing. *Cleopatra* was by far the highest-grossing film of 1963, but at a cost of $44 million, it took several years to become profitable.

While *Cleopatra* lit up screens around the world, it also enriched the coffers of countless attorneys. In violation of Rex Harrison's contract, Fox covered a Times Square billboard with a photograph of Antony and Cleopatra, with nary a Caesar in sight. "Is Rexy Not Sexy Any More?" asked *Variety,* and Harrison's lawyers sued to get his image included. In June 1963 Walter Wanger sued Fox, for breach of contract. In August, Skouras sued Wanger for libeling him in his account *My Life with Cleopatra.* Skouras also wanted to sue Brodsky and Weiss for their portrayal of him in *The Cleopatra Papers,* but his lawyers talked him out of it. A corporation owned by Elizabeth Taylor and Eddie Fisher sued Twentieth Century Fox for failing to distribute profits under terms of its contract, and in April 1964 Fox sued Taylor and Burton for $50 million, charging breach of contract and depreciation of the film's commercial value attributable to their "scandalous" conduct.

Joe framed a *New Yorker* cartoon showing two matrons standing in front of a poster for the picture, captioned, "What annoys me is that I <u>know</u> I'm going to see it." But he was crushed by the experience and regretted everything about it, from taking it on in the first place to returning to finish it. "I should have stayed fired," he observed later. He was so embarrassed by the version that survived that he asked *Who's Who* to remove *Cleopatra* from his entry and refused to talk about it for years afterward.

CHAPTER 24

The Honey Pot(boiler)

JOE STRUGGLED THROUGHOUT 1963 TO REGAIN HIS EQUILIBRIUM, BUT on August 28 he escaped for an exhilarating couple of days. He joined Sidney Poitier, Paul Newman, Marlon Brando, Charlton Heston, and about fifty other members of the entertainment community in what its organizers were calling a March on Washington for Jobs and Freedom. No one knew what to expect or even if it would turn violent, as many were predicting, but when Harry Belafonte organized the group, Joe was in. As part of the crowd of 250,000, he listened, enthralled, to Martin Luther King Jr.'s "I Have a Dream" speech and treasured the experience for the rest of his life.

To build on the momentum, Joe suggested that movie and television personalities boycott segregated theaters, nightclubs, and concert halls, and Brando and a few other actors with enough clout followed through, trying to insist on such a restriction in their film contracts. Brando sent Joe a list in February 1964, of about fifty writers, including Samuel Beckett, Arthur Miller, and Harold Pinter, who had instructed their agents to insert a clause barring future performances of their work "where discrimination is made among audiences on grounds of color," writing that he expected more to follow.

Despite his low spirits, Joe received submissions nearly every day. Would he like to work on a musical version of *Mr. Smith Goes to Washington*? A play in French? A film adaptation of the life of Benedict Arnold ("Another of my projects someone else was bound to come upon before I could start," he grumbled). Then he read Frederick Knott's play *Mr. Fox of Venice*, along with the novel from which it was adapted, Thomas Sterling's *The Evil of the Day*, both based on Ben Jonson's seventeenth-century *Volpone*.

Joe was intrigued enough to option it, and, with time out for a couple of other activities, he spent most of 1964 writing "Mr. Fox of Venice."

One of the other activities was directing a made-for-television movie. Former assistant secretary of defense Anna Rosenberg asked him to help with a Xerox-sponsored television series promoting the United Nations, and he agreed to direct its first episode, which was to be written by Rod Serling. Unfortunately, instead of an extended *Twilight Zone*, Serling's "Carol for Another Christmas" was a preachy dystopia based on Charles Dickens's *Christmas Carol*, and even Joe's direction and the combined skill of Sterling Hayden, Ben Gazzara, Peter Sellers, and Eva Marie Saint could not redeem it. But at Joe's suggestion, they hired Don Mankiewicz to write for the series as well, and Don's *Who Has Seen the Wind?* starred Gypsy Rose Lee and Edward G. Robinson.

Joe and Rosemary also moved. They had long admired the home of Bennett Cerf's Random House cofounder, Donald Klopfer, and his wife, Florence, in Westchester County's Pound Ridge. A converted dairy barn set amidst ponds, the house was comfortable and peaceful, with low ceilings, odd attic rooms, a stone fireplace, a swimming pool, and even a small cottage that Joe could use as an office. So when the Klopfers decided to sell, Joe and Rosemary bought it and named it Willow Ponds. When they sold the townhouse, they also bought a Sutton Place apartment, but they sold it a few years later. Two residences were too expensive to maintain.

Joe's "Mr. Fox" screenplay was long and intricate but hewed to Jonson's basic plot. Volpone ('sly fox') is a Venetian gentleman who pretends to be dying, and, aided by his servant Mosca (fly), he summons three men who all hope to inherit his fortune. Sterling and Knott had turned one of the fortune hunters into a woman, given her a traveling companion, and added a murder. Joe made all of them former mistresses: Merle McGill, a fading Hollywood actress; Princess Dominique, a European jetsetter; and Lone-Star Crockett Sheridan, a Texas millionaire and hypochondriac who brings along her nurse, Sarah Watkins.

Joe's Cecil Fox is a contemporary English millionaire obsessed with time and money, who lives in a Venetian *palazzo* and dreams of ballet dancing to "Dance of the Hours" (the famous melody from the opera *La Giaconda* that accompanies the dancing hippos in *Fantasia*). Fox hires William McFly, a gigolo and sometime-actor, to help him reenact Jonson's play, then summons the mistresses to his deathbed. After Lone Star announces that as Fox's common-law wife, she must inherit, she is found dead, and Sarah suspects McFly. McFly locks her up, but Sarah escapes, and when she surprises Fox dancing, she realizes Fox is not really dying. Actually, it was Fox who killed Lone Star himself, and once he is exposed, he drowns himself in a canal. The enigmatic Sarah inherits both Lone Star's fortune and the handsome McFly.

Joe always relished complicated construction, but this time, his complications were the point. His postmodern structure interspersed the story with dream sequences for each major character, a play within a play, and a film within a film. In voiceover, industry executives and theater owners react to the story on screen, allowing Joe to comment on issues like censorship, the nature of time, and life lousing up the script. Joe loved his offscreen Pirandello-esque voices, but with his first draft over six hundred pages, he knew many of his cherished words were doomed.

In early December 1964, he showed it to Rex Harrison, who was so taken with the concept that the two spent five hours trading ideas. In January 1965 he sent scripts to United Artists; Charles Feldman, who was coproducing; and Doc Erickson, whom he wanted as production manager. The UA executives immediately focused on the need to shorten it. Feldman considered the framing device too confusing. Both parties agreed Joe should eliminate the commentary and stick with the plot.

Eventually Joe gave in and shot the comedy-mystery UA and Feldman liked. He retained only the mistresses' dream sequences from his original concept, and though he shot them, he later had to cut those as well, for length. Even then he regretted it, and in later years when his original ideas became commonplace, Joe would say he had shot the wrong script. But he was still demoralized and insecure from *Cleopatra*, and he could hardly disagree with the need for massive cuts. Feldman, who was more focused on sales than creativity, thought Joe should add "A) more sex. Fox should actually lay Merle and Dominique. B) a more exciting death for Fox. 'Maybe a real heart attack while dancing.' C) a masquerade ball." Feldman also urged Joe to cast one of his previous mistresses, former French model Capucine, as Princess Dominique.

By March 1965 Joe was exasperated with Feldman. He was one of the first agents to package film deals for his clients, and he had negotiated an executive producer credit for himself. His title was to read: "Charles K. Feldman Presents." But Feldman wanted it both ways, maximum authority and minimum responsibility: he did not want to work during the production period, but he wanted to control post-production marketing and promotion.

Joe wanted it both ways, too—the other way. He wanted to run production with Doc Erickson and let United Artists make the major deals with the artists, and besides retaining complete artistic control and the $2.5 million budget his contract guaranteed, Joe wanted final authority on marketing for himself. But if there were producer responsibilities Feldman could shoulder, Joe wanted him to earn his credit. He also warned United Artists about Feldman's lavish spending habits, cautioning them to take care that Feldman didn't finance his expenses with their production funds.

Then Rex Harrison began doing what he always did: raising financial questions, issuing demands regarding the script, and thrusting himself into casting decisions. Up to a point, Joe considered Harrison worth the trouble (writer Robert Gore-Langton called him "the alpha male silverback" in the "jungle of high comedy"), but he eventually became so obstinate that Joe and Feldman started exploring alternatives like Paul Newman, Steve McQueen, and Peter Ustinov.

At one point, Harrison's agent, Laurence Evans, informed them that Harrison now wanted to play McFly instead of Fox. Agreeing Harrison was "mad," they enlarged the circle of potential Foxes to include Christopher Plummer, Cary Grant, and Robert Redford. With a bit of probing, they learned that Harrison's concerns were threefold: the Fox character was "too repugnant" and "too unpatriotic." McFly's part was "too good." And Harrison wanted a scene with Lone Star Sheridan.

Excerpts from Joe's summary of April, 1965:

April 1 COMMITMENT REX
April 2 REX NOT SET
April 13 REX SET AGAIN
April 14 NEW REX CRISIS
April 23 REX OUT
April 26 USTINOV IN
April 29 REX IN

The April 14 "New Rex Crisis" began when Harrison said his wife, actress Rachel Roberts, wanted to play Lone Star's nurse. Fresh from winning his Oscar for playing Henry Higgins in *My Fair Lady*, Harrison and Roberts stopped for a victory lap in New York on their way home, and Joe joined the delegation of UA executives visiting Harrison's hotel. They all sat through (as Joe put it) "Rex's egomaniacal chicken-shit dialogue points," in order to persuade him that Rachel Roberts would not work in the role. Forty-five minutes after they left, Harrison called Joe to ask him to break the news to his wife.

Joe returned to the St. Regis bar for an evening of "many scotches and much horseshit" that "wound up in love and understanding—and exhaustion." Or so he thought. The following day, Joe received a call from Ted Ashley, head of his agency. Harrison again insisted, "It will mean a divorce unless Joe puts Rachel in the part."

Not only would he not cast Roberts, Joe told Ashley, but if he cast Maggie Smith, Ashley was to "inform (not ask his approval) but inform Rex immediately." Ashley should also remind Harrison that Maggie Smith had been Harrison's original suggestion.

By then Joe was so fed up with Feldman that he talked to United Artists and his own lawyers about cutting Feldman out of the deal. Feldman, who was in London and already considered Joe a spoiled ingrate, got wind of Joe's intrigues and angrily told his colleagues: "Mankiewicz got a deal that United Artists didn't want to give him. . . . U.A., time and again, told me that they had made a terrible deal and wished the hell I hadn't gotten them into it."

Still furious the following day, Feldman wired his office, "ADVISE BIENSTOCK I HAVE ONLY MY TIME TO SELL AND MY TIME IS AS IMPORTANT AS JOE'S FOR 5 YEARS I HAVE SERVED HIM WITHOUT RECEIVING ONE CENT FOR MY TIME AND MY EXPENSES FOR TRIPS TELEPHONE HOTELS EXCEEDED FIFTY THOUSAND DOLLARS FOR THIS AND CLEOPATRA JOE MADE OVER MILLION DOLLARS CLEO CAPITAL GAIN. I GOT NOTHING NOT EVEN REPAYMENT EXPENSES STOP."

Harrison was still insisting on cast approval when Joe flew to London, and once he and Feldman were in the same room, their common enemy united them in a reconciliation so ardent that Feldman suggested Joe cut United Artists out of the deal. He also suggested substituting William Holden for Harrison. Or even better, wouldn't Joe like to postpone the "Fox" project and do *Casino Royale* for him instead?

Joe was disgusted, but Feldman was shameless. If not *Casino Royale,* how about William Holden for McFly, suggested Feldman, right after telling Joe that Harrison did not want McFly played by an actor of "star status." Not only was Holden a star, but he had succeeded Feldman in Capucine's affections, and the two had recently broken up. Working together might be uncomfortable for one or both of them, but to Feldman it was all just business.

Not to Joe. "I have no objection [to Holden]," he wrote Feldman, "but I do now object to Rex Harrison." Feldman assured Joe he had "laid down the law" and Rex would be calling him momentarily.

"I won't hold my breath," thought Joe, which was fortunate, since Harrison did not call. "Rex is out," Joe told Feldman the next day. But Feldman was now playing triple agent. He made a show of pursuing

Fox alternatives but instead of relaying Joe's ultimatum to Harrison, he disclosed Joe's casting choices to Harrison. At the same time, he and his agency colleagues schemed to steer Joe away from Christopher Plummer for McFly and toward a lesser actor, like Craig Stevens, "who might be more palatable to Rex in view of no name value or anyone else in this category."

Harrison adored the intrigue, but he dallied with Joe for so long that Feldman eventually had to tell him he was out. Only then did Harrison call Joe.

Joe refused to take the call.

Harrison sent a wire.

Joe continued his silence.

Feldman called Harrison, ran through the entire cast list, then told Harrison to contact Joe and demonstrate great remorse and respect for Joe's authority.

Eventually, Joe relented. Harrison stayed in and casting continued. They cast Susan Hayward as Lone Star; Edie Adams as Merle McGill, the movie star; Capucine as Princess Dominique; Cliff Robertson, McFly; and Maggie Smith as Lone Star's nurse. Joe had found Smith so "enchanting" that he wanted Feldman to option her on his behalf so he could make her a star. The closest Smith had been to Hollywood was a trip to Palm Springs with her friend Julie Andrews, but Feldman thought Joe had blown his chance by his too-obvious enthusiasm. As it turned out, shortly after *The Honey Pot*, she played Desdemona in Laurence Olivier's film version of *Othello*, and all four principals received Academy Award nominations. Smith didn't need Joe to make her a star, but they became lifelong friends.

They shot at Cinecittà to save money, and Harrison continued his irritating habits. Noticing how much more relaxed the cast and crew appeared when Harrison was absent, Joe observed, "The atmosphere when Harrison appears on stage can be cut with a knife and some day will be." Yet Harrison was nothing if not dedicated. In one seven- or eight-minute scene, Fox and McFly had to shuffle stacked decks of cards and play poker while exchanging lines, a feat even Harrison found a bit like rubbing his head and patting his stomach. He prepared by working with an Italian magician and a card shark.

Cliff Robertson, whose "boysieness" worried Joe at first, was overwhelmed by the dialogue and asked if Joe would make some of McFly's speeches more comfortable. Joe refused but put him at ease so tactfully

The Honey Pot (1967) was Joe's fourth film with Rex Harrison, and he kept his promise to himself, his wife, and his agent that it would be his last. It was his only picture with Maggie Smith, but they became friends for the rest of Joe's life.

that Robertson later told a reporter, "Any time mastermind Mankiewicz lifts the phone in the future, I'll come running." He had no idea that call would never come. Joe considered Robertson hopelessly wooden.

Edie Adams and Capucine also disappointed him. Adams did not look as sexy as he had hoped, and Joe found Capucine's constant stream of complaints about her wardrobe, hair, makeup, car, expense allowance, dressing room, and still-photograph approval ("all the demands and pretentions of a typical star") particularly irritating, considering her "almost total lack of talent." Extracting "any kind of performance" was like "pumping up a tire with a slow leak."

Both Joe and Harrison were thrilled with Maggie Smith, and Joe continued to respect Susan Hayward's professionalism. Hayward's husband was so ravaged from years of drinking that when he became ill, she asked Joe to shoot around her so she could take him home to Florida. When she tried to return, he lapsed into a coma and died during the second week in January 1966. Less than two weeks later, Hayward flew back to Italy to finish her scenes.

More worrying than the actors' limitations was the photography. The sets were visually sumptuous, but the rushes looked terrible. Joe had replaced their original cinematographer with Piero Portalupi, and he was reluctant to switch again unless he was sure they could do better. Eventually he felt he had to, and hired Gianni Di Venanzo, who had worked for Michelangelo Antonioni (whose work Joe hated) and Federico Fellini (whose work Joe revered). Di Venanzo, forty-three, immediately captured the lush interiors, but soon after he started, he had to be hospitalized. He died on February 6, 1966, of misdiagnosed hepatitis, leaving the cast and crew desolate. Joe finished with Di Venanzo's assistant, Pasqualino De Santis, who went on to become a respected cinematographer himself, working with Italian directors like Franco Zeffirelli, for whom he shot *Romeo and Juliet.*

Rachel Roberts almost raised their death toll to three when she overdosed with sleeping pills. The fourth of Harrison's six wives, Roberts could be as difficult as her husband, and when Harrison spurned her attempt at reconciliation in 1980, Roberts tried again and succeeded, making her the second woman in Harrison's life to commit suicide.

Joe started editing in London in March 1966 but broke off to be in New York with Rosemary for the birth of their daughter, Alexandra Kate, on April 30. Chris also became a father in 1966, and Eric Reynal and his wife had their second child. Joe joked about starting a Fathers After Fifty-Five club with Cary Grant, John Wayne, Otto Preminger, and Stavros Niarchos, but for the first time in his life, his family became a refuge and source of comfort.

Joe never really recovered from *Cleopatra,* and his depression lifted only intermittently, but he enjoyed fatherhood in a way he had not with his sons. He was more mature, but Alexandra's being a girl also helped. After a lifetime of observing females of all ages, he now had one of his own to observe from the very beginning, and he relished the opportunity. Not that he changed completely. He still needed to win every argument (Rosemary called it "steamrolling"), and though Alexandra (later, Alex) was clearly an artist, Joe consistently said she was going to be a writer. Rosemary pursued her own interests while making very few demands on Joe and skillfully tailored their lives around his needs and wants. As the product of an upper-middle-class English family, Rosemary considered an adult-centered family life natural, so Joe could avail himself of as much or as little of parenthood as he wished.

The Honey Pot opened in London in March 1967 to mixed reviews that predictably awarded Rex Harrison and Maggie Smith highest marks. When virtually everyone derided the film's two-and-a-half-hour length, Joe resigned himself to cutting, preferably before its US premiere in May. Before beginning he flew to Paris for the first night of a two-week "homage" to his work, organized by France's film museum, La Cinémathèque Française, and hosted by its founder Henri Langlois. Joe basked in the admiration and enthusiasm of young film fans, whose regard was especially satisfying, given that his wordy films lacked subtitles. Still wounded and hungry for affirmation, he found the event, "a touching and gratifying evening."

After cutting about twenty minutes, including the dream sequences, he returned to promote the film in the US. During interviews, he disparaged his usual targets, but, fresh from France, he added American critics, whom he now derided as performers. French critics, by contrast, "caught all the nuances [of his films], even some subtle ones that may not have been intentional." Many of the American critic-performers were indeed less enthusiastic. They generally echoed their British counterparts in praising Harrison and Smith, while complaining that the picture just had too many words, even if many of them were witty.

By then Joe was eager to move on and started discussions with David Merrick about producing *The Meteor*, a bleak comedic play by Swiss playwright Friedrich Dürrenmatt. Perhaps they could get either Lee J. Cobb or Jason Robards Jr. to star. It never happened.

CHAPTER 25

Ironic Western

JOE CONTINUED TO YEARN FOR WORK IN THE THEATER, BUT HE WAS still too vulnerable to face the risk of critical opprobrium. He was so used to believing in his own superiority that he lacked the ability to shrug off the defeat. He had always been plagued by various physical complaints, but all the drugs during *Cleopatra* had taken a further toll. Once he had emergency intestinal surgery on Christmas Eve 1967, foregoing the kind of money only motion pictures could provide seemed too risky.

Whatever Joe's internal fragility, the outside world continued to regard him as a formidable talent, and proposals continued to stream in. He left Feldman and switched agents several times, from Robby Lantz to the William Morris Agency to Richard (Dick) Gregson, a young English friend of Tom's who was engaged to Natalie Wood. Wood was a longtime close friend of Tom's, but Joe had directed her as Gene Tierney's little daughter in *The Ghost and Mrs. Muir.* Gregson planned to find him a multipicture contract at one of the studios, so in January, despite the surgery, Joe, Rosemary, Alexandra, Alexandra's nanny, and Brutus, their yellow Labrador retriever, flew to Palm Springs as planned.

Gregson informed Joe that though he had a reputation as an "object of terror," they had meetings at Paramount, Columbia, and CBS, as well as with independent producer Sam Spiegel. But after a few days of meetings, Joe fled back to Palm Springs and the relaxation of socializing. The town was full of friends and acquaintances like Truman Capote, Lee Bouvier Radziwill, the Kirk Douglases, the Bill Goetzes, the Irving "Swifty" Lazars, Claudette Colbert, Jean Simmons, and Richard Brooks, whose names Joe carefully recorded. He celebrated his fifty-ninth birthday with Capote, the Goldwyns, and Christopher Isherwood, among others. When he could fit it in, he worked on an adaptation of John Updike's *Couples* for television producer David Wolper.

In March 1968 Joe signed with Warner Bros.-Seven Arts, which had several properties he liked. He loved Anthony Burgess's concept of a musical about Shakespeare, though he considered its working title, "The Bawdy Bard," "dreadful." And he was intrigued by "Hell," a western written by former *Esquire* writers Robert Benton and David Newman. Warner's had grudgingly produced the pair's first picture, *Bonnie and Clyde* (1967), and to the amazement of everyone, including Benton and Newman, it became an enormously popular and critical sensation and attracted ten Academy Award nominations. Now they had a three-film contract, and like *Bonnie and Clyde*, "Hell" was an unconventional mix of comedy, irony, and violence (Warner's was especially keen on the violence).

Joe liked the concept, the writers, and the idea of directing a new genre. Benton and Newman's 1960s version of the nineteenth century Wild West pitted Woodward Lopeman, a liberal, well-intentioned sheriff, against Paris Pitman, an evil-but-charming robber (they favored Dickensian names). Soon after Lopeman has arrested Pitman, he becomes the warden at Pitman's prison, and while he idealistically works at reforming the criminals by improving prison conditions, Pitman organizes a motley group of fellow prisoners for an escape. The denouement piles one cynical surprise on top of another, culminating with the good Lopeman going bad.

As they worked on the script, Benton, Newman, and Joe settled into a mutual love fest. Joe found the young writers stimulating, and they appreciated his vast knowledge. "He was very patient with us and delightful," Benton recalled. "We learned a lot of craft, though we could derail Joe very easily by asking him to tell us stories about Victor Fleming or Ernst Lubitsch or the studios or whoever." They also knew not to argue when he pushed them for rewrites. "I'd rather argue with Mao Tse Tung or Vladimir Putin. Joe could shred you in two seconds. His humor could be both loving and caustic, and you wanted to stay away from the caustic part."

Newman and Benton became so fond of their professorial raconteur that they paid him the ultimate compliment. In their next picture, *Bad Company*, they created a fat, pipe-smoking, self-indulgent-but-likeable outlaw gang leader named Big Joe Simmons (David Huddleston). Benton, who formed a lifelong friendship with Tom Mankiewicz after seeking his advice on the character, later wished they had made more of Big Joe. "*Bad Company* was about the relationship between two partners, two guys going west and getting into the movie business [in the movie, they're getting into the outlaw business; Big Joe is already a full-fledged

Collaborating on *There Was a Crooked Man* (1970), David Newman and Robert Benton considered Joe a great teacher.

outlaw]. Joe taught us indirectly. He let you know he had enormous affection for you without complimenting you." When Joe saw the movie he said, "My only problem with my character is that we're both surrounded by incompetents."

Charlton Heston refused even to read the script and eventually they cast Henry Fonda as Lopeman and Kirk Douglas as Pitman, along with an equally strong group of reprobates: the brutal, not-too-smart outlaw Floyd (Warren Oates); the formerly prominent Missouri Kid, now aged lifer (Burgess Meredith); the inscrutable but merciless Chinese Ah-Ping (Olympic decathalon winner C.K. Yang); bickering gay con-artists Cyrus McNutt and Dudley Whinner (John Randolph and Hume Cronyn); and handsome male ingénue Coy (Michael Blodgett). Unable to agree on a title they all liked, they finally settled on *There Was a Crooked Man*, after the nursery rhyme.

Joe shipped his Thunderbird to California and after spending New Year's Eve, 1968, in one of Frank Sinatra's Palm Springs villas, the family moved to their own villa, with Hume Cronyn and Jessica Tandy in their pool house. By the time shooting began on March 5, 1969, the picture's expenses had ballooned, partly because of the $300,000 prison set Joe had them build in the Joshua Tree National Monument. The national park had never allowed filming, and they had to haul in eighty loads of rocks for the prisoners' rock piles (and later remove the very same rocks).

Working as assistant to executive producer Doc Erickson, Sid Ganis (future producer and Academy president), was "petrified" at the prospect of working for a man he considered a legend, but Joe put him at ease immediately. Ganis watched admiringly as Joe adapted to life without legions of aides and a studio car and driver at his disposal. Warner's softened the blow a bit by assigning him Harry Warner's old bungalow at the studio, but on his own, Joe got lost in the desert one day and had to be rescued by Brutus.

Actually, Joe was a mass of nerves. Six weeks into shooting, he slipped a disk and spent the rest of the time encased in a corset, directing from a wheelchair. Even more upsetting, Cronyn was diagnosed with cancer of the optic nerve. Joe's closest friend (they were godfathers to each other's daughters), Cronyn needed surgery, sooner rather than later, but he insisted on finishing his scenes before leaving. Joe and Erickson went to see Kirk Douglas about rearranging the schedule and Douglas exclaimed, "I've got an idea. Why don't we do all my scenes and get them out of the way, and then do all of Hume's?"

Joe and Erickson could only gape.

Joe was also shaken by the development of a musical based on *All About Eve*, by composer Charles Strouse and lyricist Lee Adams. Because Twentieth Century Fox had denied them the rights to Joe's script, they had bought the theatrical rights to Mary Orr's story. That meant they could not use any of the characters Joe had created, and the script they had commissioned pleased no one, including Lauren Bacall, who wanted to play Margo. The entire situation was so disturbing that Joe tried to put it out of his mind. But Strouse, Adams, and the producers wouldn't leave him alone, and Joe finally agreed to meet with them.

Strouse, Adams, director Ron Fields, and producer Joe Kipness flew out and spent all of Saturday, June 14, imploring Joe to write the show's book. Joe liked the score enough to be mildly tempted, but because they wanted the book completed in six weeks and needed him to stay with the production until March 1970, he felt he had to turn them down.

At the end of that draining, upsetting day, Sam Spiegel called, asking Joe to fly east to discuss directing *Nicholas and Alexandra*. When Joe declined, Spiegel came to him. Joe admired Spiegel's talent as a producer, but he found the man so personally repellent that he wanted to refuse to see him. Take the meeting anyway, urged his new agent Freddie Fields, shrugging, "Sure Sam's rude. But you gotta remember—he's also insane."

Joe couldn't tolerate more than an hour with Spiegel, but he liked the idea, and he liked the script, which had been written by Jim Goldman (William's older brother and a talented writer himself). So three weeks after shooting *Crooked Man*, Joe flew to the south of France to join Goldman on Spiegel's enormous yacht. The writers spent a pleasant week working together as they sailed around the Côte d'Azur along with passengers like Shirley MacLaine and Yul Brynner. Then Joe left abruptly. He simply couldn't take another minute with Spiegel.

He also could not stop thinking about the musical. He hired Strouse to write the theme for *Crooked Man*, and as the two men became friendly, Strouse suggested Joe talk to his lawyer. They had hired Betty Comden and Adolph Green to write the book, and as the play, now called *Applause*, inched toward opening, Joe learned he was to receive neither compensation—which he had not expected—nor recognition or credit of any kind, which shocked him, especially now that Fox had finally granted them the rights to his screenplay. While he began to consider legal action, he distracted himself for a few days, working on a tribute to Martin Luther King Jr.

He still treasured his experience at the March on Washington, and even six years after the event, Joe leapt at the opportunity to join Sidney Lumet and Doc Erickson in helping producer Ely Landau with a documentary about the fallen leader. Warner's loaned them a sound stage, so in October 1969 Joe worked on *Crooked Man* post-production during the day and on *King* production at night. He and Lumet directed a number of entertainers and politicians reading scripted parts for the picture. Joe found Bill Cosby unimpressive ("No like. A 'whitey hater'") and was not surprised when Cosby threw a fit and walked out. They filmed Burt Lancaster, James Earl Jones, Ben Gazzara, Sammy Davis Jr., Clarence Williams III, and Sidney Poitier on the first night. The second night, they shot Davis again, along with Diahann Carroll, Charlton Heston, Anthony Quinn, Darren McGavin, and Walter Matthau. Over three nights, they captured eighteen minutes of film, and *King: A Filmed Record... Montgomery to Memphis* was screened all over the country for one night only, March 24, 1970.

Early in 1970 Joe received a call from Sara, who was upset about a profile on Joe by Andrew Sarris in the March 1970 issue of *Show* magazine. The foremost American proponent of the auteur theory, Sarris had relegated Joe to the "Less than Meets the Eye" category in his influential 1968 study of directors, *The American Cinema: Directors and Directions 1929–1968*, citing Joe's devotion to content over film technique, his lack of a recognizable style, and the unevenness of his oeuvre. Sarris had since revisited the films Joe had directed, and in his *Show* piece, he applauded: "I saw emerging a pattern of intelligence, charm and subtlety that I had tended to take too much for granted in the days I thought that intelligence, charm, and subtlety would always be with us." Sarris also described Joe as "always too New York for Hollywood in temperament and always too Hollywood for New York in training."

Sara was so furious about Joe's reference to Herman's drinking and his failure to defend Herman's authorship of *Citizen Kane* more vigorously that she had written Pauline Kael, "Have you by chance seen an ignoble interview with Joe M in the March issue of an ignoble magazine, Show? I am glad now that you had the intuitive good sense not to interview him about Herman."

Joe, who believed he had fully supported Herman's authorship, and considered Herman's drinking hardly a secret, had no idea Sara was worried about how Kael was going to portray Herman in the piece she was writing about *Citizen Kane*. The day after Sara's call, Joe mailed her his annual $1,000 support check, along with a note that made no reference to her anger.

No slouch at passive aggression herself, Sara returned the check immediately, accompanied by a letter explaining that she was returning it "not because I am angry and disappointed and deeply hurt—all of which I am—but because I have already made other arrangements." She would raise the money by depleting her principal instead and if she needed more, she would sell the Mt. Tremper house. After asking for Joe's assurance that he would leave the "brooding" painting of Pop to one of her children in his will, she closed, "I hate family feuds—they are undignified and hurtful. This is my first in my seventy-two years, and I don't like it. Tomorrow, being a sad anniversary for us [Herman's death], I will ask Herman to forgive you. My love to Rosemary & Alexandra. Always, Sara."

Considering the letter "paranoid," Joe contacted Fred Hacker, who remained close to Sara, and Hacker promised to deal with it. Not long afterward he heard that Pauline Kael did not like him. He knew that Kael was working on a *New Yorker* piece about Herman, but he was puzzled. "I've never met her," he mused. About two weeks later, he heard Kael was telling people, "Joe and his family don't get on," and connected the dots to Sara.

Joe and Rosemary were home the night *Applause* opened. *Show*'s editor had invited Joe to attend a preview and review it for the magazine, but Joe had declined, and no one connected with the show had thought to invite him or even offer him a ticket. Even so, Joe had dutifully sent opening-night telegrams to Lauren Bacall, Betty Comden, Adolph Green, Charles Strouse, and Lee Adams. The next day's rave reviews were simultaneously gratifying and painful, and he was bewildered when only Stuart Ostrow called to say how much the show owed him. Joe waited around the rest of the day, but the phone never rang. "It seems I had nothing whatever to do with *All About Eve*," he recorded miserably.

He sank deeper into gloom when the *New York Times* ran a follow-up interview with Comden and Green that Joe considered "remarkably ungracious." Finally, Strouse called to arrange a meeting between Joe and Lauren Bacall, and *Applause* producer Lawrence Kasha called to exclaim, "Aren't you excited?" Only then did Kasha mention that he would be delighted for Joe to see the show.

By then Abe Bienstock had hired Harriet Pilpel, a prominent civil rights and First Amendment attorney, to look into Joe's legal situation. After the show had opened, she called to say that Joe probably had waived his rights to credit or participation in the show by his "graciousness and cooperation with all concerned." Until talking to Pilpel, Joe hadn't thought it possible to feel worse.

Finally, two weeks after the opening, Joe, Rosemary, and the Bienstocks went to see *Applause*. They visited the cast backstage afterward and even met Strouse and Lauren Bacall for drinks at "21" before their long, dispirited drive back to Pound Ridge. Four nights later, Joe and Rosemary sat in front of a television with the Cerfs and the Hornblows, watching *Applause* sweep the Tony Awards: best actress, best direction, best choreography, and best musical. Not one recipient mentioned Joe, an oversight Strouse later said he felt terrible about, though at the time, no one bothered to call Joe and apologize. At that point Joe decided he was no longer depressed, he was angry. But sad or mad, he still had no recourse. Several months later Comden and Green begged Joe to meet with them. He went and listened to them insist they didn't want him to be "mad at them." Joe "gave whatever reassurance I could" and tried to put it behind him.

Owner and management changes at Warner's delayed *Crooked Man*'s release until mid-1970, and when Warner's finally distributed it, their promotion was disappointingly low-key. They opened overseas first, and Joe went to London for the July opening. English reactions were mixed,

Some of their reprobates: Mr. Lomax (Arthur O'Connell) addressing prisoners Paris Pitman Jr. (Kirk Douglas), Floyd Moon (Warren Oates), Whiskey (Victor French), Tobaccy (Alan Hale Jr.), Dudley Whinner (Hume Cronyn), Coy Cavendish (Michael Blodgett), and Ah-Ping (C.K. Yang).

but the French, now Joe's favorite audience, liked it. Joe noted happily in his diary that *Paris Match* had called him "Le grand seigneur du cinema."

Benton and Newman were equally upset with Warner's treatment of their film, and Joe urged them, "Start screaming. I'm hoarse." When *Crooked Man* finally opened in the US at the end of 1970, reviews were mixed-to-negative. The *New York Times*'s Vincent Canby did not ignore its shortcomings but described it as a "movie of the sort of taste, intelligence and somewhat bitter humor I associate with Mr. Mankiewicz who, in real life, is one of America's most sophisticated, least folksy raconteurs, especially of stories about the old Hollywood." He added, it was "full of what seem to be (but aren't) the old-fashioned virtues of commercial moviemaking." Andrew Sarris chose it one of his ten best films for the year and applauded the New Hollywood's relaxed censorship that finally allowed Joe, as one of the "Old Hollywood sophisticates," the opportunity to portray overt homosexuality with subtlety and sensitivity.

Unlike *Bonnie and Clyde*, *Crooked Man* was not a hit. Warner's promotion was lackluster, but the picture's hybrid nature was also a problem.

Their likeable con man puzzled audiences, and in retrospect the filmmakers were probably ahead of their time. The disappointment registered with Joe only minimally, because most of the time he was too depressed to care. He could not get beyond the injustice of being erased from the history of *Applause* and was still smarting from the public humiliation over *Cleopatra*.

Every day he walked down to the beautiful office he and Rosemary had fashioned, determined to tackle a variety of projects. Instead he sat, paralyzed. "My mind teeming with countless ideas—unable to concentrate on any of them," he wrote on September 5, 1970. On October 3 he recorded "great trouble with constant weariness." On October 24: "Very low, indeed, these days. Physically, & emotionally, (in regard to my 'work')."

In December he talked with producer Harry Saltzman about doing a picture about the dancer Nijinski and even met with Rudolf Nureyev as the possible lead. Joe found Nureyev "a bit sulky, but fascinating to look at," though he had no idea if the dancer could act. Saltzman, who had made a fortune on James Bond films, never made the film, but Joe and Rosemary enjoyed visiting him in Acapulco, and when his partner, Albert (Cubby) Broccoli, hired Tom to rewrite their next Bond film, *Diamonds Are Forever*, they jump-started Tom's career.

CHAPTER 26

Of Page and Screen

WITH *APPLAUSE* STILL IN THE WORKS DURING FALL 1969, THE BOOST TO Joe's spirits from working on the King documentary was short lived. But in November a Random House editor called to say Bantam Books planned to reissue *All About Eve*'s screenplay and that he hoped Joe would write an introductory essay. Joe was pleased to be asked, but spring turned into summer of 1970, and Joe was still so depressed that he couldn't manage even to get started. Finally the publisher suggested they hire film journalist Gary Carey to interview Joe and write an introduction. Then Joe could edit it. That sounded more manageable to Joe, so after conducting two long interviews, Carey started a draft in fall 1970.

Also that fall an editor from Praeger Publishers called to ask Joe if he would meet with a film writer named Kenneth Geist, who wanted to publish a monograph on his work. When Geist arrived he explained that he was actually writing an article for *On Film*, a magazine published by the Film Society of University of California. A couple of weeks later, the Praeger editor called again. Would Joe be interested in writing a book himself? Joe was always interested—he had toyed with the idea of a memoir about his Hollywood experiences for years—but at the moment, he was both too depressed and too busy to consider it. He had started another picture.

After *Cleopatra*, Joe liked to say he wanted to make a film with two actors and a telephone booth. Even plays with only two characters were rare, and a two-character major film was practically unimaginable. And yet Joe got exactly that, and it happened very quickly. He and Rosemary had been impressed by Anthony (Tony) Shaffer's hit thriller *Sleuth* when they saw it in London during the summer of 1970. Its high comedy, intricate plot switches, and witty dialogue appealed to Joe; and its treatment of some of Joe's favorite tropes, like class and a young upstart challenging the old order, made it an obvious fit.

Its producers agreed. Palomar, a production company led by Edgar Scherick, a former television executive, and Morton Gottlieb, *Sleuth*'s Broadway producer, and financed by Bristol-Myers, owned the movie rights and offered Joe $200,000, plus 15 percent of the net profits, to help Shaffer write the screenplay and then direct it. The play was on its way to Broadway in April 1971, when Joe began meeting with Shaffer.

In the play Andrew Wyke, a wealthy writer of detective fiction who loves games and surrounds himself with antique toys and devices, pits himself against Milo Tindle, an immigrant's son who has been Wyke's wife's hairdresser and lover and now plans to marry her. When Milo accepts Andrew's invitation to his baronial mansion, Andrew convinces him to help stage a fake robbery so that Andrew can defraud his insurance company. From there, the dangerous games begin, evolving into a murderous power struggle.

The usual approach to a screen adaptation would have been to open up the two-character, one-set play, but Joe had a different vision. Aside from adding a few exterior shots, he wanted to keep the film relatively confined and employ the sets as almost a third character. That meant design was crucial, and Palomar hired Ken Adam, who had designed several James Bond films, including *Diamonds Are Forever* (written by Tom). Adam located a collection of automata, mechanical dolls and animals that Joe could utilize, both to comment on the story and to cut away periodically from the actors. Adam also designed a maze through which Milo would seek Andrew in the opening scene, providing one of the picture's many metaphorical devices.

Joe flew to London in June 1971, and he, Gottlieb, Shaffer, and Shaffer's wife, Caroline, drove to Oxford for the opening of Laurence Olivier's production of Jean Giraudoux's *Amphytrion 38*. Joe considered the play "simply dreadful," but the actual purpose of their mission was to see if sixty-four-year-old Olivier seemed up to playing Andrew Wyke (Joe was sixty-two). Olivier, who was directing rather than acting, had suffered some health problems, but he seemed fine to them. And though Olivier had called *Sleuth* "a piece of piss" after seeing it in Brighton, he happily accepted Palomar's offer.

After Joe and Shaffer worked together for a few days at the Connaught Hotel, Shaffer (forty-five) invited Joe and actor John Hurt (thirty-one) to spend a weekend in Winchester, where he and Caroline had a cottage. The cottage looked more like a shack to Joe ("cold and barely livable"), so he was relieved to be quartered at a nearby hotel, even if Shaffer's motive seemed to be cadging a hotel dinner for Hurt and himself at Joe's expense.

After accompanying Shaffer and his children on a round of "boring" Saturday errands, they returned to the cottage, where they were joined by Tony's twin, playwright Peter (who later wrote *Equus* and *Amadeus*), playwright/director Paul Giovanni (thirty-eight) and writer Howard Smith (thirty-four) for an evening of dinner and serious pot smoking. The senior member of the pot party recorded proudly that it had "no effect whatsoever," on him, but that "John Hurt passed out about 2 A.M. His 'wife' Lise became a walking zombie. Peter, Paul and Howard and I reached the hotel about 3:15 A.M."

A Sunday afternoon visit to a haunted sixteenth-century house was more to Joe's taste, but he was relieved to escape back to his beloved Connaught on Monday.

In August they were still searching for Milo. After Albert Finney rejected them, they agreed to pursue Michael Caine, Peter O'Toole, and David Hemmings, in that order, though after screening *The Wrong Box* (1966), Joe began to worry about Caine's accent, and Shaffer preferred Malcolm McDowell. Joe vetoed Sean Connery, and when Scherick asked about Rex Harrison, he said, "Not on your life." After Alan Bates turned them down, and Peter O'Toole was unavailable, Joe, Shaffer, and Gottlieb went to Rome to meet with Caine, and Joe decided he would be fine.

Joe had brought along Gary Carey's draft for his *All About Eve* introduction and worked on it intermittently. At the end of September 1971, Kenneth Geist called to say Praeger had given him a contract to write a book about Joe and his films. Joe agreed to cooperate, and when he returned to the US, he gathered materials, wrote Geist a letter of introduction to help him obtain interviews, and sat for long interviews when he could fit them in.

Back in London in February 1972, Joe found Shaffer chafing at some the changes he had insisted upon. Joe not only overrode Shaffer's objections, he begrudged the playwright the office he had managed to wangle for himself at Pinewood Studios, where they would be shooting. Shaffer's "mournful presence" annoyed him.

Joe had pushed Shaffer to heighten the class struggle within the story and was pleased that his cast would actually embody that class difference and other differences as well, even acting styles. The cockney son of a fish market porter and a cleaning woman, Michael Caine was at the forefront of a new breed of British actors who no longer disguised their working-class origins. Caine had appeared in numerous television programs and a couple of dozen films, including *Alfie* (1966), but the Harry Palmer films (*The Ipcress File* [1965], and *Funeral in Berlin* [1966]) had made him a star. His understated style of acting reflected both his habitual media—film and television—and his generation.

Lord Laurence Olivier was a classically trained clergyman's son who had been knighted in 1947; in 1970 he became the first actor in English history to be awarded a life peerage. Olivier periodically deigned to work in pictures, but he had dominated the stage for years. In addition to being probably the world's foremost actor, he had run England's cherished Old Vic company and had devoted the past ten years building up the National Theatre. After all that producing and directing, Olivier was known to play his roles his own way, no matter what the director had in mind, and to expect the rest of the cast and crew to adapt to him.

Joe never doubted his ability to exert directorial authority over the formidable Baron Olivier of Brighton, but Caine was intimidated. He even fretted about how to address his co-star. "My lord," though proper, seemed unthinkable. Fortunately, Olivier kindly wrote to him a couple weeks before rehearsals started, suggesting that he be called Lord Olivier once, when they met, and after that, just Larry. (A relieved Caine curtsied as he greeted "m'lord," and Olivier cracked up.)

Caine also worried about being able to hold his own with Britain's most acclaimed actor, and just before they started work, he appeared on Joe's doorstep one night to voice his apprehensions. Joe invited him in and reassured him with logic. "Listen. It's you and I against Larry, isn't it?" When Caine looked at him skeptically, Joe pointed out, "If you're not as good as Larry, I don't have a picture."

Joe, whose interest in class did not prevent him from living like a lord when the opportunity presented itself, motored back and forth to Pinewood in a chauffeur-driven Rolls-Royce (during post-production he economized with an Austin). Sometimes he gave Tom a lift, as *Live and Let Die* was to be shot at Pinewood. *Sleuth* occupied one stage; the Bond picture required seven, and Tom proudly showed his father their enormous underground cave, lagoon, and mechanical shark. He later regretted bragging to his father, but Joe actually was amused and proud of his son's success (it probably helped that Joe had no interest in Tom's kind of film). That June, Joe and Rosemary gave Tom a thirtieth-birthday party, and Joe brought down the house by toasting, "It's your thirtieth birthday, and I think it's time for me to tell you that it's okay to masturbate."

Joe was pleased with rehearsals, but Olivier became increasingly frustrated by his inability to get a handle on his character. Shaffer had described Andrew Wyke as "a man who has only good taste left with which to bully others," and that didn't satisfy him. He kept searching for new bits of business, new movements, and new intonations for himself and everyone else—who, in this case, included only Michael Caine. In his memoir, Caine recalled the morning Olivier announced that he had diagnosed the problem:

> "And what was that?" Joe was eventually forced to ask, as Larry left a pregnant pause that almost had a miscarriage.
>
> "I can't act with my own face!" Larry yelled. "I always need some sort of disguise."

Olivier had decided a mustache was the key to his character, and when he stuck it on his upper lip, even Joe was fascinated by the actor's transformation from "businesslike to manic enthusiasm."

The night before shooting started, Joe was tense and apprehensive, and by the second day, his back ached so painfully that he sent for a corset. That afternoon Olivier started forgetting his lines, but Joe was unconcerned. Olivier was almost sixty-five. He would simply adjust the shooting schedule.

However, Olivier was worse the next day, and as the week wore on, his memory continued to deteriorate, along with Joe's back. Olivier had just finished playing James Tyrone in Eugene O'Neill's demanding *Long Day's Journey into Night,* so he clearly could manage much more dialogue than he needed for filming. Joe was mystified. Then he learned that the National Theatre would be replacing Olivier as director with Peter Hall. Although Olivier had planned to step down, he had been kept in the dark about plans for his successor until almost the last minute. Once he saw Olivier frantically devoting most of his off-set time and energy to the situation, Joe realized what considerable stress he had been under. Then shortly after that revelation, they learned that Olivier had been taking Valium for his stage fright and that it was also affecting his memory. Once he went off Valium, Olivier charged back so powerfully that Caine suggested maybe he should go back on medication—for Caine's sake.

Physical problems continued to plague Joe. In addition to his back pain, he fell and punctured a leg. After he continued working for the rest of the day, the wound had swelled to the size of "two eggplants (both in color and size)." The following morning he continued work from a wheelchair, but as the day wore on, he became paler and paler. Finally someone realized Joe had severed a femoral vein, and they had to shut down production

Laurence Olivier taught Alexandra, six, to sneer.

for a week. Joe went to physical therapy and regained his strength and, naturally, took advantage of the time to tinker with the script.

Back at work, Joe worked at balancing the actors' performances. The entire plot was a battle between two antagonists, and both actors were nervous. Caine told Olivier, "There's no way I can override you, but I'm not going to back off, either." Olivier agreed with the need for balance—in theory. In practice, he was an incorrigible camera hog, which Joe considered typical of Olivier's generation. Caine also noticed that when one of his lines interfered with one of Olivier's movements, Olivier suggested Joe cut the line, and when they had scenes together, Olivier situated himself so that Caine had to play around him.

When Caine finally gathered the courage to complain, Joe assured him he was well aware of Olivier's machinations and urged him not to worry. He reminded Caine that when Olivier asked him to cut a line, he left it in and said he would take care of it in editing. As for camera hogging, Joe, who had seen it all, especially from Rex Harrison, had a suggestion. The next time Olivier upstaged him, Caine should turn all the way around so his back was to the camera. Then Joe would go around and shoot a close-up of Caine over Olivier's shoulder. Remember, he told Caine, "this isn't the theatre—we do have editing and close-ups."

Caine found Joe's suggestions so helpful that he used them in subsequent films, and he treasured the extraordinary experience of working with Laurence Olivier. "It was frightening the way he bore down on me—and just kept coming! He was like a force of nature. Suddenly he was this other person, this young performer showing his mettle, and I realized that was what all the risks and danger were about."

In one scene, Andrew tries to convince Milo to wear a disguise when he pretends to rob Andrew's wife's jewels, and in rapid succession, Andrew imitates Charlie Chan, a monk ("Brother Light Fingers"), a French nobleman, and Mrs. Danvers of *Rebecca* (Olivier had played Max de Winter in the 1940 film). When Milo eventually dons a clown costume, Andrew parodies Charlie Chaplin. It is a tour de force.

While shooting another scene in which Andrew was to violently sweep objects off a table, Olivier cut his hand badly, and though the injury was obvious, he kept going until they finished. Then he glared up at Joe. "You bastard. Why didn't you cut?"

"You bastard. Why didn't you stop?" Joe replied. He used that take in the film.

Caine dreaded his most difficult scene, when Andrew holds a gun to Milo's head and Milo breaks down in hysterics. After they finished, Olivier hugged Caine and whispered, "When we started on this film, I thought of you as a very skilled assistant." After pausing for dramatic effect, he added, "I now see that I have a partner." Out of the corner of his eye, Caine saw Joe wink, but he considered Olivier's declaration the greatest compliment of his life.

Joe loved the experience, too. "If you direct Larry for forty days, you're directing forty different actors . . . there are new combinations, same colors. Directing Larry was strenuous but very exciting."

"Directing Michael was even more exciting. He worked his ass off." Joe was particularly proud of Caine's accents. Using that primary marker of English class, Joe worked with Caine on every nuance of every speech so that Milo could start with an upper-class veneer when he meets Andrew and then, under stress, lapse into cockney intonations and lower-class words. As Joe later told the press, Caine was a better actor than Caine himself realized, and well able to hold his own with the formidable Olivier.

After shooting this scene for *Sleuth* (1972), Olivier promoted Michael Caine from "skilled assistant" to "partner."

Sleuth opened in the US in December 1972, to critical and popular success, and made many reviewers' ten-best lists for the year. Princess Margaret attended their London premiere. Olivier, Caine, Joe, and their composer, John Addison, all received Academy Award nominations, which allowed Joe to say that *Sleuth* was the only film ever to have its entire cast nominated for Oscars. Caine was particularly gratified, because the critics' surprised approbation had irritated him: "They don't realize I never was Alfie. . . . They're shocked that I turned out to be an actor. I'm shocked they didn't know before."

Working on his *All About Eve* introduction when he could, Joe had found editing more time-consuming than he had anticipated, but he was pleased to be writing again; he was even more pleased to realize he was enjoying it. A succession of ego-boosting honors in early 1971 raised his spirits as well. Yale Law School honored him with a film festival; Danny Kaye asked him to serve as pipe master at his Players Club roast; critic Judith Crist gave him a Great Filmmaker award. By the time he sat next to Lauren Bacall at a dinner, he had recovered enough of his sense of humor to note that Bacall was becoming "more and more Margo by the day." Even Sara came around. After Pauline Kael's essays for *Raising Kane* appeared in the February 1971 *New Yorkers*, she was so embarrassed by the grandiosity of Kael's claims on Herman's behalf that she called Joe to reconnect and make peace.

When Joe turned in the first fifty pages of his introduction, his editor, Nan Talese, expressed her "delight." Robby Lantz considered it so brilliant that he hoped to place it in the *New Yorker*—or maybe *Harper's*—prior to publication. Only Gary Carey failed to share their enthusiasm. As he later wrote in a *Film Comment* review of the two brothers' biographies, Joe had retitled the introduction a "colloquy," a word Carey considered so affected that he observed, "Even the Radcliffe-educated Karen Richards might find it slightly *de trop*."

Joe's "editing" had doubled the piece's original length, and where Joe saw profundity, Carey saw "labored" pontifications, "redundant explication," and "a few factual errors." Joe had also "added ventriloquism to his long list of accomplishments. I discovered that I was saying things I didn't believe. But what really ticked me off was that I had been cast as a dumb Plato lapping up the wisdom of the Beverly Hills Socrates."

Carey complained to the editor. The editor remonstrated with Joe. Joe threatened to remove Carey's name from the book. "Beautiful," Carey told the editor. "Let him call it 'a colloquy by Joseph L. Mankiewicz with Joseph L. Mankiewicz.'" Eventually Joe accepted most of Carey's changes, though at one point, Carey recalled, Joe "narrowed his eyes and said, 'I have a feeling your opinion of *Eve* has dropped somewhat.' I denied this, and truthfully so, since my opinion of *Eve* had never been as high as his."

However, to Joe's great joy, *More About All About Eve: a colloquy by Gary Carey with Joseph L. Mankiewicz together with his screenplay All About Eve* appeared in December 1972, about the same time as *Sleuth*'s release. Into his 110-page introduction, Joe had crammed Hollywood history, theatrical history, his own professional history, analyses of actors' and actresses' psyches, the story behind the making of *All About Eve*, and his thoughts and intentions for the picture. Joe hoped this would not be his only book, and he had not given up on writing plays. But for now, he was content to reclaim as his own a screenplay so valuable that its adaptation was the toast of Broadway.

Furthermore, the timing was felicitous. When Joe wrote the screenplay in 1949, he had relished the opportunity to write about the theater. But even then, he also had consciously created female protagonists who embodied particular aspects of the female condition. With the women's movement gathering steam in the early 1970s, his Margo and Karen characters seemed both prescient and relevant. (Eve was basically an ambitious villain, an actress who needed success because there was no other "there" there.) Margo's concerns about her identity and her fear of aging were accurate depictions of genuine problems faced by many women, but especially actresses. And Joe was most proud of Karen Richards, "the one for whom I have always felt the greatest compassion . . . the 'wife to—.'"

As he wrote of the women Karen represented:

> They're in waiting, all right, these 'wives to—.' . . . For the axe, the heave-ho, the marital pink slip. . . .
>
> When they were both very young. . . . She wasn't 'wife to—' back then. No, sir. Back then she was—right out of the catalogue—wife. Meaning also: mother; cook/laundress; childbearer; accountant; partner and professional consultant; whipping post (with understanding: 'an Artist has to take it out on somebody,' right?) for his frustrations and failures; sexually, whenever and whatever he wanted. . . .

Once the husband makes it, however, her utility is lost.

> Remember those services she'd performed as wife—so desperately needed by the Artist. . . . "Mother"? The mass Audience will replace her, there. They'll give suck to him, spoil, scold, cuddle, and even reject him. . . . Cooks and house-cleaners will be hired now . . . and her domestic duties will become that of personnel manager for backward delinquents.
>
> Childbearer? . . . among theatre-folk, children become almost always the sole responsibility of the non-performing parent; there is almost always too large an area of competition between the child and the performing parent.
>
> What else? Partner—wailing wall—even whipping post? Forget it. What with producers, packagers, lawyers, agents, business managers, publicity men, secretaries—his professional life and income will become so compartmentalized. . . . [that she] will become one of the smaller moving parts in a mechanism.
>
> Sex? No need to go into that, why belabor the obvious. It's not surprising, really, the readiness with which the 'wife to—' adjusts to sexual infidelity by her spouse. . . .
>
> What she does dread, lives in terror of, is—serious, emotional involvement on his part. It could happen any day. . . . Her man. . . . goes off to a fun fair where he's the brass ring on the

> merry-go-round; a nonstop Miss Universe contest and the one he smiles on goes into orbit. . . . At the studio, the audition, the rehearsal—. . . An Eve in the car alongside. Meanwhile, back at home, the 'wife to—' can do nothing but wait. . . .
>
> . . . I can't think of, I couldn't dream up, a human being more truly helpless than the 'wife to—,' . . . among theatre-folk.
>
> She is completely helpless. Without weapons. Her physical attractions are faded; at their best, they were no match for those, the best in the world, that now beguile her husband relentlessly.

Ironically, Joe had dedicated the 1951 edition of the screenplay to Rosa, the wife-to whose plight he so articulately and compassionately described in 1972 (though as Chris said, there was a great deal of Rosa in Margo as well).

All About Eve had not been forgotten during the previous twenty years, but once videocassette tapes in the 1970s and digital video discs in the 1990s allowed audiences of the next twenty years to appreciate the film, it became even more of a cultural touchstone. Even after Joe's death, *Eve*'s influence in the culture continued to flourish. In 2000 St. Martin's Press published *All About "All About Eve": The Complete Behind-the-Scenes Story of the Bitchiest Film Ever Made*. "I like to think of my work as 'fan scholarship,' or even 'camp scholarship,' and why not?" wrote author Sam Staggs, a journalist who had covered gay life and gay issues for many years. "Surely a book about a particular movie should echo the 'voice' of the movie itself." Staggs chronicled the film's popularity through the second half of the twentieth century, contending that it had endured "precisely because of what wasn't obvious at first. The subtext has beguiled several generations of devotees, largely gay men, who have 'read' the film as though it beamed a limelight into the closet of their hearts."

The gay community actually had claimed *All About Eve* years before, memorizing the picture, performing it for one another, and all but drowning out the dialogue by talking along with it at screenings. "Fasten your seatbelts . . ." was de rigueur for female impersonators and readers pored over the script like Kremlinologists teasing out every hint of gay and lesbianism in the film—line readings, costumes, and of course, whole characters. Pedro Almodóvar named his 1999 film *All About My Mother* in tribute.

Eve's most ambitious artistic tribute has to be the 650-page *Phoebe 2002: An Essay in Verse* by poets Jeffery Conway, Lynn Crosbie, and David Trinidad (Turtlepoint Press, 2003). Their postmodern deconstruction of the work zooms in and out of the entire screenplay, imagining scenarios, creating dialogues, and riffing on all manner of connections, including the authors' own emails.

THE REAL EVE: A CODA

After Joe's introduction was excerpted in the October 16, 1972, issue of *New York* magazine, ("All About the Women in All About Eve"), Joe received a letter from a psychologist who was distantly related to the real Eve—the understudy who had attached herself to Elisabeth Bergner and therefore became the basis for Mary Orr's story after she heard of it from Bergner. That woman, whom the psychologist had known since childhood, had lived in orphanages and foster homes until she was declared a neglected child and sent to a "training school" that lumped together both neglected and delinquent children. "Are you aware . . . that the bulk of the younger chronic mental hospital patients have similar backgrounds? Those who do not end up "insane" become psychopaths, as you describe "Eve," hollow inside and not knowing who they are," she wrote to Joe.

She added that years after the real "Eve's" encounter with Elisabeth Bergner, she had insinuated herself into the graces of opera soprano Renata Tebaldi, but unlike Bergner, Tebaldi had dismissed her after three months. "Perhaps opera singers are wiser than actresses," his correspondent speculated.

Fifteen years later, Joe and Rosemary were packing to leave Venice after being honored at a film festival, when he received a telephone call at the hotel. A woman calling herself Martina Laurence, now sixty-six and living in Venice, explained that she was the real Eve and wanted to meet him. Joe declined the invitation, but she wrote to him at home and enclosed both the portion of Elisabeth Bergner's memoirs that described the incident and her own thirty-three-page version of the experience.

Not lacking in irony, she had drawn her pseudonym from "Martina Lawrence," a character of Bergner's in *Stolen Life*, a 1939 British film in which one identical twin sister steals the other's identity. Laurence portrayed herself as the incident's injured innocent, so resentful of Joe's benefiting from her experience that she had looked into a lawsuit against him.

Translating Bergner's German, Joe learned that Laurence was hardly the only one who resented having her experiences used. He already knew that Mary Orr had been angry for years. Now he learned that Bergner had been, as well. Her account concluded:

> [T]he author of this magazine story was Mary Orr—that shy quiet girl to whom all these stories were told on that night in Vermont. . . . Hollywood bought the story for Bette Davis [*sic*], added a little love intrigue, and it became the film *All About Eve*. That film (AAE) achieved a world-wide success, even as a musical comedy. And Mary Orr and the other participants became very rich. The only ones who received nothing were the true participants: Martina Laurence, Paulus [her husband, Paul Czinner] and I.

Across the bottom of his translation, Joe wrote:

> (AND J.L.M., WHO WROTE EVERY WORD OF THE SCREENPLAY AND DIRECTED EVERY FRAME OF IT?)

CHAPTER 27

Honors but No Dough

EVEN THE TWIN TRIUMPHS OF *SLEUTH* AND *MORE ABOUT ALL ABOUT EVE* failed to keep Joe's despondence at bay, and he sank back into depression. He couldn't sleep and he couldn't write. Then, in the middle of the night on July 25, 1974, he and Rosemary were awakened by a call from Don Mankiewicz. Josie, thirty-six, had been killed by a taxicab that ran into her on a Greenwich Village sidewalk, just outside her building. Only an hour before, she had been interviewed and photographed for *New York Post* coverage of the paperback edition of her first novel, the autobiographical *Life Signs*.

Josie had worked her way up to become one of *Time*'s few female writers before leaving in 1972 to work on her novel. She, Peter Davis, and their sons, Tim, eleven, and Nicholas, nine, had just returned from living in Malibu while Peter finished *Hearts and Minds*, a documentary about the Vietnam War (it won the Best Documentary Oscar the following March). Tom, who had loved being with Josie and the boys over the summer, told Sara he was too heartbroken to come to Josie's funeral.

Everyone who knew her was devastated, not only because she was so young, but because Johanna Mankiewicz Davis was such a singular personality. Sam Jaffe, who had known her all her life, described Josie as funny like Herman and wise like Sara. A few weeks after her death, the *New York Times Book Review* ran a memorial tribute by novelist/memoirist Richard Brickner. He never mentioned Herman and probably never knew him, but anyone who had must have thought of Herman while reading Brickner's description of his daughter: "She was a writer almost all of the time . . . the most literary person imaginable, in the sense that she was a natural story-teller and a natural story. She was all alertness, all poised eye, ear, and tongue. She invented incessantly, she read people incessantly, and she narrated incessantly in conversation."

Afterward, Sara surprised no one by her strength. As usual, Joe compartmentalized, though the loss further eroded his strength and deepened his malaise. He continued to try to rouse himself, and offers of work continued to pour in. Around that time he began a treatment of *Jane,* a bestselling novel by Dee Wells that seemed tailor-made for him. The eponymous heroine is a young American living in London who becomes pregnant by one of her three lovers and has no idea whether the father is an English peer, an African American lawyer, or the cockney thief she caught burglarizing her flat. Joe loved the story, but even as he signed a contract with Columbia Pictures, he admitted to himself "how little in my heart, I want to continue in the film business—and how large my apprehension that I'm simply too old to write the things I want to write."

Even so, he was stunned the following July 1975, when Columbia executives rejected what he had written as too late and too long and ordered him to return his advance. On the heels of that unprecedented insult, they had the effrontery to ask if he wanted to supervise another screenwriter. That, at least, allowed Joe the pleasure of responding, "Screw you."

He tried to interest himself in a number of other projects, but he continued to brood over *Jane,* and a few years later, Tom proudly announced that he had optioned the rights for Joe. At that point Tom had his own production company on Warner's lot, so he was in a position to promise his father he could write and direct the picture with complete artistic control. He was crestfallen when Joe turned down the offer and only overcame his hurt feelings by deciding that his father had simply become too afraid of failure to make another picture. If Joe stopped with *Sleuth,* he could be sure of going out on top.

Ironically, Joe's last big battle was over his biography. In 1974 Geist told Joe he thought Joe's life and work might require two volumes instead of one. Joe, who privately referred to the book as Operation Futility, wished the number could be 'none' and was relieved when Geist told him in 1975 that Praeger had cancelled his contract. Imagining that he might use them for a book of his own, he offered to buy Geist's interview tapes. However, shortly afterward, Charles Scribner's Sons picked up Geist's book and issued a press release alleging that Joe's lawyers had tried to pay Geist to stop publication.

Furious at the misrepresentation, Joe hired Charles Rembar, a prominent First Amendment lawyer, to threaten a libel suit, and Scribner's eventually issued a retraction. As the book began inching toward publication, Joe, Joe's lawyers, Geist, and Scribner's lawyers started wrangling over everything from the book's title to the galleys' contents. (Geist wanted to call it "The Oldest Whore on the Beat: The Life and Films of Joseph L. Mankiewicz").

Both men were distraught. Geist had devoted five and a half years to what he hoped would be his masterpiece, and he feared Scribner's would defer to his prominent subject and his prominent subject's powerful attorney. Joe had always worried about Geist's ability to damage his professional reputation. Figuring that a lawsuit would sell more copies, Abe Bienstock counseled, "Unfortunately, Joe, there aren't that many people interested in reading a book about you anyway. Why don't you let it just come out and disappear?"

Joe had no intention of spending the money to sue, but he was willing to pay for enough of Rembar's time to make Scribner's think he might. Meanwhile, he parsed the galleys and sent Rembar point-by-point objections to what mattered most to him, most of which was personal rather than professional. That was hardly surprising, since Geist's admiration for Joe's work was the book's raison d'être, while his personal characterizations began by describing Joe as a "crotchety country squire like Evelyn Waugh in his later years," then proceeded to portray him—usually accurately—as a complicated individual markedly different from Joe's own image of himself.

Over the years, Joe and Geist had shared many hours of intense and relatively frank discussions about Joe's work, both his successes and his disappointments. Then in his sixties, Joe was still bursting with ideas, and Geist challenged him about his habitual characterization of himself as the oldest whore on the beat. Joe actually had very high standards for what he would and would not do, so why disparage himself that way?

Joe admitted he sometimes said it to evoke protests to the contrary, but he also described his disappointment.

> I've done so little original work in my life. I haven't written things that I really should have done. I haven't written a couple of books that I should have . . . I've pissed away what I had. . . . I don't know whether I'll go down as a leading film director of my time. I don't know if I'll even go down as a leading film writer of my time. There's narcissism in there . . . but I think I am a good writer . . . and I say to myself, if you are a good writer, why haven't you written? And what have you written? I don't nearly miss the films I didn't direct, as the things I haven't written.

Trying to work beneath Pop's portrait.

The biography appeared in the spring of 1978, around the same time as Richard Meryman's biography of Herman. They were sometimes reviewed together, though Joe's attracted more attention and seemed to spark new interest in his oeuvre. Film festivals and retrospectives, both in the US and abroad, lifted his spirits intermittently, though he continued to bemoan what might have been. In a 1983 television documentary, he admitted to French critic Michel Ciment, "I want to direct and write for theater, but I'm fearful. It sounds pretentious, but I don't feel good enough."

If Joe's brand of *théâtre filmé* was languishing by the 1980s, at least it could have been a time to look back with pride at his body of work as a whole. He had always overflowed with ideas and insights and creative methods of conveying them, employing complex structures not to dazzle, but to enrich his narratives. He always had something sophisticated and witty and interesting to say, even if sometimes there was too much of it. He had stuck with his resolve never to write an unmotivated character and had worked hard to develop plots out of character, even in the pictures he directed but did not write.

Colleagues appreciated his professionalism; actors wanted to work with him. He had tackled practically every genre, from gothic to film noir to spy story to Shakespeare to musical to spectacle to western to (of course) high comedy. What they shared was an unsparing adult sensibility and his recurring themes. The perennial observer of the human condition examined questions of character, time, perception and reality, intellect and emotion, expectation and disappointment, sex, class, consciousness and self-consciousness, performance, ambition, rivalry, fulfillment.

Even some of the films from Joe's so-called black years as a producer, like *The Philadelphia Story*, should have been a source of pride. But when he wasn't obsessing about writing for theater, Joe had spent much of his life lamenting his inability to make the great films he envisioned, because of all the impediments: the commercial nature of the medium, the studios, the censors, the theater owners, Darryl F. Zanuck . . . the obstacles were infinite.

As he aged, Joe became even more irascible, more embittered. He had defined himself by his work, and he was no longer writing. He had many interests but no hobbies. He had complained about Hollywood since the 1930s, but as the studios declined and collapsed, the bad old days morphed into the good old days. "They don't know what they are doing now," he would growl to interviewers, waving his hand toward the mantel and the trophies he supposedly scorned, his Oscars, his Sarah Siddons statuette, an Edgar Award for *Five Fingers*. He had been a bit of a fogey even as a young man. Now he complained, "*All About Eve* couldn't get made today. There's no sex, no violence, no car chase." Or, "I don't do intergalactic war." Or, referring to a film like *Blazing Saddles*, "It's amazing, the praise you can get for saying 'shit' and 'fuck' on film. I can't imagine how much money I would have made or how many dinner parties would have been thrown for me if I'd been willing to have the actors curse all the time."

While Joe was in Italy in 1965, about to start shooting *The Honey Pot*, Chris, almost twenty-five, had written his father about several job opportunities in the motion picture business. Ambition had been one of Joe's recurring themes for years, and in addition to analyzing the pros and cons of each job, Joe offered Chris some Pop-like advice: "A man's 'career' is the <u>end result</u> of his early efforts. One starts out with a goal in view—and one starts off in its general direction. The road to one's goal is practically never a straight line. There are detours, side-roads, set-backs, and sometimes fortunate short cuts. But it is absolutely <u>essential</u> to keep moving—one cannot simply 'wait' for that clear freeway to one's hoped-for destination."

In other words, life would almost certainly louse up the script, but the script was still worth writing. After *Sleuth*, Joe was stuck on his journey and despaired of his destination. Even so, he was never completely cut off, and old friends continued to seek him out as a father confessor/wise man/amateur therapist—almost as if Joe were their director, but without a picture. Anne Baxter came to him when her husband died in 1977. Paul Newman did the same after his son's death in 1978. Both spent hours on the Joe's sofa, talking to Joe as he sat in his chair, smoking his pipe and trying to comfort them. Hume Cronyn and Elia Kazan and even Jennifer O'Neill also looked to him for counsel.

Joe was seventy-eight in 1987, when his daughter, Alex, graduated from Williams. Although she was clearly a talented artist, she majored in theater in addition to earning an art degree, because, after a lifetime of listening to her father revere theater as the true art form and mourn his failure to conquer it, she felt she almost had to. After graduation Alex lived mostly overseas, working as a print maker in Kyoto, and on film festivals and film in Paris. Despite Joe's continued declarations that she was a writer, she wrote only enough professionally to placate him. However, she visited regularly. Always conscious of his age, she wanted to make the most of whatever time they had left together.

In 1992 Alex joined her parents at the American Film Festival in Deauville, France, where she was working, as well as at festivals honoring Joe that year in San Sebastian, Spain, and Lyon, France. On her way to move to Los Angeles that October, she stopped in Bedford for a couple of weeks. "Dad had just come back from Europe, last stop, Paris, where he had what I think he knew would be his last osso bucco in a cafe one night in Montparnasse. One day I walked into his study, mid-afternoon, and he was sitting at his unused writing desk/typewriter staring out the window. He said, 'I'm having an epiphany.'"

"I'll come back," Alex said, and returned a while later with Rosemary.

Joe was still looking out the window, gazing at the trees Alex knew he loved. "Look at these trees, this house," he said. "They're mine. There's a life I've made. And you know, I've made some great films, and they've given people a lot of pleasure."

Alex and her mother nodded and muttered encouraging noises, both thinking, "Oh god, finally."

"And I'm a good writer. I've touched more people with my movies—it's a more lasting legacy than if I'd written one or two lousy novels. Or plays."

They continued to nod, afraid to break the spell.

"It was what we'd been hoping to hear for years," Alex recalled. "What so many of his friends, from Kazan to Hume, had tried to coax out of him. But one can only reach that conclusion alone. Up to that point, he had been incapable of writing a Christmas card. But from the next morning, no exaggeration, he started on long neglected correspondence and his thoughts on autobiography with Stefan Petrucha, his assistant. To my mind, he finally got out from under the gaze of Pop."

The movie-going world had already recognized Joe's contributions. Now it seemed that he, too, had made peace with both the magnitude and the limitations of his achievements. In November 1992 the New York Film Forum honored him with a five-week retrospective, and the *New York Times* ran an interview by cultural critic Mel Gussow, who had written a biography of Darryl Zanuck and hoped to write Joe's. As usual, Joe complained about the abysmal state of contemporary films and continued to state (and believe), "I've lived without caring what anybody thought of me. I followed very few of the rules." But for the first time, he publicly acknowledged pleasure in his accomplishments and, by implication, the medium that comprised his life's work. "I think I've written some good screenplays, gotten some good performances and made some good movies."

Finally.

As 1993 began, Joe, as usual, started a new diary. His heart was slowing, and as his activities became more circumscribed, this most reflective of men turned increasingly inward, recording his physical deterioration in progressively wavery handwriting. Of his profound personal contentment, there was no doubt. On New Year's Eve he wrote in a shaky hand, "as <u>ever</u>—Ro & Joe, her champagne, his good red wine, their very fine (the best) caviar, baked potato, sour cream and onions—one cat, one dog—and a kitchen full of love."

On New Year's Day his anxiety returned. "Ro off to (2) Christmas parties. JLM to serious contemplation of his memories . . . content, structure and style. Problems, lots of problems." Joe's concerns were existential: health, wealth, and the meaning of life—his. In addition to his heart problems, his dentist never seemed to stop working on his teeth, even as the number of teeth steadily dwindled. "Surely, there cannot <u>exist</u> much more to do with a completely <u>toothless</u> mouth," he mused. He was so weak that on the second day of the year he noted, "Breakfast below stairs for the first time. The equivalent, I suppose . . . at the ending of a life—to the baby's first steps as a beginning."

Finances had been a concern his entire life. Since his twenties Joe had supported his parents; his Uncle Benny Blumenau; Erna, once she was widowed; Herman, Sara, and Josie; Rosa's mother and brother; Elizabeth

and Eric; his own children; his grandson's schooling; European refugees; various friends in distress. Tom called him a reluctant Don Corleone. Now he worried about providing for Rosemary and Alex. Rosemary was in her early sixties and in excellent health, and Alex was twenty-six. He was cautiously optimistic, noting, "Jonathan Reichman—my new lawyer. My high hopes for our future relationship." Three weeks later, disappointment: "Jonathan Reichman to discuss my various failures to keep any financial rewards of consequence. Up to my neck in honors—but no dough in sight."

On Tuesday, February 2, 1993, Rosemary flew to Nashville for a United States Golf Association annual meeting. She helped rate golf courses for the organization, and Joe seemed well enough to leave for a few days, especially with his young writer-assistant staying at the house. The night she left, Petrucha, who considered Joe a "puckish curmudgeon," told Joe he looked tired. Joe unnerved him by concurring, "Yes, and I have less time than I thought."

By Friday morning, Joe felt so ill that his doctor came to the house, and afterward Joe told Petrucha to call Rosemary. She flew back immediately and reached the house by one o'clock that afternoon. The two of them talked for about an hour before Joe sank into congestive heart failure. "I don't think I'm going to make it this time," he told her and Petrucha, as they practically carried him downstairs.

Driving "like a madwoman," Rosemary reached the hospital in six minutes, but by then, Joe's pulse was undetectable. Struggling to get him onto the stretcher, the emergency room attendants dropped him on the ground, but Rosemary knew it no longer mattered.

Exactly thirty-nine years and eleven months after Herman's death, Joe had gone to meet his co-maker.

EPILOGUE

CHAPTER 28

What They Wrought

AFTER FLYING OVERNIGHT FROM CALIFORNIA, ALEX ARRIVED TO FIND Rosemary in the kitchen, fielding an endless string of telephone calls from friends, acquaintances, and media. On the counter lay the tabloid *New York Daily News*, which Joe had devoured, cover to cover, along with his beloved *New York Times*. Alex glanced down at the front page, and there, smiling up at her, was her father's face, accompanied by his usual pipe. Even more surreal, the headline in huge black letters read:

FOR HELMER MANKIEWICZ IT'S A WRAP

Joe's death also wrapped the Herman and Joe story. The era of the Mankiewicz Brothers of Old Hollywood now had its conclusion. As for what happened next, Joe was clearly destined to live on through his films, at least for the foreseeable future. But what of Herman? Aside from cameo appearances in accounts of *Citizen Kane*, was Herman fated to be but a "parenthesis in the listings for Joe," as Pauline Kael put it, in her attempt to rescue him from that very fate?

It had been an article of faith among Pop, Joe, and Herman's sons that Herman would have been a splendid political columnist or historian. Herman's actual career—as opposed to their hypothetical scenario—did have its moments, but Herman was not a splendid screenwriter. That he frittered away his talent is indisputable. So is the fact that he also squandered a fortune and destroyed his health.

On the other hand, Herman always loved show business. He relished the creativity of make-believe, and from his arrival at college at not quite sixteen, Herman turned out humor, short fiction, criticism, and reportage; plays; and of course, screenplays, throughout the rest of his life. Forty years spent dwelling in the land of his imagination should hardly be dismissed as an unfortunate detour. That creativity was as essential a part of Herman as his talent for the bon mot.

In addition to the comedic plays, which Herman inevitably valued more than any motion picture he wrote, he did attempt to create works of meaning. He labored for years over *We, the People*. He wrote *Mad Dog of Europe* in an effort to save lives. He pushed to excel with *Citizen Kane* and, later, with *Woman on the Rock*. But aside from *Citizen Kane*, when collaborative synergy elevated his work, Herman never sustained the effort necessary to achieve excellence. He could cloak that failure of will with disdain during his screenwriting years, but it was just as characteristic of his New York years, when Herman respected his peers and valued his medium.

Herman was too astute a critic not to have examined the quality of his own work, and when his efforts failed to achieve greatness—or even critical or commercial success—Herman never seemed to try harder. He never really knew if his reach exceeded his grasp, because for any number of reasons, Herman never completely challenged his reach.

Obviously, there are other measures of a man. Herman embraced life. No one denied that he was difficult, but Herman loved and was loved. He was kind and helped many. In life and in art, Herman exposed, entertained, amused. After death, he was greatly mourned and greatly missed. Ben Hecht regretted that his memoir, *A Child of the Century*, was published the year after Herman died, too late for his beloved "Manky" to know what he had meant to Hecht. "When I remember . . . his thrown-away genius, his modesty, his shrug at adversity; when I remember that, unlike the lords of success around him, he attacked only the strong with his wit and defended always the weak with his heart, I feel proud to have known a man of importance."

As for his career, Herman's contributions to *Citizen Kane* are more than most people leave behind. Many of his contributions to films are invisible, which does not make them negligible but merely uncredited, as they say in the movies. A guiding hand on Marx Brothers pictures. A suggestion to start *Wizard of Oz* in black and white but mostly gray. He wrote and contributed to many motion pictures that gave pleasure to millions. If the definition of Herman's contributions expands to include those of his children and his children's children, then books and magazines and film and television have benefited from his legacy. It was not enough, but it was not nothing.

Sara was fifty-five when Herman died, in 1953, and to use Josie's description of the mother in her autobiographical novel, *Life Signs*, she "fairly bloomed with widowhood." She hosted Sunday-afternoon salons that attracted an interesting intellectual group. She survived Josie's death by eleven years and reached out to younger family members, including Chris and Tom, who were warmed by her affection. She never remarried, but she had at least one affair (with a prominent, married rabbi). Joe, Don, Frank, Sam Jaffe, John Houseman, George Cukor, and various Aaronson relatives contributed annually to a Sara Support Fund that sustained her in enough comfort to allow her to continue her daily French lessons. Cukor, who later remembered Sara in his will, took her to Israel in 1979.

Age did not diminish her spirit. Frank's son Josh recalled riding with his grandmother in her purple Mustang when a policeman pulled her over for running a stop sign. "There was no stop sign there," Sara said indignantly.

"Actually, there is. We put it in about two months ago," he replied.

"Look," Sara told him. "I am seventy-six years old. I've been driving here for a long time. I do not see as well as everybody else. It's unreasonable for you to think I'm going to see every single new sign you put up, every time you put it up. I'm going to miss some of them. So we can stop pretending I'm going to be seeing them all, because I'm not."

Josh watched the officer process his grandmother's unique argument. "Right," he finally replied. "You have a good day, Mrs. Mankiewicz." No ticket, no warning. Off they drove.

Sara outlived Herman by thirty-three years and died in 1985, at the age of eighty-eight.

All of Herman's children, Joe's three younger children, and many of their grandchildren experienced what Josie described in *Life Signs* as "the famous father syndrome (a weariness with blushing and scuffing at the ground and admitting yes, yes, Simon Liszt's kid, yes the screenwriter, yes some brilliant scripts, and all the time wondering why the fame never pleased him, what the hell it was he wanted and never got), the unspoken but they-might-as-well-have-been-engraved-in-stone demands for excellence, the need to Achieve, Be Someone, Pay Off the Investment, most of all Show Your Genes."

After a long, successful career, Don died in April 2015, at the age of ninety-three. He reviewed books, mostly for the *New York Times*, worked on the *New Yorker* staff, and wrote three novels, including the Harper Prize–winning *Trial*, for which he also wrote the screenplay. Among his many television screenplays were the pilots for *Marcus Welby, M.D.*, and *Ironside*, though he specialized in dramas and wrote a number of *Profiles in Courage* adaptations and creations. He adapted F. Scott Fitzgerald's *Last Tycoon* for *Playhouse 90*.

Don ran unsuccessfully for a seat in the New York State Assembly in 1952, and when he served as a delegate to New York State's 1967 constitutional convention, several attendees sought him out to tell him how much Pop had changed their lives. After he and Ilene divorced in 1972, Don married Carol Guidi, and they adopted two daughters from Colombia, Jan (1971) and Sandy (1972). He was an active union organizer throughout his career, and when the Writers Guild of America struck in 2007, he marched in the picket line at the age of eighty-five, with his son, John, his cousin Tom, and his nephew Tim Davis.

Don's children from his marriage to Ilene Korsen are Jane (1950), who lives in New York, and John (1954), who lives in Los Angeles. Both were third-generation contributors to the *New Yorker*, where Jane wrote fiction (she published elsewhere as well, including the *Atlantic Monthly*). John, whose middle name is Herman, still writes occasional "Talk" pieces, between writing and producing numerous television programs, including *House of Cards* and, in 2019, the innovative nonlinear crime drama *Interrogation*. John and his wife, Katie Bergin, have a daughter, Molly (1988), who works in film production at MGM. Their son, Jack (1991), is a playwright and documentary filmmaker who sometimes works for his cousin, Nick Davis. Don and Carol's daughters, Jan and Sandy, are both married, and Sandy's two daughters are Sara (2000) and Rebecca (2003).

Frank was a much-quoted wit with a career Herman would have loved. He earned a master's degree in journalism at Columbia and a law degree at Berkeley and worked as both journalist and lawyer. He ran unsuccessfully for California state office in 1950. He left a Los Angeles entertainment law practice to head the Peace Corps in Peru and later oversaw the Peace Corps' entire Latin American operations. As Senator Robert Kennedy's press secretary during his 1968 run for president, Frank announced Kennedy's death to the world. After cowriting a syndicated column with Tom Braden, he ran Senator George McGovern's 1972 campaign for president.

He published two books about President Nixon, and after an unsuccessful run for a Maryland congressional seat, he ran National Public Radio from 1977 to 1983. He wrote another book about the influence of television and spent his last three decades in public relations at Gray and later, Hill & Knowlton, where he became vice chair. After his divorce from Holly, he married journalist/novelist Patricia O'Brien. He died in October 2014, at the age of ninety.

Frank's sons, Josh (1955) and Ben (1967), appear on television almost nightly. Josh has been a television journalist since 1975, when he was still in college, and has been with NBC's *Dateline* since 1995. He lives in Los Angeles with his wife, Anh Tu Dang. Ben hosts classic movies, including Herman's and Joe's, on Turner Classic Movies (TCM) and discusses politics on the Young Turks network. Ben and his wife, Lee, live in Los Angeles with their daughter, Josie (2013).

Josie's widower, Peter Davis, continued to make films and published several books, including *Girl of My Dreams*, a 2015 novel about Hollywood in the 1930s. He and his second wife, Karen Zehring, have two children, Jesse (1980) and Antonia (1981). He lives in Maine with his third wife, Alicia Anstead. Josie and Peter's son Tim (1963) lives in Los Angeles and has written for a number of television series, including *Jack and Jill*, *Summerland*, and *Men in Trees*. He and Gigi de Pourtales have a son, Ryder (1999), and a daughter, Tess (2004). A filmmaker, writer, and former improvisational comedian, Josie and Peter's son Nick (1965) runs a New York production company and is writing a book about the Mankiewicz brothers and their legacy. He and his wife, Jane Mendelsohn, have two daughters, Lily Johanna (1999) and Isabel Grace (2003).

Joe's first wife, Elizabeth Young Mankiewicz Reynal Walker Darbee, died in 2007 in Sarasota, Florida, at the age of ninety-three.

Rosemary remained in Westchester County for many years after Joe died and continued her enthusiasm for golf (she was always better than Joe). She appeared at various film festivals to discuss Joe's work and now lives in Connecticut.

Eric Reynal was adopted by his stepfather, Eugene Reynal, shortly after Joe ceded custody to Elizabeth. Elizabeth never spoke to him about his father, and Eric's only childhood memory of Joe was a vague recollection of the smell of his pipe. When Elizabeth and Eugene Reynal divorced, Eric stayed with Eugene, and after Eugene remarried, his wife Katharine Beall (Kay) determinedly reintroduced Eric to Joe when Eric was in high school. After a successful career in international banking, Eric and his wife, Carmen, retired to England, where he began writing for pleasure. Joe and Rosemary maintained a warm relationship with Eric and his wife as well as with their three children, William, Carmen, and Michael, and their five grandchildren.

Chris worked as a writer, assistant director, actor and producer on a number of motion pictures, including *Runaway Jury* and *A Perfect Murder*, but his real passion and expertise was classical music. He lives in Los Angeles with his second wife, Nancy. With his first wife, Bruna, Chris had

Joe's daughter, Alex, and three of Herman's grandsons, Josh, John, and Ben, after they share stories of "Growing Up Mankiewicz" at the TCM Classic Film Festival, April 2018. © Turner Classic Movies, Inc.

one son, Jason (1966), who heads a health services company and lives in Florida and Paris with Veronique Grunler and their two children, James (2015) and Anna Rosa (2017).

Tom expanded his successful career as a screenwriter of James Bond films to become a script doctor, director, and producer of film and television, including *Dragnet, Superman,* and *Hart to Hart.* He taught film at Chapman University, and once his father died, Tom never wrote again. He was such a beloved habitué of The Palm in Beverly Hills that his caricature hung on the wall, and when he died at sixty-eight of pancreatic cancer, the restaurant kept his regular booth empty for a night. He never married ("I am owned by two cats") and lived with a succession of actresses, including Tuesday Weld, Elizabeth Ashley, and Margot Kidder, in a pattern he attributed to "always chasing my mother—if they were crazy, I was with them." He owned thoroughbred racehorses and, after maintaining a home in Kenya for years, became an enthusiastic board chairman of the Los Angeles Zoo. Tom liked to say of the Mankiewicz family, "Our idea of affection isn't so much hugging each other as caressing each other with one-liners."

Alex lives in Australia and works as an artist and illustrator specializing in graphic narratives—essentially, she draws her own films. Like Tom, Alex stopped writing when her father died.

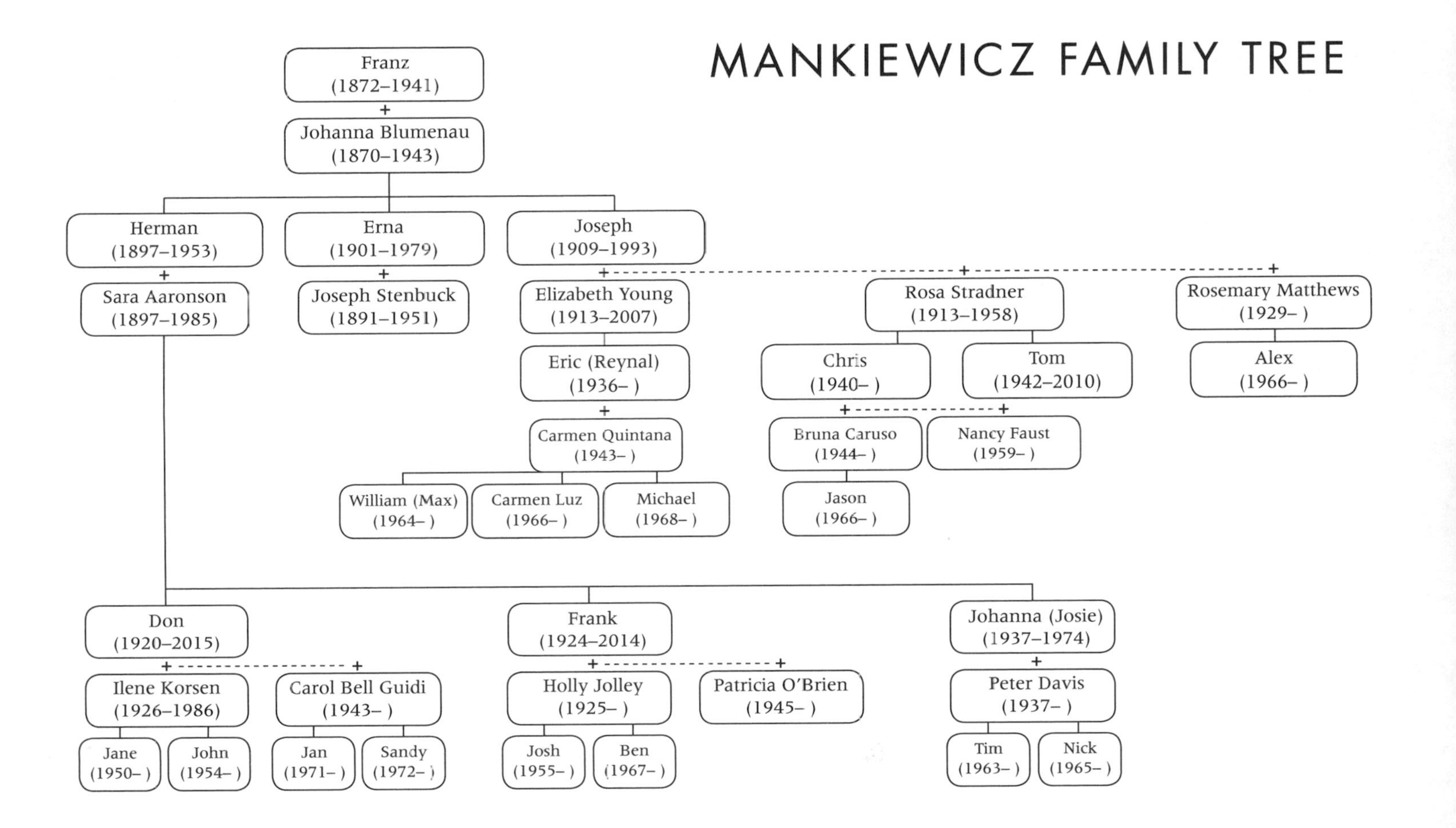
MANKIEWICZ FAMILY TREE
Franz (1872–1941)
+
Johanna Blumenau (1870–1943)
Herman (1897–1953)
+
Sara Aaronson (1897–1985)
Erna (1901–1979)
+
Joseph Stenbuck (1891–1951)
Joseph (1909–1993)
+
Elizabeth Young (1913–2007)
+
Rosa Stradner (1913–1958)
+
Rosemary Matthews (1929–)
Eric (Reynal) (1936–)
+
Carmen Quintana (1943–)
William (Max) (1964–)
Carmen Luz (1966–)
Michael (1968–)
Chris (1940–)
+
Bruna Caruso (1944–)
Jason (1966–)
Tom (1942–2010)
+
Nancy Faust (1959–)
Alex (1966–)
Don (1920–2015)
+
Ilene Korsen (1926–1986)
+
Carol Bell Guidi (1943–)
Jane (1950–)
John (1954–)
Jan (1971–)
Sandy (1972–)
Frank (1924–2014)
+
Holly Jolley (1925–)
+
Patricia O'Brien (1945–)
Josh (1955–)
Ben (1967–)
Johanna (Josie) (1937–1974)
+
Peter Davis (1937–)
Tim (1963–)
Nick (1965–)

NOTES

Richard Meryman's posthumous biography, *Mank: The Wit, World, and Life of Herman Mankiewicz* (New York: William Morrow) and Kenneth L. Geist's *Pictures Will Talk: The Life & Films of Joseph L. Mankiewicz* (New York: Charles Scribner & Sons), both published in 1978, were important resources, as were my conversations with their authors. Recordings of Ken Geist's interviews are at the American Film Institute (AFI), and when I quote interview material he did not use in the book, I cite the source's name and "to KLG."

In 2009 Rosemary Mankiewicz donated Joe's papers to the Academy of Motion Picture Arts and Sciences (AMPAS). They now constitute the Joseph L. Mankiewicz Papers, Margaret Herrick Library, Academy of Motion Picture Arts and Sciences, which I cite as "JLMP." I cite other material from the library as "AMPAS." Rosemary kindly allowed me access to Joe's diaries, logs, journals, letters, wires, and other unpublished material still in her possession. Materials without a location citation are courtesy of Rosemary or other Mankiewicz family members.

Herman Mankiewicz stories are beloved legends of Hollywood history, and because Hollywood is the land of storytelling, Herman stories have been retold, embellished, and reprinted so repeatedly that citing sources is relatively meaningless. I provide some anyway, using contemporaneous sources when I could find them, in hopes that they were as close to the originals as possible.

I retain the brothers' spelling when it adds flavor but in most cases, I correct spelling and obvious wire transmission errors rather than use *sic.*

OTHER ABBREVIATIONS

AFI	Louis B. Mayer Library, American Film Institute
Columbia	Columbia Center for Oral History Archives, Rare Book & Manuscript Library, Columbia University Libraries
Lilly	Lilly Library, Indiana University, Bloomington, Indiana
USC	Twentieth Century Fox Collection, Cinematic Arts Library, University of Southern California, Los Angeles, California
NYT	*New York Times*
NYTR	*New York Tribune*
NYHT	*New York Herald Tribune*
LAT	*Los Angeles Times*

WP	*Washington Post*
HJM	Herman J. Mankiewicz
JLM	Joseph L. Mankiewicz
EMS	Erna Mankiewicz Stenbuck
SAM	Sara Aaronson Mankiewicz
RMM	Rosemary Matthews Mankiewicz
DMM	Don Mankiewicz
FFM	Frank Mankiewicz
CM	Chris Mankiewicz
TM	Tom Mankiewicz
AM	Alex Mankiewicz
KLG	Kenneth Geist
SLS	Author

CHAPTER 3. THE REAL BEGINNING

9 "a nice man who lived on a hill nearby": FFM to SLS. In fact "wicz" is Slavic for "son of," and despite Pop's Germanophilia, he retained the "wicz" rather than Germanicizing it to "witz." During the 1930s some of the relatives fleeing Europe whom Herman and Joe helped changed or Americanized their names. When Joe asked one why, he explained that getting ahead with a name like Mankiewicz would be impossible. The brothers were amused.

9 "You can't tell me": EMS to KLG.

9 "a round little woman": Robert Coughlan, Fifteen Authors in Search of a Character Named Joseph L. Mankiewicz," *Life*, Mar. 12, 1951, 163.

9 Hanna was a born storyteller. One of the children's favorites was when Franz was almost arrested for kidnapping his own son. Trying to cross a crowded street, he became so impatient at Hanna's hesitation that he snatched baby Herman and, holding him like a football, rushed through the crowds of people and vehicles. When Hanna ran after him screaming, "Stop! Stop!" bystanders joined the chase, and after policemen grabbed Franz and protected him from the angry mob, Hanna had trouble convincing them the miscreant actually was the baby's father, because he kept railing loudly at the police, the bystanders, the city government, and the entire capitalist system.

10 "The intermittent times": JLM unpublished.

10 "When you go to a rich man": EMS to KLG.

11 "Where are the other eight points" "Don't tell me": EMS to KLG.

12 "Dr. Salzman says": EMS to KLG.

13 His parents refused to replace it: Herman's lost bicycle has achieved mythic proportions, but according to Wilkes-Barre newspaper reports, a week before Herman's twelfth birthday, the police recovered a bike belonging to Herman that had been abandoned by burglars after a failed robbery attempt. So perhaps reports of Herman's bikelessness have been exaggerated. Or maybe twelve-year-old Herman's bike was a replacement bike. Or maybe it was the original, lost for two years and then recovered. Such is the stuff that art is made of.

CHAPTER 4. HERMAN'S LIFE BEGINS

17 "people were pretty rude": Meryman, *Mank,* 32.

17 He demonstrated no interest in activism: Herman's only quasi-political activity was curtailed. Herman volunteered when Columbia science professor and honorary Serbian consulate Dr. Michael Pupin organized a mission to send twenty-five Columbia students to Serbia during the summer of 1915, to help 600,000 stranded Serbians. Ford Motor Company was donating twenty-five crated automobile chasses, and each student would build an automobile out of the chassis crate. Pupin assured parents the trip seemed safe—after all, the typhus sweeping the area was practically gone. The parents were unconvinced. Citing the ongoing war (triggered, after all, by the assassination of Archduke Ferdinand of Austria-Hungary by a Serbian), they forced Herman and most of the others to pass up the opportunity. *NYTR,* June 2, 1915; *WP,* Dec. 26, 1915, MS8.

17 "Mank was not a joiner": Howard Dietz, *Dancing in the Dark* (New York: Quadrangle Books, 1974), 30.

18 "Blame everything on conditions": "Not One Blush for 'Dynamite,'" *NYTR,* Mar. 4, 1916, 5.

19 "A great deal of theatrical practice": Reminiscences of Henry Myers: oral history (1959) *Popular Arts Project,* II. Columbia.

19 *The Peace Pirates* spoofed: Details of *The Peace Pirates* from *NYTR,* Apr. 13, 1916, and a program, courtesy of Hammerstein's daughter, Alice Hammerstein Mathias.

19 "put the pie": HJM, "Opening Chorus," *The Peace Pirates* (New York: Ray Perkins, 1916), 8. For the full flavor: "He's the guy that put the pie in pirate—Be careful lest you get the captain irate."

20 "Mr. Hart did a strong imitation": *NYTR,* Apr. 13, 1916, 9.

22 "During the busy parts": HJM, "The Hot Sands of Broadway," *NYTR,* July 29, 1917, C1.

22 "Madelein, it was plain": HJM, "The Uptown Ghetto: The Tubercular Cow," *American Jewish Chronicle,* Sept. 20, 1918, 488–89.

23 "a fat, elocuting Nora" "By the time": Meryman, *Mank,* 35.

24 "saw the German army in retreat": HJM to Papa, Beaune, Apr. 19, 1919.

25 "Some painter, I believe" "German debacle": HJM to Papa, Altwied, Jan. 1, 1919.

25 "My other faculties": Meryman, *Mank,* 39.

26 "It is only fair": HJM, "The University in Khaki," *World Tomorrow: A Journal Looking toward a Christian World,* Jan. 1920, 17–19.

26 "I am now teaching": HJM to Mama, Beaune, France, May 11, 1919.

27 "Erna's line about the death": HJM to Papa, Beaune, Apr. 19, 1919.

CHAPTER 5. GLORIOUS ADVENTURES

Quotations and accounts in this chapter are from Meryman, *Mank,* unless otherwise cited.

29 "that I'm a decent enough sort of person": HJM to Papa, Aug. 18, 1919.

32 "Berlin was prophetic": Edna Ferber, *A Peculiar Treasure* (Garden City, NY: Doubleday, Doran, 1939), 273.

CHAPTER 6. CENTRAL PARK WEST VOLTAIRE

37 "the foremost newspaper reporter": Marion Meade, *Dorothy Parker: What Fresh Hell Is This?* (New York: Penguin Books, 1989), 113.

40 "We had a big dressing room": Kenneth Tynan, "The Girl in the Black Helmet," *New Yorker*, June 11, 1979, 68.

40 "inhumane executioner of the bogus": Louise Brooks, *Lulu in Hollywood* (New York: Alfred A. Knopf, 1982), 6.

40 "Shoot her": Marc Connelly, *Voices Offstage: A Book of Memoirs* (New York: Holt, Rinehart & Winston, 1968), 75.

40 "Claude, this is Herman": Myers, Reminiscences, 25.

41 "American Ambassador of Artistry": "The London Stage," *NYT*, June 24, 1923, X1.

43 "constantly cock-eyed": Ring Lardner to F. Scott Fitzgerald, Aug. 8, 1925, *Letters of Ring Lardner*, ed. Clifford M. Caruthers (Alexandria, VA: Orchises Press, 1995), 181–82.

43 "Among the Woollcottians": Ben Hecht, *Charlie: The Improbable Life and Times of Charles MacArthur* (New York: Harper & Brothers, 1957), 110.

43 "could puncture egos": Ben Hecht, *A Child of the Century: The Autobiography of Ben Hecht* (New York: Simon & Schuster, 1954), 393–94.

45 "the *nice* Kaufman": Scott Meredith, *George S. Kaufman and His Friends* (Garden City, NY: Doubleday, 1974), 135.

45 "Sick mother": Meryman, *Mank*, 85.

45 "Call a strike": An oft-repeated quip.

45 "The play ran late": "The Theatre," *New Yorker*, Apr. 4, 1925, 14: "And it was Ashton Stevens, as reported by Mr. [Percy] Hammond, who said maliciously of a revue known as 'Round the Town' that the show ran late but the audience early." Unsigned, but by HJM.

46 "Nothing Coming In": Malcolm Goldstein, *George S. Kaufman: His Life, His Theater* (New York: Oxford University Press, 1979), 130.

46 "a born kaffeeklatscher": Reminiscences of Marc Connelly: oral history (1979) *Popular Arts Project*, 54. Columbia.

48 "The part-time help of wits" "God knows I had both kinds": James Thurber, *Years with Ross* (Boston: Little, Brown, 1959), 22.

49 "Miss Gladys Wallace": Meryman, *Mank*, 77.

49 "The brocaded broadcoats": "Prime Adepts in Scandal's School," *NYT*, Oct. 24, 1925, 19.

50 "decidedly spotty": "Critique: The Theatre," *New Yorker*, Dec. 5, 1925, 15.

50 "Chicago has no waggish weekly": HJM, "A New Yorker in the Provinces," *New Yorker*, Feb. 6, 1926, 16.

51 "Herman Mankiewicz was one of the most brilliant": Morris Fishbein, MD, *Morris Fishbein: An Autobiography* (Garden City, NY: Doubleday, 1969), 358. When Fishbein and his wife found themselves in Los Angeles over the holidays a few years later, Herman and Sara included them in their New Year's Eve party, where they met celebrities like Charlie Chaplin and actress Kay Francis. Francis sat in Fishbein's lap and told him that she, too, was from Chicago and that she, not Lilyan Tashman, was really the best-dressed person in Hollywood.

51 "low, dirty piece of behavior": HJM to Harold Ross, Feb. 10, 1926. *New Yorker* records, ca. 1924–1984. New York Public Library.

52 "I will not discuss the merit": Harold Ross to HJM, Feb. 16, 1926, *New Yorker* records, ca. 1924–1984. New York Public Library.

53 "After Mank's 'But you *can't* fire me'": Meryman, *Mank*, 125–26.

CHAPTER 7. IN SEARCH OF LUMP SUM

57 they lived next door to actor Edmund Lowe: They socialized with Lowe and his wife, actress Lilyan Tashman, who played a villainous Broadway star in *Take Me Home* (1928), a silent film Herman titled. Herman's title for her character: "Derelys Devore, the star, rose from the chorus, because she was cool in an emergency—and warm in a taxi."

58 "Look! No hands!" Meryman, *Mank*, 129. Don told me other stories of Herman's terrible driving.

59 losers, mostly actors who were better seen than heard: One picture really is worth a thousand words. *Singin' in the Rain* (1952) portrays movies' transition to sound through the irresistible performances of Gene Kelly, Donald O'Connor, and Debbie Reynolds.

59 "He could improvise": Nunnally Johnson. Oral history interview by Thomas R. Stempel, 1968–1969, 192. AFI

60 "When the producer says to you": Meryman, *Mank*, 160.

60 "If this play fails": Howard Teichmann, *George S. Kaufman: An Intimate Portrait* (New York: Atheneum, 1972), 95.

60 "Let's switch audiences": Teichmann, *George S. Kaufman*, 303.

61 "AFTER STUDYING THE PLAY": HJM to Connelly, wire, Aug. 16, 1927.

61 "YOU HAVE WORKED": HJM to Connelly, wire, Sept. 13, 1927.

61 "BEST WISHES": HJM to Dr. Frank Mankiewicz, Sept. 13, 1927.

62 "My dear Brother and Gossip": JLM to HJM, Easter 1927.

62 "He needed it": JLM to HJM and SAM, Dec. 29, 1927.

62 "Will you accept": Hecht, *Child of the Century*, 466.

63 "I want to point out to you": Hecht, *Child of the Century*, 479.

64 "I was about twenty-three": Nora Johnson, *Flashback: Nora Johnson on Nunnally Johnson* (Garden City, NY: Doubleday, 1979), 51–52.

64 "I've got to find five writers": Wells Root to Lee Server, *Screenwriter: Words Become Pictures* (Pittstown, NJ: Main Street, 1987), 173.

65 "little girl with the curl": Mordaunt Hall, *NYT*, Feb. 5, 1928, 113. A rejected alternative to Herman's "very, very good" line about "flames of war" also survives. At the request of Paramount chief Jesse Lasky, Herman employed Jesse Jr. as an "apprentice 'title writer'" during the summer, and Herman's boss's boss's son suggested, "On the far-flung borders of Russia a demoralized army struggled to hold back the German storm, while another storm took form behind it. Red Revolution!" Jesse L. Lasky Jr., *What Ever Happened to Hollywood?* (New York: Funk & Wagnalls, 1975, 79).

67 "Mary and I said just what came into our heads": *LAT*, June 30, 1929, 18.

67 Joe also joked: Joe's playwright scolds Margo Channing: "I shall never understand the weird process by which a body with a voice suddenly fancies itself as a mind! Just when exactly does an actress decide they're *her* words she's saying and *her* thoughts she's expressing?" Margo retorts, "Usually at the point where she's got to rewrite and rethink them to keep the audience from leaving the theater!"

68 "roamed through the cinematic vineyards": "News and Gossip of the Broadway Sector: 'We, the People,' as Mr. Erskine's Next Production," *NYT*, Oct. 26, 1930, X1.

68 "I have been conducting some inquiries": "In the Dramatic Mail Bag," *NYT*, Nov. 2, 1930, X4.

69 "Don't worry, Arthur": This is probably the most-recounted Herman anecdote. Years later, Marietta Tree told Don Mankiewicz she had been Herman's date on that occasion. Arthur Hornblow's son, Michael, told me he never heard his father mention the story but considered it plausible. Joe wrote next to Meryman's account, "next day's line," so perhaps Herman said it the following morning. Any attempt to set the record straight would not be complete without noting that, Joe and Marietta Tree notwithstanding, Howard Dietz claimed it was he, not Herman, who said it at a 1936 bachelor dinner given by journalist Lucius Beebe (Dietz, *Dancing in the Dark*, 79–80). Perhaps one coined it and the other stole it. Understandably, the story stuck to Herman, because it was so completely in character.

69 "They can't fire me": Meryman, *Mank*, 137.

69 "I know you just learned": an oft-repeated quip, including Sidney Skolsky, *WP*, June 27, 1936, 16; and Leonard Lyons, *WP*, Apr. 17, 1938, TT2.

69 "I have absolutely no money": HJM to Lewis Milestone, Sept. 11, 1929, Lewis Milestone papers, AMPAS.

69 "there were seven other players": Milestone to HJM, undated, Lewis Milestone papers, AMPAS.

69 "John Worth Kern": Leonard Lyons, "The Lyons Den," *New York Post*, June 27, 1944, 14.

70 "Poor Sara": Another of Herman's most famous. In 1945 Ben and Rose Hecht gave Herman and Sara a twenty-fifth anniversary party and pinned a Purple Heart on Sara for "twenty-five years of being uninterruptedly wounded," Earl Wilson, "It Happened Last Night: Be Calm, Mrs. Mankiewicz," *New York Post*, Jan. 30, 1946, 43.

70 "Remember me to the kids": HJM to SAM, New York, Apr. 29, 1927.

72 "I don't know how complimentary": SAM to Howard Suber, transcript from UCLA Class 208B, Feb. 25, 1969, 6. Kael Mss., Lilly. Suber, an assistant professor researching the history of *Citizen Kane*'s screenplay, had invited Sara and others connected with the film to address his class.

72 "I couldn't imagine anyone": HJM, testimony, *Ferdinand Lundberg v. Orson Welles, Herman Mankiewicz and RKO-Radio Pictures*, Nov. 30, 1950, 47.

74 One day when Schulberg called them: Sam Jaffe's unpublished memoir. Courtesy of Judy Jaffe Silber.

74 "a large, Teutonic individual" "proceed as fancy dictated": S. J. Perelman, *The Last Laugh* (New York: Simon & Schuster, 1982), 153.

74 "cold-eyed vultures": Perelman, *Last Laugh*, 155.

74 "It stinks": Perelman, *Last Laugh*, 157.

75 "written chiefly by": Joe Adamson, *Groucho, Chico, Harpo and Sometimes Zeppo: A History of the Marx Brothers and a Satire on the Rest of the World* (New York: Simon & Schuster, 1974), 137–38.

75 the family's Passover seders: Despite his contempt for religion, Herman conducted their family seders respectfully and with complete seriousness—except at the end. After they proclaimed, "Next year in Jerusalem," he would mutter, "Oh sehr" (German for "yeah, right"). FFM and his former wife, Holly Jolley, to SLS.

75 "If Groucho and Chico": Adamson, *Groucho, Chico,* 136.

75 "In *Cocoanuts*": Adamson, *Groucho, Chico,* 145.

76 "Each one of the brothers": John Scott, "It's Not So Funny to Direct Them," *LAT,* Sept. 20, 1931, B11.

76 "anarchical troupe": Perelman, *Last Laugh,* 158.

78 "You're a middle aged Jew": Meryman, *Mank,* 148. S. J. Perelman's version recalls Arthur Sheekman and himself ("two pale-faced young men twitching with fright") awakening Herman from an afternoon nap because they were "kind of perplexed" about the psychology of the Brothers' characters. "We—we wondered if you could analyze or define them for us."

"Oh you did, did you?" he grated. "O.K., I'll tell you in a word. One of them is a guinea, another a mute who picks up spit, and the third an old Hebe with a cigar. Is that all clear, Beaumont and Fletcher?" Perelman, *Last Laugh,* 159–60.

78 "she's old and has big tits": Adamson, *Groucho, Chico,* 223.

CHAPTER 8. GOLD SAFE, HOWEVER

80 "midget in a family ": JLM unpublished, as is the rest of his description of his childhood in this chapter unless otherwise cited.

82 "Contrary to papa's ideas": JLM to HJM and SAM, May 13, 1928. Joe also wrote that the family was "very tickled to find your name in the Who's Who in Jewry but our glee was just a wee bit lessened by the fact that Eva Blum's brother Sol is also included and a greater failure than he, hath no man."

82 "my campaign to dislodge": JLM to HJM and SAM, May 26, 1928. Joe also enclosed a clipping from the *Times* about a play, *The People,* that sounded suspiciously like Herman's *We, the People,* "with a few gulps in my throat. It would seem that either Herman is Clarke Silvernail (nobody ever had that name), or that he has been showing We, The People around too much, or that somebody has been through your closets."

83 "absolute intoxication of theater": Geist, *Pictures Will Talk,* 22.

83 "This is my third day here": JLM to HJM, Paris, Nov. 22, 1928.

84 "TWO HOURS LATE": JLM to Mankiewicz, Jan. 17, 1929.

85 "one of the nicest men": Reminiscences of Edward Albert Sutherland: oral history (1959), *Popular Arts Project,* 88–89, Columbia. The anecdote is from this source.

86 "Sutherland wants you" "That was the first time": Geist, *Pictures Will Talk,* 29.

88 *Skippy* and its sequel *Sooky*: Many years later, Joe wrote:
"Skippy. The dog died. A hit.
Sooky. The mother died. A flop. You couldn't top the dog."

88 "Joe Mankiewicz ruins you": Geist, *Pictures Will Talk,* 39.

88 the children worked harder for that twenty cents: Some of them never saw the rest. After Jackie Coogan's profligate parents spent the estimated $4 million Jackie earned as a child, California passed the Child Actors Bill, which was called the

Coogan Law. Parents were not the only exploiters. To induce his nephew to cry on camera, Taurog pretended he was actually going to kill the dog in the picture. Jackie Cooper never forgave him.

89 "an old-time, famous screenwriter" "somewhere between $75 and $100": Geist, *Pictures Will Talk*, 40–41.

90 his delighted discovery of Benzedrine: Joe was given the experimental amphetamine by one of his closest friends, Dr. Marcus Rabwin, who had delivered Judy Garland and remained close to her. Joe remained interested in medicine and psychiatry all his life and was always ready to try the latest drugs.

91 "a minor 'B' double-feature": JLM marginalia, responding to Myers' quotes in his copy of Geist's galleys, 48–49. JLMP

91 "Klopstokia . . .": According to Myers, Herman wrote the new opening titles, though Joe wrote "JLM" next to that statement in Geist's galleys. JLMP

92 "a Marx Brothers comedy without the Marx Brothers": "The New Pictures," *Time*, July 18, 1932, 23.

93 After they finished shooting: Joe's account is from Geist, *Pictures Will Talk*, 52–53. See also James Curtis, *W. C. Fields: A Biography* (New York: Alfred A. Knopf, 2003), 243–48.

94 "a little larger than Mussolini's": Meryman, *Mank*, 157.

94 Ted Healy. A former vaudevillian, Healy used to drink with Herman when they worked together at Paramount, and according to Nunnally Johnson, one day Healy said, "I cannot be happy with a fellow until I've got him pegged. Now I've got you pegged." "Well, what is it?" Herman asked. "You're an Irish bum," Healy told him. "Jewish, but an Irish bum." Johnson considered that "a perfect description of Mank." Nunnally Johnson oral history, 187, AFI.

95 "It's not that I liked it": Seaton attributed this response to Herman when telling Meryman (*Mank*, 157); to Joe when telling Geist (*Pictures Will Talk*, 65 fn); and to Selznick in his own oral history, "Reminiscences of George Seaton: oral history" (1958), 101. *Popular Arts Project*, Columbia.

95 "a well-intentioned disaster": Geist, *Pictures Will Talk*, 59.

95 "partial nervous breakdown": Geist, *Pictures Will Talk*, 51.

95 "David, you cast the movies": Interview with Peter McCrea, "Remembering Frances Dee," http://www.francesdeemccrea.com/peter-mccrea/

96 "Some time later Mankiewicz confessed": Geist, *Pictures Will Talk*, 51.

CHAPTER 9. MAD DOGS

97 *The Mad Dog of Europe*: Although Herman had asked to have his name removed, Al Rosen copyrighted the script on December 26, 1933, as "written by Herman J. Mankiewicz, dramatization by Lynn Root." I treat the script as Herman's.

100 "anti-Hitler motion picture": *Hollywood Reporter*, July 12, 1933, 4.

100 "pants pressers, delicatessen dealers": Karl K. Kitchen, "What's the Matter with the Movies?" *Columbia*, Apr. 1922, 6. Quoted in Thomas Doherty, *Hollywood's Censor: Joseph I. Breen & the Production Code Administration* (New York: Columbia University Press, 2007), 201. For more on this issue, see, among others, Neal Gabler, *An Empire of Their Own: How the Jews Invented Hollywood* (New York: Crown, 1988); and J.

Hoberman and Jeffrey Shandler, *Entertaining America: Jews, Movies, and Broadcasting* (New York: Jewish Museum, and Princeton: Princeton University Press, 2003).

101 "an industry largely financed": Francis G. Couvares, "Hollywood, Main Street, and the Church," *Movie Censorship and American Culture*, ed. Francis G. Couvares (Washington, DC: Smithsonian Institution Press, 1996), 152. Quoted in Hoberman and Shandler, *Entertaining America*, 53.

101 "these men left the country willingly": *Hollywood Reporter*, April 20, 1933, 1, quoted in Thomas Doherty, *Hollywood and Hitler 1933–1939* (New York: Columbia University Press, 2013), 43.

101 Pre-Code Hollywood: For more on this period, see Thomas Doherty, *Pre-Code Hollywood: Sex, Immorality, and Insurrection in American Cinema 1930–1934* (New York: Columbia University Press, 1999); and two books by Mick LaSalle: *Complicated Women: Sex and Power in Pre-Code Hollywood* (2000) and *Dangerous Men: Pre-Code Hollywood and the Birth of the Modern Man* (2002), both published by St. Martin's Press.

102 "a scarehead situation" "esthetic tastes": "Jaffe and Mankiewicz Flout Hays 'Mad Dog' Ban," *Hollywood Reporter*, July 18, 1933.

102 officially, the organization opposed it: Richard Gutstadt to Leon Lewis and others, August 28, 1933, Jewish Federation Council of Greater Los Angeles Community Relations Committee Collection, Part 1, 1921–1937. Series II, Subseries E, Oviatt Library, Special Collections and Archives, California State University, Northridge. Readers should know that ADL leader Leon Lewis was leading a group that was secretly investigating and trying to counter local Nazi and anti-Semitic activity. See Laura B. Rosenzweig, *Hitler's Spies: The Undercover Surveillance of Nazis in Los Angeles* (New York: NYU Press, 2017), and Steven J. Ross, *Hitler in Los Angeles: How Jews Foiled Nazi Plots against Hollywood and America* (New York: Bloomsbury, 2017). The Hollywood studio chiefs financed much of that effort, and Joe was one of MGM's representatives in the group overseeing their work, the Executive Committee of the Los Angeles Jewish Community Committee, Hollywood Branch. Its chair was Walter Wanger, and Leo Rosten and Eugene Zukor were among the other members. See Jewish Federation Council of Greater Los Angeles Community Relations Committee Collection, Part 2, circa 1920–1950. Series I, Subseries E.

103 "newsreel type" picture: Lewis to Gustadt, September 1, 1933. Jewish Federation Council of Greater Los Angeles Community Relations Committee Collection, Part 1, 1921–1937. Series II, Subseries E.

103 "Because of the large number of Jews" "It is to be remembered": Joseph Breen to Al Rosen, originally written in 1934. Sent to Sol Lesser, Nov. 25, 1936. MPAA: PCA Records, AMPAS. In 1932 Breen had written to a priest friend, "These Jews seem to think of nothing but money making and sexual indulgence. People whose daily morals would not be tolerated in the toilet of a pest house hold the good jobs out here and wax fat on it. . . . Ninety-five percent of these folks are Jews of an Eastern European lineage. They are, probably, the scum of the scum of the earth." Breen to Rev. Wilfrid Parsons, S.J., October 10, 1932, Parsons Papers, Georgetown University, Washington, DC. Quoted in Doherty, *Hollywood's Censor*, 199.

103 they sent German consul Dr. Georg Gyssling: However, Gyssling also played a mixed game. See Rosenzweig, *Hitler's Spies*, and Ross, *Hitler in Los Angeles*.

104 "photoplays written by Herman J. Mankiewicz" "contained no references": "Reich Bans Film Writer, "*NYT*, July 13, 1935, 16.

104 a caper starring Myrna Loy: Louis B. Mayer reluctantly allowed Loy to star in the first *Thin Man* picture, but only if the director promised to have her available for *Stamboul Quest*.

104 "by Herman Mankiewicz" "because of the incident": *Motion Picture Daily*, July 26, 1937, 9.

105 "fair" representation: Joseph Breen to Al Rosen, Apr. 15, 1939. Motion Picture Administration of America, Production Code Administration records, The Mad Dog of Europe, AMPAS.

106 "Somewhat over-simplified": HJM to Irving Berlin, Oct. 9, 1941, *Irving Berlin collection*, Library of Congress. (He also apologized for owing Berlin money and eventually repaid him.) The discussion of Herman's politics in this chapter is based on Meryman, *Mank*, 232–35, and SLS interviews with DMM and FFM. Subsequent quotations in this chapter are from Meryman unless otherwise cited.

107 "His views changed a lot": DMM to SLS. Furthermore, some of his friends encouraged him. While Herman was in New York, George Oppenheimer wrote, "You'd better come back soon. Several of your friends have gotten decided opinions on the European situation and it's going to take a hell of a lot of screaming for you to straighten them out again." Oppenheimer to HJM, June 8, 1938. (Oppenheimer's letter opened, "As one of my closest friends, I want you to be the first to know of my engagement to your wife, Sara. Naturally, we're both terribly happy—and the children are already calling me Daddy.")

108 "and all other dangerous isms": Leo C. Rosten, *Hollywood: The Movie Colony, The Movie Makers*. (New York: Harcourt, Brace, 1941), 139.

108 "Oscar Hammerstein and Philip Dunne": DMM to SLS.

109 "at Quantico, Virginia, on July 12, 1919": HJM to Brigadier General Robert Denig, Aug. 9, 1942.

CHAPTER 10. THE TIFFANY OF STUDIOS

110 with his own secretary: Herman originally brought his Paramount secretary, Rachel Linden, but the Marx Brothers, to whom he had loaned her for the previous two years, started calling the day she left, begging her to come back. She continued to resist until one day a bookcase fell over and the room began to roll. Harpo called again and asked, "Now will you come back?" Linden capitulated, though the culprit was actually a 6.3-Richter-Scale earthquake. Rachel Linden, as guest columnist for Harrison Carroll, *Los Angeles Evening Herald-Express*, Sept. 3, 1940.

111 "You have to care about your work": DMM to SLS.

112 "He didn't do anything more": *King Vidor, A Directors Guild of America Oral History* Interviewed by Nancy Dowd and David Shepard (DGA) (Metuchen, NJ: DGA & Scarecrow Press, 1988), 148.

112 "banal and synthetic": Geist, *Pictures Will Talk*, 69.

113 "My boy, instead of Loretta Young": Geist, *Pictures Will Talk*, 70.

113 "Quite marvelous, Joe, dear": Bob Thomas, *Joan Crawford: A Biography* (New York: Simon & Schuster, 1978), 106–7.

113 "fashion layout": Joan Crawford with Jane Kesner Ardmore, *A Portrait of Joan: The Autobiography of Joan Crawford* (Garden City, NY: Doubleday, 1962), 108.

113 "The collective efforts": Richard Watts Jr., "On the Screen," *NYHT*, Dec. 26, 1934, 9.

114 "a new type of actress": Edwin Schallert, "News and Reviews of the Stage, Screen and Music; Gossip of Studios and the Theater," *LAT*, Apr. 22, 1933, A7.

116 "Herman Mankiewicz, writer": (AP) "Herman Mankiewicz to Wed," *NYT*, May 17, 1934, 29.

116 "Here lies Herm—I mean Joe—Mankiewicz": Geist, *Pictures Will Talk*, 35.

117 "You can't have a literature": DMM to SLS.

117 "Chasen's can dispense": Meryman, *Mank*, 171.

118 "We're both making": unidentified clip, Mankiewicz family files.

118 "A five day week?" DMM to SLS

118 Morrie Ryskind, like Herman, worried: On the left at that time, Ryskind moved from far left to far right in the 1940s.

118 "My brother was a large man": Nancy Lynn Schwartz, *The Hollywood Writers' Wars* (New York: Alfred A. Knopf, 1982), 78. Schwartz cited Maurice Rapf.

119 "ROSE: It's life": Unpublished script: THE MEAL TICKET: A New Play by Herman J. Mankiewicz; Copyright, 1936, by the author, 1936, 2-1-12, 2-1-13. Courtesy of DMM.

120 "I knew that no one as witty": Hecht, *Child of the Century*, 393.

120 "Dear *Miss Hepburn*": HJM to Katharine Hepburn, Aug. 21, 1934, Katharine Hepburn Papers, AMPAS.

121 "My dear Kate": HJM to Katharine Hepburn, Dec. 14, 1934, Katharine Hepburn Papers, AMPAS.

122 "She was the only player": Lawrence J. Quirk, *Margaret Sullavan: Child of Fate* (New York: St. Martin's Press, 1986), 128.

123 "Mrs. Herman Mankiewicz, the wife of one of the ace writers": "Hollywood Highlights," *Movie Classic*, May 1936, 56. Even when they relocated, Frank recalled, "We were not living in tenements. They were always below Sunset and above Olympic [Boulevards]." FFM to SLS.

123 "Never pay bills on time": DMM and FFM to SLS. When his landlord's agent wrote that "apparently there were not sufficient funds on hand and non-payment has been protested," Herman reprimanded him, "I find this communication unwarrantably insolent," elaborating, "There is no such thing as apparently insufficient funds. Funds are either sufficient or not sufficient." HJM to Canada Trust Company, Chatham, Canada, Mar. 3, 1942.

123 "Pick a subject for debate": Sam Marx to KLG.

124 "When I sit still": I usually use Meryman's versions of Herman stories, but this time I did not, because of Joe's marginalia. He drew a line through Meryman's account and wrote, "Destroy anecdote. Wrong circumstances – happenings and HJM's punch line." Also, "HJM would hate this account." The usual punch line is, "Imagine, the whole world wired to Harry Cohn's ass." I used Geist's interview with Sam Marx; Samuel Marx, *A Gaudy Spree: The Literary Life of Hollywood in the 1930s Hollywood When the West Was Fun* (New York: Franklin Watts, 1987), 178–80; and Bob Thomas, *King Cohn, The Life and Times of Hollywood Mogul Harry Cohn* (Beverly Hills: New Millennium Press, 2000), 136–38. William Perlberg, who was Cohn's executive producer at that time, told Thomas that Cohn, who loved bargains, was able to hire Herman at $750 a week instead of his previous $2,500. Even if present, Marx and Perlberg may have embellished. If everyone who claimed to have witnessed

Herman's most famous ripostes were actually present, the events would have required the Hollywood Bowl.

124 "at Sara, his father, the Establishment": Meryman, *Mank*, 197, with comments from Joe's marginalia.

124 "When Herman kept demanding money": Meryman, *Mank*, 177.

125 "I found myself not unhappy": JLM unpublished.

127 "to emphasize the grey nature": Aljean Harmetz, *The Making of the Wizard of Oz* (New York: Alfred A. Knopf, 1977), 27.

127 "too valuable to play": Harmetz, *Making of the Wizard of Oz*, 29.

CHAPTER 11. JOE'S BLACK YEARS

128 "wretchedly unhappy": JLM unpublished writing, probably a draft for his quotations in Coughlan, "Fifteen Authors," Mar. 12, 1951.

128 Producers . . . were writers' favorite targets: Donald Ogden Stewart's depiction of producer Hunt Stromberg with a script is typical:

> He would read it, then pick up a riding crop and stride back and forth, spitting fiercely as he moved and more fiercely as he talked. "Son," he would say, "I like it [spit]. I think it's a fine scene [spit]. But how about that dumb Scranton miner? Would *he* understand it?" Hunt had never been in Scranton and I don't think he had ever seen a miner. . . . Charlie MacArthur and I once tried to get a friend in Scranton to send us out a real miner, but he claimed he couldn't find one dumb enough. Every producer, incidentally, seemed to have some similar signature-tune for use in conferences with writers. Irving [Thalberg] would constantly toss and catch a coin. Others would have their nails manicured, their shoes shined, or their hair trimmed. (Donald Ogden Stewart, *By a Stroke of Luck! An Autobiography*, London: Paddington, 1975, 197–98)

129 their parents were Jewish but they were not: FFM to SLS. Not that Herman was entirely consistent. For all his jokes about Jews and his insistence that Judaism was a religion not a race, whenever he mentioned Otto Kahn, he added, "the Jew who became an Episcopalian." FFM to SLS. Groucho Marx had another approach. Refused membership in a country club because he was Jewish, he asked if his daughter, who was only half Jewish, could go in the swimming pool if she only went in up to her waist.

129 Joe's status in the outside world rose: To say Joe's status rose when he was no longer a writer is redundant, since the low status accorded writers in Hollywood was a constant source of jokes as well as anguish; I mean the world outside the motion picture industry.

129 "twenty-nine year old Metro producer": "Hollywood Is on the Brink of Civil War," London *Daily Express*, June 25, 1938. JLMP.

130 "pencil-picking-up producer": Sam Marx to KLG.

130 he was very good at it: Not everyone agrees, of course. For a more critical look at Joe's oeuvre as a producer, see Tag Gallagher, "The Swine Who Rewrote F. Scott

Fitzgerald: Joseph L. Mankiewicz as Producer," *Senses of Cinema*, Oct. 2003, no. 28, http://sensesofcinema.com/2003/feature-articles/joseph_mankiewicz/.

130 "the one thing": Geist, *Pictures Will Talk*, 75.

130 "Well, fellows this ought to convince you": Joe told this story many times. I used Sam Marx's letter to editor, *LAT*, Aug. 9, 1976, D6.

130 "New, different, enchanting": Geist, *Pictures Will Talk*, 75.

130 "Young man, I knew Andreyev": Geist, *Pictures Will Talk*, 89.

131 "L.B. didn't want me to make that picture": Eileen Creelman, "Joseph L. Mankiewicz Talks of Producing Dickens's 'A Christmas Carol,'" *New York Sun*, Dec. 17, 1938.

131 "All right, Harvard College": JLM at Festival d'Avignon, July 29, 1980. Transcript of the interview at the Verger: Rough, Uncut Footage Partially Used in French Television, 15.

131 That telephone conversation earned Krasna: A June 8, 1936, Sidney Skolsky column describes Krasna dictating while Joe has an MGM secretary take it down in shorthand. But in *Spencer Tracy: A Biography* (New York: Alfred A. Knopf, 2011), 924, James Curtis cites, "Norman Krasna's original story, as dictated from memory by JLM, is in the MGM collection at USC, along with story conference notes and draft screenplays by Leonard Praskins and Bartlett Cormack."

131 "The Iron Butterfly": Curtis, 281. The rest of the anecdote is from Curtis, based on a JLM interview with Selden West.

132 "well worth seeing": Harry Robinson, "Hollywood Picture Indicts Lynch Law," *Sunday Worker*, New York, June 7, 1936.

133 "You destroyed my movie": JLM in interview for *Preminger: Anatomy of a Filmmaker* (1991), American Academy of Motion Picture Arts and Sciences, Academy Film Archive.

133 "You're the only one": Bob Thomas, *Joan Crawford: A Biography* (New York: Simon & Schuster, 1978), 107.

133 "I was madly in love": Geist, *Pictures Will Talk*, 89.

134 "Joe was the first producer": Geist, *Pictures Will Talk*, 82.

134 "Forget those snobs": Thomas, *Joan Crawford*, 107.

134 "She woke up like a movie star": Jane Ellen Wayne, *Crawford's Men* (New York: Prentice Hall Press, 1988), 139.

134 "You'd have to watch the way she came in": Geist, *Pictures Will Talk*, 82.

135 "restores Miss Joan Crawford": Frank S. Nugent, "The Screen: Joan Crawford and Spencer Tracy in 'Mannequin' at Capitol," *NYT*, Jan. 21, 1938, 15.

135 "Joan Crawford Is Herself Again": Nelson B. Bell, "About the Showshops," *WP*, Jan. 19, 1938, X9.

135 "Somehow his hand always touched": JLM to KLG. Also Thomas, *Joan Crawford*, 116.

136 "No more goddam shopgirls": Thomas, *Joan Crawford*, 116.

136 "I'd rather be a supporting player": Crawford with Ardmore, *Portrait of Joan*, 122.

136 "almost a good film": Geist, *Pictures Will Talk*, 99.

136 "Cukor flattered them": CM to SLS.

136 "This should have been mine": Geist, *Pictures Will Talk*, 81. This anecdote in Geist's galleys infuriated Joe, who wrote in the margin, "Johnny Mahin would, I'm sure, if pressed, admit this grotesque bit of mythology to have been inspired whilst in

the midst of an alcoholic hallucination—one of the many he enjoyed at the time." Joe added that their affair had ended by then, "by mutual recognition of its non-durability," but Joe's friend Marcus Rabwin supported Mahin's story to KLG. Even if their affair had ended, Crawford's dramatic declaration was certainly in character.

137 "some hits, some runs": JLM to KLG.

138 "goddamnedest caterwauling": Geist, *Pictures Will Talk*, 94.

139 "I feel like a good many writers . . . Oh, Joe, can't producers ever be wrong?" F. Scott Fitzgerald to JLM, Jan. 20, 1938. Quoted by, among others, Arthur Mizener, *The Far Side of Paradise: A Biography of F. Scott Fitzgerald* (Boston: Houghton Mifflin, 1951), 278; Andrew Turnbull, *The Letters of F. Scott Fitzgerald* (New York: Charles Scribner's Sons, 1963), 563; Tom Dardis, *Some Time in the Sun* (New York: Charles Scribner's Sons, 1976), 39. And just about any other book about Fitzgerald, as well as their reviews.

140 "The thing will be": Fitzgerald to Harold Ober, Mar. 4, 1938. F. Scott Fitzgerald, *As Ever, Scott Fitz--: Letters between F. Scott Fitzgerald and His Literary Agent Harold Ober, 1919–1940*, ed. Matthew J. Bruccoli, Jennifer McCabe Atkinson, asst. (Philadelphia: J. B. Lippincott, 1972), 357.

140 "I love Mank": Frances Kroll Ring, *Against the Current: As I Remember F. Scott Fitzgerald* (Berkeley, CA: Creative Arts, 1987), 23.

141 "Hard times weed out": Fitzgerald to Max Perkins, April 23, 1938. *Dear Scott/Dear Max: The Fitzgerald–Perkins Correspondence*, ed. John Kuehl and Jackson R. Bryer (New York: Charles Scribner's Sons, 1971), 246.

141 "a series of mediocre offerings": Sheilah Graham, "Hollywood Today: Joan Crawford Faces 'Crisis' of Career; Star's Will-to-Win Is Big Asset," *Atlanta Constitution*, Mar. 20, 1938, 7B.

141 "an ignorant and vulgar gent": *Correspondence of F. Scott Fitzgerald*, ed. Matthew F. Bruccoli and Margaret M. Duggan, Susan Walker, asst. (New York: Random House, 1980), 516.

141 "Monkeybitch": Fitzgerald, *As Ever*, 380.

141 "You realize that if you rewrite it": DMM to SLS. Don adapted *The Last Tycoon* for *Playhouse 90* in 1957. In 1958 he reviewed Sheilah Graham's memoir, *Beloved Infidel*. Attempting a bit of historical corrective, he described it as "a partisan account, written by one in whom objectivity would have been disloyalty" ("Kathleen Remembers," *NYT Book Review*, Nov. 30, 1958, 26).

142 "people thought I was spitting on the flag": Aaron Latham, *Crazy Sundays: F. Scott Fitzgerald in Hollywood* (New York: Viking, 1971), 123.

142 "ruined lines he probably did not even understand": Latham, *Crazy Sundays*, 136.

142 "the swine who rewrote": Geist, *Pictures Will Talk*, 90, quoting "People Will Talk," BBC-TV, Mar. 13, 1967.

143 "least-deserving-of-praise": Stewart, *By a Stroke of Luck*, 253.

143 "Be in your office": Douglas W. Churchill, "Katharine Hepburn's Persuasive Sales Technique—Signs of a Sports Cycle," *NYT*, Jul. 27, 1941, X3.

143 resembling Dorothy Thompson: When the film appeared, Thompson countered the inevitable comparisons: "In the picture, the columnist is young and beautiful. I'm not. She can't cook. I can. And she speaks Slovenian. I don't" (Leonard Lyons, "Outside of That, Yes!" *WP*, Mar. 19, 1942, 9).

144 "Mr. Tracy, I think you're a little short for me" "he'll cut you down to size," "they could turn to their schmuck husbands": Geist, *Pictures Will Talk*, 105–7.

145 "suit the comedy conventions of the time" "strong exponents of male dominance": Meryl Secrest, "The Male Chauvinist Flicks." *WP/Times Herald*, Nov. 1, 1970, K-2.

145 "worst piece of shit": Geist, *Pictures Will Talk*, 107.

145 "the best screen actor": JLM to KLG.

147 "How much would it cost me": Geist, *Pictures Will Talk*, 96 fn. Joe was not the only one to claim this response to Young's fines.

147 "Oh, we won't have to change the silver": RMM to SLS.

150 "emotional security": Elizabeth Reynal to JLM, Feb. 18, 1943.

151 "(a) How much do you yourself love the child": Karl Menninger, M.D. to Dr. Z. Rita Parker, Mar. 24, 1943.

151 "once more a beautiful martyr": JLM to Menninger, June 7, 1943.

152 "The Life of Judy Garland": Not everyone was so blasé about the affair. Joe's infidelity naturally pained Rosa, and some of Garland's friends worried about Garland's emotional wellbeing. Marcus Rabwin, who had delivered Garland and felt very protective of her, wrote Joe a long letter about how destructive he considered the relationship. Then he tore it up and said nothing.

153 "little hunchback": Gerold Frank, *Judy* (New York: Da Capo Press, 1999), 72.

153 "Christ almighty": Geist, *Pictures Will Talk*, 111.

153 "like a piece of equipment": Gerald Clarke, *Get Happy: The Life of Judy Garland* (New York: Random House, 2000), 182.

153 "She had a fresh kind of a foresty look": Clarke, *Get Happy*, 181. When Clarke interviewed him, Joe also said, "I felt protective as hell. And I think the one thing she did get from me was a little bit of grown-up conversation." JLM to Clarke, interview transcript, Nov. 14, 1990, 21, JLMP.

154 "He talked to me about God": Clarke, *Get Happy*, 185–86.

154 "I'm not speaking to you like a father" "Actually, you've been neither": Clarke transcript, 13.

154 "I don't think for a minute": Clarke transcript, 17.

155 "Without saying a word": Albert Rosen, Unpublished manuscript, ca. 1978, "Oscars Are Not for Agents," 187–88, Al Rosen Papers, AMPAS.

155 "I don't think this studio is big enough": Clarke transcript, 15.

155 "keeping other people from grief": Clarke transcript, 25.

156 "You must present": Clarke transcript, 4.

156 "You can write down": Clarke, *Get Happy*, 181.

CHAPTER 12. CITIZEN KANE

157 "written in letters of fire" "somewhat in the posture": Meryman, *Mank*, 240.

158 "Write it in the first person": Alice Duer Miller to HJM, dated "Sunday."

158 "amazingly civilized and charming": John Houseman to SAM, undated but written in 1953, a few weeks after Herman's death.

160 "4-way movie contract": Leonard Lyons, "The New Yorker," *WP*, Feb. 28, 1940, 18.

161 "The basic plot conception": HJM, Testimony, *Ferdinand Lundberg v. Orson Welles, Herman Mankiewicz and RKO-Radio Pictures*, Nov. 30, 1950, 82.

161 "a whirling pagoda": HJM, Testimony, *Ferdinand Lundberg v. Orson Welles, Herman Mankiewicz and RKO-Radio Pictures*, Nov. 30, 1950, 83.

161 "I have always thought" "I suppose I would remember": Meryman, *Mank*, 247.

162 John Dos Passos included a section about Hearst. Like *Citizen Kane*, Dos Passos's novels weave newspaper items and short biographies of actual people into his narratives. Welles denied Dos Passos any influence on the script, saying he had never read Dos Passos, but Herman certainly would have.

163 "No pair of internal revenue agents" John Houseman, *Run-Through: A Memoir* (New York: Simon & Schuster, 1972), 450–51.

163 "Mrs. Alexander, one of your duties": Meryman, *Mank*, 250.

164 "(W)e were not working in a vacuum": Houseman, *Run-Through*, 454.

164 "When we were together": Meryman, *Mank*, 260–61.

165 "I happened to be discussing": HJM to Harold Ross, June 11, 1943. Kael Mss., Lilly. Herman went on to suggest he write the piece.

165 "Orson had a way of crawling": Patrick McGilligan, *Young Orson: The Years of Luck and Genius on the Path to Citizen Kane* (New York: HarperCollins, 2015), 626.

166 "Do you suppose": Meryman, *Mank*, 262.

167 "There all resemblance ceases": Joseph Cotten, *Vanity Will Get You Somewhere* (San Francisco: Mercury House, 1987), 39.

167 "a sinister and idle figure": Houseman, *Run-Through*, 433.

167 "It isn't a who": Meryman, *Mank*, 19.

169 "very much UFA": George Cukor. Oral history interview by Gavin Lambert, Oral History Collection, 2B6. AFI.

170 "We used to go up to Victorville": Richard Wilson to Howard Suber, transcript, UCLA Class 208B, Feb. 11, 1969, 29. Kael Mss., Lilly.

171 "She looks precisely like the image": Dorothy Comingore to Howard Suber, transcript, UCLA Class 208B, n.d.,14, Kael Mss., Lilly.

172 "juvenile delinquent credit stealer": Herbert Drake to Orson Welles, Aug. 26, 1940. Welles Mss., Lilly.

172 "unsympathetic looking man": Drake to Welles, "Further Telephone Conversation with Herman J. Mangel-Wurzel re Cut Stuff He Saw," Aug. 26, 1940, Welles Mss., Lilly.

173 "Orson Welles Broadcast": Hadley Cantril to Orson Welles, Apr. 11, 1940. Welles Mss., Lilly.

173 He usually used phrases like "a few scenes": Welles also implied to one of his first biographers that John Houseman had "stolen" his idea to make a film version of Shakespeare's *Julius Caesar* (produced by Houseman, written and directed for MGM by JLM). Peter Noble, *The Fabulous Orson Welles* (London: Hutchinson, 1956), 124.

173 "Mankiewicz says the last thing": Drake to Welles, Sept. 5, 1940, Welles Mss., Lilly.

173 "I have reason to believe": Arnold Weissberger to Welles, Sept. 6, 1940, Welles Mss., Lilly.

174 "I like to believe he did": Pauline Kael, "Raising Kane," in *The Citizen Kane Book* (Boston: Little, Brown, 1971), 50.

174 "I do not suppose that you intend": Weissberger to Welles, Sept. 23, 1940, Welles Mss., Lilly.

175 "Orson is delighted with the progress": Richard Baer to Weissberger, Sept. 26, 1940, Welles Mss., Lilly.

175 "I gather that you feel": Weissberger to Welles, Oct. 1, 1940, Welles Mss., Lilly.

175 By then, Welles had agreed to share credit: The RKO files at UCLA Library Special Collections include a June 4, 1941, legal department production record listing writers' times on the project. Herman's records fifteen days between December 7 and December 23, 1939; seventy-one days between February 19 and May 11, 1940; and twenty-five days between June 18 and July 27, 1940, for a total of 111 days. Welles's entry follows Herman's with the identical dates and figures. John Houseman is credited with eighty-seven days between February 21, 1940, and June 1, 1941. Apparently constructed to satisfy some requirement—budgetary or Oscar submissions, perhaps—it was obviously constructed retroactively. However, some later researchers used it as evidence that Herman and Welles contributed equally to the script.

In fact, when Welles did not feel threatened, he could be very generous with credits. He emulated his idol, John Ford, by sharing his director's title card with cinematographer Gregg Toland (Ford shared it for *The Long Voyage Home*, 1940), and he fought to get his makeup artist an on-screen credit. That credit was denied because of union rules.

176 Lederer . . . always insisted: Besides consideration for his aunt's feelings, another possible motive for sharing the script could have been animus toward Orson Welles. Lederer had recently married Welles's ex-wife, Virginia.

176 "I don't believe in lawsuits": Louella O. Parsons, *Tell It to Louella* (New York: G. P. Putnam's Sons, 1961), 132. Parsons added that when "Herman Mankiewicz, who wrote the screenplay . . . was quite ill . . . [h]e said, 'Louella, I'm sorry about the picture. I hope you'll forgive me for my part in it.' Of course I did."

176 "Harpo ordered me the other day": HJM to Alexander Woollcott, July 7, 1941. Alexander Woollcott Correspondence, ca. 1856–1943 (MS Am 1449). Houghton Library, Harvard University.

180 "fictionized" stories: Samantha Barbas, *The First Lady of Hollywood: A Biography of Louella Parsons* (Berkeley and Los Angeles: University of California Press, 2005), 225–26.

180 "It is with exceeding regret": John O'Hara, "Citizen Kane," *Newsweek*, March 17, 1941, 60.

180 "not only a great picture": Howard Barnes, "On the Screen," *NYHT*, May 2, 1941, 16.

180 "not truly great": Bosley Crowther, "The Ambiguous 'Citizen Kane,'" *NYT*, May 4, 1941, X5. His ten-best list was in "In the Charmed Circle," *NYT*, Dec. 28, 1941, X5.

180 "so-called innovations": Richard Watts Jr., "The Theaters," *NYHT*, May 9, 1941, 14.

181 "This movie was not written": Ben Hecht, "1001 Afternoons in New York," *Newspaper PM*, Mar. 14, 1941.

181 "seems to have been overlooked": Lemuel F. Parton, "Who's News Today," *New York Sun*, May 10, 1941, 27.

181 "our long conspiracy": John Houseman to SAM, 1953.

181 "DEAR MANKIE": Orson Welles to HJM, wire, May 3, 1941.

181 "HERMAN CLAIMS": SAM to Welles, wire, May 5, 1941.

182 "there isn't one single line": Meryman, *Mank*, 270.

184 "Mank! Mank!": Meryman, *Mank*, 272, and FFM to SLS.

185 "He's got the Oscar": Geist, *Pictures Will Talk,* 109.

185 "best wishes": George Schaefer to HJM, Feb. 27, 1942.

185 "Here's what I wanted to wire": Welles to HJM, Rio de Janeiro, Apr. 5, 1942, Welles Mss., Lilly.

186 "He wrote several important scenes": Juan Cobos, Miguel Rubio, and Jose Antonio Pruneda, *Cahiers du cinema,* No. 165, Apr. 1965. Translated by Rose Kaplin *for Cahiers du cinema in English,* no. 5, 1966. Reprinted in Andrew Sarris, ed., *Hollywood Voices: Interviews with Film Directors* (Indianapolis: Bobbs-Merrill, 1967, 1971), 177–78.

187 "The whole thing is idiotic": John Houseman, transcript, Professor Stephen G. Handzo's class on film, Apr. 19, 1974, 50. Reminiscences of John Houseman: Oral history, 1974. Columbia. Considering Kael's characterization of Welles as a credit hog, her treatment of the young UCLA assistant professor Howard Suber was ironic as well as reprehensible. Suber had contracted to write an essay about the screenplay for another book about *Citizen Kane.* When Kael suggested that instead, he write one for Bantam to run alongside hers, he was thrilled. Kael sent Suber $375; he sent her his research and his essay. Then she stopped taking his calls and used his research without crediting him. See Brian Kellow, *Pauline Kael: A Life in the Dark* (New York: Viking, 2011), 156–67. Dr. Suber (now a beloved UCLA professor emeritus) confirmed the story in 2012.

187 "if we shall always remember Welles": Andrew Sarris, "films in focus: CITIZEN KAEL VS. 'CITIZEN KANE' (IV)," *Village Voice,* June 3, 1971, 67. Reprinted in its entirety in Sarris, *The Primal Screen: Essays on Film and Related Subjects* (New York: Simon & Schuster, 1973), 111–36. Peter Bogdanovich's response, "The Kane Mutiny" (*Esquire,* Oct. 1972, written mostly by Welles), was frequently anthologized, including in Bogdanovich's compendium of his interviews with Welles, *This Is Orson Welles* (HarperCollins, 1992). That book, in turn, was edited and annotated by critic Jonathan Rosenbaum, a longtime Welles scholar. Rosenbaum's nuanced review of Kael's book appeared in *Film Comment* (Spring 1972, vol. 8, no. 1, 70). There were many other responses, but beyond mentioning a couple of excellent websites, www.wellesnet.com and www.jonathanrosenbaum.net, I leave interested readers to pursue them. The bibliography includes a sampling of the voluminous literature on Welles and *Citizen Kane.*

187 "His principal contributions": Robert L. Carringer, *The Making of Citizen Kane* (Berkeley and Los Angeles: University of California Press, 1996 rev.), 35.

187 "You may think it's over": Richard Meryman to SLS.

188 "Herman was the most knowledgeable man": JLM, interviewed by Lawrence Pitkethly, New York Center for Visual History, July 12, 1991 for ten-part American Cinema series, PBS/BBC, transcript, 5–6.

CHAPTER 13. APPRENTICE DIRECTOR

189 "one of the great poker players": Geist, *Pictures Will Talk,* 96n.

189 "as honest and gentlemanly" "Darryl was away liberating Africa": Geist, *Pictures Will Talk,* 114.

190 "I always thought Zanuck had a Geiger counter": Tom Stempel, *Screenwriter: The Life and Times of Nunnally Johnson* (San Diego: A. S. Barnes, 1980), 47.

191 "You have done a magnificent job": Zanuck to JLM, Dec. 20, 1943, JLMP.
191 "In GRAPES OF WRATH we took out": Darryl F. Zanuck, "Conference with Mr. Zanuck" on temporary script of October 21, 1943, Dec. 21, 1943, USC.
191 "her husband Joe Mankiewicz in a spot": Hedda Hopper, "Hedda Hopper's Hollywood," *LAT*, Feb. 14, 1944, 11.
193 "I can imagine": JLM, Synopses and Comments, Twentieth Century Fox, Nov. 3, 1943, JLMP.
193 "not exactly my cup" "would have written and directed": JLM unpublished writing. He frequently said that about Ernst Lubitsch.
193 "The characters talk and talk and talk": Zanuck to Ernst Lubitsch and JLM, Dec. 6, 1944, USC.
193 Believing that less beautiful actresses: Later in life Joe made the same point in notes for a book about actresses. "As my old friend Sir Basil Whitehill (Bernie Weisberg, before he was knighted) once opined, 'Flat chested actresses usually get the best notices.' Very true. That's because they're spared that shattering, inevitable confrontation with the fact that, in truth, talent is not spelled t-i-t-s—and thus settle down from the very beginning to the study and practice of their craft, which is acting—not 'flashing.'"
195 "What have I done?" Gene Tierney with Mickey Herskowitz, *Self Portrait* (New York: Wyden Books, 1979), 143.
196 "insight into character": Vincent Price to JLM, undated, JLMP.
196 "Now, Vincent. Are you ready?": Vincent Price to audience, AMPAS tribute to JLM, Beverly Hills, May 6, 1991.
196 "wild mad crush": Geist, *Pictures Will Talk*, 128.
197 "Writing and directing": JLM, "Film Author! Film Author!" *Screenwriter*, May 1947, 25. Joe began the piece with a review of French filmmaker Jean Benoit-Lévy's 1946 book, *The Art of the Motion Picture*, in which Benoit-Lévy casually used the term "film auteur" to mean, in Hollywood terms, a writer-director. A number of writers responded to Joe's piece in the next issue, including Philip Dunne, who wrote that good writers lacked the time to write originals because their studios kept them busy writing adaptations.
198 "Actors have the advantage": Rex Harrison to KLG.
199 "always either inwardly or outwardly nervous": Rex Harrison to KLG.
199 "pure unaffected direction": John Ford to JLM, undated, JLMP.
199 "the highest award I could have asked for": JLM to John ("Jack") Ford, May 19, 1948, JLMP.
199 "I REALIZE THAT YOU ARE OCCUPIED": Zanuck to JLM, wire, Aug, 6, 1947, JLMP.
199 "Your use of the word 'occupied'": JLM to Zanuck, Aug. 6, 1947, JLMP.
200 "J. Arthur [Rank]": JLM to William Perlberg, Oct. 2, 1947, JLMP.

CHAPTER 14. PROMISED LAND

201 "I knew I had looked upon the Promised Land": Coughlan, "Fifteen Authors," 170.
201 "For Chrissake, that arrogant bastard": Geist, *Pictures Will Talk*, 138.
202 "In view of what appears": JLM to Zanuck, Oct. 3, 1947, JLMP.
202 "FADE OUT, THE END": JLM Diary, Apr. 17, 1948. Hereafter, "Diary."

202 "magnificent, one of the best": Zanuck to Sol Siegel, May 24, 1948, JLMP.

202 "almost bloodless operation": Coughlan, "Fifteen Authors," 170.

205 Fox had signed Monetta Eloyse Darnell as a fifteen-year-old: Darnell was officially a member of Frank Mankiewicz's Beverly Hills High School graduating class, but Frank never saw her there. She was educated on the Fox lot. FFM to SLS.

205 "Dillinger has a sunburned nose": Ronald L. Davis, *Hollywood Beauty: Linda Darnell and the American Dream* (Norman, OK: University of Oklahoma Press, 1991). 113.

206 "Darling . . . I haven't slept" "Everything under control": Davis, *Hollywood Beauty*, 114.

206 "Rosa's opening": Diary, Oct. 21, 1948.

207 "He has made a film": Bosley Crowther, "Advice to Ladies," *NYT*, Jan. 30, 1949, X1.

207 "YOU'VE SET TELEVISION BACK": Charles Brackett and Billy Wilder to JLM, telegram, Dec. 3, 1948, JLMP.

207 "honest and realistic characterization": C. B. Hanson to JLM, Office of the Superintendent of Schools, San Diego, July 1, 1949, JLMP.

207 "It's always good to see improvement": Arthur B. Adelman to JLM, Jan. 22, 1949, JLMP.

207 "all the other movies": Paul Osborne to JLM, undated, JLMP.

207 "one of the best things": Gene Kelly to JLM, Mar. 14, 1949, JLMP.

208 "the women's clubs": Philip K. Scheuer, "Mankiewicz Sees New Film Targets after Dissecting Home and Marriage," *LAT*, Feb. 13, 1949, D1.

208 "violently opposed to the concept": Eric Hudgins, "A Round Table on the Movies," *Life*, June 27, 1949, 93.

209 "We're different": Hudgins, "A Round Table on the Movies," 94.

209 "Things are working out for me": JLM, unpublished. Probably Joe's draft for Coughlan.

210 "he walked out on me": Sol Siegel to KLG.

210 "obstinately ignore": Sol Siegel to KLG.

211 "Joe Mankiewicz tried to put his name": Alan K. Rode, "The Philip Yordan Story," *Noir City Sentinel*, Nov./Dec. 2009, 13.

211 "We must conscientiously avoid propaganda": Zanuck to Lesser Samuels and Philip Yordan, Feb. 1, 1949, USC.

212 "Linda's admiration for Joseph L. Mankiewicz": Philip K. Scheuer, "Darnell Pulchritude Hard to Hide in Film," *LAT*, Aug. 6, 1950, D1.

213 "Hey, we're actors": Sidney Poitier to audience, panel moderated by Ben Mankiewicz, An Academy Salute to Joseph L. Mankiewicz, Pantages Theatre, Beverly Hills, May 21, 2009.

213 "tap dancing, superstitious, crap-shooting lackey[s]": A. S. "Doc" Young, "Hollywood Digs 'Black Gold,'" *Chicago Defender*, Dec. 17, 1949, 1.

214 She later said she hadn't realized: Ruby Dee to audience, interviewed by Foster Hirsch, A Centennial Salute to Joseph L. Mankiewicz, Academy Theater, New York City, Sept. 21, 2009.

214 "a kind of inflammatory flavor": Joseph I. Breen to Col. Jason Joy, Oct. 6, 1949, USC.

214 Yordan's "obvious, unimaginative and crude" effort: JLM to Screen Writers Guild, Nov. 12, 1949, JLMP.

215 "I find it highly commendable": "Movie of the Week: No Way Out – Hollywood Takes Its Roughest, Rawest Look to Date at Race Conflict," *Life*, Sept. 4, 1950, 46.

215 "intellectual fog belt": Coughlan, "Fifteen Authors," 173.

CHAPTER 15. ALL ABOUT EVE

216 Mary Orr's 1946 *Cosmopolitan* story: Orr based her story on an actual experience related to her by actress Elisabeth Bergner. An understudy had insinuated herself into Bergner's life and exploited Bergner and her producer husband.

216 "a very funny and penetrating high comedy": JLM to Darryl F. Zanuck, Apr. 29, 1949, JLMP.

216 he created a fictitious Sarah Siddons Society: Life copied art. To Joe's amusement, after the picture's release, a group of Chicago women formed an actual Sarah Siddons Society to annually honor an actress in a Chicago theatrical production.

217 "subjective, internal, emotional existence": JLM to Zanuck, June 19, 1950. JLMP

218 "I know Jeanne to be": JLM to Zanuck, Jan. 18, 1950, JLMP.

219 his focus was the female characters: Joe liked to say *All About Adam* could be done as a short.

219 "as close to Irene Dunne": JLM to Zanuck, Jan. 26, 1950, JLMP.

219 "Mr. Zanuck only knew about virgins": Celeste Holm to KLG.

219 "I never thought I'd live": JLM to Zanuck, March 8, 1950, JLMP.

220 "deliberately wanted to ruin her career": Hedda Hopper, "Looking at Hollywood," *Chicago Daily Tribune*, Sept. 14, 1950, B4. Hopper was applauding Davis's *All About Eve* performance and quoting herself from an earlier column.

220 as the Academy's first woman president . . . encountered such intransigence: The attitudes Davis faced may be inferred from one of the reports of her resignation after two weeks in office: "Bette's election was a grave mistake. The academy presidency is not an honorary post, but one cluttered with long hours and hard work—a job best suited to a man. (Harold Heffernan, *Atlanta Constitution*, Jan. 5, 1942, 10).

220 "in case [Joe wrote Zanuck]": JLM to Zanuck, March 8, 1950, JLMP.

220 "the kind of dame": Bette Davis, *The Lonely Life: An Autobiography* (New York: G. P. Putnam's Sons, 1962), 277.

221 "She is the perfect actress": Charlotte Chandler, *The Girl Who Walked Home Alone: Betty Davis, A Personal Biography* (New York: Alfred A. Knopf, 2006), 184.

221 "the interrelationship of the children": Holm to KLG. Kirk Douglas described Joe in almost exactly the same words, calling him "detached . . . an observer. That's how I visualize him in life—puffing on his pipe and observing. Then making a wry comment." Kirk Douglas to KLG.

221 "*Eve* was the only picture": Judith Crist, *Take 22: Moviemakers on Moviemaking* (New York: Viking, 1984), 46.

222 "For three years I was solely a wife": Davis, *Lonely Life*, 294. The rest of the anecdote is from this source. "Mrs. Craig" refers to the title character in the film *Harriet Craig*, a 1950 adaptation of George Kelly's 1925 Pulitzer Prize–winning play, *Craig's Wife*. Mrs. Craig (played by Joan Crawford) is a perfectionist, obsessed with her household.

222 "like two kids who'd learned to spell": Geist, *Pictures Will Talk,* 169.
222 "all the nuances": Anne Baxter to KLG.
222 "As you get angry": Chandler, *Girl Who Walked Home Alone,* 186. The rest of the anecdote is from this source.
223 "skullduggery and bitchcraft": Geist, *Pictures Will Talk,* 162.
223 "Joe knows more about women": Baxter to KLG. (Some of this is in Geist, *Pictures Will Talk,* 171).
223 "horse that runs all out": Baxter to KLG.
224 "We're making a fucking picture": Geist, *Pictures Will Talk,* 170.
224 "That girl is going to be a very big star": Celeste Holm to KLG. The anecdote is from Holm.
224 "the loneliest person": JLM, *More About All About Eve: A Colloquy by Gary Carey with Joseph L. Mankiewicz Together with His Screenplay* All About Eve (New York: Random House, 1972), 79.
224 "Even then she struck me": George Sanders, *Memoirs of a Professional Cad* (New York: G. P. Putnam's Sons, 1960), 70–71.
225 "She was 'discovered'": "Portrait of Marilyn," *Chicago Daily Tribune,* Aug. 20, 1950, D10.
225 "When Marilyn called": Philip K. Scheuer, "Wolves Howl for 'Niece' Just like Marilyn Monroe," *LAT,* Aug. 27, 1950, D1.
225 "narrated, or unreal, portions": JLM to Zanuck, June 27, 1950, JLMP. Includes all comments about scoring.
225 "I want to read your script": Arthur Hornblow Jr. to JLM, Nov. 10, 1950, JLMP.
226 "In the thirty odd years": Michael Charles Levee to JLM, Nov. 10, 1950, JLMP.
226 "So, now I join the parade": Gloria Swanson to JLM, Nov. 24, 1950. JLMP.
226 "so obviously right for it" "I was absolutely amazed": Robert Sherwood to JLM, June 29, 1951, JLMP.
227 "very ambitious" "I've been an influence": Coughlan, "Fifteen Authors," 163–64.
228 "the Scott Fitzgerald of his medium": Our Cinema Correspondent, "Film Notes: Actors in Aspic," *Irish Times,* Feb. 5, 1951, 4.
228 "One of Joseph Mankiewicz's talents": Margaret Farrar, Crossword Puzzle, *NYT,* June 21, 1951, 25.
229 "I always had to do": Mason Wiley and Damien Bona, *Inside the Oscars: The Unofficial History of the Academy Awards* (New York: Ballantine Books, 1996), 207.

CHAPTER 16. BREAKING AWAY

230 radio advertisements to help defeat Upton Sinclair: According to Gregg Mitchell, Joe had polished "GOP campaign speeches and anti-Sinclair radio scripts. One of the radio melodramas warned rich folks that Governor Sinclair might confiscate their swimming pools." Mitchell, *The Campaign of the Century: Upton Sinclair's Race for Governor and the Birth of Media Politics,* (New York: Random House, 1992), 332.
230 "as politically knowledgeable": Geist, *Pictures Will Talk,* 174.
231 his membership on the executive committee: Rosenzweig, *Hitler's Spies,* 140–41.
231 "In response to telegrams": "SDG Non-Red Oath Disclaimed: Prez Mankiewicz Says He Wasn't Consulted," *Daily Variety,* Aug. 25, 1950, 13.

231 "I cannot understand why": *Los Angeles Examiner*, Aug. 28, 1950.

232 Whatever Joe's initial hesitations: I am indebted to the late Sherlee Lantz for her extensive analysis of Rosa's and Joe's effects on each other.

232 "bitter debate": "SDG Schism on 'Blacklist': Mankiewicz Will Not Sign Oath": *Daily Variety*, Oct. 11, 1950, 1.

233 "What do you have in common": JLM at Avignon, 1980, 73.

233 "a fucking recall action": Geist, *Pictures Will Talk*, 185.

233 "pitted himself against": Text of Oct, 13, 1950 telegram, typed copy, JLMP

234 "the most dramatic evening": Geist, *Pictures Will Talk*, 191.

234 "In your tabulation": Kevin Brianton, *Hollywood Divided: The 1950 Screen Directors Guild Meeting and the Impact of the Blacklis*t (Lexington: University Press of Kentucky, 2016), 54.

234 "My name is John Ford": Brianton, *Hollywood Divided.*, 67.

235 "vindication and sanctification": Frank Capra to Members of the Board of Directors, SDGA, Both Those Elected and Those Appointed for A Short Interim, Nov. 1, 1950. I am indebted to Kevin Brianton for this letter.

235 "The twenty-five": JLM at Avignon, 76. See Brianton, *Hollywood Divided*, for the history of this much-recounted story and an important corrective to the myths that developed over the years.

235 "had his finger up the pulse": Geist, *Pictures Will Talk*, 173.

236 "When you are both": Zanuck to JLM, Dec. 20, 1950, JLMP.

236 "the picture was essentially": JLM at Avignon, 1980, 44.

238 "humor, sex and excitement": Geist, *Pictures Will Talk*, 212.

238 "the most obvious looking villain": Geist, *Pictures Will Talk*, 213 fn.

239 "Airmail in Turkish": Ronald Davis, *Hollywood Beauty*, 126.

239 "no man is a hero": Fred Majdalany, "The Old School Spy," *Daily Mail*, Apr. 4, 1952.

240 "Mankiewiczian moment": Dave Kehr, "Critic's Choice: New DVDs: DVD Decision, 2006," *NYT*, Dec. 26, 2006, E9.

241 "long, evasive talk": Diary, Jan. 3, 1951.

241 "it was only possible": David Thomson, *Warner Bros: The Making of an American Movie Studio* (New Haven: Yale University Press, 2017), 28–29. Running through that rivalry is Pop. Samuel Goldwyn Jr. to SLS: "Look at the father. The father is the key to understanding the Mankiewicz brothers."

241 "one of Herman's few gentle emotions": Nunnally Johnson, in essay on JLM, Roddy McDowall, *Double Exposure* (New York: Delacourte Press, 1966), 196.

243 "tragic figure in our times": John Houseman, "'Julius Caesar' on Film: Movie of Shakespeare's Play Attempts to Develop Its Characters Roundly," *NYHT*, Mar. 29, 1953, D3.

244 "muttering and grumbling": "Et Tu, Brando?" *Time*, Oct. 27, 1952, 89.

244 "You sound exactly like June Allyson": JLM at Avignon, 89.

245 "screaming fight" "You will never work": Geist, *Pictures Will Talk*, 234.

246 "Caesar's statue broods": Otis L. Guernsey Jr., "Movie Mystery: Which Version Did You See?" *NYHT*, Nov. 8, 1953, D1.

246 "I have no style or technique": JLM to KLG.

246 "to punctuate dramatically": JLM at Avignon, 1980, 53–55.

246 "Those who came to mock": Philip Hope-Wallace, ""Julius Caesar": A Faithful Film, *Manchester Guardian*, Nov. 4, 1953, 3.

247 "fake D'Artagnan horseplay" "would have loved my idea": JLM to KLG.
247 "they fall into each other's arms": *Time*, "Puccini & Fizz," Jan. 5, 1953, 42.
247 "walk across the stage": JLM to KLG.
248 "when Mimi had no lap": JLM to KLG.
248 "flung into the air": Geist, *Pictures Will Talk*, 240. Quoting JLM, "La Bohème: Décor and Decorum," for a catalogue accompanying an exhibit of Gérard's theater work.
248 comparisons to Gilbert and Sullivan: Olin Downes, "'Boheme' in English Is Offered At 'Met,'" *NYT*, Dec. 28, 1952, 40.
248 "commercial show-business" "appalling" taste: Virgil Thomson, "Opera: La Boheme," *NYHT*, Dec. 28, 1952, 19.
248 "I came through the stage door": JLM, Interview, Nov. 16, 1990, for *Preminger: Anatomy of a Filmmaker* (1991), AMPAS, Academy Film Archive.

CHAPTER 17. EXIT HERMAN

249 "At that time Ohio State University": James Thurber, *My Life and Hard Times* (New York: Harper & Bros., 1933, Perennial Classics, 1999), 67.
250 "I seem to become": HJM to "Bart," Feb. 8, 1942. Letter, courtesy of the Mankiewicz family.
250 "Sam wanted a bridge game": "Mank Loaned to Sam to Bridge Story Gap," *Hollywood Reporter*, Oct. 31, 1931. Joseph Kennedy said that Herman and Sam Goldwyn were the only two men in Hollywood with real family lives. Samuel Goldwyn Jr. told me that when he met Herman at his parents' dinner table, he had no idea Herman was the father of his brilliant Beverly High schoolmate Frank, a "big man on campus."
250 Goldwynisms: Like Yogi Berra, Goldwyn had an understandable logic. He called *Guys and Dolls'* Sky Masterson 'Sky Madison' and Marilyn Monroe 'Marlene Monroe.' Abe Burrows, *Honest Abe: Is There Really No Business Like Show Business?* (Boston: Atlantic Monthly Press, 1980), 292.
251 "not a baseball picture": Nelson B. Bell, "Mr. Goldwyn Explains about That Gehrig Film," *WP*, Feb. 3, 1942, 16.
251 "You ought to be ashamed": Richard Maibaum in Pat McGilligan, *Backstory: Interviews with Screenwriters of Hollywood's Golden Age* (Berkeley and Los Angeles: University of California Press, 1986), 278.
252 "like an old woman tossing a hot biscuit": Ray Robinson, *Iron Horse: Lou Gehrig in His Time* (New York: W. W. Norton., 1990), 277.
252 That story lasted until 2013: For an account of Shieber's detective work, see http://baseballresearcher.blogspot.com/2013/02/the-pride-of-yankees-seeknay.html.
252 "emitting sounds from every orifice": Meryman, *Mank*, 281.
252 "who never could qualify": Leonard Lyons, "Broadway Potpourri," *WP*, Nov. 15, 1945, 8.
253 "Be Calm, Mrs. Mankiewicz": Earl Wilson, "It Happened Last Night," *New York Post*, Jan. 30, 1946, 43.
253 "the pattern of sober, gentlemanly behavior": Leonard Lyons, "Broadway Potpourri," *WP*, Feb. 11, 1946.

253 "I am drunk": "Writer Will Face Felony Complaint," *Los Angeles Examiner*, Mar. 13, 1943.

254 "Felony Charge Filed against Mankiewicz": *Los Angeles Examiner*, Mar. 14, 1943.

254 "Mankiewicz Intoxicated, Police Charge": *Los Angeles Examiner*, May 21, 1943.

255 "Tell Mrs. Gershwin": Meryman, *Mank*, 284.

255 "had been dragged": HJM to Harold Ross, June 11, 1943. Kael Mss., Lilly.

255 noir enthusiasts came to admire it: Alongside such classics as *Vertigo*, *Psycho*, and *In a Lonely Place*, James Harvey devoted an entire chapter to *Christmas Holiday* in *Movie Love in the Fifties* (New York: Alfred A. Knopf, 2001).

256 Herman liked it: *Enchanted Cottage* was Don's least favorite of Herman's films, because it was so saccharine, but Robert Young was so fond of it that he named his house for the picture and years later tried to talk Dorothy Maguire into a remake with the two of them playing older characters.

256 "I'll never dare go": "An Interview with DeWitt Bodeen," Frank N. Magill, ed., *Magill's Cinema Annual 1982* (Englewood Cliffs, NJ: Salem Press) 9. Provided by Ned Comstock, Senior Library Assistant, USC.

256 "When I want a pirate": Paul Henreid with Julius Fast, *Ladies' Man: An Autobiography* (New York: St. Martin's Press, 1984), 167.

256 "Forget it" "a different kind of story": Henreid, *Ladies' Man*, 169.

257 "I gave you a terrific script": Henreid, *Ladies' Man*, 170.

257 "two of the most violently self-destructive" "companion and guardian": John Houseman, *Front and Center* (New York: Simon & Schuster, 1979), 177, 183.

257 RKO under Hughes: FFM to SLS.

258 Ray, who married her: When Ray became convinced Grahame was cheating on him, he hired private detectives, but in a scene worthy of both their films, Ray himself caught Grahame with his son from a previous marriage. She and Tony Ray later married and had two children.

258 "Heartbreak, heartbreak": Meryman, *Mank*, 281.

259 "Lester didn't seem to get much": DMM to SLS.

260 "Don't try to get the Baltimore relatives": DMM to SLS.

260 "There are actually two Saras" "How did you do that" "Don't tell Sara": Holly Jolley to SLS.

260 "Johanna is rapidly becoming": HJM to DMM, Jan. 27, 1939.

261 their group's "arbiter": Jill Schary Robinson, *With a Cast of Thousands* (Los Angeles: Wimpole Street Books, 2016), 123. Robinson's memoir, originally published to great acclaim in 1963, contains entertaining descriptions of some of Hollywood's adult circles, including the one surrounding the Mankiewiczes (123–26).

261 She made national news: The incident was very hurtful to her dedicated math teacher, however, who was made to seem incompetent, and the school required Josie to make amends.

261 "tendentious, one dimensional tract": HJM, testimony, *Ferdinand Lundberg v. Orson Welles, Herman Mankiewicz and RKO-Radio Pictures*, N.Y., Nov. 30, 1950, 65.

262 "someplace along the way": Coughlan, "Fifteen Authors," 168.

262 "I don't know how it is": Meryman, *Mank*, 315.

263 "old hand" Herman's "nice mixture": Hollis Alpert, "SR Goes to the Movies: A Mixed Bag," *Saturday Review*, May 17, 1952, 25.

263 "tolerable" and "bad": JLM to EMS, Mar. 13, 1953. Subsequent Joe-to-Erna quotations are also from this letter.

263 "You know I've never had a bad steak": TM to SLS.

263 "my co-maker": JLM, an oft-repeated story.

264 "Wednesday, the 4th": JLM to EMS, Mar. 13, 1953.

264 "In lieu of flowers": DMM to SLS.

265 "Let it all end" "I will never forgive you": Holly Jolley to SLS.

265 "When a friend leaves you": Nunnally Johnson, "Eulogy," Mar. 5, 1953.

266 "By writing, one makes an attempt": Fred Hacker to SAM, June 26, 1953. This and the remaining letters quoted in this chapter are courtesy of the Mankiewicz family.

CHAPTER 18. HOLLYWOOD CINDERELLA: A CAUTIONARY FAIRY TALE

271 "a little bit of everything": Geist, *Pictures Will Talk*, 240n.

271 "originally had planned": Thomas M. Pryor, "Metro and Lanza Reach Settlement," *NYT*, May 12, 1953, 32.

272 "The character [Harry Dawes]": JLM to Gary Cooper, June 12, 1953, JLMP.

273 "I spoke to Gary Cooper": JLM to Bert Allenberg, June 12, 1953, JLMP.

273 Gardner was probably Schary's favorite female star: Robinson, *With a Cast of Thousands*, 88.

274 "very sultry": Allenberg to JLM, Oct. 16, 1953, JLMP.

274 "Don't you know, dear boy": Allenberg to JLM, Oct. 27, 1953, JLMP.

274 "Ava has now become": Allenberg to JLM, Oct. 30, 1953, JLMP.

274 "I know you like everything": Allenberg to JLM, Nov. 17, 1953, JLMP.

275 "You must light me carefully": Ronald Bergan: "Jack Cardiff: To Cinematographer Key to the Success of Many Powell and Pressburger classics," *Guardian*, Apr. 22, 2009.

275 "AVA GARDNER ITALY BOUND": Lee Server, *Ava Gardner: "Love Is Nothing"* (New York: St. Martin's Press, 2006), 272.

276 "I'M NOT AN IDIOT": JLM to Allenberg, wire, Nov. 25, 1953, JLMP.

276 "Sinatra insisted Ava's place": Jane Ellen Wayne, *The Leading Men of MGM* (New York: Carroll & Graf, 2005), 344.

276 "FRANKIE TELLS ME": Allenberg to JLM, wire, Dec. 8, 1953, JLMP.

276 "EVER SO GRATEFUL": JLM to Allenberg, wire, Dec. 8, 1953, JLMP.

276 "ANSWER SOONEST POSSIBLE": JLM to Allenberg, Dec. 14, 1953, JLMP.

276 "The following is a breakdown": JLM to Allenberg, Dec. 15, 1953, JLMP.

278 "I immediately went over to Metro": Allenberg to JLM, Dec. 22, 1953, JLMP.

278 "Ava had been planning": Wayne, *Leading Men of MGM*, 344.

280 "a simply wonderful opera singer": JLM to Robby Lantz, Feb. 5, 1954, JLMP.

280 "I do wish you didn't feel": Allenberg to JLM, Mar. 29, 1954, JLMP.

280 "Howard likes you": Geist, *Pictures Will Talk*, 248.

281 "snicker and laugh": Arnold Picker (United Artists) to JLM, Nov. 13, 1954, JLMP.

281 "one of the most brilliant": Jean-Luc Godard, *Godard on Godard: Critical Writings by Jean-Luc Godard*, ed. and trans. Jean Narboni and Tom Milne (New York: Viking Press, 1972), 13.

281 ""It is a daring, novel, and most satisfying": François Truffaut, *The Films in My Life*, trans. Leonard Mayhew (New York: Simon & Schuster, 1975), 131.

CHAPTER 19. NEW YORK CROOKS AND SHOWGIRLS: AN AMERICAN FAIRY TALE

282 "Mr. Goldwyn and I have been exchanging": JLM to Allenberg, June 14, 1954, JLMP.

282 "The old boy is real pleased": Allenberg to JLM, June 24, 1954, JLMP.

282 "GUYS AND DOLLS is, in its concept": JLM, "Tentative Outline of Screenplay," 1–2, JLMP.

283 "PRACTICALLY CERTAIN I WILL WRITE": JLM to Marlon Brando, copy of June 26, 1954, wire enclosed in JLM to Allenberg, June 26, JLMP.

283 "Of course, he's never seen him": Allenberg, July 2, 1954, JLMP.

285 "I got the only contract": Louis Sobol, "New York Cavalcade: Among the Runyon Lads," *New York Journal American*, Apr. 30, 1955.

285 "I nearly asphyxiated": Marlon Brando with Robert Lindsey, *Brando: Songs My Mother Taught Me* (New York: Random House, 1994), 215.

286 "the mating call of a yak": Philip K. Scheuer, "Goldwyn Bets Big Bankroll on His 'Guys and Dolls,'" *LAT*, Nov. 13, 1955, D1.

287 "We'll do it my way": Susan Loesser, *A Most Remarkable Fella: Frank Loesser and the Guys and Dolls in His Life* (New York: D. I. Fine, 1993), 119.

287 "Abe, they put a tiny turd": Burrows, *Honest Abe*, 294.

287 Burrows did not like: Laurie Burrows Grad to SLS.

287 "two major flaws": Steve Sondheim, "Guys and Dolls," *Films in Review*, Dec. 1955, 523–25.

CHAPTER 20. JOE REWRITES GRAHAM GREENE

290 "petty, snide little polemic" "aging man [giving himself] a noble motive": JLM to KLG.

290 "Greene's inability to keep": JLM to Laurence Olivier, Jan. 13, 1956, JLMP.

290 "charming, empty": JLM Diary, Jan. 17, 1957. Subsequent quotations in this chapter are from this diary unless otherwise cited.

290 He was also co-opted: Contrary to legend, Lansdale was not Greene's model for Pyle. However, Lansdale was the basis for Eugene Burdick and William Lederer's 1958 novel, *The Ugly American*.

291 "I find that in exonerating": Olivier to JLM, Apr. 24, 1956, JLMP.

292 "Frog Face with Pipe": William Russo, *A Thinker's Damn: Audie Murphy, Vietnam, and the Making of The Quiet American* (William Russo, 2001), 152.

292 "MY FINGER IN DIKE": JLM, wire, Feb. 11, 1957, JLMP

293 "What the hell": Michael Redgrave, *In My Mind's I: An Actor's Autobiography* (New York: Viking, 1983), 216.

294 "travesty": Our Correspondent, "The Quiet American: Film 'Travesty' of the Novel," *London Times*, Jan. 8, 1957.

294 "they will make only the more obvious": Graham Greene, Letter to Editor, "The Film of the Book: Case of the 'The Quiet American,'" *London Times*, Jan. 29, 1957.

294 "I feel like telling him": Redgrave, *In My Mind's I*, 216, quoting Redgrave's own Mar. 21, 1957, diary entry.

295 "long incredibly revealing": JLM to Ronald Kubie, wire, July 16, 1957.

296 "eliminate two destructive outlets": JLM to Ronald Kubie, Aug. 17, 1957. In actuality, not only was he involved with Rosemary, but he had never stopped seizing the moment when opportunities arose. Besides a brief involvement with Jean Simmons while shooting *Guys and Dolls*, Joe had a two-day fling with the young Piper Laurie in the previous year.

296 "gas lighting": CM to SLS. Tom described his experience to me as, "I never knew which Mother I would find."

297 "They sat through it in stony silence" "They were unanimous" "chunks": JLM to Robby Lantz, Bert Allenberg, Abe Bienstock, Aug. 15, 1957, JLMP.

297 "You are reported as feeling": JLM to Arthur Krim, Sept. 27, 1957, JLMP.

298 "inalienable right of the screenwriter": James O'Neill Jr., "A Director's View: Mankiewicz Backs Right to Alter Novels for Screen," *Washington Daily News*, Jan. 8, 1958, 24.

298 "Americans stationed abroad": Inez Robb, "Americans Abroad 'Live in Red, White and Blue Ghettoes,'" *New York World Telegram and Sun*, Jan. 20, 1958.

298 the word "assassination" was used: *Sunday Times*, March 30, 1958. The anonymous reviewer wrote, "Much though I deplore the habit of expecting a film to be a replica of a book or a play, I look for adaptation, not assassination."

298 "audacious manner [of Joe's reversal]": David Robinson, "The Quiet American," *Sight and Sound*, Spring 1958, 201.

298 "what is missing": Godard, *Godard on Godard*, 82–84.

299 "Apparently my films": an oft-repeated remark, including AM to SLS.

299 "the most extreme" "I am vain enough": Graham Greene, "The Novelist and the Cinema: A Personal Experience," *International Film Annual No. 2*, ed. William Whitebait (Garden City, NY: Doubleday, 1958), 55. Reprinted in *The Graham Greene Film Reader: Reviews, Essays, Interviews and Film Stories*, ed. David Parkinson (New York: Applause Books, 1995), 443. At a London retrospective in 1984, Greene was still disgusted with Joe's picture – along with many of the other twenty-three films based on his books or stories. John Ford's *The Power and the Glory* was "intolerable." George Cukor's *Travels with My Aunt* was "very bad." *The Comedians* was "a disaster." *The Quiet American* was "a propaganda piece for American policy in Vietnam." ("Greene Criticizes Film Adaptations of His Books," London, September 5 [AP], *Times of India*, Sept. 6, 1984, 10).

Neither Joe nor Greene lived to see Philip Noyce's 2002 version, starring Michael Caine. It hewed more faithfully to Greene's warning about US meddling in faraway countries but demonstrated another risk in political filmmaking. Noyce's film was screened the day before New York's World Trade Center was bombed, and Harvey Weinstein delayed release indefinitely. Weinstein only released it in limited distribution a year later, after Caine refused to promote his next Miramax film unless he did.

299 "very bad film I made": Derek Conrad, "Putting on the Style," *Films and Filming*, January 1960. Reprinted in Brian Dauth, ed., *Joseph L. Mankiewicz: Interviews* (Jackson: University Press of Mississippi, 2008), 25.

CHAPTER 21. EXIT ROSA

300 "a mess": Diary, Oct. 6, 1957.

300 "Don't worry, Moss": Henry Ephron, *We Thought We Could Do Anything: The Life of Screenwriters Phoebe and Henry Ephron* (New York: W. W. Norton), 1977, 96.

300 "George would never say": Tom Mankiewicz, "Joseph L. Mankiewicz (1909–1993)," *Scenario: The Magazine of Screenwriting Art*, vol. 3, no. 3, Fall 1997, 107. Actually, it sounds exactly like Kaufman.

301 shooting his wife's lover in the crotch: Despite his own infidelities, Wanger was so angry at his wife's (actress Joan Bennett's) affair with her agent, Jennings Lang, that he shot Jennings in a parking lot in 1951. Using a temporary insanity defense, attorney Jerry Giesler got him a four months' jail sentence, and after serving three, Wanger set about resurrecting his career.

302 "real facts of life": Josie Mankiewicz to KLG. Josie's quotes in this chapter are from this interview.

303 Watching Joe revisit some of Pop's patterns: When Sam Jaffe met Pop, he was delightedly amused to observe the source of so many of Herman's mannerisms. Pop sneered at Herman in the same way Herman sneered at others and continually said, "I know," rather than, "I think." (Jaffe to KLG)

303 "Addison DeWitt in spades" "permanent war machine": CM to KLG. As an adult, Chris retained both his ability to charm and his tendency toward provocation. Tom dubbed him "Herman without Portfolio." TM to SLS.

304 "Mankiewicz says the note": Geist, *Pictures Will Talk*, 285.

305 "description of how people destroy": Fred Hacker to KLG.

305 "the entire proceedings": Diary, Nov. 19, 1958.

305 "LIFE, one is urged": JLM, *Record*. Joe kept this journal from November 19 to December 22, 1958. All remaining quotations in this chapter are from this journal except Josie's letter.

306 "Your point has been made": Josie to JLM, Nov. 30, 1958.

CHAPTER 22. SOUTHERN GOTHIC HORROR STORY

309 "Frankly, Lew": JLM to KLG.

309 "Grand Guignol": For example, "it pretends to be significant whereas, in fact, it is just Grand Guignol in a pseudo-Freudian idiom." Anonymous reviewer, *Guardian*, May 14, 1960, 5.

310 psychoanalysis with Lawrence Kubie: Besides Rosa and Williams, Kubie treated a number of prominent creative people, many of them struggling with their homosexuality, such as Leonard Bernstein. Vladimir Horowitz credited Kubie with "curing" him.

310 Z. A. Nook: DMM to SLS.

310 "who steals from the rich": Natasha Fraser-Cavassoni, *Sam Spiegel: The Incredible Life and Times of Hollywood's Most Iconoclastic Producer* (New York: Simon & Schuster, 2003), 4.

311 "the profits were as good": Tennessee Williams, *Memoirs* (Garden City, NY: Doubleday, 1975), 176.

311 "Isn't it interesting": Fraser-Cavassoni, *Sam Spiegel*, 205.

311 "truffle nose": Fraser-Cavassoni, *Sam Spiegel*, 204.

311 "Montgomery Clift has arrived": JLM to (J)ohanna: (C)hris: (T)om, "SUBJECT: SUDDENLY SAM SPIEGEL – OR WHY THE HELL DON'T YOU WRITE. IT'S BEEN A WHOLE MONTH AWREADY!" May 14, 1959. Courtesy of TM.

312 "You better get over here": Fraser-Cavassoni, *Sam Spiegel*, 207.

312 "a bag of dead mice": William J. Mann, *How to Be a Movie Star: Elizabeth Taylor in Hollywood* (New York: Houghton Mifflin Harcourt, 2010), 268.

312 "SORRY TO DISAPPOINT": JLM to Louella Parsons, telegram, June 6, 1959, JLMP.

312 "bog of tics and tremors": Fraser-Cavassoni, *Sam Spiegel* 208. Quoting Jack Hildyard.

313 "haughty eccentricity": Geist, *Pictures Will Talk*, 297.

313 "You're just a pig in a silk suit": Barbara Leaming, *Katharine Hepburn* (New York: Crown, 1995), 481–82.

313 a bit of a bully: Heidi Vanderbilt to SLS. The Vanderbilt children were also fascinated by the magnitude of Elizabeth Taylor's stardom. In Spain to shoot the beach scenes, the group attended a bullfight, and afterward, the audience across from them parted and poured toward Taylor. Taylor's bodyguards were prepared for the waves and encircled her to move her out. It seemed to Heidi as if the coliseum had tipped, with them at the bottom, and all the people were falling onto them to get to Taylor. That image is not dissimilar to the beach urchins' attack on Sebastian.

314 "It made me throw up": Boze Hadleigh, *The Lavender Screen: The Gay and Lesbian Films—Their Stars, Makers, Characters, and Critics* (New York: Citadel Press, 2001), 27.

314 "abortion": John Lahr, *Tennessee Williams: Mad Pilgrimage of the Flesh* (New York: W. W. Norton, 2014), 424. Quoting Williams's letter to Katharine Hepburn, Jan. 5, 1961.

314 "Eating People Is Wrong": Arthur Knight, "SR Goes to the Movies: Eating People Is Wrong," *Saturday Review*, Jan. 2, 1960, 31.

314 "the only movie": "The New Pictures: Suddenly, Last Summer," *Time*, Jan. 11, 1960, 64–65.

315 "a structure": Philip K. Scheuer, "Stewart, Hepburn Top Poll of Critics," *LAT*, Dec. 28, 1959, C9.

315 "intellectual fog belt": Harold Heffernan, "Successful Film-Maker Voices Dislike of Movietown," *Daily Boston Globe*, Jan. 3, 1960, A11.

315 "I never thought about homosexuality": Scheuer, "Stewart, Hepburn Top Poll of Critics."

315 "Suddenly last summer . . . Cathy knew she was being used": *Chicago Daily Tribune*, Jan. 10, 1960, E9.

CHAPTER 23. THE TOUGHEST THREE PICTURES I EVER MADE

316 "Cleopatra was conceived": JLM press conference, New York, Oct. 30, 1962.

317 "Hold your nose": Geist, *Pictures Will Talk*, 310.

318 "I think it would be a wonderful gift": Geist, *Pictures Will Talk*, 310.

318 "bloodcurdling": Diary, Feb. 3, 1961.

318 "dreadful": JLM Log, Feb. 2, 1961. On January 22, 1961, Joe started a log, in addition to his diary, though there is overlap and duplication. Subsequent quotations in this chapter are from one of these sources unless otherwise cited.

320 "WHAT IS OBVIOUS": JLM to Spyros Skrouras, teletype, May 18, 1961, JLMP.

320 "For God's sake, get something": Walter Wanger and Joe Hyams, *My Life with Cleopatra* (New York, Bantam Books, 1963), 88.

322 "huge cannonball pats": Rex Harrison, *Rex: An Autobiography* (New York: William Morrow, 1975), 180.

322 "They forgot their lines": Harrison, *Rex*, 182.

323 "very well-trained sprinter": Harrison, *Rex*, 187.

323 "It's not for sale": Wanger and Hyams, *My Life*, 109.

323 "I treat my servants": Wanger and Hyams, *My Life*, 112.

323 "I will not go into details" "makes and unmakes decisions": JLM to Abe Bienstock, Dec. 6, 1961, JLMP.

324 "ANY CONCEIVABLE CHANCE": JLM to Charles Feldman, cable, Dec. 29, 1961, Charles Feldman Papers, AFI.

325 "I've got to don my breastplate": Geist, *Pictures Will Talk*, 321.

325 "She hasn't even finished her champagne": Mann, *How to Be a Movie Star*, 16.

326 "Liz and Burton are not just playing": Wanger and Hyams, *My Life*, 121 and JLM log, Jan. 27. Wanger and Hyams date Joe's revelation as Jan. 26, and quote Joe as sitting on a volcano. Joe's Jan. 27 Log entry: "Decided to acquaint Wanger with most of the facts. I cannot [*sic*] longer accept the responsibility of sitting alone on this potential powder keg."

327 "Hope your second year": JLM Log, Feb. 1, 1962.

327 "as a genius": JLM Log, Feb. 12, 1962.

328 "If she can count them": Mann, *How to Be a Movie Star*, 30.

329 "When you're in a cage": Jack Brodsky and Nathan Weiss: *The Cleopatra Papers: A Private Correspondence* (New York: Simon & Schuster, 1963), 43.

329 "He will never be": Wanger and Hyams, *My Life*, 137.

329 "FISHER BOUNCED SYBIL FLYING" "PAPERS ARE FILLED": Brodsky and Weiss, *Cleopatra Papers*, 51.

330 "It gets more incredible": Brodsky and Weiss, *Cleopatra Papers*, 52.

330 "The real truth": *Time*, Apr. 13, 1962, 42. The previous month, *Time* had relayed gossip that Taylor was "using Burton rumors to shield the real truth: that she is mad, mad, mad for her personable director . . . who, however, is very busy shooting all day and scripting all night." *Time*, Mar. 2, 1962, 78.

330 "Madam" "erotic vagrancy": "Liz Warned on 'Erotic Vagrancy' by Vatican," *LAT*, Apr. 13, 1962, 4.

330 "Communists chuckle": "Miss Taylor, Burton Stir Mrs. Blitch," *Baltimore Sun*, May 23, 1962, 3.

331 "It used to be": Tom Mankiewicz and Robert Crane, *My Life as a Mankiewicz: An Insider's Journey through Hollywood* (Lexington: University Press of Kentucky, 2012), 63.

331 "wan and haggard": Philip Dunne, *Take Two: A Life in Movies and Politics* (New York: McGraw-Hill, 1980), 307. When Hume Cronyn dropped by Joe's room one night, he found Joe, in white gloves because of another eczema flare-up, looking like "a dissolute butler recovering from a particularly vicious dinner party, pouch-eyed and sullen" Hume Cronyn, *A Terrible Liar: A Memoir* (New York: William Morrow, 1991), 328.

331 "*Cleopatra*: Well you sure were a mess": Dunne, *Take Two*, 308.

332 "the first indoor movie": Brodsky and Weiss, *Cleopatra Papers*, 116.
332 "whims" of stars: Murray Schumach, "Fox Aide Assails 'Whims' of Stars," *NYT*, June 11, 1962, 38.
332 "PHILIPPI CONSISTS": JLM to Rosenman, copies to Skouras, Levathes, Feldman, June 29, 1962, Feldman Papers, AFI
333 "I do not believe": Murray Schumach: "Move by Zanuck Awaited at Fox," *NYT*, July 2, 1962, 22.
334 "slight edge of contempt" Ranald MacDougall to KLG.
334 "who has advanced the literature": Philip K. Scheuer, "Director of 'Cleopatra' Wins Writers' Award," *LAT*, May 8, 1963, A2.
334 "I have been told": Zanuck to JLM, Aug. 31, 1962, JLMP.
334 "an experience which violated": JLM to Zanuck, Sept. 5, 1962, JLMP.
336 "It was not the fault": Zanuck to JLM, Oct. 21, 1962, JLMP.
337 "I am, I suppose, an old whore": JLM to Zanuck, Oct. 22, 1962, JLMP.
338 "complete control": William C. Wing, "Zanuck Hints Caesar Tinsel Rubbed Off on Mankiewicz," *NYHT*, Oct. 27, 1962, 7.
338 "I'm much too old a cotton picker": "As 'Cleopatra' Story Appears to Mankiewicz," *NYHT*, Oct. 31, 1962, 17.
338 "I'd feel self-conscious": "Mankiewicz Denies Charges by Zanuck, but Won't Fight," *Hollywood Reporter*, Oct. 31, 1962.
339 "I guess we might as well": RMM to SLS.
340 "you're the only living human being": EMS to JLM, Dec. 7, 1962.
340 "that fiendish golfer": Howard Dietz, Dec. 27, 1962.
340 "Apparently she is holding out": FFM, Jan. 5, 1963.
341 "HOW SOON CAN YOU GET HERE": RMM to SLS
342 "If any woman ever acted to me": JLM to KLG. A favorite of anecdote JLM's, who attributed it to Zanuck while they were in Paris. It does not appear in his contemporaneous log, however.
342 "The picture was a very good movie": Barbara McLean. Oral history interview by Thomas R. Stempel, Darryl F. Zanuck Research Project, 1970–1971, 112–15, AFI.
342 "the toughest three pictures": Howard Thompson, "Unveiling 'Cleopatra,'" *NYT*, June 9, 1963, 121.
342 "one of the great epic films": Bosley Crowther, "The Screen: 'Cleopatra' Has Premiere at Rivoli," *NYT*, June 13, 1963, 27.
342 "The mountain of notoriety": Vincent Butler, "'Cleo' Opens and Critics Are Divided," *Chicago Tribune*, June 13, 1963, C4.
342 "staggers around": "Cinema: Just One of Those 'Things'": *Time*, June 21, 1963, 90.
342 "common touch": Alistair Cooke, "Cleopatra, a Working girl's Dream," *Guardian*, June 14, 1963, 11.
342 "old war horse": Francis Russell, "Movies: Roman in the Gloamin'," *National Review*, Aug. 13, 1963, 117.
343 "Is Rexy Not Sexy": *Variety*, Feb. 13, 1963, 3.
343 "scandalous" conduct: Edward Ranzal, "Miss Taylor and Burton Sued for $50 Million on 'Cleopatra,'" *NYT*, Apr. 23, 1964, 1.
343 "I should have stayed fired": JLM to KLG.

CHAPTER 24. THE HONEY POT(BOILER)

344 "where discrimination is made": Marlon Brando to JLM, telegram Feb. 21, 1964, JLMP.

344 "Another of my projects": Diary, Oct. 18, 1963.

346 "A) more sex": JLM Journal, Feb. 4, 1965, JLMP. Joe kept a journal on *The Honey Pot* from February 1 to June 15, 1965, with entries more expansive than those of his diary. After June 15, I return to his diaries. Subsequent quotations are from these sources unless otherwise cited.

347 "alpha male silverback": Robert Gore-Langton, "He Watched a Lover Die Rather than Call for Help, He Drove Two Women to Suicide, Meet Rex 'The Rotter' Harrison," *Daily Mail*, Apr. 5, 2008.

347 Honey Pot summary, JLM, Apr. 1965.

348 "Mankiewicz got a deal": Charles Feldman to Deane Johnson, transcribed tape, dictated Apr. 17, 1965, Feldman Papers, AFI.

348 "ADVISE BIENSTOCK": Feldman to Office, wire Apr. 18, 1965, Feldman Papers, AFI.

349 "who might be more palatable": Jack Gordean to Feldman, wire, Apr. 27, 1965, Feldman Papers, AFI.

349 "enchanting": Journal, Apr. 22, 1965. When Smith starred on Broadway in *Lettice and Lovage* in 1990, she spent most weekends with Joe and Rosemary, where she and Joe companionably solved crossword puzzles in ink.

350 "Anytime mastermind Mankiewicz": *Box Office*, June 5, 1967, 7.

350 "all the demands": Diary, Sept. 20, 1965. Actually, Capucine suffered from manic depression and attempted suicide several times before succeeding in 1990.

351 second woman in Harrison's life to commit suicide: The other was actress Carol Landis, in 1947. Although she was still alive when Harrison found her, Landis died during the half hour Harrison spent searching for the name of her private doctor instead of calling an ambulance, in hopes of avoiding a scandal.

351 "steamrolling": AM to SLS.

352 "caught all the nuances": Joseph Gelmis, "Just Don't Call Him Producer," *Newsday*, May 23, 1967, 3A.

CHAPTER 25. IRONIC WESTERN

353 "object of terror": Diary, Jan. 20, 1968. Subsequent quotations in this chapter are from JLM diaries unless otherwise cited.

354 "He was very patient" "*Bad Company* was about the relationship": Robert Benton to SLS.

355 "My only problem with my character": Robert Benton to SLS.

356 "petrified": Sidney Ganis to SLS.

356 "I've got an idea": Doc Erickson to SLS.

357 *King: A Filmed Record*: *King* was nominated for an Oscar for best documentary and appeared occasionally in theaters and on television. On its fifty-year anniversary in 2013, it was shown in theaters on a limited basis.

358 "I saw emerging" "always too New York": Andrew Sarris, "Mankiewicz of the Movies," *Show*, Mar. 1970, 27–30, 78.

358 "Have you by chance seen": SAM to Pauline Kael, Feb. 24, 1970. Later that year Sara must have heard about Herman being characterized as a son-of-a-bitch to—or by—Kael, and wrote to put the record straight:

> He was not a "son-of-a-bitch" at any time in his life. Reckless, profligate with his money & talent, impatient with mediocrity of any kind, which made him violently furious & perhaps excessively insulting. But he was also the kindest person I've ever known & his readiness to help anyone who needed assistance at the expense of his position, pocket-book or resources was sometimes hard on me but I would not have wished it otherwise. Of course he jeopardized his own status & his well-being, but that was part of his greatness. . . . I don't want you to make him a paragon of virtues. I want you to show him as he was, a fiery, sentimental & explosive personality. I don't want to be as you said to Frank, "one of those widows who want their husbands pictured in soft colors." (SAM to Kael, Oct. 15, 1970). Kael Mss., Lilly.

358 "not because I am angry": SAM to JLM, Mar. 4, 1970.
360 "movie of the sort of taste": Vincent Canby, "Screen: 'There Was a Crooked Man . . .' and a Myth," *NYT*, Dec. 26, 1970, 13.
360 "Old Hollywood sophisticates": Andrew Sarris, "films in focus," *Village Voice*, Dec. 31. 1970.

CHAPTER 26. OF PAGE AND SCREEN

363 "simply dreadful": Diary, June 15, 1971. Subsequent quotations in this chapter are from JLM diaries unless otherwise cited.
363 "a piece of piss": Nigel Fountain, "Obituaries: Anthony Shaffer," *Guardian*, Nov. 7, 2001, 20.
365 "Listen. It's you and I": TM to SLS. Also, TM to audience, An Academy Salute to Joseph L. Mankiewicz, Pantages Theatre, May 21, 2009. And Michael Caine, *What's It All About?* (New York: Random House, 1992), 333.
365 "It's your thirtieth birthday": Recounted by Jill St. John at Tom's Memorial Service, 2010. Video recording courtesy of RMM.
366 "a man who has only good taste": Starkey Flythe Jr., "It's Your Move, Larry," *Holiday*, Nov./Dec. 1972, 58.
366 "'And what was that'": Caine, *What's It All About?*, 334.
367 "There's no way I can override you": Donald Spoto, *Laurence Olivier: A Biography* (New York: HarperCollins, 1992), 366.
368 "this isn't the theatre": Caine, *What's It All About?*, 336.
368 "It was frightening": Spoto, *Laurence Olivier*, 366.
368 "You bastard": AM to SLS.
368 "When we started on this film": Caine, *What's It All About?*, 336. Caine recalled Joe's wink at the AMPAS Tribute to JLM, May 6, 1991.
368 "If you direct Larry": JLM to KLG.
369 "They don't realize": Carol Kramer, "A Class Struggle That Asks: Can a Cockney Best a Lord?" *Chicago Tribune*, Jan. 14, 1973, E5.

370 "Even the Radcliffe-educated Karen": Gary Carey, "Joseph L. and Herman J., the Hollywood Mankiewits," *Film Comment*, Nov./Dec. 1978, 66–68.

370 However, to Joe's great joy: Bantam also published *The Citizen Kane Book*, which includes notes by that same Gary Carey.

371 "They're in waiting, all right": *More About All About Eve*, 34–40.

372 "I like to think of my work": Sam Staggs, *All About "All About Eve": The Complete Behind-the-Scenes Story of the Bitchiest Film Ever Made* (New York: St. Martin's Press, 2000), ix.

372 "precisely because of what wasn't obvious": Staggs, *All About "All About Eve,"* 241.

373 "Are you aware": Mildred Teich to JLM, Oct. 31, 1972.

374 "The author of this magazine story": Elisabeth Bergner, *Bewundert viel und viel gescholten — Elisabeth Bergners unordentliche Erinnerungen* (*Admired a Lot and Scolded a Lot: Elisabeth Bergner's Messy Memories*) (Munich: Bertelsmann, 1978). Not only was "Martina Lawrence" one of Bergner's roles in *Stolen Life* (1939), but Bette Davis starred in the 1946 remake.

CHAPTER 27. HONORS BUT NO DOUGH

375 "She was a writer": Richard Brickner, "Johanna Davis Remembered," *NYT Book Review*, Aug. 18, 1974, 31.

376 "how little in my heart": Diary, May 21, 1974. Subsequent quotations in this chapter are from JLM diaries unless otherwise cited.

377 "The Oldest Whore on the Beat": KLG to Robert Dahlin at Scribner's, Nov. 23, 1977.

377 "Unfortunately, Joe, there aren't that many": TM to SLS.

377 "crotchety country squire": Geist, *Pictures Will Talk*, 3.

377 "I've done so little original work": JLM to KLG.

378 Meryman's biography of Herman: Partly to allay Joe's fears that he would be characterized negatively, Meryman showed Joe his finished manuscript, though, he wrote to Joe, "I feel a little like Herman showing Citizen Kane to Charlie Lederer" (July 7, 1977).

378 They were sometimes reviewed together: Joint reviews included Patricia Bosworth's, for the Nov. 12, 1978, Sunday *New York Times Book Review*. Ken Geist told me that Bosworth told him she had submitted a long, glowing review of his book. Before it ran, Charles Rembar called to invite her to lunch, but when Bosworth learned he was representing Joe, she said she would not talk to him. Rembar scoffed, telling her that the *New York Times* was his client and would do what he told them. The review that appeared was considerably shorter than what she had filed and looked as if it had been cut down at the last minute—each spread-out paragraph was surrounded by white space. Bosworth did not recall the incident (of forty years ago) but saw no reason to dispute Geist's account.

378 "I want to direct and write for theater": Luc Béraud and Michel Ciment, *All About Mankiewicz*, Janus Film/Filmedis (France) Documentary, 1983.

378 even if sometimes there was too much of it: Not everyone thinks they say too much. Speaking of Joe's work, Quentin Tarantino told an interviewer, "The use of the word 'talky' like it's a bad thing really irks me. His "All About Eve" is most

definitely 'talky.' It's also most definitely brilliant." Roger Ebert, Aug. 17, 2009, https://www.rogerebert.com/interviews/quentin-tarantino-glouriously-basterdizes-world-war-two). Tarantino told another interviewer, "He could have held the script for All About Eve up against every play ever written for the American stage and said, 'Suck my dick!' It's that good." Sean O'Hagan, "Missing in Action," *Guardian,* Aug. 8, 2009.

379 "*All About Eve* couldn't get made": Josh Mankiewicz to SLS, echoing many similar accounts.

379 "A man's 'career'": JLM to CM, Aug. 31, 1965.

380 "Dad had just come back from Europe": AM to SLS.

381 "I've lived without caring": Mel Gussow, "The Sometimes Bumpy Ride of Being Joseph Mankiewicz," *NYT,* Nov. 24, 1992, C13.

382 a reluctant Don Corleone: TM to SLS.

382 "puckish curmudgeon": Stefan Petrucha to SLS.

383 "I don't think I'm going to make it" "like a madwoman": RMM to SLS.

CHAPTER 28. WHAT THEY WROUGHT

387 "parenthesis in the listings": Kael, "Raising Kane," 83.

388 "When I remember": Hecht, *Child of the Century,* 394.

389 "fairly bloomed with widowhood": Johanna Davis, *Life Signs* (New York: Atheneum, 1973), 6.

389 Chris and Tom, who were warmed by her affection: CM and TM to SLS.

389 "There was no stop sign": Josh Mankiewicz to SLS.

389 "the famous father syndrome": Davis, *Life Signs,* 73.

392 "I am owned by two cats" "always chasing my mother": TM to SLS.

FILMOGRAPHY

Throughout their many decades at studios, Herman and Joe contributed without credit to countless films, both produced and unproduced. This filmography includes only a few of their uncredited contributions to motion pictures, and only to films that were actually produced. Furthermore, because they were writers above all else, readers may assume that both Herman and Joe contributed writing to the films they produced.

HERMAN J. MANKIEWICZ

1926
The Road to Mandalay, MGM, Story with Tod Browning
Stranded in Paris, Paramount, Adaptation with John McDermott

1927: Paramount
The Spotlight, Titles
A Gentleman of Paris, Titles
The City Gone Wild, Titles
Honeymoon Hate, Titles with George Marion Jr.
Figures Don't Lie, Titles
The Gay Defender, Titles with George Marion Jr.
Fashions for Women, Adaptation with Jules Furthman
The Flaming Youths, Titles

1928: Paramount
The Mating Call, Titles and Uncredited Actor
The Big Killing, Titles
Avalanche, Screenplay with J. Walter Ruben and Sam Mintz, Titles
The Barker, Titles

Gentlemen Prefer Blondes, Titles with Anita Loos
Take Me Home, Titles
Three Week Ends, Titles with Paul Perez
The Drag Net, Titles
His Tiger Lady, Titles
The Last Command, Titles
Love and Learn, Titles
The Magnificent Flirt, Titles
A Night of Mystery, Titles
Something Always Happens, Titles
The Water Hole, Titles
What a Night! Titles
Abie's Irish Rose, Titles

1929: Paramount
Thunderbolt, Dialogue
The Canary Murder Case, Titles
The Love Doctor, Titles
The Mighty, Titles
The Dummy, Adaptation and Dialogue
The Man I Love, Original Story, Screenplay with Percy Heath, Dialogue
Marquis Preferred, Titles

1930: Paramount
Ladies Love Brutes, Screenplay and Dialogue with Waldemar Young
Honey, Screenplay, Dialogue
Love Among the Millionaires, Dialogue
Men Are Like That, Adaptation with Marion Dix, Dialogue
True to the Navy, Dialogue
The Vagabond King, Adaptation, Additional Dialogue
Laughter, Producer

1931: Paramount
The Royal Family of Broadway, Adaptation with Gertrude Purcell
Dude Ranch, Additional Dialogue
Man of the World, Original Story, Screenplay
Ladies' Man, Screenplay, Dialogue
Monkey Business, Associate Producer

1931: Caddo Corporation (Howard Hughes and Lewis Milestone producing)
The Front Page, Uncredited Actor

1932: Paramount
Dancers in the Dark, Screenplay
Million Dollar Legs, Producer
Horse Feathers, Associate Producer

1932: RKO
The Lost Squadron, Dialogue with Wallace Smith
Girl Crazy, Screenplay with Tim Whelan, Dialogue with Whelan, Edward Welch, and Walter DeLeon

1933: MGM
Meet the Baron, Story with Norman Krasna
Dinner at Eight, Screenplay with Frances Marion
Another Language, Screenplay with Gertrude Purcell, Dialogue with Donald Ogden Stewart

1934: MGM
Stamboul Quest, Screenplay
The Show-Off, Screenplay

1935: MGM
Rendezvous, Contributing Writer
After Office Hours, Screenplay
It's in the Air, Uncredited Writer
Escapade, Screenplay

1936
Love in Exile, Gaumont British Picture Corp, Screenplay with Ernest Betts and Roger Burford
The Show Goes On (in England, *The Three Maxims*), Herbert Wilcox Productions, Adaptation, Screenplay

1937
John Meade's Woman, Paramount, Screenplay with Vincent Lawrence
The Emperor's Candlesticks, MGM, Uncredited Writer
My Dear Miss Aldrich, MGM, Original Story, Screenplay

1939: MGM
The Wizard of Oz, Uncredited Writer
It's a Wonderful World, Original Story with Ben Hecht

1940: MGM
Keeping Company, Original Story
Comrade X, Uncredited Writer

1941
Rise and Shine, Twentieth Century Fox, Screenplay
Citizen Kane, RKO, Screenplay with Orson Welles, Uncredited Actor
The Wild Man of Borneo, MGM, Based on Play written with Marc Connelly

1942
This Time for Keeps, MGM, Based on Characters Created By, for *Keeping Company*
The Pride of the Yankees, Samuel Goldwyn Productions, Screenplay with Jo Swerling

1943
Stand by for Action, MGM, Screenplay with John Balderston and George Bruce
The Good Fellows, Paramount, Based on Play written with George S. Kaufman

1944
Christmas Holiday, Universal, Screenplay

1945: RKO
The Enchanted Cottage, Screenplay with DeWitt Bodeen
The Spanish Main, Screenplay with George Worthing Yates
Cornered, Based on Treatment written with Ben Hecht and Czenzi Ormonde

1949
A Woman's Secret, RKO, Screenplay, Producer

1952
The Pride of St. Louis, Twentieth Century Fox, Screenplay

JOSEPH L. MANKIEWICZ

1929: Paramount
The Dummy, Titles
Close Harmony, Titles
The Man I Love, Titles
The Studio Murder Mystery, Titles
Thunderbolt, Titles
River of Romance, Titles
Dangerous Curves, Titles with George Marion Jr.
The Mysterious Dr. Fu Manchu, Titles
The Saturday Night Kid, Titles
The Virginian, Titles
Fast Company, Dialogue
Woman Trap, Uncredited Actor

1930: Paramount
Slightly Scarlet, Screenplay and Dialogue with Howard Estabrook
The Social Lion, Adaptation, Dialogue
Only Saps Work, Dialogue

1931: Paramount
The Gang Buster, Dialogue
Finn and Hattie, Dialogue
June Moon, Scenario with Keene Thompson, Dialogue with Keene Thompson and Vincent Lawrence
Skippy, Scenario with Norman McLeod, Dialogue with Norman McLeod and Don Marquis
Newly Rich (retitled *Forbidden Adventure*), Scenario with Edward E. Paramore Jr. and Norman McLeod, Dialogue with Norman McLeod
Sooky, Scenario and Dialogue with Sam Mintz and Norman McLeod

1932: Paramount
This Reckless Age, Scenario and Dialogue
Sky Bride, Scenario and Dialogue with Agnes Brand Leahy and Grover Jones
Million Dollar Legs, Original Story; Screenplay with Henry Myers
If I Had a Million, Screenplays for some episodes; Contributed to other episodes and to framing story

1933: RKO
Diplomaniacs, Original Story, Screenplay with Henry Myers
Emergency Call, Screenplay with John B. Clymer

1933: Paramount
Too Much Harmony, Scenario
Alice in Wonderland, Screenplay with William Cameron Menzies

1934: MGM
Manhattan Melodrama, Screenplay with Oliver H. P. Garrett
Forsaking All Others, Screenplay

1934: Viking Production
Our Daily Bread, Dialogue

1935: MGM
I Live My Life, Screenplay
After Office Hours, Contributed Dialogue

1936: MGM Producer
Three Godfathers
Fury
The Gorgeous Hussy
Love on the Run

1937: MGM Producer
The Bride Wore Red
Double Wedding
Mannequin

1938: MGM Producer
Three Comrades
The Shopworn Angel
The Shining Hour
A Christmas Carol

1939: MGM Producer
The Adventures of Huckleberry Finn (retitled *Huckleberry Finn*)

1940: MGM Producer
Strange Cargo
The Philadelphia Story
The Wild Man of Borneo

1941: MGM Producer
The Feminine Touch
Woman of the Year

1942: MGM Producer
Cairo
Reunion in France

1944: Twentieth Century Fox
Keys of the Kingdom, Screenplay with Nunnally Johnson, Producer

1946: Twentieth Century Fox
Dragonwyck, Screenplay, Director
Somewhere in the Night, Screenplay with Howard Dimsdale, Director

1947: Twentieth Century Fox
The Late George Apley, Director
The Ghost and Mrs. Muir, Director

1948: Twentieth Century Fox
Escape, Director

1949: Twentieth Century Fox
A Letter to Three Wives, Screenplay, Director
House of Strangers, Screenplay (uncredited) with Philip Yordan, Director

1950: Twentieth Century Fox
No Way Out, Screenplay with Lesser Samuels, Director
All About Eve, Screenplay, Director

1951
People Will Talk, Twentieth Century Fox, Screenplay, Director

1952
Five Fingers, Twentieth Century Fox, Dialogue (uncredited), Director

1953

Julius Caesar, MGM, Screenplay, Director

1954

The Barefoot Contessa, Figaro/United Artists, Screenplay, Director, Producer

1955

Guys and Dolls, Samuel Goldwyn/MGM, Screenplay, Director

1958

The Quiet American, Figaro/United Artists, Screenplay, Director, Producer

1959

Suddenly, Last Summer, Horizon Films/Columbia Pictures, Director

1963

Cleopatra, Twentieth Century Fox, Screenplay with Ranald MacDougall and Sidney Buchman, Director

1967

The Honey Pot, Charles K. Feldman/Famous Artists/United Artists, Screenplay, Director, Producer with Charles K. Feldman

1970

There Was a Crooked Man, Warner Bros., Director, Producer

King: A Filmed Record... Montgomery to Memphis, Commonwealth United/Martin Luther King Film Project, Director of segments

1972

Sleuth, Palomar Pictures International/Twentieth Century Fox, Director

SELECT BIBLIOGRAPHY

In addition to books already cited in the Notes, the following were valuable resources.

BY AND ABOUT MANKIEWICZES

Dick, Bernard F. *Joseph L. Mankiewicz*. Boston: Twayne, 1983.

Lower, Cheryl Bray, and R. Barton Palmer. *Joseph L. Mankiewicz: Critical Essays with an Annotated Bibliography and a Filmography*. Jefferson, NC: McFarland, 2001.

Mankiewicz, Frank, with Joel L. Swerdlow. *So as I Was Saying . . . My Somewhat Eventful Life*. New York: St. Martin's Press, 2016.

COLUMBIA AND 1920S NEW YORK

Erskine, John. *The Memory of Certain Persons*. Philadelphia: J. B. Lippincott, 1947.

Gallagher, Brian. *Anything Goes: The Jazz-Age Adventures of Neysa McMein and Her Extravagant Circle of Friends*. New York: Times Books, 1987.

Harriman, Margaret Case. *The Vicious Circle: The Story of the Algonquin Round Table*. New York: Rinehart, 1951.

MacAdams, William. *Ben Hecht: The Man behind the Legend*. New York: Charles Scribner's Sons, 1990.

Meade, Marion. *Bobbed Hair and Bathtub Gin: Writers Running Wild in the Twenties*. New York: Doubleday, 2004.

Mordden, Ethan. *All That Glittered: The Golden Age of Drama on Broadway, 1919–1959*. New York: St. Martin's Press, 2007.

HOLLYWOOD HISTORY AND MOVIES

Balio, Tino. *United Artists: The Company That Changed the Film Industry*. Madison: University of Wisconsin Press, 1987.

Berg, A. Scott. *Goldwyn: A Biography*. New York: Alfred A. Knopf, 1989.

Bernstein, Matthew. *Walter Wanger: Hollywood Independent*. Berkeley and Los Angeles: University of California Press, 1994.

Bordwell, David, Janet Staiger, and Kristin Thompson. *The Classical Hollywood Cinema: Film Style & Mode of Production to 1960*. New York: Columbia University Press, 1985.

Brown, Peter Harry, and Pat H. Broeske. *Howard Hughes: The Untold Story*. Cambridge, MA: Da Capo Press, 2004.

Brownlow, Kevin. *The Parade's Gone By*. New York: Alfred A. Knopf, 1968.

Burton, Richard. *The Richard Burton Diaries*. Edited by Chris Williams. New Haven: Yale University Press, 2013.

Carey, Gary. *All the Stars in Heaven: Louis B. Mayer's M-G-M*. New York: E. P. Dutton, 1981.

Caspary, Vera. *The Secrets of Grown-Ups: An Autobiography*. New York: McGraw-Hill, 1979.

Chrissochoidis, Ilias, ed. *The Cleopatra Files: Selected Documents from the Spyros P. Skouras Archive*. Stanford: Brave World, 2013.

Coleman, Terry. *Olivier*. New York: Henry Holt, 2005.

Corliss, Richard. *Talking Pictures: Screenwriters in the American Cinema*. New York: Penguin Press, 1975.

Crowther, Bosley. *The Lion's Share: The Story of an Entertainment Empire*. New York: E. P. Dutton, 1957.

Douglas, Melvyn, and Tom Arthur. *See You at the Movies: The Autobiography of Melvyn Douglas*. Lanham, MD: University Press of America, 1986.

Eisenschitz, Bernard, *Nicholas Ray: An American Journey*. Trans. by Tom Milne. London: Faber & Faber, 1993.

Eyman, Scott. *Ernst Lubitsch: Laughter in Paradise*. New York: Simon & Schuster, 1993.

Eyman, Scott. *Lion of Hollywood: The Life and Legend of Louis B. Mayer*. New York: Simon & Schuster, 2005.

Farber, Stephen, and Marc Green. *Hollywood on the Couch: A Candid Look at the Overheated Love Affair between Psychiatrists and Moviemakers*. New York: William Morrow, 1993.

Fisher, Eddie. *My Life, My Loves*. New York: HarperCollins, 1984.

Gomery, Douglas. *The Hollywood Studio System*. New York: St. Martin's Press, 1986.

Goodman, Ezra. *The Fifty-Year Decline and Fall of Hollywood*. New York: Simon & Schuster, 1961.

Graham, Sheilah. *College of One: The Story of How F. Scott Fitzgerald Educated the Woman He Loved*. New York: Viking, 1967.

Graham, Sheilah. *The Real F. Scott Fitzgerald, Thirty-Five Years Later*. New York: Warner Books, 1976.

Graham, Sheilah, and Gerold Frank. *Beloved Infidel: The Education of a Woman*. New York: Henry Holt, 1958.

Gussow, Mel. *Don't Say Yes until I Finish Talking: A Biography of Darryl F. Zanuck*. New York: Pocket Books, 1972.

Harvey, James. *Romantic Comedy in Hollywood, from Lubitsch to Sturges*. New York: Alfred A. Knopf, 1987.

Haskell, Molly. *From Reverence to Rape: The Treatment of Women in the Movies*. 3rd ed. Chicago: University of Chicago Press, 2016.

Haver, Ronald. *David O. Selznick's Hollywood*. New York: Alfred A. Knopf, 1980.

Hayward, Brooke. *Haywire*. New York: Alfred A. Knopf, 1977.

Hopper, Hedda. *From under My Hat*. Garden City, NY: Doubleday, 1952.

Koszarski, Richard. *Hollywood on the Hudson: Film and Television in New York from Griffith to Sarnoff*. New Brunswick: Rutgers University Press, 2008.

Lambert, Gavin. *On Cukor*. New York: G. P. Putnam's Sons, 1972.

Lasky, Bessie Mona. *Candle in the Sun*. Los Angeles: DeVorss, 1957.

Loos, Anita. *Kiss Hollywood Good-By*. New York: Viking, 1974.

Louvish, Simon. *Monkey Business: The Lives and Legends of the Marx Brothers*. New York: St. Martin's Press, 2001.

Malone, Aubrey. *Maureen O'Hara: The Biography*. Lexington: University Press of Kentucky, 2013.

Marmorstein, Gary. *A Ship without a Sail: The Life of Lorenz Hart*. New York: Simon & Schuster, 2012.

McGilligan, Patrick. *George Cukor: A Double Life*. New York: St. Martin's Press, 1991.

McGilligan, Patrick. *Nicholas Ray: The Glorious Failure of an American Director*. New York: HarperCollins, 2001.

Mordden, Ethan. *The Hollywood Studios: House Style in the Golden Age of the Movies*. New York: Simon & Schuster, 1988.

Navasky, Victor S. *Naming Names*. New York: Penguin Books, 1981.

O'Hara, Maureen, and John Nicoletti: *'Tis Herself: An Autobiography*. New York: Simon & Schuster, 2005.

Oppenheimer, George. *The View from the Sixties: Memories of a Spent Life*. New York: David McKay, 1966.

Powdermaker, Hortense. *Hollywood the Dream Factory: An Anthropologist Looks at the Movie-Makers*. Boston: Little, Brown, 1950.

Rollyson, Carl. *Marilyn Monroe: A Life of the Actress*. Rev. ed. Hollywood Legends Series. Jackson: University Press of Mississippi, 2014.

Ross, Steven J. *Hollywood Left and Right: How Movie Stars Shaped American Politics*. Oxford: Oxford University Press, 2011.

Sarris, Andrew. *The American Cinema: Directors and Directions 1929–1968*. New York: Da Capo Press, 1996, originally Dutton, 1968, amended Chicago: 1985.

Sarris, Andrew. *"You Ain't Heard Nothin' Yet": The American Talking Film, History & Memory, 1927–1949*. New York: Oxford University Press, 1998.

Schary, Dore. *Heyday: An Autobiography*. Boston: Little, Brown, 1979.

Schatz, Thomas. *The Genius of the System: Hollywood Filmmaking in the Studio Era*. New York: Pantheon, 1988.

Schulberg, Budd. *Moving Pictures: Memories of a Hollywood Prince*. Chicago: Ivan R. Dee, 2003.

Selznick, Irene Mayer. *A Private View*. New York: Alfred A. Knopf, 1983.

Shipman, David. *Marlon Brando*. London: Sphere Books, 1989.

Solomon, Aubrey. *Twentieth Century-Fox: A Corporate and Financial History*. Lanham, MD: Scarecrow Press, 2002.

Spoto, Donald. *A Girl's Got to Breathe: The Life of Teresa Wright*. Jackson: University Press of Mississippi, 2016.

Spoto, Donald. *Laurence Olivier: A Biography*. New York: HarperCollins, 1992.

Stempel, Tom. *FrameWork: A History of Screenwriting in the American Film*. New York: Continuum, 1991.

Taylor, Elizabeth. *Elizabeth Taylor*. New York: Harper & Row, 1964, 1965.

Thomas, Bob. *Thalberg: Life and Legend*. Garden City, NY: Doubleday, 1969.

Thomson, David. *Showman: The Life of David O. Selznick*. New York: Alfred A. Knopf, 1992.

Viertel, Salka. *The Kindness of Strangers*. New York: Holt, Rinehart and Winston, 1969.

Zukor, Adolph, with Dale Kramer. *The Public Is Never Wrong: The Autobiography of Adolph Zukor*. New York: G. P. Putnam's Sons, 1953.

ORSON WELLES, *CITIZEN KANE*, AND HEARST

Bogdanovich, Peter. *The Cinema of Orson Welles*. New York: Film Library of the Museum of Modern Art, 1961.

Brady, Frank. *Citizen Welles: A Biography of Orson Welles*. New York: Charles Scribner's Sons, 1989.

Callow, Simon. *Orson Welles: Hello Americans*. New York: Viking, 2006.

Callow, Simon. *Orson Welles: The Road to Xanadu*. London: Jonathan Cape, 1995.

Davies, Marion. *The Time We Had: Life with William Randolph Hearst*. New York: Ballantine, 1977.

Gottesman, Ronald, ed. *Focus on Citizen Kane*. Englewood Cliffs, NJ: Prentice-Hall, 1971.

Gottesman, Ronald, ed. *Focus on Orson Welles*. Englewood Cliffs: Prentice-Hall, 1976.

Gottesman, Ronald, ed. *Perspectives on Citizen Kane*. Boston: Twayne, 1996.

Guiles, Fred Lawrence. *Marion Davies*. New York: McGraw-Hill, 1972.

Leaming, Barbara. *Orson Welles: A Biography*. New York: Viking, 1985.

Lundberg, Ferdinand, *Imperial Hearst: A Social Biography*. New York: Equinox, 1936.

McBride, Joseph. *Orson Welles*. New York: Da Capo Press, 1996.

McBride, Joseph. *What Ever Happened to Orson Welles? A Portrait of an Independent Career*. Lexington: University Press of Kentucky, 2006.

Naremore, James, ed. *Orson Welles's Citizen Kane: A Casebook*. Oxford: Oxford University Press, 2004.

Nasaw, David. *The Chief: The Life of William Randolph Hearst*. Boston: Houghton Mifflin, 2000.

Rosenbaum, Jonathan. *Discovering Orson Welles*. Berkeley and Los Angeles: University of California Press, 2007.

Thomson, David. *Rosebud: The Story of Orson Welles*. New York: Alfred A. Knopf, 1996.

ACKNOWLEDGMENTS

To my regret, several of the most important contributors died before this book was finished. I hope I adequately conveyed my appreciation to them during our time together. Foremost are Herman's sons, Don and Frank, and Joe's son, Tom, who each spent many hours sharing candid recollections of their fathers.

I am grateful to be able to thank many other family members for their generosity. Rosemary Mankiewicz, who was married to Joe for over thirty years, was a tremendous supporter of this project and made available her opinions, her memories, and her voluminous papers, especially Joe's diaries and personal musings. Along with Tom, Joe's other three children, Eric Reynal and Chris and Alex Mankiewicz, were invaluable contributors—intelligent, perceptive, and honest. Alex deserves special thanks. Over the years she became a true partner in my quest to understand her complicated father and bring him to life.

Because Herman died more than half a century ago, finding people who knew him was a challenge. Frank's first wife, Holly (mother of Josh and Ben, see the family tree, page 393), was an important source of firsthand memories of her beloved father-in-law. Don's second wife, Carol, was a terrific source of Hollywood history, and she certainly made Sara come alive (as a mother-in-law from hell, actually, seconding Holly's experience). Frank's second wife, Patricia O'Brien, contributed several of Frank's favorite stories. Herman and Sara's nephews, John Fox and his wife, Gretchen, Jonathan Silverman and his wife, Berry, and Reuben Aaronson added unique stories about their uncle. Don's son, John, and Frank's son, Josh, shared their memories of their grandmother and their recollections of family lore. Ben and his wife, Lee, shared valuable family documents, and Ben provided—on his cellphone, no less—my only opportunity to hear Herman talk, nine minutes into *The Front Page* (1931).

Herman and Sara also had a daughter, Johanna (Josie), born in 1937. She died tragically young in 1974, but a number of her friends shared their vivid recollections. Judy Jaffe Silber—who qualifies more as family than friend—set aside an entire day to talk and invited Frank to join us, so they could jog each other's memories. She also shared her father, Sam Jaffe's, memoirs and oral history. Judy's sister, Barbara Kohn Katz, as well as Josie's childhood friends Louisa Wallace Jacobs, Susan Kohner Weitz, Jill Schary Robinson, and Caroline Veiller Saltzman, and Josie's college friends Anne Rogin and Ann Hamilton were enormously helpful. Neighbors and lifelong family friends, Danny Selznick and the late Alice Hammerstein Mathias shared important memories.

Herman's and Joe's biographers, Richard Meryman and Kenneth Geist, were alive during much of the time I worked on this book, and both kindly discussed their findings with me. Ken was particularly generous in going to great pains to provide me with copies of his recorded interviews, and I thank also the American Film Institute (AFI) for their efforts in making those copies.

I am very grateful to Lee Adams, Robert Benton, Kevin Brianton, Al Connable, Tandy Cronyn, James Curtis, Ruda Dauphin, Ronald Davis, Doc Erickson, Brian Gallagher, Sidney Ganis, Julie Garfield, Samuel Goldwyn Jr., Laurie Burrows Grad, Stephanie Wanger Guest, Michael Hornblow, Evelyn and George Idelson, Sherlee Lantz, Piper Laurie, Patrick McGilligan, Chris O'Sullivan, Kathy Sachs, Elaine Schreyek, Sandra Schulberg, Charles Strouse, David Thomson, Alfred Vanderbilt III., Heidi Vanderbilt, Jeanne Vanderbilt, and Charles Ziarko. I regret that not all of them are still alive to accept my thanks. To those who helped me over the years and whose names I have inadvertently omitted, please accept my apologies as well as my gratitude.

Librarians and archivists have been patient and enterprising guides. Special thanks to Robert Vaughn and Emily Wittenberg at AFI. To Jenny Romero, Louise Hilton, Faye Thompson, Kristine Krueger and, indeed, the entire staff at the Margaret Herrick Library, Academy of Motion Picture Arts and Sciences. To Barbara Hall and Hilary Swett at the Writers Guild Foundation (and to Barbara for her help during the years she was at the Herrick Library). To the very special Ned Comstock and Dace Taube at the Cinematic Arts Library, University of Southern California. To Rebecca Baumann and the staff of the Lilly Library at Indiana University. To Julie Graham and the staff at the Charles E. Young Research Library, UCLA Library. To Ashley Swinnerton at the Film Study Center of the Museum of Modern Art, as well as the entire staffs at the Billy

Rose Theatre Division, New York Public Library for the Performing Arts and the Rare Book and Manuscript Library, Columbia University. And to those who helped from long distance at the Oviatt Library, California State University at Northridge; Archives and Special Collections, University of Nebraska-Lincoln; Harry Ransom Center, University of Texas at Austin; Wisconsin Historical Society Archives, University of Wisconsin; and the Library of Congress.

I am very grateful to University Press of Mississippi director Craig Gill for his guidance and enthusiasm. Thank you also to Emily Bandy, Pete Halverson, Valerie Jones, Kristin Kirkpatrick, and everyone else at the Press who shepherded the manuscript through to finished book with such excellence and attention to detail. Most special thanks to my knowledgeable and creative copy editor, Lisa Williams, to Cliff Stern for his website assistance, and to series editor, Carl Rollyson, and my agent, Sam Stoloff, who were advocates and advisers every step of the way.

Of all my friends, Deirdre Bair deserves special thanks. Her constant encouragement is nourishing, and her wise counsel invaluable. In addition to Deirdre, Mary Dearborn, Dolores Eyler, Barbara Fisher, Diane Jacobs, Kristin MacQuarrie, Victoria Olsen, and Mary Test took the time to read my manuscript and provide advice. Each improved it in a different way—how fortunate was I. Marion Meade was my go-to expert on the Algonquins and a fount of wisdom on biography in general. The biography/memoir seminar Women Writing Women's Lives (which kindly allowed me to remain a member, even when my subjects were not women) provided intellectual stimulation and professional inspiration, as well as warm companionship that ameliorated the isolation of writing. Special thanks to members Pat Auspos, Louise Bernikow, Betty Caroli, Kathy Chamberlain, Kate Culkin, Dorothy O. Helly, Marnie Mueller, Dona Munker, Jill Norgren, and Julie Van Haaften, who alerted me to new information and provided extra insights, and to Carla Peterson for also leading me to my terrific agent. I also benefited from members of the New York University biography seminar, especially Patty O'Toole, a role model as well as a friend.

Above all, I thank my first and last reader, my husband, Jon, to whom I dedicate this book. Yet again, Jon bore with good nature and grace a book's near-total occupation of our time, our living space, and my attention. After years of failing his pre-credits quizzes at the end of the many old movies we have watched together, I am finally passing a few. You can take that string off your finger now, Uncle Billy.

PHOTO CREDITS

Photographs without citations were provided by Mankiewicz family members.

Aviva Slesin Collection of Research and Production Materials for The Ten-Year Lunch: The Wit and Legend of the Algonquin Round Table, Billy Rose Theatre Division, The New York Public Library: pp. 38, 42, 44, 47, 48, 63, 66 (bottom photo), 71, 77.

© John Swope Trust / mptvimages.com: p. 244

Margaret Herrick Library, Academy of Motion Picture Arts and Sciences: pp. 24, 66 (top photo), 73, 76, 86, 90, 94, 111, 144, 152, 194, 195, 198, 203, 204, 226, 239, 251, 285, 293, 314, 315, 326, 350, 355, 360.

Courtesy of The Museum of Modern Art: pp. 122, 132, 137, 140, 147, 148, 166, 168, 171, 192, 213, 369.

Photofest: pp. 39, 88, 91, 114, 191, 237.

The Columbian, 1918, University Archives, Rare Book & Manuscript Library, Columbia University Libraries: p. 20

© Turner Classic Movies, Inc. A WarnerMedia Company. All Rights Reserved: p. 392

INDEX

References to illustrations appear in **bold**.

ABOUT THE AUTHOR

© Erin Silber Photography

Sydney Ladensohn Stern worked as a reporter for *Fortune* and *Money* magazines and as an editor and award-winning columnist ("Suburban Exposure") for the *Scarsdale Inquirer* before she started freelancing for numerous publications including the *New York Times*. Her first book, *Toyland: The High-Stakes Game of the Toy Industry*, was a Featured Alternate for Book of the Month and Fortune Book clubs. Her first biography was *Gloria Steinem: Her Passions, Politics, and Mystique*. She lives in New York City. For more, see sydneylstern.com.